Runaway and Homeless Youth

Stephen J. Morewitz

Runaway and Homeless Youth

New Research and Clinical Perspectives

Springer

Stephen J. Morewitz
Nursing and Health Sciences
California State University, East Bay
Hayward, CA, USA

ISBN 978-3-319-30861-6 ISBN 978-3-319-30863-0 (eBook)
DOI 10.1007/978-3-319-30863-0

Library of Congress Control Number: 2016940243

Printed on acid-free paper

This Springer imprint is published by Springer Nature
The registered company is Springer International Publishing AG Switzerland

Preface

Runaway and Homeless Youth: New Research and Clinical Perspectives analyzes up-to-date research about runaway and homeless youth based on results from the national Runaway Youth Project (RYP), which is part of the larger Missing Persons Project (MPP) (see Appendix A).

This book uses social sciences theories to explain why children and adolescents run away and become victimized. This work focuses on an ecological theory approach to explain the ways in which individual, social, peer, family, and school factors increase the risk or protect against youth running away from home. This book also offers new insights about the social and behavioral profiles of runaway and homeless children and adolescents when they go missing and live on the streets.

Chapter 1 describes the experiences of children and adolescents who run away from home or become homeless for other reasons. This chapter examines why youth who are disconnected from their family, peers, classmates, and teachers may be at increased risk of running away from home. Chapter 1 evaluates the extent to which child sexual, physical, and emotional abuse and neglect, domestic violence, school difficulties, and peer problems are determinants of running away from home.

In Chap. 2, the process of eloping from substitute care such as foster care is assessed. This chapter analyzes the institutional conditions and the demographic, social, psychological, and behavioral conditions that may increase at the probability that young people elope from substitute care settings.

Chapter 3 focuses on street youth's survival strategies associated with obtaining food while on the streets and the problems associated with food insecurity. This chapter assesses where young people on the streets get their food and their types of food and nutrient content.

In Chap. 4, the employment activities and other income sources of street young people are assessed. This chapter assesses various conditions such as community views toward runaway and homeless youth that may affect the extent to which these children and adolescents are able to engage in employment while on the streets.

The remaining 17 chapters analyzes the diverse experiences of street youth in the USA and other countries, focusing on such problems as physical victimization; sexual risks, including rape, sexually transmitted infections and human immune virus/acquired immunodeficiency syndrome, and other health problems; adolescent pregnancy; sexual minorities; violent and delinquent behavior; suicidal behaviors; self-mutilation; and mortality rates. In addition, the remaining chapters highlight such issues as the school difficulties that young people encounter while on the streets, the role and impact of the police, courts, secure detention, and social service agencies in responding to runaways. Other chapters focus on interventions and policies that have been implemented to deal with the problems of runaway and homeless youth.

Hayward, CA Stephen J. Morewitz

Contents

About the Author

Stephen J. Morewitz is president of the consulting firm, STEPHEN J. MOREWITZ, Ph.D., & ASSOCIATES, Buffalo Grove, IL, and San Francisco and Tarzana, CA, which was founded in 1988. His firm consults in curriculum development, program development, and litigation. He is a lecturer in the Department of Nursing and Health Sciences at California State University, East Bay, and is a lecturer in the Department of Sociology, San Jose State University. Dr. Morewitz has been on the faculty or staffs of Michael Reese Hospital and Medical Center, the University of Illinois at Chicago, the College of Medicine and School of Public Health, DePaul University, Argonne National Laboratory, and the California School of Podiatric Medicine. He is founder of the Forensic Social Sciences Association, an interdisciplinary and international association. Dr. Morewitz is the author of 100 publications, including the San Jose State University Faculty Author award-winning book, *Kidnapping and Violence: New Research and Clinical Perspectives* (New York: Springer Science+Business Media, LLC, 2016); the San Jose State University Faculty Author award-winning book, *Handbook of Forensic Sociology and Psychology* (New York: Springer Science+Business Media, LLC, 2014) (coedited with Dr. Mark L. Goldstein); *Death Threats and Violence: New Research and Clinical Perspectives* (New York: Springer Science+Business Media, LLC, 2008); the Society for the Study of Social Problems (SSSP) Crime and Delinquency Division award-winning book, *Domestic Violence and Maternal and Child Health* (New York: Kluwer Academic/Plenum Publishers/Springer Science+Business Media, LLC, 2004); the SSSP Crime and Delinquency Division award-winning book, *Stalking and Violence. New Patterns of Trauma and Obsession* (New York: Kluwer Academic/Plenum Publishers/Springer Science+Business Media, LLC, 2003); and *Sexual Harassment and Social Change in American Society* (Bethesda, MD: Austin & Winfield, Rowman and Littlefield Publishing Group, 1996). He is past chair of the SSSP Crime and Delinquency Division and has served on a variety of SSSP committees. He was elected to Sigma Xi, the Scientific Research Society, and to Pi Gamma Mu, the International Honor Society in Social Sciences. Dr. Morewitz earned his A.B. and M.A. from the College of William and Mary in Virginia and his Ph.D. from the University of Chicago.

Chapter 1
Runaway Youth at the Time of Their Disappearance

This chapter presents data on the prevalence of runaway behaviors and the social, demographic, and behavioral characteristics of youth who run away, become homeless, or are thrown away by their parents or guardians. Findings from self-report narratives and the Runaway Youth Project (RYP), which is based on a random sample of 200 missing persons reports, are used to evaluate the demographic, social, psychological, and behavioral characteristics of runaway and homeless children and adolescents (Morewitz and Sturdy Colls 2016, forthcoming). This chapter analyzes risk factors such as socioeconomic status (SES), demographic characteristics, conduct disorder, sexual orientation, sexual and physical abuse and neglect, and family dysfunction that may increase the likelihood that children and adolescents will run away or become homeless. In this chapter, characteristics of the runaway episode such as duration, season, alterations in the runaway youth's appearance, travel patterns, and peer and adult involvement are evaluated. This chapter also analyzes the hazards faced by street youth such as human trafficking, prostitution, physical and sexual victimization, depression, suicidal behavior, and substance abuse. In this chapter, the criminal history and substance abuse patterns of runaway youth are discussed.

Researchers are evaluating the prevalence of runaway behaviors and the social, demographic, and behavioral characteristics of youth who go run away or become homeless (Hammer et al. 2002; Thompson and Pillai 2006; Luthar 1999). Data from self-report narratives and the RYP, which is based on a random sample of 200 missing persons reports, are used to describe the demographic, social, psychological, and behavioral characteristics of runaway and homeless children and adolescents (see Appendix A).

S.J. Morewitz, *Runaway and Homeless Youth*,
DOI 10.1007/978-3-319-30863-0_1

Prevalence

Running away from home is a prevalent behavior in the USA. According to NISMART, 1,682,900 runaway/thrown-away incidents occurred in 1999 (Hammer et al. 2002; Sedlak et al. 2002). In the USA, about 1.3 million young people live on the streets daily (Family and Youth Services Bureau, National Clearinghouse on Families and Youth n.d.). In other countries, the prevalence of street youth is also high.

Socioeconomic Status Factors

Low SES is one of the factors that increase the risk that children will become delinquent and enter the juvenile justice system (Bright et al. 2014). Young people who run away from home are from all SES groups (Posner 1992; Johnson 2010). However, Posner (1992) indicates that a majority of runaway are from lower-SES groups. Posner (1992) attributes to the trend that disadvantaged families suffer more stress associated with a lack of resources, which adds more stress to the family environment.

According to Thompson and Pillai (2006), runaway youth come from families who are struggling with different complex social problems such as poverty, unemployment, homelessness, child abuse, partner violence, substance abuse, and mental disorders. Children and adolescents are a particularly vulnerable group who respond to their families' difficult social problems by running away. In fact, a number of these youth respond to their families' social problems by running away on a chronic basis.

Luthar (1999) also stated that youth from lower-SES groups are at increased risk of running away and participating in other high-risk behaviors than youth from higher-SES groups. Certain ethnic/racial groups have lower-SES background and as a result face a variety of complex social problems such as poverty, unemployment, child abuse, substance abuse, and suicide (Thompson and Pillai 2006). For example, Native Americans have had high rates of poverty and Native American children and teens are more likely to suffer various complex social problems such as runaway episodes, school dropout, alcohol abuse, depression, and suicide than youth from other ethnic/racial groups (US Department of Commerce 1993; Liu et al. 1994).

Youth who run away from home or substitute care have a higher probability of having conduct disorder (CD), which involves repeated antisocial behaviors such as bullying, fighting, starting fires, and committing theft. Children and adolescents with CD often come from lower-SES family backgrounds (Chen et al. 2007; Moffitt 1993; Patterson and Yoerger 1997). Youth with CD frequently are raised by single parents who often have lower SES because of their parental status. Moreover, children and adolescents with CD are raised by families that have impaired parental practices.

Lower-SES youth, especially runaway youth, are at greater risk of developing physical health problems (Thompson and Pillai 2006). For example, lower-SES young people may be more likely to suffer malnutrition than upper-SES youth.

Runaway children and adolescents may be more likely to have lower educational attainment than non-runaway youth, which may be partly due to their family's lower-SES background. Youth who run away may be more likely to have gone to alternative schools or have had dropped out of school (Thompson and Pillai 2006; Kurtz et al. 1991a).

Runaway/thrown-away young people may be more likely to have missed school days, jeopardizing their academic achievement (Hammer et al. 2002). In an analysis of estimated runaway/thrown-away incidents, Hammer et al. (2002) discovered that 4 % of the episodes (70,500 incidents) involved children who were enrolled in school at the time of the incident who had missed at least 5 school days.

To what extent are youth at the time that they runaway, are kicked out of the home, or become homeless in other ways having school problems? However, studies indicate found that runaway youth, especially chronic runaways, encounter a variety of school problems, including missed school days, school suspensions, school truancy, low school achievement, and school failure (Hammer et al. 2002; Warren et al. 1997; Greene et al. 1997a, b; Thompson and Pillai 2006; Rogers et al. 1994).

Age

Age factors may increase the risk that children and adolescents will run away from home (Hammer et al. 2002; see also Appendix A). The results of the NISMART indicated that young people ages 15–17 accounted for two-thirds of the estimated runaway/thrown-away episodes (Hammer et al. 2002). In 18 % of the runaway/thrown-away incidents, the juvenile was 13 years or younger.

In the RYP, young people classified as "endangered runaways" had an average of 15.7 years, while those classified as not endangered had an average age of 23.3 years (see Appendix A). These runaways had still not returned home and may never do so.

Age also may be a factor in running away from substitute care. According to Courtney et al. (2005), a majority of the youth (90 %) who ran away from their placement were ages 12–18. However, according to the National Runaway Switchboard (2008), children under 12 years of age constitute the fastest growing age group who called crisis switchboards. Between 2000 and 2007, crisis calls by this age group increased by 172 %.

Older youth may elope from placement for longer periods than their younger counterparts (Courtney et al. 2005). In Courtney et al.'s (2005) analysis, 12 % of 12-year-old runaways eloped from placement for more than 5 weeks compared to nearly 38 % of 18-year-old runaways who eloped from care for the same period.

Gender

Gender factors may predict whether some youth run away from home. Female children and adolescents are at high risk of being abused in the family environment, which increases their likelihood of running away. However, in Hammer et al.'s (2002) analysis of the NISMART data on runaway/thrown-away incidents, girls did not have a higher probability of running away.

In contrast, in the RYP, girls were almost twice as likely as boys to run away from home (66 % vs. 34 %) (see Appendix A). Various factors may help to account for gender differences in running away. For example, as noted above, in instances of sexual abuse, girls may be more likely to run away than boys. However, in the RYP, data on the prevalence of child sexual, physical, and emotional abuse and neglect are not available (see Appendix A).

Gender factors also may be associated with running away from substitute care (Crosland and Dunlap 2014; Courtney and Zinn 2009; Courtney et al. 2005). One investigation of youth running away from substitute care showed that girls had a higher probability than boys of running away from out-of-home placements (Courtney et al. 2005).

Racial and Ethnic Factors

Racial and ethnic characteristics of youth may be associated with an increased probability of running away from home. In Hammer et al.'s (2002) research, 66 % of the estimated runaway/thrown-away incidents involved White young people. Non-Hispanic Black and Hispanic youth accounted for as much as 15 % and 14 % of the estimated incidents, respectively. Five percent of the episodes involved youth from other racial/ethnic backgrounds.

The results of the RYP revealed different racial/ethnic characteristics (see Appendix A). Whites constituted about 34 % of the runaways. Hispanics and African Americans each made up about 31 % of the sample of runaways. Asians accounted for 2 %, and other racial/ethnic groups made up 3 % of the sample. More research should be conducted to determine the extent to which racial and ethnic issues affect the extent to which young people run away or are thrown out of their home.

Sexual Orientation

Gay, lesbian, bisexual, and transsexual or transgender (GLBT) young people may be more likely to run away than heterosexual youth. According to Whitbeck et al. (2004), GLB young people had a higher likelihood of being kicked out by their parents or leaving because of conflicts over their sexual behavior or sexual orientation.

Residence (Region)

Investigators have not focused on geographical factors that may increase the likelihood that youth will run away from home. In the RYP, 45 % of the runaway children and adolescents resided in the south (see Appendix A). About 20 % of the runaway youth resided in the west. About 13 % of the runaway young people lived in the southwest region and 11 % lived in the Midwest. About 8 % resided in the north, and 5 % lived in the eastern region. More research is needed to ascertain if residential region influences the risk and nature of runaway behavior.

Did Runaway Youth Tell Their Families That They Were Running Away?

Researchers know little about whether children and adolescents tell their family, friends, and others that they are running away. In some cases, they vanish without telling their families and friends. P.J., a 14-year-old girl from New Orleans, LA, in RYP Case # 216, reportedly did not notify her family that she was running away (see Appendix A). Her grandmother stated that she became worried after P.J. did not come home.

In RYP Case # 398, J.G., a 16-year-old boy from Monroe, MI, vanished after he left his family's home for school in the morning hours (see Appendix A).

Witnesses may see the youth traveling and provide information to law enforcement personnel. In RYP Case # 553, a witness reported seeing L.W., a 15-year-old boy, leaving a youth academy in an automobile (see Appendix A).

Leaving Home Without Identification or Cash

Runaway children and adolescents may disappear without any identification or money. In RYP Case # 398, J.G. reportedly ran away from home without any identification or money (see Appendix A). John failed to pick up his pay check from his part-time job.

Duration That Runaway Youth Is Reporting Missing

Results from the NISMART reveal that the duration of most runaway/thrown-away incidents is short (Hammer et al. 2002). Fifty-eight percent of the estimated runaway/thrown-away episodes (975,700 episodes) lasted from 24 h to less than 1 week. Eighteen percent of the estimated incidents lasted from 7 h to less than 24 h, and 15 % lasted from 1 week to less than 1 month. Seven percent of the estimated incidents lasted from 1 month to less than 6 months.

However, other research shows that runaway youth may stay away for long periods and even permanently. The RYP results showed that young people may stay for long time periods or do not ever return home (see Appendix A). Youth who were classified as endangered runaways had been missing an average of 2.6 years. Those young people classified as non-endangered runaways had been missing an average of 8.8 years.

Seasons When Young People Run Away from Home

Seasonal factors may affect the likelihood that children and teens will run away. During the summer months, outdoor conditions such as warm temperatures allow many young people to survive on the streets and these conditions may encourage youth to run away during the summer months. Similarly, parents may kick out their children during the summertime because they feel that they can survive on the streets during this season.

The results of NISMART indicate that 39 % of the estimated runaway/thrown-away episodes occurred during the summer months (Hammer et al. 2002). In the NISMART investigation, 20 % of the estimated runaway/thrown-away incidents occurred in each of the other seasons. In less than 1 % of the incidents, no information was available about the season when the runaway/thrown-away incidents took place.

The RYP results had different seasonal patterns of running away from home (see Appendix A). Children and adolescents were most likely to run away from home during autumn (40.5 %). About 25 % of the youth reported running away during the spring and 23 % ran away during the summer months. Youth were least likely to run away during winter, suggesting that young people may be less likely to run away during periods of poor weather conditions.

Runaway Youth May Use Hair Dye to Alter Hair Color or Alter Their Appearance in Other Ways

Runaway children and adolescents at the time that they disappear may dye their hair a different color or alter their appearance in other ways. In RYP Case # 448, M.L., a 17-year-old girl with sandy hair color, reportedly may dye her hair a darker color (see Appendix A).

In RYP Case # 450, M.S., a 14-year-old girl with brown hair, reportedly used blonde highlights (see Appendix A). L.S., a 16-year-old, blond-hair girl from Eugene, OR, in RYP Case # 528, allegedly dyed her hair black at the time that she had run away from home (see Appendix A).

Runaway youth may wear disguises such as wigs. For example, in RYP Case # 528, L.S. allegedly also may have worn a wig at the time that she disappeared (see Appendix A).

Use of Nicknames/Alias Names

Runaway young people may use nicknames and alias names to avoid detection by law enforcement personnel. The RYP findings revealed that about 23 % of the runaway youth uses an alias or nickname (see Appendix A). For example, M.L., in RYP

Case # 148, reportedly may be using the nickname R. (see Appendix A). In RYP Case # 450, M.S. allegedly may be using the alias name S.A. (see Appendix A).

Use of Alias Birthdates

Runaway children and adolescents may use alias birthdates to help avoid detection by the police. For example, L.J., a 14-year-old girl from Philadelphia, PA, in RYP Case # 507, used an alias date of birth (see Appendix A). Her real date of birth is June 20, 1991, while her alias date of birth is May 20, 1990.

Runaway Youth in the Company of Peers

Young people who run away often are in the company of peers at the time that they run away from home. Young people who run away in the company of peers may benefit from the social support and resources of these traveling companions.

Running away from peers also may reflect the significance of peer influence during childhood and adolescence. Runaway youth may be in the company of same-sex or mixed-sex peers. Running away in the company of a same-sex peer is illustrated by RYP Case # 514 (see Appendix A). In this runaway missing person case, M.C., a 17-year-old girl from Leesburg, VA, may be running away with a juvenile female.

Runaway Youth in the Company of Adults

Running away with adult companions may illustrate the importance of adult role models for youth who are running away. These adults may, in a sense, act as replacements for the runaway youth's parents.

The adult travel companions' gender may be the same or different from that of the runaway youth. Adult male companions may reflect father issues that the runaway youth is struggling with. In contrast, adult female companions may reflect mother problems that the runaway youth is grappling with. An example of running away in the company of an adult of different sex is illustrated by RYP Case # 518 (see Appendix A). In this case, T.A., a 14-year-old girl from Dallas, TX, may be running away with an adult male.

According to the RYP, 11 % of the youth ran away from home with one or more adults (see Appendix A). In RYP Case # 421, H.A., a 15-year-old boy from Bloomington, CA, may be running away in the company of an adult male (see Appendix A).

In some cases, law enforcement may possess some information about the adults who are accompanying the runaway youth. For example, in RYP Case # 455, S.H., a 17-year-old girl from Newport News, VA, reportedly was running away with an adult White male with the name Harry (see Appendix A).

Runaway Youth in the Company of Both Juveniles and Adults

Children and adolescents who run away from home may be in the company of both juveniles and adults. For example, in RYP Case # 463, W.S., a 16-year-old boy from Knob Noster, MO, may have been in the company of a juvenile female and an adult female (see Appendix A).

Runaway Youth in the Company of Relatives

Children and adolescents who disappear may be in the company of relatives and others. J.G., a 14-year-old girl from Winston Salem, NC, in RYP Case # 575, allegedly ran away from home in the company of a male and a juvenile female relative (see Appendix A).

Do Runaway Youth Stay in the Local Area?

To what extent do runaway young people stay in their local areas at the time that they run away from home? Hammer et al. (2002) discovered that in 38 % of the estimated runaway/thrown-away incidents, the juvenile had run away 10 miles or less. The investigators found that in 31 % of the estimated incidents, young people had run away more than 10 but no more than 50 miles. In 10 % of the estimated episodes, the youth had run away more than 50 but no more than 100 miles. Young people had run away more than 100 miles in 13 % of the estimated runaway/thrown-away incidents. No information was available for 9 % of the estimated runaway/thrown-away episodes.

Results from the RYP showed that some young people may be staying in the local area (see Appendix A). In the RYP, 27 % of the runaway youth may be staying in their local area, according to law enforcement personnel. For example, in RYP Case # 457, J.R., a 13-year-old boy, from Bakersfield, CA, may still be staying in the Bakersfield, CA, area (see Appendix A).

In RYP Case # 460 involving P.T., a 15-year-old girl from Montgomery County, Maryland, law enforcement personnel thought that patience may frequent a residential community in Montgomery County, Maryland (see Appendix A).

In other instances, law enforcement personnel have information to believe that the runaway youth may be staying in the local area or traveling to another destination. For example, in RYP Case # 160, the police reported that S.A., an 18-year-old girl from Sarasota, FL, may still be in the local region or she may go to Miami, FL (see Appendix A).

Motor Vehicle Used to Run Away

Young people use a variety of ways to run away from home depending on their resources and access to different modes of transportation. In the RYP, 4 % of the young people used a motor vehicle to run away from home (see Appendix A).

Did the Runaway/Thrown-Away Youth Leave the State?

What percent of runaway/thrown-away youth leave the state? Hammer et al. (2002) discovered that in 9 % of the estimated runaway/thrown-away incidents, children and adolescents traveled out of state.

Results from the RYP showed that about 14 % of the sample reportedly may have traveled to another state (see Appendix A). Young people may have travel companions to help them deal with the challenges and uncertainties of running away to another state.

Travel Destinations in the USA

Investigators are beginning to analyze the specific travel destinations of runaways. San Francisco is considered a popular destination for runaway youth. In the RYP, about 13 % of the runaway young people reportedly traveled to Texas and 13 % to Newberry, South Carolina (see Appendix A). Runaway young people also left for Miami, Florida, Salt Lake City, Utah, and Baltimore, Maryland (8 % each).

Travel to Another Country

How often do children and adolescents run away to another country? The RYP results indicated that about 4 % of the youth may have traveled to another country (see Appendix A). In the RYP, 3 % of the youth ran away to Mexico.

Youth in the USA who live in states that border Mexico or are in a state close to Mexico may be likely to run away from home and travel to Mexico. Youth who are of Hispanic heritage, especially Mexican heritage, and who have family, friends, and acquaintances may be likely to run away to Mexico. In some instances, young people also may go across many states to reach Mexico.

Young people who travel to another country may run away with peers or adults. Being in the company of peers or adults may help the runaway youth adjust to the challenges of running away to another country. For example, in RYP Case # 456, S.C., a 14-year-old Hispanic girl from Las Vegas, NV, may have run away to Texas or Mexico (see Appendix A). S.C. may be traveling with an adult male.

In other instances, the young person may run away to another country such as Mexico without having a traveling companion. In RYP Case # 513, for example, another Hispanic girl, C.V., 15-year-old from San Diego, CA, may have left the USA and headed to Mexico without a traveling companion (see Appendix A).

Travel Plans Unknown

Law enforcement personnel may be unaware of the travel plans of runaway youth. For example, in RYP Case # 472, the travel plans of S.B., a runaway girl from Virginia Beach, VA, was unknown to the police (see Appendix A). In RYP Case # 579, the police did not know the travel plans of a runaway girl, M.E., from Fairfax County, VA (see Appendix A).

Emotional Status at the Time of Their Disappearance

During childhood and adolescence, youth may be impulsive at times, and those who run away may do so out of impulse. In other instances, youth may plan their escape from home. They may select their travel companions and destination; obtain necessary resources, including money and food; and plan other details to facilitate their successful running away from home.

Runaway Youth Suffer Distress and Painful Psychosocial Experiences

Children and adolescents frequently run away in response to feeling severe distress. Their feelings of distress result from experiencing the pain and trauma of abuse, neglect, humiliating events, and exploitation (Hyde 2005; Paradise and Cause 2002; Tyler and Johnson 2006; Peled and Cohavi 2009).

Suicidal Behaviors

Runaway and homeless children and adolescents may be exposed to severe trauma and lack the resources and capacity to deal with this trauma, increasing their risk for suicidal behaviors (Whitbeck et al. 2000; Yoder et al. 1998; Hammer et al. 2002;

Rotheram-Borus 1993). According to Hammer et al. (2002), in 4 % of the estimated runaway/thrown-away incidents, children and adolescents had previously tried to commit suicide.

While on the streets, young people who become victims of human trafficking may be at risk for engaging in suicidal behaviors such as suicidal ideation and suicide attempts (Kiss et al. 2015).

Abuse

To what degree are children and adolescents around the time that they run away or become homeless are the victims of physical, sexual, and emotional/mental abuse? Research reports indicate that a significant percentage of children and adolescents who run away have been exposed to different forms of abuse at home (Hammer et al. 2002; Benoit-Bryan 2011). Based on an estimated 1,682,900 young people who had an endangered runaway/thrown-away episode in 1999, Hammer et al. (2002) discovered that 21 % had been abused physically or sexually in their family before the episode or were fearful of returning to the household. Verbal, physical, and sexual types of abuse may increase the chance that children and teens will run away from home. In terms of verbal abuse, Benoit-Bryan (2011) showed that youth who had reported verbal abuse in the family were more than twice as likely to have run away from home (11.7 %) than those who did not report verbal abuse (5.3 %). With regard to physical abuse, children and adolescents who reported family-related physical abuse in Benoit-Bryan's (2011) longitudinal investigation were almost three times likely to run away from home (17.4 %) than those youth who did not report physical abuse (6.3 %). Children and adolescents who reported being sexual abused in Benoit-Bryan's (2011) investigation were more than twice as likely to run away (17 %) than those who did not report being sexually abused (7.9 %).

Neglect

In addition to abuse, children and adolescents who are the victims of neglect may have a higher probability of running away or becoming homeless than those who have not suffered from neglect (Thompson and Pillai 2006; Thrane et al. 2006; Nebbitt et al. 2007; Whitbeck et al. 1997a, b).

However, based on a convenience sample of 602 adolescents, Thrane et al. (2006) discovered that adolescents who had suffered from neglect and sexual abuse were more likely to run away earlier and face victimization on the streets. According to Whitbeck et al. (1997a, b) and Nebbitt et al. (2007), youth may run away in response to parental neglect.

Other Family Problems and Dysfunction

Children and adolescents around the time that they run away or become homeless may be responding to additional family problems and dysfunction. A number of studies detail diverse family problems and dysfunction as major predictors of youth runaway and homelessness (Nebbitt et al. 2007; Thompson and Pillai 2006; Tyler et al. 2001a, b, c; Whitbeck et al. 1997a, b; Bass 1992a, b; Crespi and Sabatelli 1993; Dusenbury et al. 1994; Kurtz et al. 1991b; Rotheram-Borus 1993). Parental conflict, distrust of parents, family disorganization and instability, parental rejection, lack of parental warmth and support, poor parenting, and parental substance abuse may increase the risk of children and adolescent running away (Nebbitt et al. 2007; Thompson and Pillai 2006; Tyler et al. 2001a, b, c; Whitbeck et al. 1997a, b; Bass 1992a, b; Crespi and Sabatelli 1993; Dusenbury et al. 1994; Kurtz et al. 1991b; Rotheram-Borus 1993). The stressors that high-risk families experience increase conflict between children and adolescents at risk for running away and their parents (Dusenbury et al. 1994).

Substitute Care

Children and adolescents who have been placed in substitute care such as foster care may have a higher probability of running away from home. In Benoit-Bryan's (2011) investigation of runaway youth, more than 30 % of the individuals who had resided in foster care had run away. In contrast, a little more than 8 % of persons who had never been in foster care ran away from home.

History of Violence

Runaway and homeless young people may be at risk for engaging in violent behavior. Hammer et al. (2002) showed that in 4 % of the estimated runaway/thrown-away incidents, youth were with a violent individual during the episode.

Kim et al. (2009) discovered that running away increases the probability of subsequent violent delinquency. Similarly, Baron and Hartnagel (1998) showed that chronic homelessness and related conditions predict participation in violent crimes such as robbery. The findings of the RYP showed that 11 % of the runaway juveniles had a history of violence (see Appendix A).

Victims of Physical Assault

To what degree is youth at the time that they run away or become homeless are at increased risk of physical assault? Data from the RYP revealed that the police had reported that none of the runaway youth had been victims of a physical assault at the time that they ran away (see Appendix A).

In contrast, various investigations reveal that youth in runaway/thrown-away episodes may be at increased risk of being physically assaulted (Hammer et al. 2002). According to Hammer et al. (2002), in 4 % of the estimated runaway/thrown-away episodes, children had been physically assaulted or an individual had tried to physically assault the child during the runaway/thrown-away episode.

Delinquency/Criminal History at the Time Youth Run Away

According to various reports, children and adolescent runaways have conduct problems and participate in various delinquent behaviors such as vandalism and robbery, especially as part of their subsistence strategies (Whitbeck et al. 2000; Hammer et al. 2002; Thompson and Pollio 2006; Chen et al. 2006; Edinburgh and Saewyc 2009; McCarthy and Hagan 1992).

Runaway/thrown-away youth may spend time in areas where criminal activities are known to transpire. In the NISMART investigation, in 12 % of the estimated incidents of runaway/thrown-away incidents, the youth spent time in a location where criminal behaviors were known to occur (Hammer et al. 2002).

Hammer et al. (2002) discovered that 11 % of children and adolescents who ran away had participated in criminal conduct during their runaway episode. Based on their analysis of youth at shelters, Thompson and Pollio (2006) revealed that 16 % had engaged in misdemeanors. According to an investigation carried out by the Federal Youth Services Bureau, two-thirds of youth in shelters and four-fifths of young people on the streets had attempted or completed a theft (Greene et al. 1995).

Runaway and homeless youth frequently suffer from hunger and food insecurity and steal food as part of their subsistence strategy. In their study of homeless youth on the streets, McCarthy and Hagan (1992) discovered that 47 % of the adolescents in the survey indicated that they had stolen food.

In the RYP, only 2 % of the runaways had a criminal history (see Appendix A). In 2 % of the RYP runaway incidents, law enforcement personnel also classified the runaway case as involving possible foul play (see Appendix A).

Human Trafficking, Prostitution, and Survival Sex

Runway/thrown-away and homeless children and adolescents may be kidnapped, forced, or tricked into becoming victims of sex, forced labor, and organ trafficking (International Labour Organization n.d.; UNHCR n.d.; Family & Youth Service Bureau, National Clearinghouse on Families & Youth n.d.; National Human Trafficking Resource Center n.d. a, b; Ark of Hope for Children 2014, February 22; Morewitz 2008, 2016). Human traffickers may use money, food, and other rewards to lure the street youth into sex, forced labor, and organ trafficking. Street youth are especially susceptible to human traffickers because of their desperate need for basic survival on the streets and lack of family and social support.

Human trafficking is a multibillion dollar enterprise and is increasing and is present in 50 US states (Ark of Hope for Children 2014, February 22). Globally, two million children are trafficked for the sex trade. As many as 300,000 Americans under age 18 are trafficked annually for the sex trade (Ark of Hope for Children 2014, February 22). According to the United Nations Office on Drugs and Crimes (UNODC), in 2012, the percentage of child victims increased over a 3-year period from 20 to 27 % (Ark of Hope for Children 2014, February 22).

According to the Family & Youth Service Bureau and National Clearinghouse on Families & Youth (n.d.), during the first 72 h that male and female children are on the streets, they are solicited to participate in prostitution. Girls become prostitutes for the first time on average between 12 and 14 years of age. Among female youth on the streets, 55 % engage in sex work. Seventy-five percent of these girls have a pimp. Approximately 20 % of these girls engage in prostitution as part of national crime networks. They are kidnapped, coerced, or tricked into moving far away from their families and are kept separated from friends and family members.

Runaway and homeless youth are often coerced, kidnapped, or tricked into human trafficking (Family & Youth Service Bureau, National Clearinghouse on Families & Youth n.d.). Human traffickers may threaten these young people with death or threaten to kill their family members and friends if they try to escape sex and forced labor trafficking (Morewitz 2008). The human traffickers may use both verbal and non-verbal forms of communication to make these death threats. Human traffickers also may use blackmail to coerce the street youth into participating in sex, forced labor, and organ trafficking.

Friends of the street youth may participate in the targeting and kidnapping of the victims (Morewitz 2016). For example, in one self-report, T, a 14-year-old girl, reported that an older boyfriend coerced her into human trafficking (Family & Youth Service Bureau, National Clearinghouse on Families & Youth n.d.). Runaway and homeless young people may also be human trafficking victims even if no obvious kidnapping, coercion, or deception is involved (UNHCR n.d.).

Runaway and homeless young people may participate in survival sex, e.g., exchanging sex for food, money, drugs, shelter, or other resources (McCarthy and Hagan 1992; Hammer et al. 2002). In their sample of homeless young people, McCarthy and Hagan (1992) discovered that 29.7 % had participated in prostitution.

Runaway and homeless young people are also kidnapped, coerced, or tricked into participating in forced labor (Morewitz 2016; International Labour Organization n.d.; National Human Trafficking Resource Center n.d. a, b; UNHCR n.d.). Human traffickers may pretend to be friends with the runaway and homeless young people and take advantage of their vulnerabilities, e.g., the youth's desperate need for food, clothing, and shelter. Human traffickers will select their targets at transportation centers, runaway shelters, and other street locations where runaway and homeless youth congregate.

Use of Alcohol and Other Illicit Drugs at the Time They Ran Away

Researchers have analyzed the patterns of substance use and abuse after children and adolescents run away (Van Leeuwen et al. 2004; Ginzler et al. (2003); Greene et al. 1997a, b; McCarthy and Hagan 1992). Substance use and abuse is prevalent among these individuals. According to Hammer et al. (2002), in 19 % of the estimated runaway/thrown-away incidents, children were dependent on drugs. The researchers discovered that in 17 % of the estimated episodes, youth were taking hard drugs. In addition, during 18 % of the estimated runaway/thrown-away incidents, 18 % the youth were with an individual who was known to be abusing drugs. In another investigation, McCarthy and Hagan (1992) revealed that 80 % of their study participants indicated that they smoked marijuana since becoming homeless.

Medical Condition and Mortality

Children and adolescents may have or develop a life-threatening medical condition and die from this condition during a runaway/thrown-away episode (Roy et al. 2004). According to the RYP results, about 3 % of the runaways had a medical condition (see Appendix A). Young people on the streets who become human trafficking victims may have untreated medical problems (National Human Trafficking Resource Center n.d. a, b).

Female runaways may have a history of pregnancy or become pregnant while on their own. Halcon and Lifson (2004), based on a sample of 203 homeless youth ages 15–22, showed that 53 % of the female reportedly had at least one pregnancy and 28 % had two or more pregnancies. About 43 % had an abortion. One or more live births occurred in 24 % of the females.

Disability

Runaway and homeless youth may suffer from mental disorders and/or developmental disabilities (Hammer et al. 2002; Whitbeck et al. 1999, 2000). During runaway and homeless episodes, street experiences such as victimization and interacting with nonconventional peers may increase the likelihood of depressive symptoms. Young people on the streets who are victims of human trafficking may suffer from depression (Kiss et al. 2015). Whitbeck et al. (1999) discovered that street experiences increased the young people's adverse impact of their childhood abuse and symptoms of depression.

According to the RYP, 1 % of the runaway young people reportedly had a mental disability (see Appendix A). In the RYP sample, no symptoms of depression were reported (see Appendix A). No physical disabilities among runaways in the RYP were noted (see Appendix A).

Runaway and homeless children and adolescents may engage in self-mutilation. For example, in one investigation, Tyler et al. (2003) discovered that homeless youth had a high prevalence of self-mutilation; 69 % had engaged in self-mutilation at least one time. In their study, 12 % indicated that they had received medical care for their self-injurious behaviors.

Contacts with Law Enforcement

In NISMART, the police were contacted in 32 % of the estimated runaway/thrown-away incidents. Given the ongoing subsistence strategies and illicit drug use of runaway and homeless youth, they are at increased risk of being arrested and incarcerated (Chen et al. 2006; McCarthy and Hagan 1992; Warren et al. 1997; Bass 1992a, b). Using a sample of 428 homeless and runaway young people, Chen et al. (2006) revealed that more than 50 % of the adolescents reported having been arrested at least one time after running away initially. The teens reported an average of 4.4 arrests.

Based on their investigation of homeless young people, McCarthy and Hagan (1992) showed that 46 % of their study participants had been jailed at least one time since running away or becoming homeless in other ways. Runaway children and adolescents face extensive juvenile justice entanglement stemming from their status offenses and participation in stealing, burglary, prostitution, and other offenses.

Contact with Social Services

Youth around the time that they runaway or become homeless may be more likely to have a history of social service contacts, reflecting their past and current exposure to life-threatening abuse and neglect. However, findings from the RYP did not reveal any evidence that the endangered runaway had contacts with social services (see Appendix A).

Runaway/Thrown-Away Incident Outcomes

According to NISMART, in more than 99 % of the runaway/thrown-away episodes, the child returned home (Hammer et al. 2002). In the remaining runaway/thrown-away incidents, the child was located but did not return home, the child was neither located nor did she or he return home, or no information was available.

In contrast, the RYP results showed that the entire sample of 200 runaway children and adolescents had not returned home (see Appendix A). In addition, the runaway youth had not been definitively located.

Chapter 2
Running Away from Substitute Care

This chapter evaluates the possible reasons why young people are placed in substitute care such as foster care, the prevalence of eloping from substitute care, and the duration of eloping from these out-of-home settings. In this chapter, the institutional conditions of substitute care and the demographic, social, psychological, and behavioral conditions that may increase at the probability that young people will elope from substitute care settings. This chapter discusses organizational issues such as the differences in social service agencies' classification of elopement and the resources available to agencies in locating and returning youth who have gone absent without leave. This chapter discusses the role of emergency runaway shelters for youth who have eloped from substitute care. The conditions that increase the risk that youth will elope from substitute care are also presented. Such factors as placement instability or disruption, substitute care neglect and abuse, demographic characteristics of the youth in substitute care, peer influence, and family issues are discussed. This chapter also analyzes the impact of frequent elopement from out-of-home placement settings on the youth's future social, educational, and employment status. This chapter also discusses interventions to improve substitute care.

Substitute care, also known as out-of-home care, involves the placement of youth in different living arrangements (Sigrid 2004; Crosland and Dunlap 2014). Youth in substitute care may be placed in foster care, family or relative foster care, group homes, residential settings, and emergency shelters (Crosland and Dunlap 2014; Slesnick et al. 2009; Nebbitt et al. 2007). Children and adolescents are placed in substitute care for a variety of reasons. Their parents may be unable to care for them because of parental death, poverty, incarceration, or other circumstances (Crosland and Dunlap 2014). In addition, youth are placed in substitute care because they are victims of abuse, neglect, or lack of supervision. A court order will remove a child from her or his home and the child then becomes a ward of the state. Child welfare or social service then places the child in substitute care based on the best needs of the child.

Children and adolescents run away from both home and substitute care settings such as group homes and foster care (Johnson 2010). Running away from substitute care is referred to as elopement or going absent without leave (AWOL). According to

S.J. Morewitz, *Runaway and Homeless Youth*,
DOI 10.1007/978-3-319-30863-0_2

the Administration for Children's Services (1992), running away is an event in which a child who is under the care of a state-licensed social service agency voluntarily or involuntarily goes missing without the permission of the designated caregiver.

Disagreement exists among child welfare organizational officials about when a child in substitute care is classified as a runaway (Crosland and Dunlap 2014). Agencies and group facilities vary in their reporting of runaways. Some organizations report a child as a runaway once she or he disappears from placement without consent. In contrast, other organizations only report a child as a runaway if she or he has gone missing without permission for a minimum time period, e.g., a 24 h time period.

Once a child goes missing from placement without permission, the staff of child welfare organizations and the police attempt to find and bring back the child who has eloped (Crosland and Dunlap 2014). Child welfare organizations must use more resources and effort to successfully locate and return the runaway. The agencies must meet substantial reporting requirements within specified time periods such as within 24 h. The police use resources to try to find the runaway and must comply with paperwork related to their activities.

Schools face a loss of money when a child goes missing from substitute care and does not go to school (Crosland and Dunlap 2014). Schools can lose funding due to reduced school attendance.

Prevalence of Running Away from Substitute Care

Data on the prevalence of running away from substitute care are usually derived from investigators collecting surveys of homeless young people. In addition, researchers determine the prevalence of running away from substitute care by analyzing the discharge data from emergency homeless shelters and other organizations (Crosland and Dunlap 2014).

Many foster youth run away from their placements. The US Department of Health and Human Services found that in the USA approximately 8000 of 424,000 young people in foster care ran away from placements in 2009. According to various researchers (Sedlak et al. 2002; Biehal and Wade 2000; Crosland and Dunlap 2014), youth in substitute care constitute a large part of the runaway youth population. Sedlak et al. (2002) showed that youth in foster care are about two times as likely to run away (2.4 %) as young people in the same age range in the community (0.9 %).

According to the Runaway Youth Longitudinal Study 2011, 30 % of the youth who had been in foster care also had a history of running away from home (Benoit-Bryan 2011; Johnson 2010). In contrast, 8.1 % of those interviewed in the investigation who had not been in foster care had run away from home previously (Benoit-Bryan 2011).

Other research has shown high rates of elopement among young people in substitute care. In Courtney et al.'s (2014) analysis, between 46 and 52 % of 17-year-olds in foster care in three states, Illinois, Wisconsin, and Iowa, had run away from placement.

A significant percentage of young people in substitute care frequently run away from placement more than once (Courtney et al. 2014; Wade and Biehal 1998). For example, in one self-report, a 16-year-old girl stated that, for a period of 5 years and 5 months, she had run away three times from a group home, which is a locked facility (Mishriki 2001–2013).

According to Courtney et al. (2014), almost 67 % who eloped from placement did so more than one time. The authors found that a substantial percentage (36 %) had eloped from substitute care on three or more occasions.

Foster Care Young People in Runaway Shelters

Children and adolescents who reside in runaway emergency shelters may have eloped from foster care placements (Crosland and Dunlap 2014). In the USA, Bass (1992a, b) evaluated 170 runaway shelters and discovered that more than 25 % of the young people had come from a foster or group home facility. In addition, the author showed that 38 % of the individuals had been in a foster care setting during the year before they eloped.

According to another study that analyzed 2000 young people in 18 states, 18 % of children and adolescents from shelters had run away from foster care (Kurtz et al. 1991a). In an investigation of young people at a shelter in Seattle, MacLean et al. (1999) stated that 18 % of the shelter youth had indicated that they had run away from care. In addition, another study of young people from shelters and streets in four states in the Midwest showed that 13 % of them had run away from foster care (Whitbeck et al. 1997a, b).

In Canada, one investigation of 689 homeless young people demonstrated showed that 43 % of the individuals had contact with child protect services (Raising the Roof 2009). Moreover, 68 % of the study participants had originated directly from three types of settings: foster care, group facilities, or centers for youth.

Duration of Elopement Episodes

Many children and adolescents run away from placement for a short time period. For example, one investigation showed that almost 50 % of runaway incidents were less than 1-week duration (Courtney et al. 2005). Other youth elope for longer periods. Courtney et al. (2005) discovered that nearly 25 % of elopement episodes were of 5-week duration or longer.

Why Youth Run Away from Substitute Care

Foster care has been called a “national disgrace,” and this dysfunctional foster care system produces a high rate of running away from these settings (Crosland and Dunlap 2014). Youth in these settings may be abused and/or go missing and in some cases die. In addition, Carpenter et al. (2001) found that high-risk sexual activities and increased rates of pregnancy are linked to being in placement settings. Substitute caregivers also may remove youth from their placement settings. For example, in one self-report, a runaway girl reportedly was placed in a foster home and was kicked out by her foster parents after a short stay because she would go out all night with her friends (Mishriki 2001–2013).

Young people in substitute care settings may suffer from neglect as well. In one self-report, a runaway boy indicated that he had been placed in a foster home and the foster parent, a lady, did not do anything except give him $250 a month, which was half of her monthly government check for being a foster parent (Mishriki 2001–2013). The youth claimed that the foster parent told him that he was on his own.

Demographic Factors

One investigation of youth running away from substitute care showed that girls had a higher probability than boys of running away from out-of-home placements (Courtney et al. 2005). Girls may have a higher probability of accessing shelter and hotline services (Crosland and Dunlap 2014). According to the National Runaway Switchboard (2008), 75 % of individuals calling in response to a crisis were females.

Age may be a factor in running away from substitute care. According to Courtney et al. (2005), a majority of the youth (90 %) who ran away from their placement were in the 12–18 years age group. However, according to the National Runaway Switchboard (2008), children under 12 years of age constitute the fastest growing age group who called crisis switchboards. Between 2000 and 2007, crisis calls by this age group increased by 172 %.

Older youth may elope from placement for longer periods than their younger counterparts (Courtney et al. 2005). In Courtney et al.'s (2005) analysis, 12 % of 12-year-old runaways eloped from placement for more than 5 weeks compared to nearly 38 % of 18-year-old runaways who eloped from care for the same period.

Placement Disruptions or Instability

Disruptions or instability in substitute care placements can increase the probability that youth will run away (Courtney et al. 2005; Yoder et al. 1998). For example, according to Courtney et al. (2005), young people who have a history of placement instability are more likely to run away.

Victims of Abuse, Neglect, Abandonment, and Family Conflict/Dysfunction

Because youth in foster care often have been removed from their families because of abuse, neglect, abandonment, and various forms of family conflict and dysfunction, they are likely to present challenges to foster care staff, causing them to experience placement instability or disruptions (Williams et al. 2001; Aarons et al. 2010; Keil and Price 2006; Crosland and Dunlap 2014).

Youth in substitute care who have been victims of sexual, physical, and mental/ emotional abuse; abandonment; and neglect have an increased probability of running away (Crosland and Dunlap 2014; Thompson et al. 2004; Yoder et al. 1998). Studies reveal that girls are more likely to be sexually abused than boys, which support the findings that girls tend to run away more than boys.

According to one self-report, a runaway girl who had abusive caregivers, her mother and an aunt, and an uncaring father, wrote that she was "bounced" among five placement settings (Mishriki 2001–2013). While on the streets, she got involved in drugs and was later arrested by the police.

In another case, K., a female runaway/homeless adolescent, had been in a variety of psychiatric and child welfare agency placements, including a group home (Williams et al. 2001). K. had suffered from abuse and neglect. She reportedly had been sexually and physically abused and neglected by her mother who was a drug addict. K. later was often truant from school, engaged in self-harm behaviors to deal with her emotional problems, and attempted suicide several times. Her dysfunctional history may have contributed to her intense psychosocial difficulties and multiple placements in substitute care.

Children who live at home typically are running away from their parents. In contrast, children and adolescents in foster care are eloping from their foster care settings to be with their friends, girlfriends or boyfriends, biological parents, and other family member (Crosland and Dunlap 2014; Pergamit and Ernst 2010; Biehal and Wade 2000; Johnson 2010). Foster youth run away from foster care to return to settings that are familiar to them (Crosland and Dunlap 2014). Young people who elope from foster care may seek the comfort and security of being with their friends and family and as a way to achieve a feeling of normalcy in their lives (Courtney et al. 2005). Youth may realize that their biological families are not "normal" or "healthy." Nevertheless, the youth will elope from foster care settings to be with their unhealthy families because the families give them a sense of normalcy or having a "real home."

Young people also elope from foster care so that they can obtain other desired goods and services. For example, they may want to "hang out" with their friends and eat their favorite foods that they cannot do in foster care (Clark et al. 2008; Crosland and Dunlap 2014).

Children and adolescents in substitute care may elope from their placement because they are suffering different forms of abuse and neglect in the setting. In one self-report, an 8-year-old boy wrote that he eloped from his orphanage because he and other residents would frequently get beat up (Mishriki 2001–2013).

Youth in substitute care may run away to avoid overcrowded settings and the lack of privacy (Johnson 2010). Young people may elope from placements in order to protest the poor services provided at these facilities (Johnson 2010).

Children and adolescent in substitute care may elope to seeking protection against bullying, assaults, and sexual harassment by other residents (Johnson 2010). Youth also may elope from placements to flee caregiver abuse (Johnson 2010).

Young people run away from substitute care because they do not like their caregivers or their placement setting (Crosland and Dunlap 2014; Pergamit and Ernst 2010). Angenent et al. (1991), in an investigation of foster care in the Netherlands, showed that young people who eloped from foster care were more likely to indicate that their caregivers were authoritarian and cold toward compared to young people who did not run away.

Substitute care staff in group settings who are trained in providing youth with appropriate skills in social development, education, and employment and who use effective interactional strategies have a greater chance of forming positive bonds with youth than staff who do not have such training (Willner et al. 1977). As a result of these effective bonds, youth may have a lower probability of running away from group settings.

In one investigation, Willner et al. (1977) measured youth assessments of caregiver relationships and discovered that youth were more likely to favorably rate caregivers who exhibited such behaviors as having a calm demeanor, being helpful, having a joking relationship with them, offering effective feedback, and being fair. Caregivers who engage in these types of preferred behaviors may be better able to gain compliance from youth. Young people also may have a higher probability of accepting the guidelines of staff. As a consequence, youth may have a lower chance of running away from substitute care (Willner et al. 1977; Crosland and Dunlap 2014).

The quality of educational programs and services provided to foster youth may affect their likelihood of running away. Youth in placement settings may not have individualized educational plans or actually obtain educational services. For example, White et al. (1990) discovered that 39 % of young people in placement settings had received individualized education plans. However, only 16 % of these individuals obtained these educational services. However, research is lacking on whether the lack of educational programs and services in foster care settings are linked to running away episodes.

The educational performance of youth in foster care is often low. For example, investigations reveal that a large percentage of foster care youth function below their grade level (Crosland and Dunlap 2014; Fanshel et al. 1990; Pasztor et al. 1986). Low educational attainment may contribute to elopement episodes. However, research is needed to investigate the link between educational attainment and running away frequency.

Youth who elope from placements in the first months of placement may be at increased risk of funning away in the future (Crosland and Dunlap 2014; Courtney et al. 2005; Kaplan 2004). In Courtney et al.'s (2005) analysis, foster youth were more likely to run away from foster care settings within the first couple of months of being placed.

In one self-report, an 8-year-old boy reportedly eloped from his orphanage and returned the next day after being sexually abused by a male adult who took him to his residence for the night (Mishriki 2001–2013).

According to various investigations, young people in emergency runaway shelters often have run away from foster care settings (Crosland and Dunlap 2014; Kurtz et al. 1991a; Bass 1992a, b). Based on a sample of 2000 young people in 18 states, Kurtz et al. (1991a)) discovered that 18 % of children and adolescents from shelters had run away from foster care. Based on analysis of four states in the Midwest, Whitbeck et al. (1997a, b)) discovered that 13 % of the young people in shelters and on the streets had eloped from a foster care setting. According to Bass's (1992a, b) research on 170 runaway shelters, more than a quarter of the young people had been previously in a foster care or group setting. The author reported that, some time during the year before their elopement, 38 % of the children and adolescents had been in a foster care setting. In an investigation of young people at a shelter in Seattle, according to MacLean et al. (1999), 18 % of the shelter youth had indicated that they had run away from foster care. In addition, another study of young people from shelters and streets in four states in the Midwest showed that 13 % of them had run away from foster care.

First Time of Running Away from Substitute Care

Youth who elope for the first time are at risk for future running away episodes. According to Ross (2001), the first episode of running away from substitute care increases the risk of future running away incidents.

History of Running Away

Young people who have a history of running away have a high probability of running away in the future (Thompson et al. 2004; Yoder et al. 1998).

Use of Alcohol and Other Drugs

Young people who smoke cigarettes and consume alcohol and other drugs are at increased risk of running away (Thompson et al 2004; Yoder et al. 1998; Courtney et al. 2005; Crosland and Dunlap 2014; Williams et al. 2001). Substance addiction increases the likelihood that young people will run away or experience other forms of placement instability than those who are not addicted to substances (Williams et al. 2001). For example, in one self-report, T., a female adolescent, reportedly had great difficulties in coping with her addiction to alcohol and other drugs (Williams et al. 2001). T., who was 19 at the time, had been living on and off the streets since the age of 13. She had been a frequent resident of the different runaway shelters in her community. T. distrusted people and her distrust of people may have contributed to her placement instability.

Youth who use substances may run away to be with their substance-using friends and to obtain access to cigarettes, alcohol, and other drugs. In addition, youth who use alcohol and other drugs may be more likely to be performing poorly in school, which increases their probability of running away. Use of alcohol and other drugs among young people is also linked to juvenile delinquency and arrests, which increase the likelihood that they will run away.

Having Mental Health Diagnoses

Young people who have been diagnosed with mental disorders may have a higher probability of running away of substitute care. Based on an analysis of children who ran away from out-of-home settings, Courtney et al. (2005) showed that youth who had mental health diagnoses had an increased likelihood of eloping.

Offending History Increases Risk of Running Away from Residential and Foster Care

Youth who have a history of committing offenses may have a higher probability of running away from substitute care.

Type of Placement

The type of foster care setting may affect whether a child runs away from that setting. According to Courtney et al. (2005), youth were less likely to run away from foster care if they resided with a relative. In addition, they were less likely to run away from foster care if they lived in a foster care setting with a sibling.

According to Witherup et al. (2006), young people who have obtained termination of parental rights are living with a relative in a long-term custody arrangement or who are placed in "home-type" settings have a lower probability of running away from foster care and have more stable placements than those in group facility settings.

In their analysis, Courtney et al. (2005) discovered that young people were more likely to run away from residential-type placement settings. Researchers should analyze which factors increase the likelihood that youth will elope from these types of facilities.

Access to Education

While in foster care placement settings, young people may have problems accessing the appropriate educational programs and services based on their educational needs (Crosland and Dunlap 2014).

Consequences of Running Away

Running away can have major adverse consequences for the youth. Youth who elope may face more restrictive placement settings when they are returned to foster care (Crosland and Dunlap 2014). Children and adolescents who run away may decrease their bonding with conventional adults (Kaplan 2004). For example, running away also increases the probability that young people will engage in delinquent and gang activities and get arrested (Crosland and Dunlap 2014).

Youth who run away often participate in risky survival strategies while on their own, including engaging in criminal activities such as petty theft (Crosland and Dunlap 2014; Biehal and Wade 2000). In an investigation of runaways from foster care, Biehal and Wade (2000) discovered that almost 50 % of more than 200 young people had participated in delinquent activities and had been charged with crimes. The authors showed that some of the individuals had a history of criminal behavior before they had been placed. Their criminal activities increased when they were placed in group foster care settings with other juveniles who had criminal histories.

While on the streets, runaways may be kidnapped and forced or tricked into human trafficking and engage in survival sex and prostitution in order to make money, and they risk acquiring sexually transmitted infections (STIs), including HIV/AIDS (Family & Youth Service Bureau, National Clearinghouse on Families & Youth n.d.; International Labour Organization n.d.; UNHCR n.d.; Morewitz 2016; Crosland and Dunlap 2014). These runaway youth face sexual violence victimization, which also increases their risk for STIs. According to Booth et al. (1999), both foster care youth and runaways are significantly more likely to be infected with HIV than young people who do not run away.

While on their own on the streets, runaway youth including those who participate in human trafficking, survival sex, and prostitution, face sexual violence victimization and exploitation and other crimes, such as kidnapping, robbery, stalking, and death threats (Crosland and Dunlap 2014; Kaplan 2004; Biehal and Wade 2000; Morewitz 2003, 2008, 2016; UNHCR n.d.; International Labour Organization n.d.). Runaways are vulnerable to sexual and financial exploitation and abuse by pimps and human traffickers who offer the youth money, shelter, and alcohol and other drugs (Crosland and Dunlap 2014; Farmer and Pollock 1998).

Runaways on the streets are likely to use and abuse alcohol and other drugs. Runaway young people may continue their substance use and abuse patterns that they develop prior to running away or they may use and abuse substance for the first time. Runaways who use and abuse substances are at increased risks for criminal victimization.

Running away from placement settings also can lead to the runway youth having problems interacting with others. In addition, frequent elopement from placement settings is associated with having difficulties in attending school, getting good grades, and completing their education (Crosland and Dunlap 2014). Youth in foster care already face difficulties accessing the appropriate educational opportunities based on their educational needs, and elopement episodes may worsen their educational opportunities (Crosland and Dunlap 2014). As a result, runaway young people may be less likely to acquire the academic skills necessary to acquire employment in the future. However, more research is needed to evaluate the impact of frequent elopement on the social and educational outcomes of runaways.

Youth who exit the foster care system often have poor employment outcomes. For example, according to Courtney et al. (2014), only 46 % of young adults were currently working and they had an average annual income of $13,989. Frequent elopement from placement settings may limit youth's future employment opportunities. More studies are needed to analyze the employment patterns of youth who frequently elope from placement settings.

Placement Outcomes and Interventions

Foster care settings can address organizational problems such as staff abuse, authoritarian staff, inflexible rules, overcrowding, and the lack of educational programs and services. Strategies that seek to eliminate or reduce these problems can help to reduce the rate at which youth elope from placement.

One major concern is that foster care officials must ensure child safety while at the same time allowing independence for the youth under their care (Crosland and Dunlap 2014). Allowing independence can endanger the foster care youth by exposing them to harmful influences in the world outside of the foster care system.

Foster care placements that seek to expand the child's social capital in terms of social skills, attitudes, and cognitive functioning may reduce elopement episodes and improve other social, education, and employment outcomes (Crosland and Dunlap 2014).

Engaging the parents of runaways through family therapy may be useful in decreasing the rate of running away among youth in the general population (Crosland and Dunlap 2014; Slesnick & Prestopnik 2004). However, family therapy may not be helpful for youth in foster care since they are not residing with their biological parents (Crosland and Dunlap 2014).

Clark et al. (2008) suggest that customizing interventions by assessing a young person's motivation for running away can be helpful in reducing the number of placements and increasing placement stability.

Despite the organizational difficulties facing substitute care settings and the social problems facing the juveniles in these setting, placements can produce successful outcomes. Juvenile residents may improve their education attainment and employment potential. For example, one female runaway indicated that she went back to school and achieved a higher grade level after being placed in a group home (Mishriki 2001–2013).

Chapter 3
Food Insecurity and Related Problems Among Homeless and Runaway Youth

In this chapter, street youth's survival strategies associated with obtaining food while on the streets and the problems associated with food insecurity are discussed. This chapter analyzes the prevalence of food insecurity, the social meanings associated with food insecurity, the street youth's hoarding behaviors, dietary intake patterns, use of food sources, food-obtaining strategies, types of accommodations, the amount of time since leaving home, social network characteristics, history of abuse and neglect, and related behaviors. This chapter discusses the street youth's obstacles in obtaining food such as poor health, limited food availability, and lack of clean environments. In this chapter, other factors that may increase food insecurity such as demographic characteristics, history of caretaker abuse and neglect, unstable housing, alcohol and other drug use and abuse, pregnancy, lack of social networks and social support, and human trafficking victimization are analyzed.

Food insecurity refers to reduced access to nutritional and safe foods due to limited availability or uncertain ability to obtain nutritional food using legal and socially acceptable methods and the social meaning of these barriers to nutritional food (Anderson 1990; Antoniades and Tarasuk 1998; Dachner and Tarasuk 2002; Whitbeck et al. 2006).

Studying food insecurity among homeless and runaway youth has been difficult because these transient populations are not easily accessible to investigators. Despite these problems, investigators measure food insecurity and related behaviors in different ways (Li et al. 2009; Whitbeck et al. 2006). Researchers often study child and adolescent growth and energy use patterns and ask research participants to recall their dietary intake patterns, use of food sources, food-obtaining strategies, types of accommodations, the amount of time since leaving home, social network characteristics, history of abuse and neglect, and related behaviors. Investigators also may assess the research participants' main sources of income in the last 30 days. In one study, Whitbeck et al. (2006) used three items from the USDA Food Insecurity Scale to measure "going without or cutting back food."

S.J. Morewitz, *Runaway and Homeless Youth*,
DOI 10.1007/978-3-319-30863-0_3

Adolescent Growth and Eating Patterns

Growth among adolescents is linked to substantial appetites during this period (Whitbeck et al. 2006). In addition, during adolescence, individuals often eat food indiscriminately. As a consequence, teen frequently do not follow nutritional guidelines (Grunbaum et al. 2004; Whitbeck et al. 2006).

These adolescent growth and eating patterns make the problems of food insecurity and unhealthy eating especially difficult for homeless and runaway teens. Homeless and runaway teens can engage in extensive physical activities on a daily basis, which can further increase their risks for food insecurity, hunger, and malnutrition.

Perceptions of Food

Because of their "hand-to-mouth" living conditions, homeless and runaway young people may perceive food as precious and may engage in such food-related behaviors as hoarding, storing, guarding, coveting, fighting, and sharing (Dachner and Tarasuk 2002). Individuals who suffer from food insecurity may hoard food because of their fear that they will not have a stable source of food. Runaway and homeless youth may work to obtain enough money so that they can store food for times when they are unemployed and without financial resources to buy food. In one self-report narrative, a female teen runaway, who had been sleeping under abandoned trailers and stealing money, reported that she would make enough money for several weeks and use the money to store food (Mishriki 2001–2013).

In Dachner and Tarasuk's (2002) analysis of food insecurity and daily survival among homeless young people at a homeless drop-in center in Toronto, Ontario, Canada, the researchers described a number of behaviors related to the fact that homeless youth regarded food as precious. The investigators found that at a homeless drop-in center, a homeless young person would be appointed to guard food that was left on a dining table for a short period. The authors noted that homeless youth at the drop-in center on occasions would accuse each other of stealing food, which resulted in disputes and physical altercations.

According to Dachner and Tarasuk (2002), homeless youth at the drop-in center might share their food under specific circumstances. The authors discovered that young people might share food in exchange for a favor; they might also share food as a gift for a friend. The researchers also showed that youth at the homeless drop-in center might share their food if they prepared a meal as a group. For group meals, the young people would be careful in dividing their portions. However, some youth would complain if they felt that their portion was insufficient.

Analysts evaluate the frequency in which runaway and homeless youth go hungry due to lack of money. Researchers study how often street youth reduce the size of their meals or skip meals because they do not have enough money (Dachner and Tarasuk 2002). Moreover, they may be too sick and lack the energy to obtain food.

Dachner and Tarasuk (2002) point out that when confronted with the choice of walking 5 km in the rain or staying in one location and attempting to recover from the flu, the homeless young people often will go without eating a meal.

Self-report narratives of runaway and homeless youth support the view that they suffer food insecurity. In one self-report, a young female runaway noted that she had great difficulty just surviving on the streets (Mishriki 2001–2013). The runaway girl indicated that she broke into many houses that had "for sale" signs in order to sleep in them. The constant moving and the lack of food led to her starving and feeling exhausted.

Based on a self-report narrative, a male runaway teen reported suffering food insecurity on a regular basis. The runaway boy noted that he would go for days without any food or water (Mishriki 2001–2013).

In another self-report narrative, a female 11-year-old runaway reported that she and a friend walked back to her hometown and did not eat for the first several days (Mishriki 2001–2013). During this period, the girl indicated that she and her friend would sleep in laundromats and on the streets.

In their investigation, Whitbeck et al. (2006) evaluated the extent to which a sample of 428 homeless and runaway teens in the last 30 days had reduced the size of meals or missed meals, if they had not eaten for an entire day and if they had been hungry but could not eat because they did not have enough money to purchase food. The researchers discovered that about one-third of the street youth interviewed indicated that they suffered from food insecurity during the 30 days before the interview. Food insecurity consisted of such behaviors as skipping meals, going without food for an entire day, and going hungry. In the last 30 days, 25 % of the street youth in the sample noted that on a few occasions they went an entire day without eating. In the sample, 21 % of the homeless and runaway young people reported that they had reduced the quantity of meals or skipped meals frequently during this period. The investigators found that 13 % of the street youth had cut quantities or skipped meals on a few occasions.

Whitbeck et al. (2006) also showed that in the past 30 days, 14 % of the street young people in the sample reported that they frequently went without food when they were hungry. In their study, another 17 % of the street youth noted that they went hungry on a few occasions in the past 30 days because they had no money to purchase food.

In another study, Antoniades and Tarasuk (1998) discovered that 11 % of the homeless street youth in Toronto, Ontario, Canada, indicated that they had been frequently worried about successfully finding food for their next meal. In addition, according to Antoniades and Tarasuk (1998), 48 % of the street young people in their sample stated that they, over the prior 30 days, had suffered some hunger and/or absolute deprivation of food.

Runaway and homeless young people face the risk of being the victim of sex, force labor, and organ trafficking. These trafficked youth may suffer malnourishment related to being physically abused, restrained, confined, and tortured (National Human Trafficking Resource Center n.d. a, b).

Food Insecurity and Illnesses

Food insecurity and hunger, in addition to other problems such as unsafe living conditions, lack of sleep, and over exertion can cause runaway and homeless young people to develop malnutrition and related health problems. Homeless children who suffer food deprivation, hunger, and malnutrition may be at risk for a variety of adverse social, emotional, cognitive, physical, and developmental impairments (American Psychological Association, n.d.).

Runaway and homeless youth may suffer a variety of health problems including respiratory problems, sexually transmitted infections (STIs), sleep deprivation, and injuries that may significantly impair their food- and income-acquiring strategies as well as their social and family functioning. In their study of homeless young people at a drop-in center in Toronto, Ontario, Canada, Dachner and Tarasuk (2002) found that a number of homeless youth developed respiratory infections and influenza during the winter months. In this sample, homeless young people suffered from lower extremity problems such as blisters and blisters associated with being frequently on their feet while on the streets.

Runaway and homeless youth who stay at homeless shelters may develop health problems from staying at these locations. Dachner and Tarasuk (2002) noted that a few homeless young persons in their study acquired scabies or lice, and a majority of these individuals felt that they picked up scabies or lice while staying at the homeless drop-in center.

While living on the streets, runaway and homeless young people may suffer from injuries associated with their income-acquiring strategies. In Dachner and Tarasuk's research (2002), homeless young people who participated in squeegeeing frequently reported back, neck, and arm pain associated with that income activity. In this study, a few homeless youth also reported being hit by motor vehicles, and a few suffered bruises and fractures.

Lack of stable shelter increases runaway and homeless young people's susceptibility to poor health (Dachner and Tarasuk 2002). According to Dachner and Tarasuk (2002), lack of stable shelter reduces the youth ability to recuperate from infections. The investigators note that young people in the shelter who have a cold might acquire more serious illnesses because of their lack of a stable place to live and recuperate from illnesses.

Impact of Alcohol and Other Drug Use and Abuse

Heavy alcohol and other drug use and abuse among food-insecure homeless and runaway young people, including youth who are victims of human trafficking, can have adverse health and social effects. Food-insecure runaway and homeless who heavily use and/or abuse alcohol and other drugs can suffer severe impairment in their social/family, occupational, and health functioning. Many homeless and runaway young people who heavily use and abuse alcohol and other drugs are likely to become impaired in their strategies for obtaining income and food while on the streets. As a result, their cognitive functioning, psychomotor functioning, and nutritional status can become compromised, increasing their susceptibility to health problems.

In one investigation, Tarasuk et al. (2005) found that heavy drug use by female homeless girls and young women who heavily took drugs tended to have lower levels of "vitamin B-6, thiamin, niacin, magnesium, and zinc." Female runaway and homeless youth who heavily used drugs had lower average body mass index scores. In contrast, among male homeless youth, heavy drug use did not predict differences in intake of energy or nutrients.

Heavy alcohol consumption can actually increase energy and nutrient intakes. For example, Tarasuk et al. (2005) discovered that heavy alcohol use (having more than five drinks "on at least one 24-h recall") among homeless young people predicted higher energy intakes and higher levels of vitamin B-6, thiamin, niacin, and magnesium. Female homeless who consume large amounts of alcohol had higher levels of riboflavin and phosphorous.

Heavy alcohol and other drug use and abuse also can lead to poor judgment and impaired psychomotor function that increase their risk for intentional and unintentional injuries and other types of victimization such as participation in human trafficking, prostitution, and survival sex.

In their study of homeless youth at a drop-in center, Dachner and Tarasuk (2002) found that a few of the homeless youth suffered alcohol and other drug abuses. In these situations, homeless status impaired the young person's ability to overcome their addictions to alcohol and other drugs.

Food Insecurity and Pregnancy

While on the streets, pregnancy girls and women can be especially at risk due to food insecurity. In one investigation, Antoniades and Tarasuk (1998) noted of the five female homeless youth who were either pregnant or breastfeeding, none had indicated that they had suffered absolute deprivation of food. However, one of these females did report suffering hunger in the prior 30 days.

Demographic Characteristics

Demographic factors may increase the risks of suffering food insecurity. In Whitbeck et al.'s (2006) analysis, older homeless and runaway adolescents had a greater probability of experiencing food insecurity.

Types of Accommodation and Food Insecurity

Homeless and runaway young people have different types of accommodation, and these different types of accommodation may impact their degree of food insecurity (Antoniades and Tarasuk 1998; Li et al. 2009).

According to Li et al. (2009), 61 % of homeless young people in Toronto, Ontario, Canada reported spending the previous night outside. The investigators found that 21 % stayed at a friend's residence and 7 % stayed in a squat. In their study, Li et al. (2009) showed that 6 % stayed the prior night at a shelter, and 5 % stayed in other settings such as jails, hotels, and Internet cafes.

Based on a survey of 88 street young people in Toronto, Ontario, Canada, Antoniades and Tarasuk (1998) discovered that the youth varied widely in their accommodations. Twenty-five percent reported that they resided in a hostel or shelter, 22.9 % rented an apartment either alone or with others, and 19.3 % lived in a room in a rooming house. In this sample, 17.1 % of the homeless young people indicated that they stayed with friends or relatives, and 15.9 % reported that they live on streets or live in a "squat," e.g., live in an abandoned building.

Runaway and homeless youth who are living on the streets or in squats may be particularly at risk for suffering food insecurity (Whitbeck et al. 2006; Antoniades and Tarasuk 1998). In Whitbeck et al.'s (2006) research, homeless and runaway youth who had ever "spent time" on the streets had an increased probability of suffering food insecurity. Li et al. (2009) found that 63 % of the homeless young people in their sample had lived more than 12 months away from home. Based on Whitbeck et al.'s (2006) analysis, these individuals would be especially at risk of suffering food insecurity.

Police, business owners, and others will find runaway and homeless teens living in squats or sleeping in different public and private settings and force them to move to other locations such as abandoned or vacated residences and businesses. Some runaway youth seek to avoid police detection and are constantly seeking locations to evade police detection. As a result, the instability of moving from place to place and the energy requirements needed to move around repeatedly leads to energy depletion and hunger among the homeless and runaway youth.

History of Caretaker Abuse and/or Neglect

Street youth who have a history of caretaker abuse and/or neglect may be at increased risk of suffering food insecurity. In Whitbeck et al.'s (2006) research, runaway and homeless youth who had a history of caretaker abuse and/or neglect were more likely to report food insecurity.

Social Network and Social Support

The quality and quantity of social networks and related social support may influence the likelihood that street young people will have food insecurity. According to Whitbeck et al. (2006), homeless and runaway youth who had a larger social network were less likely to suffer food insecurity. However, the researchers did not find a link between the percentage of the youth's social network from their home community and their risks of food insecurity.

Main Sources of Income

Among homeless and runaway children and adolescents, their lack of regular income is a major risk factor for food insecurity and resulting outcomes such as hunger and malnutrition (Dachner and Tarasuk 2002; Antoniades and Tarasuk 1998). Runaway and homeless youth, like other marginal groups in society, often rely on the informal and socially stigmatizing economic activities such as panhandling or squeegee cleaning vehicle windows to make money (O'Grady et al. 1998; Gaetz and O'Grady 2002; Williams and Nadin 2012).

In Li et al.'s (2009) analysis of homeless youth in Toronto, Ontario, Canada, 54 % of females and 56 % of males reported that panhandling or squeegee cleaning was their main source of income in the last 30 days.

Based on a study of homeless young people in Adelaide, South Australia, Booth (2006) demonstrated that 61 % of the youth indicated that they panhandled for food. The passage of policies such as the Ontario government's Safe Streets Act, which went into effect in January 2000, attempts to curtail these informal, socially marginal economic activities. Local jurisdictions may enact anti-panhandling and anti-loitering laws that also are designed to prohibit or discourage panhandling.

Runaway and homeless young people also participate in other economic activities such as selling handicrafts. Li et al. (2009) showed that 4 % of females and 4 % of males sold items such as handicrafts as a primary source of income in the last 30 days.

Paid employment is another main source of income for some street youth. In Li et al.'s (2009) study of homeless young people in Toronto, Ontario, Canada, 4 % of females and 1 % of males engaged in paid employment.

According to one self-report narrative, one male adolescent runaway noted that he started working full time at a local used book store in order to make enough money to pay for food (Mishriki 2001–2013).

While on the streets, runaway and homeless young people may get assistance from family and friends. According to Li et al. (2009), 4 % of those interviewed stated that they received money from friends or family as their primary source of income in the previous 30 days. In Booth's (2006) study, 34 % of the homeless youth indicated that they requested help from family and friends.

Runaway and homeless youth on the streets also may receive different types of government assistance as a main source of income. Li et al. (2009), in their research on Toronto homeless youth, found that 3 % of males and 7 % of males received government transfers.

Income from Criminal Activity

Runaway and homeless youth often engage in crimes such as theft, including stealing food, human trafficking, prostitution and survival sex, and illicit drug trade in order to get food and other desirable items and services. Various studies have shown that street young people may be victims of human trafficking and participate in prostitution and survival sex, e.g., exchanging sex for money, food, drugs, shelter, and other desired items and services (Morewitz 2008, 2016; UNHCR n.d.; International Labour Organization n.d.; Family & Youth Services Bureau, National Clearinghouse on Families & Youth n.d.).

Victims of human trafficking may be suffering from malnutrition, confinement, physical restraint, and torture (Family & Youth Services Bureau, National Clearinghouse on Families & Youth n.d.; National Human Trafficking Center n.d. a, b). Human traffickers may limit the ability of their victims to eat nutritious meals as part of a pattern of social, psychological, and financial control, domination, and physical abuse.

In Li et al.'s (2009) investigation, 19 % of the homeless youth reported sex work as their primary source of income. According to McCarthy and Hagan (1992), 29.7 % of the homeless young people admitted to engaging in prostitution since leaving home.

In one self-report narrative, a male runaway noted that he had to steal food since he did not have any money (Mishriki 2001–2013). In McCarthy and Hagan's (1992) study of homeless youth in Toronto, Ontario, Canada, 46.9 % admitted to stealing food since they had left home. According to Li et al. (2009), 13 % of the homeless youth in their study reported theft or illegal drug activity as their main source of income in the last 30 days.

In an investigation of homeless youth in Adelaide, South Australia, Booth (2006) discovered that 65 % of young people in the sample reported that they engaged in theft as a food-acquiring strategy. Likewise, Dachner and Tarasuk (2002) reported that homeless young people would steal food from grocery stores.

Various studies have shown that street young people may be victims of human trafficking and participate in prostitution, and survival sex, e.g., exchanging sex for money, food, drugs, shelter, and other desired items and services (Morewitz 2016; UNHCR n.d.; International Labour Organization n.d.; Family & Youth Services Bureau, National Clearinghouse on Families & Youth n.d.). In Li et al.'s (2009) investigation, 19 % of the homeless youth reported sex work as their primary source of income. According to McCarthy and Hagan (1992), 29.7 % of the homeless young people admitted to engaging in prostitution since leaving home.

Victims of human trafficking may be suffering from malnutrition, confinement, physical restraint, and torture (Family & Youth Services Bureau, National Clearinghouse on Families & Youth n.d.; National Human Trafficking Center n.d. a, b). Human traffickers may limit the ability of their victims to eat nutritious meals as part of a pattern of social, psychological, and financial control and physical abuse.

Number of Different Income Sources

While on the streets, runaway and homeless children and adolescents may rely on multiple methods to obtain income. According to Li et al. (2009), 20 % of the homeless youth in their sample used one income-generating strategy, 37 % used two methods, 25 % relied on three strategies, and 18 % used four income-acquiring strategies.

Runaway and homeless youth's major source of income may affect their vulnerability to food insecurity and hunger. Antoniades and Tarasuk (1998) found that street youth who derived their main source of income from squeegeeing or panhandling were most at risk for food insecurity. Likewise, Whitbeck et al. (2006) showed that street youth's use of deviant and non-deviant food-acquiring strategies were associated with an increased risk of suffering food insecurity.

Main Sources of Food

Homeless and runaway young people obtain food from different legitimate and deviant/criminal sources depending on their access to legitimate and criminal/deviant opportunity structures, level of impairment due to substance abuse and poor health, and other factors.

While on the streets, youth will often beg for food. In Booth's analysis (2006), 44 % of the homeless youth reported that they begged for food. Street youth also may use deception to obtain food for free. For example, Dachner and Tarasuk (2002) reported that a few homeless youth would get fast-food establishment to replace their purchase by falsely stating that they had lost the food that they had bought from them.

In addition, young people on the streets also will buy their food. However, according to Dachner and Tarasuk (2002), none of the homeless youth in their study was able to live on food that they bought. These young people had limited incomes and had to spend money for other goods and services.

In Li et al.'s (2009) analysis, a majority of the homeless young people reported obtaining food from legitimate food sources. Seventy-five percent reported that they bought food, and 75 % indicated that other people gave them food.

Antoniades and Tarasuk (1998) showed that 28.4 % of the homeless youth in their investigation relied on supermarkets or large grocery stores for their primary food source. Almost 23 % used hostels or shelters where they resided as their main source of food. About 20 % of the homeless young people used fast-food facilities or street vendors as their main food source. Almost 16 % of the street youth in their study used drop-in centers as their main source of food. About 7 % relied on friends or family members, 4.5 % used convenience stories or small variety stores, and 1.1 % relied on food banks as their primary food source.

Runaway and homeless young people may combine their money to purchase food items (Dachner and Tarasuk 2002). In Dachner and Tarasuk's (2002) analysis of homeless youth at a drop-in center in Toronto, Ontario, Canada, some young people will combine their funds to buy food. Groups of youth at the drop-in center would purchase packaged food and cook it in the drop-in center's kitchen facilities.

Runaway and homeless young people frequently rely on programs and organizations that meet their basic needs such as the provision of food and consider these programs and organizations essential (Thompson et al. 2006). Food services include food trucks that offer sandwiches and meals provided by charities and drop-in centers.

Li et al. (2009) found that 51 % of the homeless youth in their sample indicated that they used a charitable program as their main food source over a 24-h period. Charitable organizations or social service organizations provide an alternative to purchasing food (Dachner and Tarasuk 2002). Booth (2006) discovered that 63 % of the homeless young people in her study reported using welfare food programs. Runaway and homeless youth may obtain food from food banks. According to Li et al. (2009), 1 % of the young people stated that they obtained food from food banks.

Dachner and Tarasuk (2002) found in a study of homeless young people at a homeless drop-in center that the youth knew about the location, times of operation, and quality of various social service and charitable organizations that provided food. Some youth in this investigation reported that they would plan their daily activities around going to these food-serving locations. The investigators discovered that certain homeless young people reported suffering food poisoning at some of these facilities and other homeless youth considered some of these facilities as "dirty." Young people in this investigation would avoid facilities that they felt were unsafe and dirty. Young people also reported that they would not go to organizations that required them to listen to sermons or pray unless they were suffering from extreme food deprivation.

In Li et al.'s (2009) analysis, 6 % of the homeless youth in their study stole food or took food from garbage (known as dumpster surfing). Mishriki (2001–2013) describe one self-report narrative about a teen runaway who slept at night behind a grocery store and would raid the dumpster behind the store to retrieve day-old bread (Mishriki 2001–2013). Dachner and Tarasuk (2002) also noted that several homeless young people rummaged through garbage cans in search of food.

In another self-report narrative, a male adolescent runaway spent a considerable amount of time evading police detection by avoiding major roads and highways. He noted that he would go through individuals' trash containers in search of food (Mishriki 2001–2013).

In some cases, runaway and homeless youth obtain day-old food from employees of food stores. In Dachner and Tarasuk's (2002) research, some homeless young people received day-old food from pizza and donut store employees.

The young people's main source of food may influence their degree of food insecurity (Antoniades and Tarasuk 1998, pp. 373, 374). According to Antoniades and Tarasuk (1998), street young people who obtained their food from fast-food restaurants and drop-in centers had the highest probability of suffering food deprivation. These youth are also more likely to live on the streets or live in squats. Likewise, Whitbeck et al. (2006) discovered that street youth's use of different food sources was linked to an increased likelihood of suffering food insecurity.

Food Intake

As homeless and runaway struggle to obtain sufficient healthy food for survival on the streets, they may frequently suffer reduced food intake. Based on interviews with 261 homeless young people in Toronto, Ontario, Canada, Li et al. (2009) showed that their average food intakes (based on 24 h dietary intake recalls) fell below Canada's Food Guide recommendations for all four groups of food and below the regular food intakes of young adults (ages 19–30 years) in the population.

Li et al. (2009) revealed that homeless youth's average regular food intake was less than 50 % of the number of fruit and vegetable servings that are eaten by young adults in the population. Compared to the food intake of young adult women in the population, homeless female youth's average regular consumption of food from two food groups, the milk and alternatives and meat and alternatives, were less than 50 % of the average number of servings.

In Li et al.'s (2009) investigation, both male and female homeless young people in their sample obtained more energy from the category of "other foods" than from any other group of food. Female homeless youth received two times the amount of energy from food classified as "other foods" compared to young adult women in the population. Male homeless young people received 39 % of their energy from "other foods" compared to young adult men in the population who obtained 26 % of their energy from "other foods."

Li et al. (2009) examined the homeless young people's mean food group intake from sources of food and demonstrated they had low mean food intakes from food obtained from charities and purchases of food. The investigators showed that increased consumption of food from either charities or purchased foods was not related to an increased intake of fruit and vegetables or grain products. Li et al. (2009) also found that among female homeless youth, the larger their percentage of total energy intake from bought food, the less likely they would consume milk products. In contrast, the percentage of total energy intake from purchased foods was not associated with consumption of milk products. Unlike among female homeless young people, among homeless male youth, the greater their percentage of total energy intake from charity food programs was associated with a greater total food consumption of meat and alternatives.

In Li et al.'s (2009) analysis, homeless young people did not follow the Canada's Food Guide recommendations regarding increased consumption of dark green or range vegetables, whole grains, leaner meats, and lower-fat milk products. In their study, Li et al. (2009) discovered that only 25 % of female homeless youth and 29 % of their male counterparts had eaten any dark green or orange vegetables. With regard to whole grain consumption, only 15 % of the female homeless young people and 16 % of the male homeless youth had eaten any whole grains throughout the day. The researchers showed that approximately 50 % of the homeless youth had consumed lean meat, fish or alternatives to meat, and lower-fat milk products throughout the day.

Li et al. (2009) showed that youth who obtained their food from charities were more likely to consume these food types than those who bought their food. However, more than 70 % of the young people who obtained their food from charities had not eaten any dark green or orange vegetables or whole grains.

In Li et al.'s (2009) investigation, 88 % of the homeless young people who consumed more than 800 kcal from bought food in a day had purchased food such as hamburgers, French fries from fast-food restaurants or hotdogs, and other food from street vendors. Homeless youth who consumed more than 800 kcal from charities in a given day often had eaten breakfast cereals with milk, coffee, fruit, and hot food consisting of pasta, rice, potatoes, meat, and vegetables.

Dachner and Tarasuk (2002) also found that homeless youth at a drop-in center who purchased food were likely to buy food that was cheap, easy to transport, and already prepared. The youth's purchased food included hamburgers, sandwiches, pizza slices, hot dogs, and ice cream. They purchased food from restaurants, stores, and street vendors.

Nutrient Intakes

Street youth who suffer food insecurity may have inadequate nutrient intakes. For example, Tarasuk et al. (2005), in their analysis of homeless young people in Toronto, Ontario, Canada, discovered that more than 50 % were nutritionally inadequate in terms of their intakes of vitamin A, vitamin C, folate, magnesium, and zinc. The researchers also demonstrated that more than 50 % of the female homeless youth were nutritionally inadequate in regard to vitamin B-12 and iron.

Weight Status

While on the streets, young people may have weight problems because of food deprivation. Tarasuk et al. (2005) found that 7 % of the homeless young people in their sample were underweight. In addition, 22 % of the homeless youth in their study were overweight or obese. Based on triceps skinfold thickness and arm circumference measures to assess mid-arm muscle area (AMA) of 87 normal and underweight young people, the authors discovered indicators of wasting in four males. The results also indicated that 17 males and two females had muscle reserves that were below the mean. Younger people who are still growing may have low AMA regardless of their nutrient intake. However, only one young person with evidence of wasting was younger than 20 years of age. None was under 18 years of age.

In addition, female runaway and homeless girls with nutritional problems who get pregnant and or are the victims of violence while on the streets may be susceptible to health problems (Morewitz 2004).

Chapter 4
Employment and Other Income Sources of Runaway and Homeless Youth

In this chapter, the employment activities and other income sources of street young people are assessed. This chapter evaluates the type and prevalence of street youth employment and income sources and various conditions such as community views toward runaway and homeless youth that may affect the extent to which these children and adolescents are able to engage in employment while on the streets. This chapter analyzes the extent to which street youth engage in panhandling on the streets for spare change or squeegee cleaning motor vehicle windows and requesting money from drivers who are stopped at traffic lights. In addition, other casual and temporary jobs such as participating in construction, working on painting jobs, and selling handicrafts and tickets for sports and concert events are examined. This chapter also discusses the other income sources of runaway and homeless young people such as reliance on government assistance and friends and family members. In this chapter, obstacles to employment such as employer financial exploitation, human trafficking victimization, police harassment, negative community beliefs, restrictive laws, and the trauma and stress of street life are presented.

In different countries, street youth, including runaways and homeless young people, may participate in various income-generating activities and receive income from other sources (Veale and Dona 2003; Rosa et al. 1992; Dewees and Klees 1995; Stephenson 2001; Ali et al. 2004). McCarthy and Hagan (1992), in their analysis of 390 homeless teens in Toronto, Ontario, Canada, discovered that 70 % were able to find some type of a job.

However, because of their runaway and homeless status and associated problems, they have difficulty working on a regular basis. Youth who run away and become homeless may work for only short periods and face being fired or laid off (Pollio et al. 2000; Dachner and Tarasuk 2002). In Pollio et al.'s (2000) investigation, 10 % of the runaway and homeless youth reported that they had been terminated from their job immediately before they had enrolled in the study.

Likewise, McCarthy and Hagan (1992) found that many of those homeless adolescents who did get jobs had only temporary ones. They discovered that 62 % of the homeless youth who had been employed were not working at the time of the study.

S.J. Morewitz, *Runaway and Homeless Youth*,
DOI 10.1007/978-3-319-30863-0_4

Homeless and runaway youth may give up trying to find work and instead return to school. In McCarthy and Hagan's (1992) investigation, 20 % of the juveniles had stopped trying to seek employment and had gone back to school.

While on the streets, many runaway and homeless young people work in the informal or illegal economy (Li et al. 2009; Dachner and Tarasuk 2002). Many runaway and homeless teens use "deviant" street subsistence strategies and/or seek casual and often temporary, low-paying employment to make money (Dachner and Tarasuk 2002; Mishriki 2001–2013; Li et al. 2009; Antoniades and Tarasuk 1998).

In terms of deviant subsistence strategies, runaway and homeless youth typically engage in panhandling on the streets for spare change or squeegee cleaning motor vehicle windows and requesting money from drivers who are stopped at traffic lights (Li et al. 2009; Dachner and Tarasuk 2002).

Runaway and homeless adolescents also have other jobs. They may have casual construction and painting jobs (Dachner and Tarasuk 2002). Homeless and runaway youth may sell handicrafts and other items (Li et al. 2009). In Li et al.'s (2009) study, 4 % of the females and 4 % of the males reportedly sold items such as handicrafts. Runaway and homeless young people may work for ticket brokers to sell tickets for sports and concert events.

In one self-report narrative, a male runaway reported that he took a job at a used bookstore in Columbus, Ohio, after walking for weeks on side roads in different areas (Mishriki 2001–2013). The adolescent runaway told the bookstore staff that his family was "in trouble" and that he needed money to help them.

In another self-report narrative, a male runaway noted that he lived with a friend and his parents for a few months after he ran away from home. While living there, he worked for a fast-food establishment (Mishriki 2001–2013). The runaway teen indicated that he worked as many hours as possible and then left this living situation and employment. A 12-year-old female runaway in another self-report narrative noted that she worked at a truck stop (Mishriki 2001–2013). While working at the truck stop, she felt that life was good.

While on the streets, young people may be coerced or tricked into sex, force labor, and organ trafficking and participation as child soldiers during armed conflicts (International Labour Organization n.d.; UNHCR n.d.; Morewitz 2008, 2016). These children may work for free or receive very little money for their services (National Human Trafficking Resource Center n.d. a, b). They may also work just for tips. Street youth who are trafficked often work very long hours or work at unusual times. These human trafficking victims often are not given breaks. In addition, they often are subject to extreme restrictions while on the job.

Human traffickers often make false promises about the nature of the work to the street youth in order to trick them into becoming human trafficking victims (National Human Trafficking Resource Center n.d. a, b). Moreover, human traffickers often force their victims into assuming a large debt that makes them unable to pay off the debt. Street youth often work in settings that have extreme security measures such as bars on windows and security cameras, which prevent them from escaping the work location.

Homeless and runaway young people have other sources of income (Li et al. 2009; Antoniades and Tarasuk 1998). Based on a study of homeless young people in Toronto, Ontario, Canada, Li et al. (2009) showed that 3 % of females and 7 % of males received government transfers. Youth on the streets also receive financial support from family members and friends. According to Li et al. (2009), 4 % of the female homeless youth obtained money from family members or friends and 3 % of their male counterparts did so.

While on the streets, young people may earn a limited income and therefore may obtain money through illegal activities such as theft, illicit drug activities, and sex work (Li et al. 2009; Dachner and Tarasuk 2002; Antoniades and Tarasuk 1998). Li et al. (2009) discovered that 13 % of female homeless youth and 22 % of their male counterparts obtained money from illegal behaviors such as theft or drug activities. Illicit drug work can involve delivering illicit drugs and other drug-related activities (Dachner and Tarasuk 2002). With regard to sex work, females in Li et al.'s (2009) study were more likely to participate in prostitution (19 %) than males (6 %).

Prevalence of Street Youth Income Activities

What is the prevalence of income-generating activities among street youth? Based on a study of 371 runaway and homeless young people using crisis shelter services, Pollio et al. (2000) discovered that 13 % were working. In Li et al.'s (2009) analysis of homeless youth in Toronto, Ontario, Canada, 4 % of females and 1 % of males reported that they were engaged in paid employment. According to Li et al. (2009), 54 % of the females and 56 % of the males had participated in panhandling or squeegeeing.

Antoniades and Tarasuk (1998), in their analysis of Toronto street youth, discovered that 14.8 % indicated that their main source of income was employment. In the sample, 13.6 % reported that they engaged in squeegeeing or panhandling. According to law enforcement and the City Council of Toronto, Ontario, Canada, about 220 street young people were squeegeers in the summer months of 1998 (Esmonde 2002).

Characteristics of Runaway and Homeless Teens Who Work

In Esmonde's (2002) analysis of homeless and runaway youth in the Toronto, Ontario, Canada who participated in squeegeeing, most of the squeegeers are between the ages of 16 and 25. In this report, about 60 % of the street youth who engaged in squeegeeing are male and 40 % are female. About 40 % of the squeegeers are from areas outside of Toronto.

Esmonde (2002) noted that a majority of the young people who squeegee are homeless. Thirty-four percent of these young people did not have any residence. Twenty-four percent of the squeegeers are squatting in abandoned buildings. Fifteen percent of the squeegeers reside with a friend or relative. Twenty-four percent rent and 3 % stay in shelters.

Runaway and homeless adolescents may differ in their employment activities on the streets based on their age. Antoniades and Tarasuk (1998) showed that street young people who engaged in squeegeeing or panhandling as their major source of income were younger than other street youth except those who relied on a personal needs allowance as their major source of income. A personal needs allowance is provided to young people who reside in some hostels.

Antoniades and Tarasuk (1998) did not find that squeegeeing or panhandling or the street youth's other main sources of income varied by gender. More research is needed to assess possible gender differences in income activities among youth on the streets.

Education, Job Training, and Job Placement Resources for Runaway/Homeless Youth

While on the streets, some runaway and homeless youth can access skill-building services such as educational, job training, employment readiness, and job placement services, which can potentially help them get off the streets (Thompson et al. 2006a; Slesnick et al. 2009; Robertson and Toro n.d.; Aviles and Helfrich 2004; Karabanow and Clement 2004). These services are essential for helping the runaway and homeless young people make the transition to living a conventional life (Robertson and Toro n.d.).

Agencies provide runaways and homeless youth with a variety of services to increase their access to employment opportunities. Service providers assist these young people with such services as identification services, clothing vouchers for employment interviews, Internet access, and financial support for rent and tuition (Thompson et al. 2006a).

Organizations offer other services such as providing food and shelter, medical and mental health services, counseling, and case management (Thompson et al. 2006a). These types of services help to stabilize the runaway and homeless youth, which can prepare them for participating in educational programs, job training, employment readiness, and job placement programs.

Experts recommend that these youth complete high school (or earn a GED) and college (Morey and Friedman 1993; National Network of Runaway and Youth Services, Inc. 1985; Robertson and Toro n.d.). Alternatively, they should participate in alternative educational programs that allow them to obtain skills for the job market.

What percentages of homeless and runaway young people access these educational and job placement services? De Rosa et al. (1999) analyzed service utilization patterns among homeless and runaway young people in Los Angeles, CA, and discovered that 14 % of the youth reported that they used employment services. The researchers also found that two individuals reported using GED services.

Obstacles to Employment and Income-Related Activities

Youth, because of their runaway and homeless status, may encounter many obstacles to working while on their own (Dachner and Tarasuk 2002). For example, Dachner and Tarasuk (2002) report that runaway and homeless young people at a construction site received less pay than they were previously promised.

Runaway and homeless young people seeking employment and those already on the job may face prejudice and limited job opportunities because of their street behaviors, clothing, body tattoos, and body piercings (Esmonde 2002; Dachner and Tarasuk 2002). Public views toward homeless and runaway youth may substantially affect street-involved youth's employment opportunities (Esmonde 2002). Many people blame homeless individuals for having deficits in their personal characters and therefore may act very prejudicial toward them (O'Grady et al. 1998). The public may consider homeless adults and young people as substance abusers and too lazy to get an education and suitable employment.

The presence of homeless and runaway youth on the streets who are squeegeeing or panhandling also may pose a threat to the security of people in public settings (Esmonde 2002). The presence of these homeless and runaway youth also may offer an unsettling picture to the public that the benefits of the economy are not equally shared across the community.

In Canada, the government introduced the Safe Streets Act in 1999 as part of a "law and order" strategy (Esmonde 2002). Although the bill did not specify squeegeeing or panhandling, the bill banned solicitations such as requesting the "immediate provision of money or another thing of value, regardless of whether consideration is offered or provided in return…" (Esmonde 2002).

Other Obstacles in Obtaining Employment

While on the streets, runaways and homeless young people are exposed to the trauma of repeated abuse. They are also under the daily stress of not having shelter, food, and other necessities. As a result, runaways and homeless young people may be unable to use education, job placement, and other employment services due to the trauma, abuse, and stress in surviving on the streets. For example, many youth on the streets suffer from food insecurity, hunger, sleep deprivation, and mental disorders, which may inhibit them from using employment-related services.

Runaway and homeless young people often do not have a mailing address so that they can apply for a job. They may lack access to facilities to take showers/baths that enable them to prepare for a job interview. They may lack access to suitable clothes for job interviews.

Runaway and homeless youth often have not completed their education and, as a result, do not meet the educational requirements for a job and also lack employment experience to qualify for a job. The age of the runaways and homeless youth also may prohibit employers from hiring them for many jobs.

Runaway and homeless young people may not be willing to use available employment, educational, and vocational services. Various studies have revealed that runaway and homeless young people have low rates of using social services and health-care programs, including employment, education, and vocational training services (Thompson et al. 2006a; Brooks et al. 2004; De Rosa et al. 1999). Runaway and homeless young people may be the victims of abuse and exploitation and are thus distrustful of service providers and other adults (Thompson et al. 2006a; Kurtz et al. 2000; Farrow et al. 1992). Young people may avoid needed services because they are afraid of getting arrested or turned over to child protective services. Youth may in fact have outstanding warrants.

Runaways and homeless young people who do wish to use services such as employment programs may lack insurance. These individuals may not have access to transportation to get to these programs. In addition, runaway and homeless youth may not know about the availability of these services (Yates et al. 1990; Thompson et al. 2006a).

Those runaways and homeless young people who do access services are more likely to access outreach programs and drop-in centers than other settings and have a greater likelihood of using health-care and mental health programs (Thompson et al. 2006a; Mallett et al. 2004; De Rosa et al. 1999).

Young people who are trafficked also may be unable to participate in legitimate employment activities. Human traffickers often will strictly control their victims' schedule, relationship with other people, and spending habits and prevent them from engaging in conventional employment (Family & Youth Service Bureau, National Clearinghouse on Families & Youth n.d.).

Impact of Income-Generating Activities on Street-Involved Youth

Some social science research shows that working at an early age can have positive effects on their child development, while other studies focus on the adverse impact of employment during childhood (Stephenson 2001). Do legitimate income-producing activities of street youth improve the functioning and quality of life of runaways and homeless young people? According to O'Grady et al. (1998), homeless and runaway young people who do leave the streets view employment as essential for increasing their "levels of social capital." Social capital consists of the ways in which people achieve information and skills to reach cultural goals during their life (O'Grady et al. 1998; Coleman 1988; Stephenson 2001). Without stable income, youth in Hagan and McCarthy's (1997) study reported that they rarely could leave the streets.

According to theories of opportunity and social control and social functioning, having employment may help reduce criminal activity (O'Grady et al. 1998). Youth on the streets who work may have improved psychosocial functioning because they are better able to develop high self-esteem, positive attachments with conventional role models, and effective behavior controls. Moreover, homeless and runaway young people who work may have less opportunity to engage in criminal behaviors.

For example, Hartnagel (1989) showed that "cumulative unemployment" among young people had a greater likelihood of suffering depressive symptoms and reduced self-esteem, which increased the probability that they would have substance-abuse problems.

However, other investigations have not found an association between employment activities and reduced juvenile delinquency. In a study of part-time employment, Tanner and Krahn (1991) youth who worked part-time had a greater chance of suffering from substance abuse. These youth may have had substance-abuse difficulties because they were imitating the behaviors of their adult co-workers.

Based on a sample of homeless young people in Toronto, Canada, O'Grady et al. (1998) evaluated the effects of engaging in squeegeeing. The investigators reported that young people who participated in squeegeeing while on the streets had a number of positive outcomes. Squeegeers exhibited better psychosocial and behavioral functioning than youth who did not engage in squeegeeing. Squeegeers reported lower levels of depression and suicidal behaviors than non-squeegee workers. Squeegee workers also had a lower probability of reporting that they "like doing nothing at all." O'Grady et al. (1998) also discovered that squeegeers had lower rates of criminal activity than homeless youth who did not squeegee. In addition, O'Grady et al. (1998) found that squeegeeing was related to more stable housing situations.

Career and Employment Outcomes of Former Homeless and Runaway Youth

Despite the barriers to finding stable employment, some runaway and homeless young people are able to leave the streets and obtain additional career-related education and training and/or stable employment. Lindsey et al. (2000) interviewed former homeless and runaway youth and found some who had completed education and obtained employment. For example, in one case study, D., a young Caucasian man, had dropped out of the 10th grade and at age 14 had left home because he reportedly had conflicts with his parents (Lindsey et al. 2000). When D. was 17, he drove into a tree while driving under the influence of alcohol. This incident caused him to contact his parents again. D. later got his general education degree and obtained secure employment.

In another case study in Lindsey et al.'s (2000) investigation, J., a young Caucasian woman, reportedly had arguments with her mother, dropped out of school, and went to live with her friends. She had lived in a shelter, used marijuana, and reportedly had been arrested several times. After she was engaged, she stopped smoking marijuana. J. eventually graduated high school and completed a medical assistant training program. She is currently employed as a medical assistant in a physician's office.

Lindsey et al. (2000) also describe a case study involving S., a 20-year-old Caucasian woman who graduated high school, took some community college classes, and wanted to obtain an undergraduate degree in elementary education. However, she was employed at a bowling alley at the time of her interview. S. was able to get additional education despite leaving her parents after a stressful adolescence. After getting raped by the father of a friend at the age of 16, attempting suicide, and later that year getting pregnant and having a miscarriage, S. had conflicts with her parents and went into a shelter. After undergoing counseling, S. returned to her parents and was living with then at the time of her interview.

Runaway and homeless youth may set high employment goals for themselves. Some young people may suffer severely traumatic experiences such as a life-threatening event and/or a history of abuse and become very ambitious as a consequence. For example, Williams et al. (2001) analyze the case of S., a 21-year-old African American woman who suffered the death of her baby at age

16, went into a coma and was placed on a ventilator, suffered betrayal and abandonment by her mother and father, dealt with substance abuse, and now has the goal of becoming an attorney.

However, some runaway youth may have limited employment opportunities as adults and suffer financially as a consequence (Benoit-Bryan 2011). A longitudinal investigation of runaways showed that former runaways as adults earned $8823 less than adults who never ran away from home (Benoit-Bryan 2011). The researchers discovered that other predictors of income were gender, age, race/ethnicity, and abuse (verbal, physical, and sexual). Females made $11,690 less, while income increased $1731 for each additional year of age. Being African American reduced income by $4557, while being Asian increased income $6363. A history of verbal and sexual abuse before the age of 18 reduced income ($2122 and $6833, respectively), while physical abuse history is associated with an increase of $2888.

Some runaway youth may be more likely to receive public assistance as adults. In Benoit-Bryan's (2011) study, adults who were former runaways had a 76 % increase in the likelihood of having a household member who was receiving public assistance. Several factors increased the probability among adults of having a household member on public assistance; being female (increase of 81 %), being African American (increase of 10 %), having a history of being in foster care (increase of 91 %), and having a history of verbal, physical, and sexual abuse increased the likelihood (increase of 21 %, 32 %, and 68 %, respectively).

In contrast, Benoit-Bryan (2011) showed that among adults, being Asian and Hispanic was associated with a decrease likelihood of having a household member on public assistance (decrease of 53 % and 18 %, respectively). Homosexual orientation decreased the odds of having a household member on public assistance (decrease of 62 %). Adults who had been born in the USA had a 3 % decrease in the probability of having a household member on public assistance.

Chapter 5
School Issues Facing Runaway and Homeless Youth

This chapter analyzes school problems facing young people who run away from home or become homeless. In this chapter, school failure, expulsion, and other adverse school outcomes facing homeless and runaway young people are discussed. Factors that increase the risk of adverse school outcomes such as school absences, school failure, suspensions, and expulsion are analyzed. This chapter examines why youth are at risk for having disruptive, behavioral problems in school, performing poorly, skipping school, failing school, being suspended or expelled from school, dropping out of school, and running away from home because they suffer from abuse and trauma and have learning disorders such as attention-deficit, hyperactivity disorder (ADHD), conduct problems, and other related behavioral and mental health problems. In this chapter, the prevalence of school problems such as truancy, school detention, and school suspension and expulsion are presented. This chapter also discusses the federal McKinney–Vento Homeless Assistance Act role in providing federal funds for homeless shelter programs in the USA to make sure that homeless young people get access to education.

According to a US General Accounting Office (GAO) (1989) investigation, 50 % of young people using runaway shelters reported that they had school problems. In China, Zhao et al. (2012) found that school-associated problems were a risk factor for running away from home or care institutions. Pollio et al. (2006) discovered that 45 % of runaway youth had experienced a recent school problem. Warren et al. (1997) also found that runaway youth have been involved in a variety of school problems.

In one self-report case, a 16-year-old female adolescent indicated that she ran away from home after bringing home a failing report card (Mishriki 2001–2013). The runaway girl reported that she had frequently skipped school.

Investigators have studied a variety of conditions that increase school failure, expulsion, and other adverse school outcomes facing homeless and runaway young people. Youth who have learning disorders, conduct problems, and other related behavioral and mental health problems are at risk for having disruptive, behavioral problems in school, performing poorly, skipping school, failing school, being suspended or expelled from school, dropping out of school, and running away from home.

S.J. Morewitz, *Runaway and Homeless Youth*,
DOI 10.1007/978-3-319-30863-0_5

Prevalence of Mental Disorders in Runaway and Homeless Youth

The rate of mental disorders and developmental disabilities among runaways and thrown-aways is substantial. Hammer et al. (2002) discovered that an estimated 24,300 runaway/thrown-away children and adolescents had a major mental disorder or developmental disability at the time of their runaway/thrown-away incident.

Young people who are exposed to severe trauma may try to cope with these traumatic experiences by being truant from school and exhibiting other maladaptive behaviors such as self-mutilation, or deliberate self-harm (DSH) and suicidal behaviors. Williams et al. (2001), in their analysis of former runaway and homeless young people, discuss the case of K., a 21-year-old African American woman. K. was a frequent school truant, participated in DSH, was hospitalized in a psychiatric facility, and had suicidal ideation possibly in response to being sexually and physically abused and severely neglected as a child by her mother who was a drug addict.

In one self-report, a male runaway teen had difficulties keeping up with his school assignments because of his poor attention span, lack of motivation, poor sleeping habits, and inadequate nutrition (Marschall 2014). The boy, who had been severely abused and neglected in a chaotic, violent, and traumatic home environment and had been robbed at gunpoint, had a history of suicidal ideation, self-harm behaviors, somatic symptoms, and other mental health problems. In another report, a female teen runaway reportedly left school and was hospitalized in a psychiatric inpatient setting and then placed in different substitute care settings (Williams et al. 2001).

Certain subgroups of youth such as those from sexual minority backgrounds may be more at risk from the chronic stress associated with verbal and physical abuse at school, which increase their risk for running away from home and various other negative behaviors (Savin-Williams 1994; Cochran et al. 2002).

Youth with conduct disorder (CD) engage in repeated antisocial behaviors such as bullying, fighting, setting fires, destroying property, committing theft, and skipping school (Turgay 2005). Oppositional defiant disorder (ODD) is somewhat similar to CD. In fact, the markers of ODD frequently occur in CD. Youth with conduct problems may have attention-deficit hyperactivity disorder (ADHD) and other learning disorders, which can be associated with childhood abuse, family violence, substance use, and other problems (Sharma and Marimuthu 2014).

Runaway youth may have both CD and ODD, making them more likely to challenge the authority of teachers and administrators. Youth who oppose their teachers and school rules and regulations are more likely to have poor school performance and drop out of school (Thompson and Pillai 2006; Quilgars et al. 2008). In some instances, youth who drop out or are expelled may miss being with their school friends. In a qualitative study of runaway girls in Israel, Peled and Cohavi (2009) describe the case of one runaway girl who reported that after she was expelled from school, she missed the fun that she used to have with her school friends.

CD is prevalent among homeless and runaway young people (Robertson and Toro n. d.; Cauce et al. 1997; Feitel et al. 1992; Robertson 1989). In fact, running away is a marker of CD. The disorder can be diagnosed using the Diagnostic Interview Schedule.

Children and adolescents with childhood-onset CD are also likely to have weak attachment to school (Chen et al. 2007; Yiu and Khong 2009; Peled and Cohavi 2009), which can lead to their disengagement from school and negative attitudes toward school and career development, school absence, truancy, school dropout, and exposure to deviant peers during school (Hammer et al. 2002; Quilgars et al. 2008).

In school settings and in other situations, negative peer interactions, including interaction with deviant peers and rejection by peers, may increase the probability of CD (Chen et al. 2007). When young people run away from home or a care institution, those with and without CD have an increased risk of getting into fights and exhibiting other forms of aggressive behaviors. In one self-report narrative, a female runaway stated that she had a fight with her best friend (Mishriki 2001–2013).

Children and adolescents with CD face barriers to obtaining legitimate jobs (Patterson and Yoerger 1997; Chen et al. 2007; Rogers et al. 1994; Peled and Cohavi 2009; Thompson and Pillai 2006; Robertson and Toro n. d.). Several reports have shown that 25–35 % of homeless young people were kept from completing a year of school (Clark and Robertson 1996; Robertson 1989).

Children and adolescents may suffer from ADHD, which can be associated with their history of physical, sexual, and emotional abuse and neglect. Children and adolescents with CD are frequently hyperactive, have impulsive and explosive behaviors, are deficient in social skills, and have comorbid conditions such as deficits in learning and cognitive functioning, including ADHD, lower intelligence quotients, and reduced capacity for verbal reasoning, planning, and organizing (Turgay 2005). CD by itself is rare. Youth with CD frequently have high rates of other comorbid conditions such as autism spectrum disorder, substance use, and anxiety and depressive disorders that may be associated with poor school performance, difficulties in peer relations, impaired family functioning, and other difficulties (Turgay 2005; Guttmann-Steinmetz et al. 2009; Booth and Zhang 1997; Cauce et al. 1997).

Substance Use and Conduct Problems

A frequent comorbid condition among youth with conduct problems is substance use. Some youth with conduct problems may have low self-control, which increases their likelihood of participating in criminal conduct including substance use (Baron 2003). Substance use increases youth's risk of performing poorly in school and being suspended or expelled. Youth who abuse alcohol and other drugs may be more likely to join gangs. For example, in one self-report, a Terry, a 19-year-old girl, reported that she quit school in the tenth grade after abusing drugs and alcohol (Williams et al. 2001). She had been involved with gangs and had already been living on the streets episodically since the age of 13.

Substance use also increases the likelihood that young people will be arrested, leading to school suspension, absence, or expulsion. Moreover, homeless and runaway young people who have low self-control and take drugs may have a higher probability of interacting with deviant peers and following deviant social beliefs and values. Runaway and homeless youth with low self-control and who take drugs may be more likely to be unemployed and homeless for longer durations.

When runaway and homeless youth with and without CD leave home, they are at increased risk of using hard drugs when they leave home. According to Hammer et al. (2002), an estimated 292,000 children and adolescents were taking hard drugs at the time of their runaway/thrown-away episode. In Hammer et al.'s (2002) analysis, an estimated 317,800 children and adolescents were substance dependent at the time of their runaway/thrown-away incident.

Homeless and runaway young people with CD may have an increased probability of using high-risk drugs that are related to sexual activity and HIV/AIDS (Booth and Zhang 1997). Booth and Zhang (1997) discovered that CD was the greatest determinant of heroin and/or cocaine use on a lifetime basis. The authors also found that CD was the best predictor of whether the homeless and runaway youth engaged in survival sex or exchanging sex for drugs, food, shelter, or money. In their investigation, CD also was positively linked to the number of sex partners and the number of drugs taken by the homeless and runaway youth.

Many runaway children may be suffering from depression, which interferes with their functioning at school and impairs other aspects of their daily functioning. A US GAO report showed that 63 % of the youth using shelter services indicated that they suffered from depression (US General Accounting Office 1989).

In one self-report narrative, a girl noted that she was failing school before she ran away from home (Mishriki 2001–2013). The girl had become depressed because she loved her brother whom she could not see. She also reported that her father beat her.

However, in other instances runaway and homeless young people may be able to overcome their behavioral difficulties and do well academically. In some instances, the runaways are able to get away from their negative peer interactions, which previously had facilitated their involvement in alcohol, drugs, and sex. They may get sent to drug rehabilitation and placed in group homes that assist the youth to give up their negative street lifestyle. For example, one female runaway, after participating in drug rehabilitation and being placed in a group home, noted that she got back to school and was doing very well because she was talking to her friends from her hometown and was no longer drinking, doing drugs, and having sex (Mishriki 2001–2013).

In another self-report story, a female teen runaway noted that despite all of the problems that she had as a teen runaway, she was able to go back and earn her GED (Mishriki 2001–2013).

Failing Grades

Runaway and homeless youth frequently experience school problems such as skipping school, having poor or failing grades, and being expelled from school. They have these school difficulties in combination with problems living in dysfunctional families that are often characterized by physical, sexual, and emotional abuse, a lack of love and emotional warmth, poor communication, and other problems. In a self-report narrative, a female teen reported that before she had run away, her grade point average had dropped from 3.38 to 0.0 (Mishriki 2001–2013).

School failure can be devastating and can be a contributing factor in teens' running away episodes. For example, one self-reported female runaway reported that the staff at a group home were wondering why she went from having passing grades to complete failure (Mishriki 2001–2013). The girl indicated that she felt like a failure and decided to run away with another girl.

Truancy

Runaway teens may have a history of truancy. In one investigation, Thompson and Pillai (2006) discovered that 56.8 % of the youth in New York and 33.5 % in Texas indicated that they had been truant or expelled from school.

According to one self-report story, a female juvenile, who was still living at home, skipped school 1 day and went to a park to hang out with friends (Mishriki 2001–2013). The youth indicated that she skipped school in order to find time "to think." The girl later ran away from home.

In another self-report narrative, an 11-year-old female runaway reported that she was charged with truancy (Mishriki 2001–2013). A 12-year-old girl in one self-report narrative stated that she "skipped" school (Mishriki 2001–2013).

Young people who run away and become homeless may face multiple truancy charges (Mishriki 2001–2013). One runaway girl reported that she had been charged with truancy two times (Mishriki 2001–2013). Runaway and homeless youth who are truant have an increased probability of meeting deviant peers and engaging in delinquent activities.

Children may be truant in order for them to be with their girlfriend/boyfriend or other friends. For example, one female adolescent reported that she became a truant in order to be with her boyfriend (Mishriki 2001–2013). In one self-report, a female runaway, who reported that she frequently would stay out late with friends, indicated that she had truant from school (Mishriki 2001–2013). In this self-report narrative, the female juvenile reported that when she was 14, she got her second charge for truancy (Mishriki 2001–2013).

Runaway and homeless children and adolescents who suffer mental health problems may be especially at risk for being truant from school. For example, in one self-report, a female runaway reportedly was often truant. She was hospitalized in a psychiatric inpatient setting and had a history of sexual and physical abuse and neglect by her mother who was addicted to drugs. The teen had a history of multiple suicide attempts and suicidal ideation.

Runaway and homeless youth who abuse alcohol and other drugs frequently are truant from schools. According to one self-report, a female runaway who was often truant indicated that she would frequently stay out late with her friends and would smoke cigarettes, use alcohol, and take other drugs (Mishriki 2001–2013).

Parents may not know that their child is truant because the child is keeping it a secret. For example, in one self-report case, a 16-year-old girl noted that she had been skipping school for 3 months, and her mother was unaware that she had been truant for so long (Mishriki 2001–2013).

Runaway youth will use various tactics to hide the fact they are truant from school (Violent Acres 2007, April 11). In one self-report, a 15-year-old female runaway described how her mother took her to school (Violent Acres 2007, April 11). The girl would walk in the school's front door with her backpack containing textbooks and school homework and 10 min later she would walk out the school's back door to be with her boyfriend.

Truancy may lead to school failure and school expulsion. In one self-report case, a 16-year-old runaway girl reported that she frequently skipped school, which resulted in her failing courses (Mishriki 2001–2013).

Truancy also provides an opportunity for juveniles to engage in other status offenses. While truant, children and adolescents have the opportunity to make plans to run away. For example, after skipping school, one 12-year-old girl planned to run away to Florida with two older male adolescents (Mishriki 2001–2013).

Truants are also more likely to be victimized during their time away from school and supervised activities. According to one self-report narrative, a 12-year-old girl reported that an older man forced her to engage in oral sex after she skipped school and was hanging out at a park (Mishriki 2001–2013).

Runaway and homeless children and adolescents who are charged with truancy may receive probation. This sanction gives youth an opportunity to change their negative behavior.

Truancy prevention programs also may help to reduce truancy rates and other deviant behavior. For example, based on an intensive home and school visiting intervention with runaway, sexually assaulted Hmong girls, Edinburgh and Saewyc (2009) discovered that the intervention project reduced school truancy.

School Detention

Youth who run away and become homeless may be more likely to have been in school detention than non-runaway/homeless young people. Pollio et al. (2006) showed that 31 % of the runaway and homeless youth in their investigation had received a detention in school.

School Suspensions

To what extent the children at the time that they runaway or become homeless have a history of being suspended from school? Pollio et al. (2006), in their investigation of 371 runaway and homeless youth who were using emergency shelter and crisis services, showed that 27 % of the youth had been suspended from school at admission into the study. According to Warren et al. (1997), school suspensions among runaway youth were associated with sexual activity.

Expulsion

Runaway and homeless young people may be more likely to be expelled from school than non-runaway/homeless youth. In Pollio et al.'s (2006) investigation, 8 % of the runaway/homeless had been expelled from school. Based on a study of runaway teens using emergency shelter services in New York and Texas, Thompson and Pillai (2006) discovered that 43.9 % had been expelled from school or truant.

Missed School Days

Because of social, educational, and financial barriers and mental and behavioral problems, many runaway and homeless young people are unable to attend school and progress academically (Rosa et al. 1992). Hammer et al. (2002) estimated that among runaway/thrown-away youth enrolled in school at the time of their runaway/thrown-away incident, an estimated 70,500 had missed at least 5 days in school.

In the USA, the federal McKinney–Vento Homeless Assistance Act offers federal funds for homeless shelter programs to make sure that homeless young people get access to education (The McKinney–Vento Homeless Assistance Act (MVHAA) of 1987 (Pub. L. 100-77, July 22, 1987, 101 Stat. 482, 42 U.S.C. § 11301 et seq.)). As a result, some runaway youth are able to go back to school. For example, in one self-report narrative, one female runaway reported that after being put in a group home, she went back to school and "got her grade 7" (Mishriki 2001–2013).

However, many street youth do not attend school. Based on a study of 371 runaway and homeless youth using crisis shelter services, Pollio et al. (2006) discovered that only 49 % were currently attending school or were recent graduates.

School attendance is a problem in many other countries. For example, in a study of street children of Recife, Brazil, Rosa et al. (1992) discovered that less than two-thirds of the sample was going to school. However, the investigators found that street youth who were enrolled in classes were behind one or two grades in terms of their expected school performance.

Runaway and homeless youth in Canada may either try to work or attend school. In McCarthy and Hagan's (1992) analysis of 390 homeless adolescents in Toronto, Ontario, Canada, 20 % had tried to get a job while on their own but had given up their job search and had come back to school.

Youth who are the victims of physical abuse at the time they runaway or become homeless may be especially at risk for missing school days. Hammer et al. (2002) showed that in 4 % of the runaway/thrown-away incidents, youth who were enrolled in school at the time of the episode had missed at least 5 days of school. In an investigation of the impact of early child maltreatment, Lansford et al. (2002) discovered that adolescents who suffered early child physical maltreatment were away from school twice as many days than adolescents who had not been physically maltreated.

While on the streets, young people who are tricked or coerced into becoming a human trafficking victim also will miss school days. Human traffickers may restrain and confine runaway and homeless youth and closely monitor and restrict their schedule, which prevents them from attending school.

Low School Achievement

According to Rogers et al. (1994), children and adolescents who ran away had a greater likelihood of lower achievement on standardized tests. Youth who have been physically maltreated at the time they ran away may be especially at risk for lower school performance. However, based on an investigation of child maltreatment, Lansford et al. (2002) found that although children who had been physically maltreated were more likely to have lower school grades and lower scores on school achievement tests and more likely to be suspended from school, the effects of physical maltreatment could be accounted for by risk factors related to physical abuse instead of physical abuse by itself.

Young people who have been trafficked may have been victims of physical and sexual abuse, physical restraints, confinement, and torture (National Human Trafficking Resource Center n.d. a, b). As a consequence, they may have a greater likelihood of performing poorly in school.

Runaway and homeless youth face school failure and other related obstacles (Greene et al. 1997b). Likewise, according to Thompson and Pillai (2006), high rates of runaway recidivism are related to school failure and other high-risk behaviors.

Participation in Special or Remedial Education

Some investigations have demonstrated that approximately 25 % of homeless youth take remedial or special education courses (Clark and Robertson 1996; Robertson 1989). Additional research is needed to evaluate the extent to which remedial or special education programs improve school outcomes for street youth.

School Alternatives

Homeschooling may be a viable alternative for some runaway and homeless youth. According to a self-report narrative, one runaway girl who had been charged with truancy noted that she received homeschooling afterward (Mishriki 2001–2013). Research on the impact of homeschooling on runaway and homeless young people is needed.

High School Completion and Attendance

Runaway and homeless youth are less likely to complete school (Benoit-Bryan 2011; Tarasuk et al. 2005; Yates et al. 1988). In an investigation of initial visits to an outpatient medical clinic, Yates et al. (1988) found that runaway youth were almost five times more likely to drop out than non-runaway youth.

In their investigation of 261 homeless adolescents and young adults, Tarasuk et al. (2005) discovered that a majority of the young people had not finished high school. Seven were going to school currently. However, only two of the individuals were attending school on a full-time basis.

Benoit-Bryan (2011) in a longitudinal investigation of former runaways revealed that adults who were former runaways had a 50 % decrease in the probability of obtaining a high school diploma or a GED. For other educational levels, former runaways also were more likely to have low educational attainment compared to those who did not run away.

Chapter 6
Substance Use Among Homeless and Runaway Adolescents

This chapter analyzes the rates and types of substance use and abuse among homeless and runaway youth and young people in the general population. In this chapter, the rates of street youth using substances such as tobacco, marijuana, alcohol, cocaine, hallucinogens, methamphetamine, ketamine, heroin, and MDMA (ecstasy) are presented. In this chapter, risk factors such as the street youth's demographic characteristics, parental use and abuse of alcohol and other drugs, family dysfunction, negative peer influence, and social networks are analyzed.In addition, this chapter studies the extent to which such conditions as the trauma and stress of family abuse and conflict may increase the probability that runaway and homeless children and adolescents may use alcohol and other drugs to cope with these stressful and traumatic problems.

The stress and trauma of living on the streets also may increase the youth's likelihood of using and abuse substances. This chapter examines the effects of housing instability and type of environmental setting on street youth's use of alcohol and other drugs. The impact of mental disorders on substance use and abuse is also discussed. This chapter also discusses the effects of using alcohol and other drugs on violent behaviors; victimization; sexually transmitted infections, including human immune virus (HIV)/acquired immunodeficiency syndrome (AIDS); and unintended pregnancies.

Researchers have analyzed the prevalence, theories, risk factors, and consequences of substance use and abuse among street youth in different countries (Noto et al. 1997; Hammer et al. 2002; Thompson et al. 2008; Rice et al. 2007; Van Leeuwen et al. 2004; Whitbeck et al. 2004; Cochran et al. 2002; Benoit-Bryan 2011).

S.J. Morewitz, *Runaway and Homeless Youth*,
DOI 10.1007/978-3-319-30863-0_6

Prevalence of Substance Abuse

In the general child and adolescent population, experimentation with alcohol and drugs is prevalent (Johnson et al. 2005). For example, according to the Monitoring the Future, 49 % of youth in 2014 had used an illegal substance by the time they left high school (Johnston et al. 2015). However, runaway and homeless youth use substances earlier in life and more frequently than children and adolescents in the general population (Johnson et al. 2005).

Researcher have analyzed the rates of substance use and abuse in among homeless and runaway youth of different sexual orientations (Cochran et al. 2002; Whitbeck et al. 2004) and in different settings (e.g., street and shelter) and for different periods of time (Johnson et al. 2005; Van Leeuwen et al. 2004; Hammer et al. 2002). Rates of substance may vary depending on which setting or time period is measured. Rates of substance use also may differ depending on the demographic and social/behavioral characteristics of the runaway and homeless youth (Kipke et al. 1997a, b; Greene et al. 1997a, b; Feitel et al. 1992; McCaskill et al. 1998).

According to Hammer et al. (2002), in 19 % of the estimated runaway/thrown-away incidents, the children were dependent on drugs. In addition, the researchers discovered that in 17 % of the episodes, youth was taking hard drugs at the time. In 18 % of the episodes, the children were with an individual who was known to be abusing drugs.

A US General Accounting Office (1989) study found that 20 % of young people using runaway shelters had substance-abuse problems. In another investigation, McCarthy and Hagan (1992) revealed that 80 % of their study participants indicated that they smoked marijuana since becoming homeless.

Johnson et al. (2005), using a longitudinal diagnostic investigation of 428 homeless and runaway youth ages 16–19 years, discovered that 60.5 % of the runaway young people had at least one of three substance disorders (alcohol abuse, alcohol dependence, and drug abuse) based on lifetime criteria. The investigators found that 48.1 % had at least one substance disorder using 12-month criteria.

Using data from 150 shelter teens in Los Angeles, CA, Feitel et al. (1992) discovered that 41 % fulfilled the criteria for substance abuse. Based on a sample of 96 shelter and street youth, Mundy et al. (1990) showed that 48 % fulfilled the DSM III criteria for alcohol abuse or dependence and 39 % fulfilled criteria for drug use or dependence.

Based on a 1-day survey of 186 homeless young people in Denver, Colorado, 75 % of whom were between the ages of 16 and 25, Van Leeuwen et al. (2004) discovered that 75 % had had used marijuana during the previous 9 months, 69 % alcohol, 30 % hallucinogens, and 25 % ecstasy. Other reported drug uses in the past 9 months included 19 % cocaine, 18 % methamphetamine, 13 % ketamine, and 12 % heroin.

Halcon and Lifson (2004) found that 51.7 % of a sample of 203 homeless young people, aged 15–22, indicated that on average they had five or more alcoholic drinks weekly. More than a third of the sample reported that they had 15 or more alcoholic beverages each week. According to the investigators, two-thirds of the sample of homeless youth reported using illegal drugs. Among these illegal drugs, homeless youth were most likely to use marijuana (56.9 %).

In Washington, D.C., based on a sample of 327 homeless young people, ages 14–21 years, Bailey et al. (1998) showed that about 75 % of the youth had used alcohol and marijuana in their lifetime. Sixteen percent of the respondents had ever used crack cocaine and almost one-third had ever taken hallucinogens. Seven percent of the respondents had ever used heroin and 4 % have been needle users. More than 25 % of the homeless youth in the study reported having three or more symptoms of dependency on alcohol or other drugs based on the DSM-IV (1994) criteria.

Using data on homeless and runaway teens from San Francisco, CA; Denver, CO; and New York City, Kral et al. (1997) reported that 97 % had taken drugs or alcohol. The researchers also found that 21 % of the study participants had been injection drug users.

In Kipke et al.'s (1997) investigation of street young people in Hollywood, CA, 93 % had used marijuana, 89 % had consumed alcohol, and 66 % had used speed. The researchers also showed that 61 % had used LSD and 50 % had taken cocaine. In addition, 45 % had taken mushrooms, 44 % had used inhalants, and 41 % had used crack cocaine.

Whitbeck and Hoyt (1999), based on a study of homeless and runaway young people in the Midwest, found that 81.2 % had taken alcohol in the last year, 69.4 % had used marijuana, 27.2 % had used amphetamines, and 25.8 % had used hallucinogens. The investigators also showed that 16.8 % had used inhalants in the last year, 16.1 % inhalants, 14.7 % cocaine, 9.2 % barbiturates, 6.8 % tranquilizers, and 6.4 % opiates.

Using a sample of runaway and non-runaway youth who had an initial visit at an outpatient medical clinic, Yates et al. (1988) discovered that 84 % of the runaway youth reported using alcohol or drugs. In their sample, 34.5 % of runaway young people indicated that they engaged intravenous drug use compared to only 3.7 % of non-runaway youth.

In addition to a higher rate of heroin use, runaway young people in Yates et al.'s (1988) investigation reported higher rates of other drugs than non-runaway young people. Runaway youth had a higher prevalence of various substances including cigarettes, stimulants, hallucinogens, and narcotics.

Homeless and runaway young people frequently smoke cigarettes and drink alcohol. A self-reported female runaway girl stated that while on the streets she lived in multiple houses and drank alcohol and smoked cigarettes (Mishriki 2001–2013).

In addition to using alcohol and other drugs, teen runaway and homeless youth may participate in illicit drug dealing (Mishriki 2001–2013). A self-reported 15-year-old female runaway stated that while on the streets she met a low-level drug dealer and started to deliver drugs for him (Mishriki 2001–2013).

Researchers have examined the onset of substance abuse among runaway and homeless youth. According to Johnson et al. (2005), more than 85 % of substance abuse and dependency takes place at the same time or after a child's first runaway incident. In the Runaway Youth Project (RYP) Case # 390, M.C., a 16-year-old girl, reportedly had been involved with drugs for 5 months before she ran away from home (see Appendix).

Possible Demographic Correlates

Runaway and homeless youth may vary in their substance use based on their age (Greene et al. 1997a, b). Using three national samples, Greene et al. (1997a, b) showed that older homeless youth (18–21) had higher rates of substance use than those in the 12–17 age group.

Use of alcohol and other drugs by homeless and runaway young people may differ based on their racial and ethnic background (Greene et al. 1997a, b). In Greene et al.'s (1997a, b) study, the investigators demonstrated that substance use was higher among Whites than African Americans.

Gender differences may influence substance use among runaway and homeless youth. For example, Johnson et al. (2005) found that male homeless and runaway teens were more likely than their female counterparts to fulfill criteria for at least three substance-abuse disorders (67.4 % vs. 55.2 %, respectively). The investigators also showed that male homeless and runaway and homeless adolescents were more likely than female homeless and runaway adolescents to fulfill 12-month criteria for having at least one of three substance-abuse disorders. According to Greene et al. (1997a, b), male homeless youth had higher rates of substance use than their female counterparts.

Familial Risk Factors

The parents of runaway and homeless young people may have risk factors that influence their child's development of substance-abuse problems. The parents of these youth frequently have alcohol and drug problems, which help to explain the high level of family dysfunction among runaway and homeless youth (Thompson et al. 2008; Mallett et al. 2005).

In Mallett et al.'s (2005) interviews with 302 homeless youth, ages 12–20 years, about 33 % stated that their family members' drug use or their own personal substance use was a major factor for their becoming homeless.

Based on an investigation of runaway and homeless young people, Whitbeck et al. (1997b) discovered that over 50 % of the youth indicated that at least one of their parents had a problem with alcohol. Almost 20 % of the study participants reported that they had two parents who had problems with alcohol. In addition, more than 33 % of the study participants revealed that they thought that at least one of their parents had difficulties with hard drugs. In Johnson et al.'s (2005) research, homeless and runaway youth had a greater probability of fulfilling criteria for substance-abuse disorders if their caretakers had been in substance-abuse treatment.

Parents' substance-abuse behaviors can result in parents' inability or reduced motivation to meet the psychosocial needs of their children. Parental alcohol problems may lead to parental rejection of their offspring. As a result, the children and adolescents of substance-abusing parents may develop a variety of psychosocial problems, including abusing alcohol and drugs, having impairments in developing and maintaining relationships, and running away from home on a repeated basis (McMorris et al. 2002; Kurtz et al. 1991a, b, c).

Runaway and homeless young people may use alcohol and other drugs to cope with the stress and trauma of their family abuse and family conflict (Thompson et al. 2008; Johnson et al. 2005). In Johnson et al.'s (2005) investigation, runaway and homeless young people who had suffered more caretaker physical or sexual abuse had a greater likelihood of fulfilling alcohol dependence criteria. McMorris et al. (2002) found that parental alcohol problems increased the risk that they would abuse their children, which led to an increased probability that the abused children would have drinking problems.

Johnson et al. (2005) also evaluated the extent to which certain parenting practices increased or decreased the risk of alcohol and other drug abuse among homeless and runaway young people. In their investigation, parents who monitored their child's activities, e.g., knew their whereabouts and knew who they were with, were more likely to reduce their child's chances of meeting criteria for substance abuse.

On-the-Street Risk Factors

Runaway and homeless youth who abuse alcohol and other illicit drugs face an increased probability of being victimized (Thrane et al. 2011; Kral et al. 1997; Hoyt et al. 1999). Using a sample of 5387 heterosexual females, ages 11–18, from the Longitudinal Study of Adolescent Health, Thrane et al. (2011) demonstrated that use of alcohol doubled the probability of being sexually assaulted. The runaway and homeless youth's risk of sexual victimization may increase when they are under the influence of alcohol or drugs during sexual intercourse. In Kral et al.'s (1997) investigation, 75 % of the homeless young people reported that during sexual intercourse, they were under the influence of alcohol or other drugs.

Runaway and homeless young people, when faced with the stress of surviving on the streets, may turn to alcohol and other drugs to help them cope with these stress. For example, one self-reported runaway youth, who reportedly ran away from home at age 15, noted that his life on the streets was hard and he got into a lot of drugs, crime, and other behaviors (Mishriki 2001–2013).

Deviant peer group and peer network influences also may lead homeless and runaway youth to get involved in alcohol and other drugs (Johnson et al. 2005; Kipke et al. 1997a, b; Rice et al. 2007; Tyler 2008; McMorris et al. 2002). According to McMorris et al. (2002), parental alcohol difficulties are linked to their offspring having alcohol problems because of parental rejection in association with the youth having nonconforming peers and high-risk subsistence strategies on the streets. McMorris et al. (2002) also showed that having deviant peer interactions and engaging in deviant subsistence strategies on the streets had the strongest direct effects on whether homeless and runaway young people used alcohol.

Based on an investigation of newly runaway and homeless youth in Los Angeles, CA, Rice et al. (2007) showed that runaway and homeless young people who have peers who have been arrested may have an increased probability of using hard drugs. The investigators also discovered that while on the streets, youth may be more likely to use hard drugs if they have peers who are in gangs. In addition, the study results indicated that runaway and homeless youth who have peers who steal from other individuals may have an increased likelihood of using hard drugs (Rice et al. 2007). The researchers also discovered that runaway and homeless young people may be more likely to use hard drugs if they have peers who suffered from drug overdoses (Rice et al. 2007).

Peer group and social networks enable homeless and runaway youth to continue their use of alcohol and other drugs. According to one self-report narrative, a teen runaway reported drinking alcohol with his friends (Mishriki 2001–2013).

Group affiliation can influence patterns of drug use and HIV-risk behaviors (Kipke et al. 1997a, b). Homeless and runaway young people may use alcohol and other drugs because they belong to groups that promote certain social and political beliefs and values. As members of these groups, runaway and homeless children and adolescents may engage in certain risk behaviors or have certain physical features. For example, Kipke et al. (1997a, b) found that homeless and runaway youth who viewed themselves members of the "punker" group were more likely to have unprotected sex and share needles during injection drug use.

Another social group, lesbian, gay, bisexual, and transsexual or transgender (LGBT) youth, may initiate or increase their use and abuse of alcohol and other drugs on the streets (Cochran et al. 2002; Whitbeck et al. 2004). They may abuse alcohol and other drugs as a part of high-risk survival strategies and to cope with the stress and trauma of street life, especially because of their sexual minority orientation.

In one study, Cochran et al. (2002) showed that homeless sexual minority youth took cocaine or crack, crack or crack mixed with amphetamines, and speed or crystal methamphetamines more often in the past 6 months than their homeless heterosexual counterparts. The researchers also discovered that homeless LGBT young people used more kinds of drugs than their heterosexual counterparts.

Whitbeck et al. (2004) discovered variations in substance abuse among homeless and runaway gay male and lesbian youth compared to homeless and runaway heterosexual youth. Homeless and runaway gay males (63.2 %) had a lower probability of abusing alcohol than heterosexual male youth (85.1 %). However, homeless and runaway lesbian youth had higher rates of both alcohol and other drug abuse than their homeless and runaway heterosexual females.

Runaway and homeless LGBT youth are more likely to get HIV/AIDS because they may be injection drug users and engage in multiple sexual risk behaviors (Marshall et al. 2010; Yates et al. 1988). For example, Lubotsky et al. (n.d.) describe the ways in which GLBT youth are initiated into prostitution and substance addiction by elder panders who provide them with highly addictive crystal methamphetamine to solidify their participation in prostitution.

According to Ennett et al. (1999a, b), not having a social network may increase homeless and runaway youth's risk for participating in HIV/AIDS risk behaviors such as taking illegal drugs, having multiple sex partners, and engaging in survival sex (Ennett et al. 1999a, b).

Housing Instability and Type of Setting

Housing instability and type of environmental setting may influence alcohol and drug use by homeless and runaway young people. The time that homeless and runaway young people spend away from home and on their own increases the odds that they will engage in survival sex, which increases HIV/AIDS risks (Janus et al. 1987a, b; Tyler et al. 2001a, b, c; Greene et al. 1999). In Chen et al.'s (2004) analysis, increased duration on the streets may increase the street youth's risk of alcohol and other drug use. In addition, increase time on the streets predicts an increased likelihood of engaging in theft and other problematic behaviors (Chen et al. 2004).

Street youth in Greene et al.'s (1997a, b) investigation had higher rates of using most types of substances than those youth in shelters. They had higher rates of using drugs such as marijuana, hallucinogens, stimulants, crack cocaine, and intravenous drugs than shelter youth.

Unstable housing among injection drug users is linked to their higher incidence of HIV (Corneil et al. 2006). One study of high HIV-risk incarcerated women showed that the larger the number of residences that they lived in, the greater their likelihood of having unprotected sex (Weir et al. 2007). Elifson et al. (2007) discovered that female drug users who stayed in unstable housing situations were less likely to reduce HIV-associated risk behaviors than those who had stable housing. According to Kipke et al. (2007) and Clatts et al. (2005), housing instability and homelessness increase sexual and drug risks for HIV among men who have sex with other men (MSM).

Human Trafficking Victimization, Prostitution, and Substance Abuse

Human traffickers may abduct and force or coerce runaway and homeless young people into sex, forced labor, and organ trafficking (Morewitz 2008, 2016). Children are also kidnapped and used as child soldiers during armed conflicts. Traffickers may use drugs to kidnap human trafficking victims (Silverman et al. 2007; Morewitz 2008). These human traffickers often get their victims addicted to alcohol and other drugs as part of their pattern of controlling and abusing their victims. Traffickers will use alcohol and other drugs to make child soldiers feel more courageous during warfare. Human trafficking victims also may turn to substance use and abuse to cope with the trauma of human trafficking victimization. Therefore, runaway and homeless young people who are trafficked are at risk for using and abusing alcohol and other drugs.

Substance use is linked to engaging in survival sex and prostitution among runaway and homeless adolescents (Greene et al. 1999; Van Leeuwen et al. 2004; Walls and Bell 2010; Yates et al. 1991). Walls and Bell (2010) found that drug use is a correlate of survival sex among homeless youth and adults in 28 states in the USA. Van Leeuwen et al. (2004) showed that 11 % of the homeless youth survey reported exchanging sex for drugs, money, food, or shelter.

These results are explained by the homeless and runaway youth's multiple risk behaviors. Runaway and homeless young people have high rates of sexual behaviors (Greenblatt and Robertson 1993; Rotheram-Borus 1993; Bailey et al. 1998). Homeless and runaway young people often engage in survival sex, e.g., having sex in exchange for drugs, money, food, and shelter and other risky sexual behaviors (Greenblatt and Robertson 1993; Rotheram-Borus 1993). They also have high rates of substance abuse (Greenblatt and Robertson 1993; Kipke et al. 1995; Pennbridge et al. 1992).

Substance Use and HIV/AIDS Risks

Among runaways and homeless young people, certain types of drug use may increase HIV/AIDS risk (Weber et al. 2002; Gleghorn et al. 1998). Street youth who are injection drug users have a higher probability of getting HIV/AIDS. Greene et al. (1997a, b) showed that 17.1 % of current street youth and 3.6 % of current shelter youth were injection drug users. Johnson et al. (1996) also showed that injection drug use was one of the risk factors for AIDS.

Among homeless and runaway youth, injection drug use can occur together with alcohol and drug use, increasing the risk of HIV/AIDS risk. In addition, substance use can co-occur with risky sexual behaviors such as survival sex, increasing HIV/AIDS risk among runaway and homeless young people. Weber et al. (2002) found that female street youth who participated in prostitution had a two times greater likelihood of binging on alcohol and five times greater probability of binging on drugs.

Homeless and runaway youth who participate in prostitution may be at increased risk of engaging in injection drug use. For example, Weber et al. (2002) demonstrated that female street youth who participated in prostitution were four times more likely to have a history of intravenous drug use. These female homeless youth had a 2.5 times greater likelihood of injecting cocaine as their drug choice.

Substance-Abuse Effects on Unintended Pregnancies

Substance use may increase the probability of unintended pregnancies (Morewitz 2004). Using alcohol and other drugs can impair judgment and coordination leading to inconsistent or nonuse of condoms and other contraceptives.

Mental Disorders and Substance Use

Homeless and runaway youth who have a conduct disorder (CD) may be more likely to use drugs such as heroin and cocaine. For example, according to Booth and Zhang (1997), CD was the greatest predictor of lifetime use of heroin and or cocaine. CD may increase the likelihood of substance use among runaway and homeless youth because it predicts participation in survival sex, which involves engaging in sex in exchange for alcohol and other drugs, food, shelter, or other valued items. In Booth and Zhang's (1997) report, CD was the best predictor of participation in survival sex among homeless and runaway young people.

Substance use may increase the risk of mental health problems such as depression, self-mutilation, and suicidal behaviors among homeless and runaway young people (Johnson et al. 2005; Bolognini et al. 2003; Olson et al. 1999). In Johnson et al.'s (2005) investigation, 93 % of the homeless and runaway teens interviewed who fulfilled criteria for a substance-abuse disorder also fulfilled criteria for at least one other mental disorder. Sherman et al. (2005) showed that substance use was positively associated ever having engaged in self-cutting using a sample of street children in Lahore, Pakistan.

In Thompson et al.'s (2008) analysis, heavy alcohol use by homeless and runaway young people and episodes of major depression were indirectly linked to an increased risk of suicidal ideation. The authors suggest that homeless and runaway youth often have more than one mental disorder, which is a "necessary but not sufficient" condition for causing suicidal behaviors.

Homeless and runaway youth with a family history of substance abuse, childhood sexual abuse, physical abuse, neglect, and family conflict and violence, in combination with the chronic trauma of living on the streets at a young age, are also susceptible to post-traumatic stress disorder (PTSD) and other mental disorders related to severe trauma (Thompson et al. 2008).

Substance Abuse, Violence, and Other High-Risk Behaviors

Substance use is linked to violence by reducing cognitive functioning and behavioral inhibitions in individuals who may be predisposed to violent tendencies (Morewitz 2004). In addition, runaways and homeless young people also may have a higher probability of violent behavior because many of them come from dysfunctional homes where violence and abuse were prevalent (Crawford et al. 2011). These youth may learn to use violence in their home environment, which later increases their chances of becoming violent while on the streets (Crawford et al. 2011). Many street youth witness violence while on the streets, including murder, and have themselves been the victims of physical and sexual violence at home and on the streets.

Street youth may fear being murdered and assaulted (Kipke et al. 1997a, b) and may become desensitized to the use of violence as a survival strategy. The street youth's persistent state of vigilance and stressful experiences increase the probability that they will resort to violence in situations that they perceive as threatening.

Young people on the streets may engage in violence, and they use and sell drugs as part of their deviant subsistence strategies (Crawford et al. 2011). Crawford et al. (2011) describe the example of a drug dealer who may be forced to intimidate people for self-protection. Intimidation can result in violence during threatening incidents. Violence is reinforced and maintained over time (Caspi et al. 1989).

Street youth who interact with violent peers may be more likely to engage in violence on the streets. Hammer et al. (2002), in the NISMART, discovered that in 7 % of the estimated runaway/thrown-away incidents, the teen runaway was in the company of a violent individual.

Drug Use and Mortality Among Homeless and Runaway Youth

Drug overdose is a cause of death among homeless youth and adults. In Roy et al.'s (2004) analysis of mortality among street youth in Montreal, Quebec, Canada, drug overdose was the second leading cause of death (five males and three males).

Substance Use Among Adults Who Were Former Runaways

What are the long-term behavioral consequences of substance use among former runaway youth? Using longitudinal data of runaways, Benoit-Bryan (2011) found that adults who were former runaways had a higher rate of smoking cigarettes in the previous 30 days (55.4 %) than adults who had never run away (35 %). Having a history of running away had the largest effect on self-reported smoking in the previous 30 days. Other characteristics that were related to an increase probability of smoking cigarettes in the prior 30 days included female gender, being Hispanic, being African American, being Asian, age, and a history of foster care and verbal, physical, and sexual abuse. Having been born in the USA and homosexual orientation were not related to an increase in the rate of cigarette smoking in the prior 30 days.

In terms of alcohol use, Benoit-Bryan (2011) showed that adults who were former runaways did not have an increased probability of consuming alcohol. The author notes that the study did not measure the frequency and amount of alcohol use, which may vary among former runaways.

With regard to marijuana use, Benoit-Bryan (2011) found that adults who had run away as juveniles had a 67 % higher rate of marijuana use in the previous 30 days than their counterparts who had never run away. Several variables predicted an increase probability of using marijuana: being an American Indian (59 % increase), bisexual (127 % increase), and homosexual (56 % increase). Having a history of physical abuse and verbal abuse also were related to an increased likelihood of using marijuana (36 % and 15 %, respectively). Being Hispanic and Asian was associated with a decreased probability of using marijuana (decrease of 77 % and 60 %, respectively).

Chapter 7
Delinquent/Criminal and Violent Behavior

This chapter analyzes delinquent and violent behaviors among runaway and homeless young people. Emphasis is on the prevalence of different types of delinquent and criminal behaviors and the risk factors that increase the likelihood that street youth will participate in these behaviors. Theft, robbery, drug trade, and status offenses such as alcohol-related violations are some of the criminal and delinquent activities discussed. This chapter discusses such risk factors as low socioeconomic status, age, family impairment, abuse and exposure to violence, gang involvement and negative peer influence, conduct disorder, neurocognitive problems, substance use and abuse, and school difficulties, duration of homelessness, and housing instability as conditions that increase the probability that runaway and homeless young people will participate in delinquent/criminal and violent behaviors. In this chapter, the process of social learning is discussed to illustrate the ways in which young people may learn to use violence in their home environment, which later increases their likelihood of exhibiting violent interactional styles while on the streets. While on the streets trying to survive using deviant subsistence strategies such as theft, survival sex, and robbery, young people may become desensitized to the use of violence as a survival strategy. The street youth's persistent state of vigilance and stressful experiences increase the chances that they may resort to violence in situations that they perceive as threatening. This chapter also assesses the effects of violence on street youth. For example, female youth on the streets who become victims of violence may be especially at increased risk of having unintended pregnancies. Violent interactions often result in the inconsistent or nonuse of condoms and other contraceptive methods.

In the USA and other countries, street youth, including children who run away or become homeless, may have a higher rate of committing delinquent and violent behaviors than young people who live at home (Benoit-Bryan 2011; Tyler 2008; McCarthy and Hagan 1992; Lalor 1999; Kipke et al. 1997a, b). Based on a longitudinal investigation of 360 runaway young people, Tyler (2008) discovered that former runaway youth exhibited a higher prevalence of delinquent activities than non-runaway youth.

S.J. Morewitz, *Runaway and Homeless Youth*,
DOI 10.1007/978-3-319-30863-0_7

Other studies show that homeless and runaway young people are at risk of engaging in delinquent/criminal and violent behaviors. Kim et al. (2009), using a sample of 416 teens from the Lehigh Longitudinal Study, found that running away from home increased the likelihood of delinquency. According to an investigation carried out by the Federal Youth Services Bureau, two-thirds of youth in shelters and four-fifths of young people on the streets had attempted or completed a theft (Greene et al. 1995).

Based on their analysis of shelter youth, Thompson and Pollio (2006) revealed that 16 % had engaged in misdemeanors. Other researchers should assess the rates of misdemeanors among street youth.

Using data from the National Incidence Studies of Missing, Abducted, Runaway, and Thrown-away Children (NISMART), Hammer et al. (2002) discovered that in 11 % of the estimated runaway/thrown-away incidents, runaway children and adolescents participated in criminal conduct.

For example, in Runaway Youth Project (RYP) no. 553, Lashawn Washington, a 16-year-old boy from Rockville, MD, reportedly was traveling in a stolen vehicle with two of his classmates at the time that they were running away from a youth academy (see Appendix).

Runaway youth may be at increased risk of engaging in violent behavior because many of them come from dysfunctional homes where violence and abuse were prevalent (Crawford et al. 2011). Street youth may have a propensity of violence because they were exposed to coercion and violence in their home environment. Through the process of social learning, young people may learn to use violence in their home environment, which later increases their likelihood of exhibiting violent interactional styles while on the streets (Crawford et al. 2011). Many street youth witness violence while on the streets, including murder, and have themselves been the victims of physical and sexual violence at home and on the streets. Many street youth fear being shot, stabbed, or sexually and physically assaulted (Kipke et al. 1997a, b). Young people on the streets may become desensitized to the use of violence as a survival strategy. The street youth's persistent state of vigilance and stressful experiences increase the probability that they will resort to violence in situations that they perceive as threatening.

While on the streets, runaway and homeless young people may develop violent interactional styles while they engage in deviant subsistence strategies (Crawford et al. 2011). Crawford et al. (2011) use the example of a drug dealer who relies on violence for self-protection. Thus, the drug dealer may have to threaten individuals for self-protection. Violent interactional styles can lead to violent confrontations, especially during threatening situations. Caspi evaluate the extent to which violent interactional styles are reinforced and maintained over time.

Association with violent peers may increase the probability that runaways will participate in violent activity while on the streets. In NISMART, Hammer et al. (2002) discovered that in 7 % of the estimated runaway/thrown-away incidents, the youth was in the company of a violent individual.

Lack of money, lack of stable employment, lack of education, lack of job skills, food insecurity, and lack of stable housing are some of the prevalent problems among homeless, and runaway youth engage in deviant subsistence strategies in order to survive on the streets (Whitbeck et al. 1999, 2006).

Homeless and runaway young people steal food in response to the problem of food insecurity and lack of money (Whitbeck et al. 2006). For example, in one self-report, Larry, who was 14 when he ran away from home, noted that he did not have any money so he would steal food when he was hungry (Mishriki 2001–2013). Larry reported that in order to eat, he would steal food from gas stations. Runaway and homeless youth may also search through trash for food, which also known as "dumpster surfing." For example, in one self-report, a runaway boy reported that he searched for food by going through people's trash (Mishriki 2001–2013).

In McCarthy and Hagan's (1992) research on 390 homeless adolescents in Toronto, Canada, 47 % indicated that they had stolen food since becoming homeless. The investigators discovered that more than 90 % of those who stole food stated that they had pilfered food from businesses at least one time. Among those who pilfered food, another 26 % reported that they had stolen food such as bread from vehicles delivering supplies to food establishments or left restaurants without paying their bill.

Booth (2006), using a sample of homeless youth in Adelaide, South Australia, showed that 65 % of the young people engaged in theft in order to acquire food while on the streets. In an investigation of 261 homeless youth in Toronto, Canada, Li et al. (2009) discovered that 22 % of males and 13 % of females indicated that they engaged in theft or the drug trade as their main source of income in the previous 30 days.

In their first weeks on the streets, runaways may steal money. For example, in one self-report, a 12-year-old runaway girl wrote that during her first week on the streets, she slept in abandoned trailers and stole money (Mishriki 2001–2013).

Besides stealing food and money, homeless and runaway youth commit theft of goods worth up to $50 and also more than $50 (McCarthy and Hagan 1992). One investigation found that 47.9 % of the homeless teens reported that they had stolen goods up to $50 in value (McCarthy and Hagan 1992). The authors showed that 41.5 % had committed theft of goods over $50. Runaway and homeless young people also commit burglaries as part of their deviant subsistence strategies (Whitbeck et al. 1999).

While on the streets, homeless and runaway youth use alcohol and other drugs in response to the trauma and despair of street life and sell drugs as a subsistence strategy (McCarthy and Hagan 1992). Hammer et al. (2002), in an investigation of runaway/thrown-away episodes, showed that 19 % of the runaways were dependent on drugs, 17 % were taking hard drugs, and 18 % were with someone who was known to be abusing drugs.

In Hagan and McCarthy's (1997) study, 80 % indicated that they had smoked marijuana since becoming homeless. Since leaving home, 55 % had reported using hallucinogens, 42 % cocaine, and 34 % amphetamines.

Homeless and runaway young people who abuse alcohol and other drugs are at increased risk of engaging in illegal and violent behavior (Crawford et al. 2011). Substance abuse may reduce their psychosocial inhibitions and worsen their violent tendencies in potentially threatening social situations. Runaway and homeless young people who abuse alcohol and other drugs may have a higher probability of engaging in various criminal activities in order to support their drug dependence and because of diminished decision making. Youth who engage in illicit drug dealing are also more likely to engage in violence as a result of their participation in illegal drug dealing.

While on the streets, homeless and runaway children and adolescents engage in survival sex and prostitution as subsistence strategies, which increase the potential for sexual assaults, rape, and other violence (McCarthy and Hagan 1992). In one investigation, 30 % of the homeless teens indicated that they had engaged in prostitution since becoming homeless (McCarthy and Hagan 1992). Homeless and runaway young people on the streets participate in other deviant subsistence strategies. For example, homeless and runaway youth may rob pedestrians (Whitbeck et al. 1999).

Violence and Unintended Pregnancies

Females who are victims of violence face an increased probability of unintended pregnancies (Morewitz 2004), and female youth on the streets who become victims of violence may be especially at increased risk of having unintended pregnancies. Violent interactions often result in the inconsistent or nonuse of condoms and other contraceptive methods.

Impaired Family Functioning

Various investigations have shown that young people from families characterized by abuse such as physical, sexual, and socio-emotional abuse have an increased probability of running away, living on one's own, and participating in delinquent and violent behaviors (Kim et al. 2009; Chen et al. 2007; Baron et al. 2001; Hagan and McCarthy 1997; Lee and Schreck 2005; Whitbeck et al. 1999). According to Whitbeck et al.'s (1999) risk amplification model, runaway children frequently were abused sexually and physically and faced other trauma in their family and are at increased risk for victimization while on the streets. Street experiences such as interacting with deviant peers and engaging in deviant subsistence strategies may increase the effects of childhood physical and sexual abuse among homeless and runaway youth (Whitbeck et al. 1999).

In Chen et al.'s (2007) study, runaway and homeless adolescents who had been victims of sexual abuse in the family had greater interactions with deviant peers. In addition, Whitbeck et al. (1999) showed that runaway and homeless adolescents who had suffered physical and sexual abuse in the family were more likely to interact with deviant peers.

Using a sample of 416 teens in Pennsylvania, Kim et al. (2009) showed that physical and psychological abuse increased the risk of running away, and running away increased the probability that youth on the streets would participate in delinquency. Chen et al. (2007) also found that young people who have weak attachment to their families also have a higher probability of participating in delinquent and criminal activities (Chen et al. 2007).

Mental Disorders and Neurocognitive Problems

Some homeless and runaway children and adolescent runaways are likely to exhibit a variety of mental health problems. They may suffer from conduct disorder (CD), which involves repeated antisocial behaviors such as bullying, fighting, harming animals, setting fires, destroying property, committing theft, running away from home or substitute care, and skipping school (Turgay 2005; Burke et al. 2002). Oppositional defiant disorder (ODD) is somewhat similar to CD. In fact, the markers of oppositional defiant disorder (ODD) frequently occur in CD.

Runaways and homeless young people may have substance-abuse problems and other mental health and neurocognitive difficulties and participate in violent and delinquent behaviors such as vandalism and robbery, especially as part of their subsistence strategies on the streets such as survival sex, e.g., exchanging sex for food, alcohol and other drugs, shelter, or other desired goods and services (Crawford et al. 2011; Chen et al. 2007; Whitbeck et al. 2000; Hammer et al. 2002; Thompson and Pollio 2006; Chen et al. 2006; Chen et al. 2007; Edinburgh and Saewyc 2009; McCarthy and Hagan 1992; Robertson and Toro n.d.). In Chen et al.'s (2007) research on homeless and runaway young people, childhood onset of CD was linked to an increased probability of engaging in sexual and nonsexual subsistence strategies and other delinquent activities.

Youth with childhood-onset CD may be at greater risk for engaging in delinquent/criminal and violent behaviors because they may be "more impulsive, shortsighted and aggressive" (Chen et al. 2007; Moffitt 1993; Patterson 1982).

Runaway and homeless young people may be at risk for anxiety and depression. In one self-report, a 12-year-old girl indicated that around the time that she ran away from home, she was suffering from depression because she could not see her brother whom she loved. In her first week on the run, the 12-year-old girl wrote that she stole money (Mishriki 2001–2013).

In addition to conduct problems, substance use and abuse, and other mental health problems, homeless and runaway youth with neurocognitive problems also are at increased risk of engaging in delinquent and criminal behaviors (Chen et al. 2007).

School Problems and Low Self-Esteem

Homeless and runaway young people, including those with childhood-onset conduct problems, may have a higher probability of having school problems such as ineffective attachment to school, class absences, truancy, school suspensions, expulsions, quitting school, school failure, and low self-esteem that create barriers for them to obtain legitimate jobs (Thompson and Pillai 2006; Patterson and Yoerger 1997; Chen et al. 2007). Based on a study of runaway young people using runaway shelter services, Thompson and Pillai (2006) revealed that 43.9 % had reported truancy/expulsion from school. Those homeless and runaway youth with a history of weak attachment to school and related school problems may have a higher probability of engaging in deviant subsistence strategies that lead to delinquent and criminal activities. In one self-report, a 12-year-old runaway girl wrote that before she ran away and began to steal money, she had failing grades in school (Mishriki 2001–2013).

Socioeconomic Status

One study found that homeless young people may come from families with higher socioeconomic status (SES) than homeless adults (Robertson and Toro n.d.). Nevertheless, many runaway and homeless young people may come from low-SES or disadvantaged families. For example, Greene et al. (1995) showed that 40 % of shelter youth and on the streets came from families that were on public assistance, while only 22 % of young people in general were from families on public assistance. Chen et al. (2007) report that homeless youth with childhood-onset conduct problems are more likely to come from disadvantaged families. These youth may have a higher probability of engaging in delinquent behavior than those from non-disadvantaged families (Chen et al. 2007). Disadvantaged families may be headed by single parents and may have impaired parenting processes. As a result, these low-SES families may be less likely to offer support, both socio-emotional and financial, to their children with conduct problems, which may result in a greater likelihood that they will engage in delinquent activities.

Age and Peer Factors

Age and other factors may influence whether runaway and homeless and runaway youth engage in delinquent, criminal, and violent behaviors. Runaway and homeless children who have early-onset CD may have an increased likelihood of engaging in delinquent, criminal, and violent activities as adolescents (Chen et al. 2007).

Some older homeless and runaway youth may be more likely than their younger counterparts to participate in delinquent/criminal and violent behaviors. One possible explanation is that older homeless and runaway youth are more likely to interact with antisocial peers. Using a sample of 696 homeless young people, Rice et al. (2008) showed older youth had a greater probability of interacting with antisocial peers, which resulted in antisocial behavior. Older homeless youth also had a lower likelihood of interacting with pro-social peers.

Older peers can contribute to the delinquency of younger peers. Runaway children and adolescents on the streets gain access to alcohol and drugs and engage in sex when they interact with older peers (Mishriki 2001–2013).

The older peers themselves can violate the law because of their relations with younger peers. For example, older males can be charged with statutory rape for having sex with female teen runaways.

Younger peers may find interacting with older peers to be exciting and fun. Hanging out with older peers may be a way for these younger runaways to feel like they are more grown up. In one self-report narrative, a female 11-year-old runaway indicated that hanging out with peers much older than her "was the life" (Mishriki 2001–2013).

Social and Behavioral Factors Associated with Homelessness and Time on the Streets

Duration of homelessness and the more time that homeless and runaway young people spend on the streets increase their exposure to antisocial peers and situational adversities and participation in deviant subsistence strategies that lead to delinquent/criminal behaviors (Chen et al. 2007; Whitbeck et al. 1999). One possible explanation is that the duration of homelessness and amount of time on the streets increase the likelihood that the youth will interact with antisocial peers and participate in deviant subsistence strategies. Based on a sample of 696 homeless young people, Rice et al. (2008) discovered that an increased duration of homelessness predicted a greater probability that the homeless youth would interact with antisocial peers. According to Chen et al. (2007), exposure to the streets increased runaway and homeless teens' likelihood of interacting with deviant peers and engaging in deviant subsistence strategies, both sexual and nonsexual.

Housing instability also increases the risk of substance abuse among homeless and runaway youth and young adults, which increases their risk for engaging in violence and other criminal/deviant activity (Clatts et al. 2005).

Homelessness may lead to interacting with violent individuals on the streets. For example, young people who run away from home may travel with companions who are potentially violent and have had previous contact with the criminal justice system. According to Hammer et al. (2002), 4 % of youth who had an endangered runaway/thrown-away episode were with a violent individual during the episode. In RYP Case # 553, L.W., a 16-year-old boy from Rockville, MD, was thought to be traveling in a stolen Ford van at the time that he and his two classmates were reportedly running away from a youth academy (see Appendix). In RYP Case # 465, R.C., a 17-year-old girl from Caddo Mills, TX, reportedly may have been traveling with an adult male, C G., who has a warrant for his arrest and may be armed and dangerous (see Appendix).

While on the streets, young people are also at risk of becoming victims of sex, forced labor, and organ trafficking. Street youth also face the risk of being kidnapped and forced or tricked into becoming members of violent gangs, especially in communities that are dominated by violent gangs. In various countries, young people on the streets face being kidnapped and coerced or tricked into becoming child soldiers.

History of Running Away Episodes

Studies show that running away increases the probability of subsequent violent delinquency (Kim et al. 2009). Similarly, Baron and Hartnagel (1998) showed that chronic homelessness and related conditions predict participation in violent crimes such as robbery.

Runaway youth may have a history of delinquent activities such as a history of running away. For example, in RYP Case # 216, P.J., a 14-year-old girl from New Orleans, reportedly had run away from home in the past (see Appendix). Similarly, in RYP Case # 390, M.C., a 16-year-old girl, had run away from home on two prior occasions (see Appendix).

Routine Activity and Lifestyle-Exposure Approach

Routine activity and lifestyle exposure affect criminal/delinquent activities and associated victimization. Cohen and Felson (1979) point out that the daily routine activities of individuals may place them at increased risk of both perpetrating delinquent/criminal activities and their victimization. Hindelang et al. (1978) analyzed the ways in which lifestyle exposure leads to both criminal activities and victimization.

Data on runaway episodes illustrates the possible role of routine activity and lifestyle-exposure factors in facilitating delinquent and criminal activities. Hammer et al. (2002) showed that in 12 % of the runaway incidents, the youth was known to be in a location where criminal behaviors were known to take place.

Peer Interactions on the Streets: Conventional and Deviant Peers

Children and adolescents who run away often spend a significant amount of time interacting with their peers in social networks. Peers are friends and acquaintances who they consider part of the group of people who they hang out with on the streets. Based on a study of runaways' and non-runaways' initial visits to an outpatient medical clinic, Yates et al. (1988) found that 50 % of the runaways reported being with their friends on the streets was their main activity compared to 19.7 % of the non-runaways.

Researchers previously thought that homeless and runaway young people participated in social networks that consisted of small, temporary groups of homeless and runaway youth with homogeneous characteristics (Whitbeck and Hoyt 1999; Ennett et al. 1999a, b; Rice et al. 2007). Newer investigations have revealed that youth on the streets participate in social networks that consist of both conventional peers from the street youth's original home environments and communities and deviant peers from the streets (Johnson et al. 2005). In addition, researchers show that some runaway and homeless young people continue to interact with their family members (Johnson et al. 2005; Milburn et al. 2005). Moreover, investigations have shown that the relationships between runaway and homeless youth and their families may be stronger than previously recognized.

Peer interactions in social networks may either enhance or decrease risky behaviors on the streets (Ennett et al. 1999a, b). For example, runaway and homeless young people who interact with friends who do not pressure them into participating in high-risk behaviors may have low rates of such behaviors. Ennett et al. (1999a, b) found that runaways and homeless youth who had social networks tended to have networks that were supportive and fostered emotional expression. These social networks often consisted of a person who used alcohol or other drugs but these social networks did not pressure street youth to engage in high-risk behaviors.

Rice et al.'s (2007) study of 183 newly homeless young people in Los Angeles, CA, revealed that conventional or pro-social peers were associated with a reduction in HIV-risk behaviors at a 2-year follow-up. However, Unger et al. (1998) showed that having social support had no association with homeless youth's likelihood of using substances.

The lack of social networks may increase the chances that young people will participate in risky behaviors on the streets. In Ennett et al.'s (1999) investigation, 26 % of runaway and homeless young people did not have a current social network. Those without a social network had a higher probability of engaging in illegal drug use, survival sex, and having multiple sex partners that put them at risk for adverse outcomes.

The social network of homeless young people may be associated with homeless female adolescents' experience of intimate partner violence (IPV). In one investigation, Petering et al. (2014) discovered that female homeless youth who suffered IPV had more male friends compared to female homeless youth who did not report IPV.

Peers Provide Assistance in Subsistence Strategies

While on the streets, homeless and runaway children and adolescents may help each other in their subsistence strategies. They may assist each other in stealing food and robbing individuals.

Participation in certain types of social networks may influence whether runaway and homeless young people engage in delinquent and criminal activities. Kipke et al. (1997a, b) discovered that youth in different subcultural peer groups affect the lifestyles and behaviors of homeless young people. For example, the investigators found that street youth in the so-called "punker" group had a greater risk of engaging in unprotected sex and sharing intravenous needles.

Peers Offer Social and Emotional Support

Street youth may offer social and emotional support to each other that help them to engage in delinquent, criminal, and violent behaviors. Some street youth may be especially vulnerable to inadequate emotional support. For example, Chen et al. (2007) suggest that the lack of support from families and social service organizations may lead runaway and homeless youth with CD to engage in illicit behaviors.

In an investigation of 432 homeless young people in Los Angeles, CA, Unger et al. (1998) discovered that social support reduced the likelihood of depression and poor health.

Low Self-Control

Runaway and homeless young people who have low self-control may have a higher probability of engaging in criminal activities and using drugs. Baron (2003) obtained some evidence to support these findings. Moreover, those homeless and runaway youth with low self-control may be more likely to associate with deviant peers and hold deviant social values. Those with low self-control also tend to be unemployed and homeless for longer durations.

Long-Term Effects on Criminal Behavior as Adults

Another issue is whether former homeless and runaway youth will have higher rates of criminal activities later as adults (Benoit-Bryan 2011). Using data from the Runaway Youth Longitudinal Study, Benoit-Bryan (2011) discovered that adults who were former runaways were more likely to be arrested after age 18 than those who had not run away (25.4 % vs. 11.7 %). Former runaways also reported a greater probability of selling drugs in the previous 12 months than non-runaway adults. The author suggests that young people who run away are more likely to be exposed to using and selling drugs while on the streets. These runaways' exposure to drugs and the drug trade result in their drug dependence while on the streets, which increases the probability that they will engage in the illegal drug trade as adults. However, Benoit-Bryan (2011) showed that adults who were former runaway youth did not have an increased chance of engaging in other criminal activities as adults compared to non-runaways. Former runaways did not differ from non-runaways in damaging private property, engaging in theft, dealing in stolen property, committing financial fraud, and perpetrating violence against persons.

Chapter 8
Runaway and Homeless Sexual Minorities

This chapter evaluates the degree to which young people who identify themselves as lesbian, gay, bisexual, and transsexual or transgender (LGBT) and those who are still questioning their own sexual identity are at increased risk of becoming a runaway, thrown-away, or homeless youth because of their minority sexual orientation. This chapter discusses the societal stigma, prejudice, discrimination, and social isolation and rejection that LGBT youth encounter because of their sexual orientation. Researchers have developed the term "gay-related stress (GRS)" to describe the chronic stresses that are related to stigmatizing minority sexual orientation victimization (SOV), e.g., harassment and physical violence suffered by individuals who are known to be LGBT or who divulge their sexual minority status. LGBT youth from disadvantaged racial and ethnic minority groups also may suffer additional chronic stress because of their racial and ethnic minority status. Their parents who are influenced by the dominant heterosexual norms and values of society may kick them out of their home, or the LGBT youth may run away because of parental rejection and conflict over their sexual minority orientation. This chapter assesses the LGBT youth's rates of running away, experiences on the streets, and socio-health risk behaviors. In this chapter, interventions for this population are also presented.

Proportion of LGBT Youth in Street Youth Populations

Researchers have difficulty estimating the size of the LGBT runaway and homeless youth population (Benoit-Bryan 2011; Lankenau et al. 2005; Whitbeck et al. 2004; Cochran et al. 2002). LGBT youth tend to face more harassment and physical abuse than heterosexuals and may be more hesitant to reveal their real sexual orientation in different studies. In other instances, many young people may be uncertain about their sexual orientation. Youth may spend time exploring their sexual orientation. In other cases, young people may hide their LGBT status.

S.J. Morewitz, *Runaway and Homeless Youth*,
DOI 10.1007/978-3-319-30863-0_8

Measurement of the prevalence of LGBT youth may vary depending on community characteristics. For example, LGBT young people may be less likely to admit to their sexual orientation in communities that are hostile toward sexual minorities. The quantification of the prevalence of LGBT population may differ depending on the ways in which the different categories of sexual minority status are classified. For example, Benoit-Bryan (2011), in a longitudinal investigation of runaway youth, used a five-point sexual orientation scale: (1) 100 % heterosexual, (2) mostly heterosexual, (3) bisexual, (4) mostly homosexual, and (5) 100 % homosexual.

Benoit-Bryan (2011) discovered that bisexuals were most likely to run away (21.7 %), followed by those who rated themselves as mostly heterosexual (17.7 %). Thirteen percent of those who classified themselves as 100 % homosexuals ran away. Individuals who indicated that they not attracted to either sex had a rate of running away of 11.8 %. Those persons who rated themselves as mostly homosexual had a rate of running away of 11.5 %. Those respondents who considered themselves 100 % heterosexual were the least likely to run away (7.6 %). In Cochran et al.'s (2002) study of 375 adolescents between the ages of 13 and 21, 84 reported themselves as a sexual minority and 71 of these sexual minority youth identified themselves as bisexual.

Using interviews with 110 runaway and 655 non-runaway youth who visited an outpatient medical clinic, Yates et al. (1988) discovered that 7.3 % of the runaway youth identified themselves as homosexual and 9.1 % bisexual. Almost 83 % of the runaway young people reported themselves as heterosexual. In addition, the sexual identity of 0.9 % was unknown, and no one was undecided in his or her sexual orientation. De Rosa et al. (1999), in their survey of 296 young people aged 13–23 years, found that 80 % reported themselves as heterosexual, 12 % bisexual, and 9 % gay.

Based on studies by Kruks (1991) and Tenner et al. (1998), the prevalence ranged from 11 to 35 %. In an investigation of 558 youth enrolled in the At-Risk Youth Study, Marshall et al. (2010) found that 13.4 % reported themselves as a sexual minority.

Gay-Related Stress Among LGBT Children and Adolescents

Researchers have developed the acronym GRS to describe the chronic stresses that are related to suffering from stigmatizing minority SOV, e.g., harassment and physical violence suffered by individuals who are known to be LGBT or who divulge their sexual minority status (Bontempo and D'Augelli 2002; Almeida et al. 2009; Rosario et al. 2002). In other instances, LGBT persons suffer SOV and GRS if their LGBT status is accidentally discovered.

In other situations, young people suffer SOV and GRS if they exhibit signs of an atypical gender even if they have not come out to their parents, friends, classmates, and others (Saewyc et al. 2006). LGBT youth from disadvantaged racial and ethnic minority groups also may suffer additional chronic stress because of their racial and ethnic minority status (Morris 2014, September 3). In one situation, James, whose mother is a divorced Latina and has three jobs, noted that he felt like an outsider because of his Latino background and his homosexual orientation (Morris 2014, September 3).

Among adolescents, suicide is the third highest cause of death and non-suicidal self-harm occurs in between 13 and 45 % among adolescents (Liu and Mustanski 2012). LGBT young people in particular may be at increased risk for depression, self-harm, and suicidal behaviors due to SOV and GRS (Almeida et al. 2009; Liu and Mustanski 2012; District of Columbia Public Schools 2007). Based on an analysis of ninth through 12th grade students, Almeida et al. (2009) discovered that LGBT young people had higher rates of depressive symptoms than their heterosexual counterparts. The District of Columbia Public Schools (2007), which used the 2007 Youth Risk Behavior Surveillance (YRBS) data for youth in Washington, D.C., discovered that 40 % of sexual minority children and adolescents indicated that they felt sad or hopeless in the past 2 weeks. Only 26 % of the heterosexual young people surveyed had indicated feelings of sadness or hopelessness in the past 2 weeks.

In addition, Almeida et al. (2009) demonstrated that LGBT youth showed higher percentage of suicidal ideation than heterosexual young people. According to the YRBS data for youth in Washington, D.C., LGB young people had more than two times the rate of considering attempting suicide in the past year than heterosexual youth (31 % compared to 14 %) (District of Columbia Public Schools 2007).

SOV, GRS, and other factors may increase the risk of self-harm and suicidal behaviors among LGBT young people. In a longitudinal evaluation of 246 LGBT young people, aged 16–20 years, Liu and Mustanski (2012) demonstrated that prospective victimization associated with sexual minority status along with low levels of social support, being impulsive, and an attempted suicide history were linked to an increased probability of suicidal ideation. The authors also showed that gender-related nonconforming behavior during childhood, victimization, gender (female), behaviors involving seeking sensations, prospective feelings of hopelessness, and a history of attempted suicide increased the probability of self-harm. In Almeida et al.'s (2009) investigation, LGBT male and female youth who perceived discrimination were more likely to suffer depressive symptoms. Perceived discrimination among LGBT males was associated with a higher risk of self-harm and suicidal ideation.

LGBT children who are rejected by their parents and other family members are more likely to suffer mental health problems. In one case, Luke, a self-reported gay young man, suffered suicidal ideation, depressive symptoms, social isolation, and panic attacks after he "came out" to his mother (Morris 2014, September). LGBT young people's victimization interacts with family support to determine the extent that sexual minority youth will experience mental health difficulties (Hershberger and D'Augelli 1995).

Other reports have shown that high rates of violence and victimization increase the risk of suicide attempts among GLBT young people (Bontempo and D'Augelli 2002; Garofalo et al. 1999; Hershberger et al. 1997; Russell and Joyner 2001).

Studies reveal that LGBT youth who face LGBT-related stigma, prejudice, discrimination, exclusion, and social isolation on a societal-wide basis may have other socio-health risk factors and socio-health risk behaviors such as high-risk sexual behaviors and abuse of alcohol and other drugs than their heterosexual counterparts (Bontempo and D'Augelli 2002; Almeida et al. 2009; Liu and Mustanski 2012; Heck et al. 2011; Jiang et al. 2010; Silenzio et al. 2007; D'Augelli et al. 2001;

Whitbeck et al. 2004; Cochran et al. 2002; Saewyc et al. 2006; Kosciw et al. 2009; D'Augelli et al. 2001; Ryan et al. 2009; Russell and Joyner 2001; Savin-Williams and Cohen 1996).

Runaway and Homeless LGBT Youth and Their Families

LGBT young people may be more likely than heterosexual youth to have left home or been kicked out by their parents because of conflict with their parents over their sexual minority status (Whitbeck et al. 2004). In one investigation, Whitbeck et al. (2004) discovered that GLB young people had a higher probability of being thrown out of their by their parents or leaving home because of tensions over their sexual conduct or sexuality. In Whitbeck et al.'s (2004) investigation, gay male youth were five times more likely to have left their families because of tensions over their sexual orientation than heterosexual male youth.

In one case, Mike, who is a self-reported gay in his late teens, "came out" to his parents (SafeHorizon n.d.). His parents were not supportive of his sexual orientation and eventually threw him out of their home.

Parents will cut off financial support for their LGBT children. In one case, Jackie, a self-reported lesbian young woman, reported that her parents cut off her credit cards and other financial support after she came out to them about her lesbian status (Morris 2014, September 3).

According to Cochran et al. (2002), young people who are LGBT also run away from home because of similar factors as heterosexual youth. The investigators discovered that conflict with parents and other family members and a desire to be free were frequently mentioned reasons for running away among LGBT young people. LGBT young people's conflict with their parents over sexual minority orientation was also reported as a factor.

Risk of Victimization and Coercion

As noted above, LGBT youth are at increased risk of violence (Saewyc et al. 2006). In the family context, because of their sexual minority status, LGBT children and adolescents may be sexually and physically abused by their parents (Whitbeck et al. 2004; Cochran et al. 2002; Savin-Williams and Cohen 1996; Ryan et al. 2009). In Whitbeck et al.'s (2004) report, homeless and runaway GLB youth had a higher probability of being sexually abused by their adult caretakers (44.3 %) than heterosexual youth (22.3 %). In addition, lesbian youth had a greater likelihood of reporting physical abuse and neglect by an adult caretaker than female heterosexual youth.

Parents may threaten to kill their LGBT children. In one case, H., a self-reported LGBT young person, reported that her mother hated her and threatened to kill her because she is not girlie enough (Morris 2014, September 3; Morewitz 2008). Deeply religious parents and other parents who hate and fear the LGBT lifestyle may make death threats against sexual minorities in general. For example, in the case of L., a self-reported young homosexual male, his father would disgustingly say that they should round up and murder all gay people (Morris 2014, September 3).

Parents who are religious may be more likely to harass and threaten their LGBT children (Morris 2014, September 3). In H.'s case, her mother was a devout Christian, and she thought that H. would not go to the "gates of heaven" because of her "sexual sins." The mother had adopted H. and told her that she regretted ever doing so.

In some households, parents may fear transmission of LGBT status and sexually transmitted infections (STIs) and physically separate their LGBT children from their heterosexual children (Morris 2014, September 3). In one instance, J., a self-reported gay young man who came out to his mother, described how his mother forced his heterosexual brother to move out of the room that they were sharing because she feared that being gay was a disease and that he would transmit it to his heterosexual brother.

Parents of LGBT children may accuse them of being sexually promiscuous and tell them that they will die of STIs. In one case, J. reported that after he came out to his mother, she accused him of being a "whore" and told him that he would die of STIs (Morris 2014, September 3).

In some cases, after their children come out as LGBT, parents will try to get them to undergo reparative therapy to replace his homosexual orientation with a heterosexual one (Morris 2014, September 3). In one case, B., a 16-year-old gay boy who is the son of a Baptist minister, reportedly was sent across the country to a Christian school and the parents looked into reparative therapy for him (Morris 2014, September 3).

Parents of LGBT youth may use financial incentives as a reward to force their sexual minority children to undergo conversion therapy. For example, in the case of J., the self-reported lesbian, her parents reportedly told her that if she participated in conversion therapy and tried to become a heterosexual, then they would provide her with financial assistance (Morris 2014, September 3).

In one case, the foster parents of T., a self-reported homosexual boy, tried to eliminate his gay orientation by getting their church to perform an exorcism (Saewyc et al. 2006). T.'s parents also reportedly used other religious rituals to try to eliminate his homosexual tendencies.

In school settings, LGBT young people may encounter discrimination, social isolation, exclusion, harassment, bullying, and other forms of violence because of their sexual minority status (Bontempo and D'Augelli 2002; Heck et al. 2011; Morris 2014, September 3). In one instance, J., a self-reported lesbian, indicated that her sorority chapter's executive board expelled her from her sorority after they discovered her lesbian sexual orientation (Morris 2014, September 3).

Likewise, LGBT youth and adults can become the victims of hate crime-related verbal threats, harassment, physical violence, and discrimination in employment, housing, and other community settings (Saewyc et al. 2006; Mays and Cochran 2001; Kosciw et al. 2009). For example, "L.," a young gay male, reportedly was bullied and molested by five men in a local community (Lubetsky et al. n.d.). He allegedly knifed one of the perpetrators in self-defense but was arrested and jailed for 10 days. After completing his jail sentence, L. reported that he felt unsafe in the community and ran away from home even though his parents were supportive of his sexual orientation.

Problems Facing Homeless and Runaway Youth While on the Streets

Runaway and homeless LGBT children and adolescents, especially those living on the streets, face threats to their social, physical, and emotional well-being. They are more likely to be victims of violence (Kipke et al. 1997a, b). While on the streets, they are at increased risk of being robbed, raped, and assaulted. In one report, Whitbeck et al. (2004) showed that GLB young people had a higher probability of being sexually victimized on the streets than heterosexual youth. The authors also discovered that runaway and homeless lesbian youth had a higher likelihood of reporting physical victimization than heterosexual female youth.

Cochran et al. (2002) also discovered that LGBT young people while on the streets were more likely to be victim of physical violence than heterosexual youth. However, the researchers found gender differences in physical victimization before and after the LGBT youth became homeless. LGBT male young people indicated that they suffered more physical victimization during the previous 3 months. In contrast, LGBT female youth reported more physical victimization since they ran away and became homeless.

In terms of sexual victimization, Cochran et al. (2002) showed that homeless LGBT young people reported more of this type of victimization from the time that they first ran away or became homeless. The researchers analyzed whether sexual victimization of homeless LGBT youth varied by gender and found that this pattern of sexual victimization only applied to male young people. The investigators also discovered that homeless LGBT young people who reported sexual victimization had 7.4 more offenders than homeless heterosexual young people.

Homeless and runaway LGBT young people may be at increased risk of engaging in survival behaviors, including survival sex and prostitution than their heterosexual counterparts (Whitbeck et al. 2004; Lubotsky et al. n.d.). Homeless and runaway GLBT youth engage in sex in exchange for money, food, drugs, and shelter (Koopman et al. 1994; Saewyc et al. 2006). Whitbeck et al. (2004), in their analysis, discovered that gay male youth had a higher probability of participating in survival sex than their heterosexual male counterparts.

In Marshall et al.'s (2010) analysis, sexual minority males had an increased risk of participating in survival sex compared to heterosexual male street-involved youth. However, compared to heterosexual females, sexual minority females were not more likely to engage in survival sex.

Lubotsky et al. (n.d.) describes the vulnerabilities of GLBT young people to being tricked into prostitution while on the streets. Homeless and runaway youth, especially younger individuals, may be "easy targets" for so-called elder panders who deceive the homeless and runaway gay youth into participating in sex work. The elder panders trick the younger homeless and runaway youth by establishing trust with them by offering food, a place to stay, and physical protection from the harsh realities of street life. The elder panders also initiate them into substance addiction by providing them with highly addictive drugs such as crystal methamphetamine. This drug increases sexual desires and appetite and reinforces the homeless and runaway gay youth's participation in prostitution.

Homeless and runaway GLBT young people are also at increased risk of engaging in sex survival because of the lack of alternatives, including safe shelters for homeless and runaway GLBT youth. Lubotsky et al. (n.d.) discusses the ways in which homeless and runaway GLBT youth are likely to suffer abuse in conventional shelters, which keeps them on the streets and engaging in prostitution and addicted to drugs.

Runaway and homeless LGBT may be more likely to engage in other high-risk sexual practices than their heterosexual counterparts, increasing the homeless and runaway LGBT youth's chances of acquiring STIs, including HIV. According to Cochran et al. (2002), homeless LGBT young people reported more sexual risk behaviors than their heterosexual counterparts. Homeless sexual minority youth were more likely to have more sexual partners in a lifetime than homeless heterosexual young people. LGBT youth were more likely to be younger at the time of their first sexual intercourse than homeless heterosexual youth. In addition, compared to their heterosexual counterparts, the homeless LGBT young people reported a higher rate of unprotected sex.

Walls and Bell (2010), based on a study of 1625 individuals, aged 10–25, showed that homeless gay, lesbian, or bisexual youth and young adults had a higher rate of engaging in survival sex than White heterosexual youth and adults.

Various cases reflect LGBT youth's participation in survival sex. For example, Colette, a 14-year-old bisexual, came out to her brother and father and her father kicked her out of the house. To stay in her basement room, which she rents, Colette reportedly has sex with her landlord in exchange for her paying the rent. Collette shares her place with her girlfriend, Jenny, who also ran away from home (Saewyc et al. 2006). In another case, Mike, a self-reported gay adolescent, was kicked out of his home after coming out to his parents. Mike then reportedly went home with strangers and had sex with them in order to have shelter for the night (SafeHorizon n.d.).

Runaway and homeless LGBT youth are at risk of acquiring HIV because they may be IV drug users, participate in survival sex and prostitution, are victims of sexual abuse and rape, and engage in multiple sexual risk behaviors (Marshall et al. 2010; Yates et al. 1988). In their investigation of runaway and non-runaway youth at an outpatient medical clinic, Yates et al. (1988) found that 34.5 % of the runaway youth reported intravenous drug use, 26.4 % survival sex, 21.8 % sexual abuse, and 13.6 % problems with sex. Among the runaway youth, 9.1 % identified themselves as bisexual and 7.3 % self-reported as homosexual.

Using a sample of 558 young people from the At-Risk Youth Study, Marshall et al. (2010) discovered that street-involved sexual minority young people in the past 6 months had inconsistent condom use with clients. They also noted that they had a greater number of clients

Runaway and homeless LGBT young people also may participate in nonsexual survival strategies. For example, Whitbeck et al. (2004) demonstrated that lesbian youth on the streets had a greater probability of using nonsexual survival strategies than heterosexual female youth. Like their heterosexual counterparts, homeless and runaway LGBT youth will work jobs such as panhandling (Saewyc et al. 2006). One female runaway adolescent, J., who lives with her girlfriend, panhandles to earn money (Saewyc et al. 2006).

LGBT youth who are homeless and runaways face many stresses and discrimination while on the streets. Like heterosexual young people, LGBT young people try to find shelter. For example, in one case, J., a self-reported lesbian college student, stayed with friends, which is called "couch surfing" (Morris 2014, September 3). In other instances, homeless and runaway sexual minority youth will hitchhike and engage in other high-risk behaviors. In one case, J., a self-reported gay adolescent, hitchhiked to distance himself from his parents who kicked him out the house because of his gay sexual orientation (Morris 2014, September 3).

Youth who runaway and become homeless are at greater risk of social difficulties and mental health problems, including depression, post-traumatic stress disorder (PTSD), self-harm behaviors, suicidal behaviors, and psychosis (Whitbeck et al. 2004; Cochran et al. 2002; Noell and Ochs 2001; Unger et al. 1997; MacLean et al. 1999; Cauce et al. 2000; Kruks 1991).

Based on the University of Michigan Composite International Diagnostic Interview, Whitbeck et al. (2004) measured major depressive episodes, PTSD, and substance abuse in a sample of GLB and heterosexual homeless and runaway youth. The investigators showed that GLB young people had a higher probability of having a major depressive episode than their heterosexual counterparts (41.3 % vs. 28.5 %). In their study, gay homeless and runaway males had a higher chance of suffering a major depressive episode than heterosexual males (42.1 % vs. 24.4 %).

Using the Achenbach's Youth Self-Report Report (YSR), Cochran et al. (2002) discovered that homeless LGBT youth had a higher degree of symptoms of depression based on the Center for Epidemiologic Studies Depression Scale (CES-D).

Case studies also show that runaway and homeless LGBT youth suffer from depression. For example, Mike, a self-reported gay adolescent, reportedly suffers from serious mental illness and depression, according to youth counselors (SafeHorizon n.d.).

Whitbeck et al. (2004) demonstrated that homeless and runaway LGB young people (47.6 %) had a higher probability of suffering PTSD than their heterosexual counterparts (33.4 %). These results were explained by the high rate of PTSD among homeless and runaway lesbian youth (59.14 %).

In Whitbeck et al.'s (2004) investigation, homeless and runaway GLB young people had a higher probability of suffering suicidal ideation than homeless and runaway heterosexual youth (73 % compared to 53.2 %). In the study, homeless and runaway lesbian youth had a higher rate of suicidal ideation (75 %) than their heterosexual counterparts (55.3 %). With regard to suicide attempts, 57.1 % of the homeless and runaway GLB young people reported attempting suicide at least one time, while 33.7 % of homeless and runaway heterosexual adolescents reported at least one suicide attempt. Home and runaway lesbian youth reported a higher rate of attempting at least one suicide (63.6 %) than homeless and runaway heterosexual females (37.1 %). Noell and Ochs (2001) also indicated that homeless sexual minority youth exhibited more suicidal behaviors than homeless heterosexual youth.

With regard to one investigation of self-mutilation among homeless youth (44 % male and 56 % female), Tyler et al. (2003) discovered that about 15 % of the participants reported themselves as gay, lesbian, or bisexual.

LGBT youth may be at risk for other social and mental health problems. In Cochran et al.'s (2002) investigation, LGBT young people exhibited more withdrawn behavior, somatic complaints, and social problems than their heterosexual counterparts. In their analysis, LGBT young people also displayed more delinquent, aggressive, internalizing, and externalizing behaviors.

However, Whitbeck et al. (2004) did not find that homeless and runaway gay males (63.2 %) were more likely to suffer conduct disorder than homeless and runaway heterosexual male youth (85.1 %). The authors concluded that homeless and runaway gay males had a higher probability of suffering internalizing behaviors and a lower probability of exhibiting externalizing behaviors than their heterosexual male counterparts.

While on the streets, GLBT young people initiate or increase their use and abuse of alcohol and other drugs and abuse these substances (Cochran et al. 2002; Whitbeck et al. 2004). These sexual minority youth may use and abuse alcohol and other drugs as a part of high-risk survival strategies and as a way to cope with the stress and trauma of street life.

In terms of the patterns of substance abuse, Cochran et al. (2002) showed that homeless sexual minority youth used cocaine or crack, crack or crack mixed with amphetamines, and speed or crystal methamphetamines more often in the past 6 months than homeless heterosexual youth. The researchers also discovered that homeless LGBT young people took more kinds of drugs than their heterosexual counterparts.

Whitbeck et al. (2004) discovered variations in substance abuse among homeless and runaway gay male and lesbian youth compared to their heterosexual counterparts. The researchers demonstrated that homeless and runaway gay males were less likely to abuse alcohol than heterosexual male youth (63.2 % compared to 85.1 %). However, the authors found that homeless and runaway lesbian young people had higher rates of both alcohol and other drug abuse than their heterosexual female counterparts. Among the homeless and runaway lesbians, 61.4 % reported abusing alcohol and 47.7 % reported abusing drugs. Only 35.5 % of the homeless and runaway heterosexual females reported alcohol abuse and 32.5 % reported drug abuse.

Chapter 9
Well-Being and Access to Health Care

In this chapter, an overview of health problems facing runaway and homeless young people is presented. Street youth often have difficulty accessing health care and have an increased probability of developing mental, social, and physical health difficulties. Runaway young people may have an increased probability of suffering from health problems such as pneumonia, scabies, depressive symptoms, post-traumatic stress disorder (PTSD), conduct disorder, prostitution, and substance use and abuse. Street youth also face the hazard of being kidnapped and coerced or lured into sex and forced labor trafficking that place them at increased risk of sexually transmitted infections (STIs), human immune virus (HIV)/acquired immunodeficiency syndrome (AIDS), depression, and other psychosocial and physical health problems. This chapter discusses the factors that increase the likelihood that homeless and runaway young people will develop health problems. This chapter evaluates the degree to which homeless and runaway young people who engage in risky behaviors such as survival sex may have a higher probability of suffering victimization and poor health outcomes such as STIs, including HIV/AIDS. Moreover, this chapter assesses the degree to which runaway and homeless youth who lack shelter and access to healthy food may face a greater likelihood of having food insecurity and related health problems. This chapter assesses the extent to which runaway and homeless youth suffer impaired functioning as a result of their health difficulties. In this chapter, the health status and level of impairment of adults who were former runaways are presented.

Youth who are on the streets often have difficulty accessing health care and have an increased probability of developing mental and physical health difficulties (Benoit-Bryan 2011; Klein et al. 2000; Craig and Hodson 1998). Klein et al. (2000), in a survey of young people in shelters and on the streets, discovered that 50 % of the youth on the streets did not have a regular source of health care. The survey also revealed that 36 % of the young people in shelters had a regular source of health care. In terms of health status, the survey showed that 25 % of the youth on the streets reported having major health difficulties in the previous 12 months. Eighteen percent of youth in shelters indicated that they had significant health problems in the previous 12 months.

S.J. Morewitz, *Runaway and Homeless Youth*,
DOI 10.1007/978-3-319-30863-0_9

As adults, former runaways may have a higher likelihood of suffering from health problems that impair their functioning. For example, Benoit-Bryan (2011) discovered that former runaways had a 44 % higher probability of suffering from health problems as adults that impair their ability to perform moderate physical activities compared to individuals who never ran away.

Former runaways may be less likely to consider themselves in good health than those individuals who never have run away. In Benoit-Bryan's (2011) investigation, runaways were much more likely to have suicidal ideation as an adult than persons who had never run away.

Various factors may affect the health status of runaway and homeless young people. Sexual orientation may affect the likelihood of harassment and stress, which can contribute to various health problems. Lesbian, gay, bisexual, and transgender (LGBT) homeless and runaway youth may be at increased risk for health problems.

Runaway and homeless youth who have a history of severe sexual, physical, and emotional abuse and neglect may be at increased risk for re-victimization on the streets and adverse health outcomes. For example, runaway and homeless youth who are victims of sex, forced labor, and organ trafficking may suffer a variety of severe psychosocial and physical health problems. While on the streets, homeless and runaway young people who engage in risky behaviors such as survival sex and criminal behaviors such as theft and assault may have a higher probability of suffering victimization and poor health outcomes. Moreover, runaway and homeless youth who lack shelter and access to healthy food may face a greater likelihood of having health problems.

Physical and Mental Health Problems

While on the streets, runaway and homeless young people suffer from both physical and mental health problems. For example, Yates et al. (1988) discovered that runaway young people had an increased probability of suffering from physical and mental health problems, such as pneumonia, scabies, depressive symptoms, and substance use.

Malnutrition and Food Insecurity

Food insecurity refers to reduced access to nutritional and safe foods due to limited availability or difficulties in getting nutritional food through legal and socially acceptable ways (Anderson 1990; Antoniades and Tarasuk 1998; Dachner and Tarasuk 2002; Whitbeck, Chen, and Johnson 2006). Like teens in general, runaway and homeless children and adolescents may have poor eating habits (Whitbeck, Chen, and Johnson 2006). Homeless and runaway youth are especially at risk for food insecurity, hunger, and malnutrition because they participate in substantial physical activities without securing the necessary quantity and quality of nutritional food. While on the streets, young people may suffer from poor health and disabilities that limit their ability to obtain food.

While on the streets, runaway and homeless young people may become victims of human trafficking and exhibit evidence of rape, malnourishment, torture, and physical confinement (National Human Trafficking Resource Center n.d. a, b; Morewitz 2016).

STIs Including HIV/AIDS

While on their own, runaway and homeless youth often are unemployed and lack income and may engage in survival sex, which increases their risk for HIV/AIDS and other STIs (Greene et al. 1999; Allen et al. 1994; Stricof et al. 1991; Halcon and Lifson 2004). The likelihood that homeless and runaway youth will participate in survival sex is also increased by HIV risks (Haley et al. 2004).

One investigation by Greene et al. (1999) showed that 27.5 % of young people on the streets engaged in survival sex compared to 9.5 % of young people in shelters. Other studies showed that the prevalence of survival sex ranged from 7.8 to 9.7 % (Huba et al. 2000) to more than 33 % of the homeless youth (Greenblatt and Robertson 1993; Kipke et al. 1995).

Runaway and homeless youth who have multiple sex partners are at risk for STIs. In addition, runaway and homeless young people who use alcohol and other drugs may be at increased risk for sexual victimization, including sexual assault that increases their risk for STIs and HIV/AIDS.

While under the influence of alcohol and other drugs, their judgment and psychomotor functioning may be impaired. As a result they often engage in other high-risk sexual behaviors such as not using a condom, using condoms incorrectly, having multiple sexual partners, and sharing needles that also increase their risk for STIs, including HIV/AIDS.

In Halcon and Lifson's (2004) research, almost 33 % of the homeless youth indicated that they had acquired at least one STI. According to other investigations, 17–28 % of homeless teens report having a STI history (Clatts and Davis 1999; Huba et al. 2000). In a study in Texas, Rew et al. (2002) found that 25 % of homeless teens had a history of gonorrhea, 8.7 % chlamydia, 8.0 % AIDS, and 3.9 % chlamydia. In 2001, Wagner et al. (2001) discovered that the most prevalent STI reported among homeless youth in Seattle was chlamydia.

MacKellar et al. (2000) and Noell et al. (2001a, b) showed that female runaway and homeless youth had higher STI rates than their male counterparts. However, Greene et al. (1999) and Kral et al. (1997) discovered that male runaway and homeless youth had higher survival sex rates than female runaway and homeless young people. In one study of outpatient medical clinics, Yates et al. (1988) runaways actually had a lower percentage of STIs than non-runaways (18.2 % vs. 29.9 %).

Youth who are victims of sex trafficking may participate in coercive sexual activities and may not use contraception. They are at increased risk for STIs, including HIV/AIDS.

As adults, former runaways may have a higher probability of suffering an STI. In Benoit-Bryan's (2011) research, former runaways were 54 % more likely to indicate that they had an STI as an adult than non-runaways. Yates et al. (1988) found that 4.4 % of runaways had pelvic inflammatory disease compared to 1.4 % of the non-runaways.

Teenage Pregnancy

Studies indicate that as many as 20 % of homeless female adolescents get pregnant (Thompson et al. 2008; Halcon and Lifson 2004). Various reports have shown that female adolescent runaways have higher rates of pregnancy compared to female youth in households. Using data from the Longitudinal Study of Adolescent Health, Thrane and Chen (2012) discovered that among girls between 11 and 17 years, the probability of pregnancy in the following year was 1.67 times more likely for runaway girls. Berry et al. (2000) found that runaway and homeless female adolescents are more than four times likely to get pregnant than their peers who do not run away or become homeless.

Researchers have investigated the pregnancy history among homeless youth. Using a sample of 203 homeless young people 15–22 years of age, Halcon and Lifson (2004) discovered that 53 % of the females reported at least one pregnancy. In this sample, 28 % indicated that they had two or more pregnancies. About 43 % had an abortion. Almost 24 % had one or more live births. Almost 10 % of those who had been pregnant were currently pregnant.

Runaway and homeless young people may be abducted, raped, and forced or tricked into sex trafficking. Female victims of sex trafficking are at increased risk for unplanned pregnancies and pregnancy-related complications.

Other homeless and runaway pregnant teens may face an increased probability of having adverse pregnancy outcomes. In Halcon and Lifson's (2004) study of homeless youth, 69 % of the pregnant adolescents reported to have one or more miscarriages.

Prior to running away or becoming homeless, girls and adolescents may have a history of rape, pregnancy, and adverse pregnancy outcomes. For example, in Lindsey et al.'s (2000) interview study of former homeless and runaway young people, the authors discuss the case of Susan, a young Caucasian woman, who at the age of 16 reportedly had been raped by a friend's father and later that year got pregnant and suffered a miscarriage.

Other Physical Health Problems among Runaway and Homeless Youth

While on the streets, children and adolescents may suffer from other physical health problems. In one self-report, a runaway adolescent reported suffering from seizures, panic attack, and migraines (Mishriki 2001–2013).

Psychosocial Problems Among Runaway and Homeless Youth

Runaway and homeless youth may suffer problems in social functioning, anxiety, depression, post-traumatic stress disorder, suicidal behaviors, deliberate self-harm, substance abuse, or other major mental health problems and/or developmental disabilities (Benoit-Bryan 2011; Chen et al. 2006, 2007; Yates et al. 1988; Hammer et al. 2002; Whitbeck et al. 1999, 2000). Runaway youth are likely to develop other health problems and related impairments in functioning (Benoit-Bryan 2011; Thompson and Pillai 2006; Peled and Cohavi 2009).

Teen runaways may have problems in developing long-term relationships (Peled and Cohavi 2009; Janus et al. 1987a, b; Olson et al. 1980). Youth who run away frequently fear intimate relationships (Peled and Cohavi 2009; Janus et al. 1987a, b; Olson et al. 1980). Runaways may often feel socially isolated (Peled and Cohavi 2009; Janus et al. 1987a; Olson et al. 1980). Low self-image and low self-esteem are prevalent among children and adolescents who run away (Peled and Cohavi 2009; Chun and Springer 2005; Smart and Walsh 1993). Feelings of sadness are common among runaway youths (Peled and Cohavi 2009; Chun and Springer 2005; Smart and Walsh 1993). In addition, runaway youth may have feelings of helplessness (Peled and Cohavi 2009; Chun and Springer 2005; Smart and Walsh 1993).

Conduct Disorder

Conduct disorder (CD), which is common in children and adolescents, consists of repeated and persistent antisocial behaviors such as violation of age-appropriate social norms and individuals' rights (Turgay 2005). CD can involve running away from home or care institutions, bullying, fighting, harming animals, setting fires, destroying property, committing theft, engaging in deceitful behaviors, skipping school, and committing other serious violations of rules. Because the markers of ODD are often present in CD, mental health professionals should not make the diagnosis of ODD if the person has CD.

Research has shown that the rates of CD among homeless youth ranged from 48 to 93 % (Cauce et al. 1997; Feitel et al. 1992; Robertson 1989). Another investigation by McCaskill et al. (1998) revealed that 39 % of young people, ages 12–17, from shelters, had disruptive behavior disorders (mostly CD). This CD rate was higher than in a sample of matched house youth.

Booth and Zhang (1997), in a study of the CD rate among runaway and homeless youth from a drop-in center that provided services to high-risk young people, revealed that 50 % of the male and 60 % of the female youth had a diagnosed CD.

The prevalence of CD in the general population is much lower. In the general population, reported rates of CD range from less than 1 to 10 %. The rates differ widely based on the type of population sampled and the methods for determining CD. The rates may have increased and urban areas may have higher rates than rural areas.

Depression

Many youth who run away suffer from depression (Peled and Cohavi 2009; Chun and Springer 2005; Smart and Walsh 1993). During runaway and homeless episodes, street experiences such as victimization and interacting with non-conventional peers may increase the likelihood of depressive symptoms. In one self-report story, a female runaway reported that she will feel very depressed and upset because of her problems in dealing with the need to survive on the streets (Rebeccas Community n.d.). In a study of runaway and non-runaway youth, Yates et al. (1988) showed that runaway young people were more likely to be depressed. Whitbeck et al. (1999) showed that homeless and runaway youth's street experiences worsened the impact of their childhood abuse in the family and their symptoms of depression.

Anxiety Disorders and PTSD

Runaway children and adolescents are at risk for post-traumatic stress disorder (PTSD) (Peled and Cohavi 2009; Martijn and Sharpe 2006; Thompson et al. 2006b, 2008). Tyler et al. (2003) revealed that about 36 % of runaway young people fulfilled the PTSD diagnostic criteria. Using a diagnostic interview measure of PTSD for a sample of 150 runaway and homeless young people in New York, Feitel et al. (1992) showed that 32 % fulfilled the lifetime criteria for the disorder. Based on another diagnostic interview protocol for a sample of 364 homeless adolescents in Seattle, WA, Cauce et al. (2000) showed that 12 % fulfilled the PTSD criteria. Cauce et al. (2000) noted, however, that their results may reflect the lower estimates of PTSD since about 7 % of their interviews left out the PTSD component due to time limitations in the study.

PTSD Risk Factors among Runaway and Homeless Young People

Researchers are analyzing possible risk factors for PTSD among runaway and homeless youth. Investigators are also evaluating possible differences in PTSD risk factors depending on study's sampling location (Thompson et al. 2008). Runaway and homeless youth frequently were abused and neglected in their family environment and exposed to extensive family conflict and dysfunction (Whitbeck et al. 1997a, b). Runaway and homeless young people who have suffered abuse and neglect and have been exposed to other substantial family problems may be at increased risk of developing PTSD.

In Thompson et al.'s (2008) analysis of runaway youth at a juvenile detention center and emergency youth shelter, runaway youth in both settings who worried about family relationships had a higher probability of suffering more severe PTSD symptoms. Parental substance abuse is a sign of family dysfunction and, not surprisingly, may increase the risk of PTSD among their children who suffer chronically from substance-abuse-related family impairment (Thompson et al. 2008). While on the streets, young people who are assaulted or injured by a weapon may be at increased risk of suffering from PTSD (Whitbeck et al. 2006). Youth who run away frequently from their home or substitute care may be at increased risk for developing PTSD (Thompson et al. 2008). In Thompson et al.'s (2007) analysis, an increased number of runaway episodes was linked to more PTSD symptoms among runaway young people at a juvenile detention center.

Suicidal Behaviors

Among children and adolescents who run away, suicidal behaviors are prevalent (Hammer et al. 2002). In one self-report story, a female runaway noted that she gets to point when she does not want to go on living because of her inability to deal with the realities of life on the streets (Rebeccas Community n.d.). She expresses the desire to just give up

According to Hammer et al. (2002), 4 % of children and adolescents who had an endangered runaway/thrown-away episode had tried to commit suicide previously. Yates et al. (1988) in their investigation reported that runaway youth were more likely to engage in suicidal behaviors. They discovered that the runaway young people had a higher probability of previously attempting suicide or to be actively suicidal compared to non-runaway young people.

A report by US General Accounting Office (1989) revealed that 12 % of runaway young people using runaway shelters may have been suicidal. Craig and Hodson (1998), in an investigation of homeless young people in London, UK, showed that 20 % of the homeless youth had attempted suicide in the previous 12 months.

Runaway and homeless children and adolescents may be exposed to severe trauma and lack the resources and capacity to deal with this trauma, increasing their risk for suicidal behaviors (Yates et al. 1988; Whitbeck et al. 2000; Yoder et al. 1998; Hammer et al. 2002; Rotheram-Borus 1993; Rebeccas Community n.d.).

Suicide attempts among female runaways are especially high (Peled and Cohavi 2009; Greene and Ringwalt 1996; Kidd 2006; Molnar et al. 1998; Votta and Manion 2004). Runaway and homeless youth may try to commit suicide multiple times. For example, in one self-report narrative, a girl who ran away when she was 14 had tried to take her life multiple times (Rebeccas Community n.d.).

While on the streets, runaway and homeless children and adolescents may use different methods to commit suicide. According to one self-report story, one girl tried to kill herself by slashing herself with a syringe (Rebeccas Community n.d.).

Former runaways may have greater odds of engaging in suicidal behaviors as an adult. In Benoit-Bryan's (2011) investigation, runaways had odds 51 % higher of having suicidal ideation as an adult than persons who had never run away. In this study, former runaways also had more than three times higher probability of attempting suicide as an adult compared to individuals who never ran away.

Feelings of Hopelessness

Feelings of hopelessness occur among runaway and homeless teens as they try to cope with the trauma of the streets and the daily need to survive.

Deliberate Self-Harm

Runaway and homeless children and adolescents may engage in self-mutilation. For example, in one investigation, Tyler et al. (2003) discovered that homeless youth had a high prevalence of self-mutilation; 69 % had engaged in self-mutilation at least one time. In their study, 12 % indicated that they had received medical care for their self-injurious behaviors. According to one self-report story, a female teen runaway would slash multiple areas of her arm (Rebeccas Community n.d.).

Runaway and homeless youth may engage in self-mutilation for different reasons. A prime reason is to cope with the overwhelming emotional pain and anxiety brought on by the trauma of living on the streets and the trauma associated with their life prior to running away.

Substance Abuse

While on the streets, many youth runaways have an increased risk of substance abuse (Peled and Cohavi 2009; Chen et al. 2004; Greene and Ringwalt 1996; Yates et al. 1988). Researcher have analyzed the rates of substance use and abuse in among homeless and runaway youth of different sexual orientations (Cochran et al. 2002; Whitbeck et al. 2004) and in different settings (e.g., street and shelter) and for different periods of time (Johnson et al. 2005; Van Leeuwen et al. 2004; Greene et al. 1997a, b; Hammer et al. 2002; Yates et al. 1988). Rates of substance may vary depending on which setting or time period is measured. Rates of substance use also may differ depending on the demographic and social/behavioral characteristics of the runaway and homeless youth (Kipke et al. 1997a, b; Greene et al. 1997a, b; Feitel et al. 1992; Mundy et al. 1990; McCaskill et al. 1998).

According to Hammer et al. (2002), 19 % of the children and adolescents who had an endangered runaway/thrown-away episode were dependent on drugs. In addition, the researchers discovered that 17 % of the youth were taking hard drugs at the time of the endangered runaway/thrown-away episode. In addition, during the endangered runaway/thrown-away episode, 18 % were with an individual who was known to be abusing drugs. In another investigation, McCarthy and Hagan (1992) revealed that 80 % of their study participants indicated that they smoked marijuana since becoming homeless.

Johnson et al. (2005), using a longitudinal diagnostic investigation of 428 homeless and runaway youth ages 16–19 years, discovered that 60.5 % of the runaway young people had at least one of three substance disorders (alcohol abuse, alcohol dependence, and drug abuse) based on lifetime criteria. The investigators found that 48.1 % had at least one substance disorder using 12-month criteria.

Using data from 150 shelter teens in Los Angeles, CA, Feitel et al. (1992) discovered that 41 % fulfilled the criteria for substance abuse. Based on a sample of 96 shelter and street youth, Mundy et al. (1990) showed that 48 % fulfilled the DSM III criteria for alcohol abuse or dependence and 39 % fulfilled criteria for drug use or dependence.

Based on a one-day survey of 186 homeless young people in Denver, Colorado, 75 % of whom were between the ages of 16 and 25, Van Leeuwen et al. (2004) discovered that 75 % had had used marijuana during the previous 9 months, 69 % alcohol, 30 % hallucinogens, and 25 % ecstasy. Other reported drug uses in the past 9 months included 19 % cocaine, 18 % methamphetamine, 13 % ketamine, and 12 % heroin.

Halcon and Lifson (2004) found that 51.7 % of a sample of 203 homeless young people, aged 15–22, indicated that on average they had five or more alcoholic drinks weekly. More than a third of the sample reported that they had 15 or more alcoholic beverages each week. According to the investigators, two thirds of the sample of homeless youth reported using illegal drugs. Among these illegal drugs, homeless youth were most likely to use marijuana (56.9 %).

In Washington, D.C., based on a sample of 327 homeless young people, ages 14–21 years, Bailey et al. (1998) showed that about 75 % of the youth had used alcohol and marijuana in their lifetime. Sixteen percent of the respondents had ever used crack cocaine and almost one-third had ever taken hallucinogens. Seven percent of the respondents had ever used heroin and 4 % have been needle users. More than 25 % of the homeless youth in the study reported having three or more symptoms of dependency on alcohol or other drugs based on the DSM-IV (1994) criteria.

Using data on homeless and runaway teens from San Francisco, CA; Denver, CO; and New York City, Kral et al. (1997) reported that 97 % had taken drugs or alcohol. The researchers also found that 21 % of the study participants had been injection drug users.

In Kipke et al.'s (1995) investigation of street young people in Hollywood, CA, 93 % had used marijuana, 89 % had consumed alcohol, and 66 % had used speed. The researchers also showed that 61 % had used LSD and 50 % had taken cocaine. In addition, 45 % had taken mushrooms, 44 % had used inhalants, and 41 % had used crack cocaine.

Whitbeck and Hoyt (1999), based on a study of homeless and runaway young people in the Midwest, found that 81.2 % had taken alcohol in the last year, 69.4 % had used marijuana, 27.2 % had used amphetamines, and 25.8 % had used hallucinogens. The investigators also showed that 16.8 % had used inhalants in the last year, 16.1 % inhalants, 14.7 % cocaine, 9.2 % barbiturates, 6.8 % tranquilizers, and 6.4 % opiates.

Using a sample of runaway and non-runaway youth who had an initial visit at an outpatient medical clinic, Yates et al. (1988) discovered that 84 % of the runaway youth reported using alcohol or drugs. In their sample, 34.5 % of runaway young people indicated that they engaged intravenous drug use compared to only 3.7 % of non-runaway youth.

In addition to a higher rate of heroin use, runaway young people in Yates et al.'s (1988) investigation reported higher rates of other drugs than non-runaway young people. Runaway youth had a higher prevalence of various substances including cigarettes, stimulants, hallucinogens, and narcotics.

Homeless and runaway young people frequently smoke cigarettes and drink alcohol. A self-reported female runaway girl stated that while on the streets she lived in multiple houses and drank alcohol and smoked cigarettes (Mishriki 2001–2013).

Runaway and homeless youth use substances earlier in life and more frequently than children and adolescents in the general population (Johnson et al. 2005). In addition to using alcohol and other drugs, teen runaway and homeless youth may participate in illicit drug dealing (Mishriki 2001–2013). A self-reported 15-year-old female runaway stated that while on the streets she met a low-level drug dealer and started to deliver drugs for him (Mishriki 2001–2013).

Risk Factors for Substance Use and Abuse Among Homeless and Runaway Youth

The parents of runaway and homeless young people may have risk factors as well as protective factors that influence whether their child will suffer from substance-abuse problems. The parents of these youth frequently have alcohol and drug problems, which help to explain the high level of family dysfunction among runaway and homeless youth (Thompson et al. 2008; Mallett et al. 2005).

In Mallett et al.'s (2005) interviews with 302 homeless youth, ages 12–20 years, about 33 % stated that their family members' drug use or their own personal substance use was a major factor for their becoming homeless.

Based on an investigation of runaway and homeless young people, Whitbeck et al. (1997b) discovered that over 50 % of the youth indicated that at least one of their parents had a problem with alcohol. Almost 20 % of the study participants reported that they had two parents who had problems with alcohol. In addition, more than 33 % of the study participants revealed that they thought that at least one of their parents had difficulties with hard drugs.

In Johnson et al.'s (2005) research, homeless and runaway youth had a greater probability of fulfilling criteria for substance-abuse disorders if their caretakers had been in substance-abuse treatment.

Parents' substance-abuse behaviors can result in parents' inability or reduced motivation to meet the psychosocial needs of their children. Parental alcohol problems may lead to parental rejection of their offspring. As a result, the children and adolescents of substance-abusing parents may develop a variety of psychosocial problems, including abusing alcohol and drugs, having impairments in developing and maintaining relationships, and running away from home on a repeated basis (McMorris et al. 2002; Kurtz et al. 1991a, b, c).

Stress, Trauma, and Family Factors

Runaway and homeless young people, when faced with the stress of surviving on the streets, may turn to alcohol and other drugs to help them cope with these stress. For example, one self-reported runaway youth, who reportedly ran away from home at age 15, noted that his life on the streets was hard and he got into a lot of drugs, crime, and other behaviors (Mishriki 2001–2013).

While on the streets, young people may use alcohol and other drugs to cope with the stress and trauma of their family abuse and family conflict (Thompson et al. 2008; Johnson et al. 2005). In Johnson et al.'s (2005) investigation, runaway and homeless young people who had suffered more caretaker physical or sexual abuse had a greater likelihood of fulfilling alcohol dependence criteria. McMorris et al. (2002) found that parental alcohol problems increased the risk that they would abuse their children, which led to an increased probability that the abused children would have drinking problems.

Johnson et al. (2005) also evaluated the extent to which certain parenting practices increased or decreased the risk of alcohol and other drug abuse among homeless and runaway young people. In their investigation, parents who monitored their child's activities, e.g., knew their whereabouts and knew who they were with, were more likely to reduce their child's chances of meeting criteria for substance abuse.

Substance Abuse and Victimization

Runaway and homeless youth who abuse alcohol and other illicit drugs face an increased chance of being victimized (Thrane et al. 2011; Kral et al. 1997; Hoyt et al. 1999). Using a sample of 5387 heterosexual females, ages 11–18, from the Longitudinal Study of Adolescent Health, Thrane et al. (2011) demonstrated that use of alcohol doubled the probability of being sexually assaulted. The runaway and homeless youth's risk of sexual victimization may increase when they are under the influence of alcohol or drugs during sexual intercourse. In Kral et al.'s (1997) investigation, 75 % of the homeless young people reported that during sexual intercourse, they were under the influence of alcohol or other drugs.

Deviant Peer Groups and Networks

Deviant peer group and peer network influences also may lead homeless and runaway youth to get involved in alcohol and other drugs (Johnson et al. 2005; Kipke et al. 1997a, b; Rice et al. 2007, 2008; Tyler 2008; McMorris et al. 2002). According to McMorris et al. (2002), parental alcohol difficulties are linked to their offspring having alcohol problems because of parental rejection in association with the youth having nonconforming peers and high-risk subsistence strategies on the streets.

McMorris et al. (2002) showed that having deviant peer interactions and engaging in deviant subsistence strategies on the streets had the strongest direct effects on whether homeless and runaway young people used alcohol.

Other Physical and Psychosocial Problems Associated with Human Trafficking Victimization

Runaway and homeless young people who are victims of sex and forced labor trafficking may be frequently isolated from friends, family, and access to health care. As a consequence, they are at increased risk of suffering physical and psychosocial problems. These youth may be fearful, suicidal, depressed, paranoid, anxious, and hypervigilant (Family & Youth Services Bureau, National Clearinghouse on Families and Youth n.d.; National Human Trafficking Resource Center n.d. a, b; Kiss et al. 2015). Human trafficking victims also may be suffering from PTSD and engaging in self-harm behaviors (Kiss et al. 2015). Trafficked runaway and homeless young people may be chronically exposed to toxic substances and have other untreated health problems including dental disease. Street youth who are trafficked also may exhibit aggressive and self-harm behaviors.

Future Substance-Abuse Problems

Former runaways may be more likely than non-runaways to have substance-abuse problems. Based on Benoit-Bryan's (2011) study results, runaways were 2.4 times more likely to be a smoker as an adult than persons who had never run away. The investigators found that former runaways had odds 67 % higher of using marijuana as an adult compared to non-runaways. However, the researcher did not find that former runaways had a higher probability of using alcohol as an adult than non-runaways.

Chapter 10
Suicidal Behavior

Investigators have studied the patterns of different types of suicidal behaviors such as suicidal thoughts, feelings, suicide attempts, and completed suicides among adolescents in the general population and among homeless and runaway youth (Jorgensen et al. 2009). This chapter evaluates the prevalence and risk factors of suicidal behaviors in the adolescent population and among street youth who cope with survival on the streets. This chapter analyzes factors such as gender, sexual orientation, child sexual and physical abuse, neglect, trauma, stress, and human trafficking victimization that may increase the probability that runaway and homeless young people will engage in suicidal behaviors. In addition, this chapter assesses the degree to which adults who are former runaways are at risk for suicidal behaviors.

Prevalence of Suicidal Behaviors in General Child and Adolescent Population

Suicide is the third highest cause of death among adolescents, and the prevalence of non-suicidal deliberate self-harm (DSH) ranges between 13 and 45 % among adolescent youth (Liu and Mustanski 2012). According to the Center for Disease Control and Prevention, 30 % were no longer engaging in their regular activities because they felt hopeless (National Center for Health Statistics 2005). The report also revealed that 17 % of young people have planned to commit suicide. In this investigation, nearly 9 % of young people tried to commit suicide. Among those who attempted suicide, 3 % required medical care for their injuries. In the United Kingdom, Craig and Hodson (1998) found that 20 % of homeless young people in London had tried to commit suicide in the prior 12 months.

The prevalence of suicidal thought among adolescents is also high (Kurtz, Kurtz, et al. 1991; Yoder et al. 1998) and suicidal thoughts are linked to suicide attempts (Kienhorst et al. 1990; Rotheram-Borus 1993).

S.J. Morewitz, *Runaway and Homeless Youth*,
DOI 10.1007/978-3-319-30863-0_10

Demographics

Some studies have revealed that girls have a 2–3 time greater likelihood of suicidal ideation and attempting suicide than boys (Cole 1989; Overholser et al. 1990; Yoder et al. 1998). According to Oates (2004), girls have a higher probability of suffering sexual abuse than boys, and researchers have shown that the correlation between sexual abuse and suicide is gendered with females having a higher risk (Brockington 2001; Lange et al. 1999; Lester 2003; Oates 2004; Jorgensen et al. 2009).

In one self-report, a runaway girl wrote that she frequently had suicidal thoughts and feelings of hopelessness (Broken 2014). The youth indicated that she is often aware about individuals who cut themselves or commit suicide. The runaway girl wrote that she would never be like one of those individuals.

With regard to race and ethnicity, some investigators have discovered that White teens are more likely to have suicidal ideation and attempt suicide than their African American and other non-White counterparts (Bolger et al. 1989; Friedman et al. 1984; Kahn 1987; Yoder et al. 1998).

According to some reports, older adolescent may have a greater chance of engaging in suicidal behaviors than younger youth (Carlson and Cantwell 1982; Rutter and Garmezy 1983; Yoder et al. 1998). However, other studies did not find a link between the youth's age and their suicidal behaviors (Brent et al. 1986; DeMan and LeDuc 1995).

Sexual Minority Youth

Some investigations have found that lesbian, gay, bisexual, and transsexual or transgender (LGBT) young people have an elevated risk of engaging in suicidal behaviors. Studies by Savin-Williams (1994) and D'Augelli and Hershberger (1993) indicate that LGB youth are at higher risk of suicidal behaviors than their heterosexual counterparts.

Sexual orientation-related violence (SOV) and gay-related stress (GRS) may cause LGBT young people to be at increased risk for depression, DSH, and suicidal behaviors (Almeida et al. 2009; Liu and Mustanski 2012; District of Columbia Public Schools 2007). Using data from the YRBS, LGB young people in Washington, DC, were more than two times likely to consider a suicide attempt in the past 12 months than their heterosexual counterpart (31 % compared to 14 %) (District of Columbia Public Schools 2007).

Family Dysfunction Including Physical and Sexual Abuse by Family Members

Family dysfunction may increase the risk of suicidal behaviors among children and adolescents. As an important agent of socialization, parents may transmit suicidal propensity to their children (Jorgensen et al. 2009). Research suggests that parenting difficulties may result in child development impairments, and these impairments can increase the likelihood of suicidal ideation (Waldvogel et al. 2008; Jorgensen et al. 2009).

Child and adolescent physical and sexual abuse and neglect are major examples of family impairment and may increase the risk of suicidal behaviors among youth (Jorgensen et al. 2009; Smyth and Maclachlan 2004; Lester 2003; Oates 2004; Yoder et al. 1998). Sexual and physical victimization and neglect often lead to mental health difficulties, which increase the probability of suicidal behaviors (Hershberger and D'Augelli 1995; Whitbeck et al. 1997a, b; Yoder et al. 1998).

Physical and Sexual Abuse Outside the Family

Youth who suffer physical and sexual victimization outside the family also are at risk for developing mental health problems, which increases their chances of engaging in suicidal behaviors (Hershberger and D'Augelli 1995; Whitbeck et al. 1997a, b; Yoder et al. 1998).

History of Family Suicide/Loss and Suicidal Behavior

Children and adolescents who have a family member, close friend, or other loved one who commits suicide or engages in suicidal behaviors may have a greater chance of suicidal behaviors themselves (Smyth and Maclachlan 2004; Jorgensen et al. 2009; Yoder et al. 1998; Rotheram-Borus 1993). Melhem et al. (2003) showed that individuals who were very close to a suicide victim had a greater probability of developing chronic mental and emotional difficulties, which result in a higher likelihood of suicidal thought.

A study by Bearman and Moody (2004) showed that youth who have a family member who attempted suicide may have an increased probability that they will have suicidal ideation. Another investigation by Gutierrez et al. (2001) also revealed that teens living in families with a history of suicidal behavior have a higher probability of having suicidal ideation and feelings.

Mental Disorders and Poor Health

Among teens, mental disorders and poor health increase the probability of suicidal behaviors (Bridge et al. 2006; Jorgensen et al. 2009; Yoder et al. 1998). According to Vladislav et al. (2003) and Wagner et al. (2003), youth with high rates of comorbid conditions have increased risks of suicidal behaviors.

Substance abuse and other externalizing behaviors have been linked to an increased likelihood of suicidal behaviors (Yoder et al. 1998; Greene and Ringwalt

1996). Studies by Bolognini et al. (2003) and Olson et al. (1999) reveal that among teens, heavy use of alcohol and drugs may indirectly affect having suicidal thoughts.

Substance abuse may increase the risk of depression among youth (Aseltine and DeMartino 2004; Walinder and Rutz 2001). Substance abuse may add to depressive ideation in high-risk adolescents (Rossow et al. 2004). Therefore, substance abuse may worsen existing symptoms, although substance abuse does not seem to directly trigger suicidal ideation (Cooper et al. 2002; Steinhausen and Winkler-Metzke 2004).

Some researchers have found gender differences in the link between adolescent substance use and suicidal behaviors. According to Kandel et al. (1991), substance abuse is associated with more suicide attempts among male youth than among their female counterparts. In contrast, Hallfors et al. (2004) and King et al. (1993) showed that among female youth, substance abuse is linked to greater suicidal thoughts.

Depression and other internalizing behaviors also may increase the probability of suicidal behaviors among adolescents (Stewart et al. 2006; Yoder et al. 1998). Youth with low self-esteem may have a greater probability of engaging in suicidal behaviors (Yoder et al. 1998).

The association between depressive symptoms and suicidal behaviors among young people may vary based on gender. Studies have shown that among male youth, substance abuse and depression predict suicidal ideation (Aseltine and DeMartino 2004; Walinder and Rutz 2001). According to Martin et al. (2004), depressive symptoms only indirectly influence the prevalence of suicidal thoughts among female youth.

Youth who suffer from other mental health disorders such as psychoticism, post-traumatic stress disorder (PTSD), and schizophrenia may increase the probability of suicidal behaviors (Vladislav et al. 2003). Other investigations have shown that a majority of youth who attempt suicide had conduct disorder and PTSD (Vladislav et al. 2003; Wagner et al. 2003; Whitbeck et al. 2000, 2004).

Adolescents with Biological Relatives Who Have Mental Disorders

Investigators have shown that teens with biological relatives who have mental disorders have a higher probability of themselves having mental disorders. As a result, these adolescents have a higher probability of engaging in suicidal behaviors (Yoder et al. 1998).

Youth with Family Members Who Abuse Alcohol or Drugs

Teens with family members who suffer from substance abuse are themselves more likely to use and abuse alcohol and other drugs. As a result, these young persons have a higher likelihood of suicidal behaviors (Yoder et al. 1998).

Personal Difficulty

Various investigations have shown that youth who encounter various types of personal difficulty have an increased likelihood of suicidal thought (Jorgensen et al. 2009; Cooper et al. 2005). Types of personal difficulty that increases the probability of suicidal ideation include lack of social support, unemployment, nonconforming behaviors, and aggressive conduct toward other people and DSH behaviors. For example, DSH behaviors are associated with an increased probability of suicide attempts (Cooper et al. 2005; Penn et al. 2003; Jorgensen et al. 2009).

Prevalence of Suicidal Behaviors Among Homeless and Runaway Youth

Homeless and runaway youth suffer from many problems while on their own such as victimization, substance abuse and other mental disorders, and food insecurity, which increase their risk for suicidal behaviors (Jorgensen et al. 2009). Studies have revealed that the rates of lifetime suicide attempts among runaway and homeless young people have ranged from about 10 to 37 % (Yoder et al. 1998; Feitel et al. 1992; Greene and Ringwalt 1996; US General Accounting Office 1989).

An analysis of data from the National Incidence Studies of Missing, Abducted, and Runaway, and Thrown-away Children (NISMART) revealed that in 4 % of the estimated runaway/thrown-away incidents (70,500), the youth had previously tried to commit suicide (Hammer et al. 2002).

Yoder et al. (1998) showed that runaway and homeless adolescents made an average of almost three suicide attempts during the 12 months before the study and made a median of two suicide attempts. An investigation by the US General Accounting Office (1989) revealed that 12 % of runaway youth using runaway shelters were "possibly suicidal" (US General Accounting Office 1989).

Gender factors may influence the rates of suicide attempts. For example, homeless female adolescents may try to commit suicide more frequently than their male counterparts. In Molnar et al.'s (1998) investigation, 48 % of the homeless female teens in the sample attempted suicide compared to 27 % of the homeless males. Among homeless female teens, the mean number of suicide attempts was 6.2 compared to 5.1 for their male counterparts.

Homeless and runaway youth use different methods to attempt suicide. In Yoder et al.'s (1998) investigation, young people were most likely to slit their wrist and/or cut or stab themselves (43.6 %), overdose on drugs (42.3 %), and attempt suicide by hanging, suffocation, or strangling (13 %).

Gender factors may affect the runaway/homeless youth's use of suicide methods. Female runaway and homeless adolescents in Yoder et al.'s (1998) research had a higher probability of slitting their wrist than their male counterparts (49.1 % vs. 26.1 %). In this study, male runaway and homeless youth were more likely to attempt suicide by hanging, suffocation, or strangling than female runaway and homeless young people (39.1 % vs. 1.8 %).

In Yoder et al.'s (1998) analysis of runaway and homeless adolescents, 53.9 % of the sample indicated that they had some type of suicidal thought in the year prior to the study.

However, investigators differ in the ways that they define and measure suicidal ideation. Yoder et al. (1998) regarded suicidal thought as involving thinking about DSH, thinking that they "would be better off dead," contemplating suicide, or making plans to commit suicide.

According to one study, Kameka, a female runaway/homeless girl, had attempted suicide several times. She had engaged in self-harm behaviors in order to deal with her emotional distress (Williams et al. 2001). Kameka was often truant from school. She had been sexually and physically abused as a child and neglected by her mother who was addicted to drugs.

Runaway and homeless youth who have been victims of abuse, neglect, and abandonment and chaotic and traumatic family environments may be at risk for suicidal behaviors. For example, in Marschall (2014), the case study of a runaway boy named M. is presented. M. had a history of suicidal ideation and had come a traumatic and chaotic family environment. He also suffered from abandonment. M. had run away from home at the age of 17 because of emotional, physical, and sexual abuse, possible neglect, and abandonment. In response to his traumatic experiences, M. had various somatic complaints and engaged in DSH behaviors by cutting himself, in addition to having a history of suicidal ideation.

Young people who runaway and become homeless may become suicidal in highly traumatic situations. Runaway and homeless youth can face traumatic situations such as leaving home or being arrested by the police and may respond with suicidal behaviors. For example, they may take their own lives after committing homicide. In one case, a runaway couple in Florida apparently committed suicide after killing a police officer (Kuo 2014, March 27).

In another case, a runaway boy reportedly cut his wrist while detained in police station in Dubai (*The National*, no date). The runaway boy revealed that he cut his wrists because he was having family problems, which caused him to hate himself. He indicated that he was not suicidal.

Suicidal Behavior Risk Factors Among Homeless and Runaway Youth

Different factors may increase the risk that homeless and runaway young people will engage in suicidal behaviors. These conditions may be the same ones that increase the risk of suicidal behaviors among youth in the general population.

Child Abuse

Different forms of child abuse among runaway and homeless youth have been linked to their increased likelihood of suicidal behaviors. Runaway and homeless children and adolescents who have a history of child sexual abuse may have an increased probability of engaging in suicidal behavior (Jorgensen et al. 2009; Plunkett et al. 2001). According to Plunkett et al. (2001), the association between sexual abuse and suicidal behaviors is high among homeless teens. Sexual abuse by a member of one's family among runaway and homeless adolescents has been found to be associated with an increased likelihood of suicidal ideation (Yoder et al. 1998). According to Rew et al. (2001), homeless and runaway young people were more likely to suffer sexual abuse, which helps to explain why they initially run away from home.

Having been sexually and physically abused as a child has been linked to an increased risk of attempting suicide among homeless and runaway youth (Molnar et al. 1998). In Molnar et al.'s (1998) analysis of street youth, being sexually and physically abused before going on their own increased the risks of attempting suicide.

Other studies have found a link between both family-based physical and sexual abuse and suicidal ideation among homeless young people (Kidd 2004; Noell and Ochs 2001; Rew et al. 2001; Jorgensen et al. 2009).

Human Trafficking Victimization

Street youth who become victims of human trafficking may be at increased risk of engaging in suicidal behaviors such as suicide ideation and attempted suicide (Kiss et al. 2015).

Substance Abuse and Other Externalizing Behavior

Substance abuse may increase the risk of suicidal behaviors among homeless and runaway young people. According to one self-report, a 15-year-old runaway girl who had a history of abusing drugs made two serious suicide attempts (Leader, no date).

Knowing a Friend Who Attempted Suicide

As in the case of adolescents in the general population, runaway and homeless young people who know a friend who has tried to commit suicide are themselves at risk for having suicidal ideation (Yoder et al. 1998).

Internationalizing Behaviors

Internalizing behaviors may increase the probability that homeless and runaway youth may engage in suicidal behaviors. For example, according to Yoder et al. (1998), internalizing behaviors increased the likelihood of suicidal thought among runaway and homeless adolescents. While on the streets runaway and homeless young people may suffer from depression, which can increase the probability that they will engage in suicidal behaviors. In one self-report, a 15-year-old girl who suffered from depression made two major suicide attempts (Leader, no date). Another example of internalizing behaviors is having feelings of hopelessness, which may increase the risk of suicidal behaviors among runaway and homeless young people (Broken 2014, November 29).

Suicidal Prevention Programs

Because young people on the streets are at risk for suicide, Molnar et al. (1998) recommends suicidal prevention programs for this vulnerable population. These interventions require evaluating suicidal behaviors such as suicidal ideation and suicide attempts. In addition, these programs should help the homeless and runaway young people with the psychosocial impact of abuse and neglect.

Suicidal Behavior Among Adults Who Were Former Runaways

To what degree are adults who are former runaways at great risk of engaging in suicidal behaviors? Based on a longitudinal analysis of former runaways, Benoit-Bryan (2011) revealed that adults who were former runaways had more suicidal ideation in the previous year than adults who had not run away from home (12 % vs. 6.6 %). The results also showed that adults who had run away had a higher percentage of suicide attempts in the prior 12 months than adults who had not run away (4 % vs. 1.4 %). In the investigation, Benoit-Bryan (2011) also discovered that several factors increased the probability of having suicidal ideation: being bisexual higher by 73%), homosexual (higher by 169 %), and having a history of verbal (142 % higher), physical (47 % higher), and sexual abuse (70 % higher).

Chapter 11
Self-Mutilation Among Runaway and Homeless Youth

This chapter examines self-mutilation, also known as deliberate self-harm (DSH), and suicidal behavior among runaway and homeless young people. These street youth may intentionally burn themselves, cut themselves on their extremities, hit themselves, bang their head against a wall, insert objects under their nails, scrape skin to draw blood, pull their hair out, or use other forms of self-mutilation (Tyler et al. 2003; Saewyc and Edinburgh 2010; Williams et al. 2001; Jorgensen et al. 2009; Favazza 1998; Smith et al. 1998). This chapter analyzes factors such as gender, sexual orientation, child sexual and physical abuse, neglect, trauma, human trafficking victimization, social isolation, and stress that may increase the probability that street youth will engage in DSH to cope with overwhelming emotions while on the streets (Tyler et al. 2003; Jorgensen et al. 2009).

Persons who engage in DSH may do so to relieve tension, respond to feelings of anger, deal with feelings of emptiness and depression, achieve self-punishment, and isolate oneself from the environment. In other instances, people cause themselves to bleed to feel alive (Oumaya et al. 2008; Bennum and Phil 1983; Smith et al. 1998; Raine 1982).

In one self-report narrative, a runaway girl, R., described her self-mutilation as cuts "all up" her arm (Homeless People-Rebecca's Story, n.d.). R. stated that she "slashed" herself to transform the pain of emotions into a physical pain that she could control.

According to another self-report, a female teen indicated that she would cut herself or run away from home in order to deal with her hard life (Mishriki 2001–2013). In another case, a runaway adolescent boy reportedly cut his wrists with a blade while he was held at a Dubai police station. The boy admitted that the cut his wrists because he was having problems with his family members and hated himself as a consequence. He denied being suicidal (The National, n.d.).

A female runaway/homeless girl, K., in another case of self-reported self-mutilation, reportedly engaged in self-harm as a way to cope with her emotional distress (Williams et al. 2001). She had been sexually and physically abused as a child and neglected by her mother who was addicted to drugs. K. had been a frequent school truant and had tried to commit suicide on several occasions.

S.J. Morewitz, *Runaway and Homeless Youth*,
DOI 10.1007/978-3-319-30863-0_11

Prevalence of Self-Mutilation and Suicidal Behaviors

Self-mutilation is most prevalent among children and young adults (Laye-Gindhu et al. 2005; Klonsky 2007; Schmidtke et al. 1996; National Institute for Clinical Excellence 2004). Self-harm behaviors begin to occur among youth ages 12–14.

Researchers have studied the rate of DSH and suicidal behaviors in children, adolescents, and individuals of other ages in the general population and in clinical-based settings (Resch et al. 2008; Tyler et al. 2003). Based on the BELLA investigation, which used a sample of 2863 families with children ages 7–17, Resch et al. (2008) discovered that 2.9 % of the adolescents in the 11–17 age group reported that they had engaged in self-mutilation or attempted suicide in the previous 6 months. Almost four percent of these adolescents indicated that they had suicidal thoughts. Among the parents of the children in the sample, 1.4 % indicated that their children engaged in self-mutilation or had attempted suicide and 2.2 % of had thoughts of suicide. For children under 11, parents reported very low rates of self-mutilation and suicide attempts.

Other investigations have found that DSH occurs in about 3–4 % of the general populations (Briere and Gil 1998; Garrison et al. 1993). Researchers have difficulty measuring the prevalence of self-harm behaviors because of the lack of monitoring systems in place and the fact that individuals do not report their DSH behaviors to health providers and others (Bowen and John 2001).

Researchers are analyzing the prevalence of self-mutilation among adolescents who attempt suicide. For example, Guertin et al. (2001) evaluated adolescents who attempted suicide between 1996 and 2000 and discovered that the most prevalent types of self-mutilation were carving one's skin and picking at a wound.

Youth and others who are jailed or incarcerated may be at increased risk for self-mutilation and suicidal behaviors (Penn et al. 2003). For example, using a sample of 289 adolescents admitted to a juvenile correctional facility, Penn et al. (2003) discovered that 12.4 % reported having a previous suicide attempt and almost 60 % used cutting behaviors and other violent methods to attempt suicide. The case involving the runaway who cut his wrists with a blade while detained in a Dubai police station supports these findings (The National, n.d.).

Data on gender differences in self-mutilation among children and adults is mixed (Briere and Gil 1998; Lipschitz et al. 1999; Tyler et al. 2003). One investigation of rates in early adolescence showed few gender differences (Garrison et al. 1993). In contrast, using a community sample of adolescents, an investigation revealed the girls have a higher rate of self-mutilation than boys (Ross and Heath 2002).

Clinical investigations have also demonstrated mixed results regarding gender differences in self-mutilating behaviors. For example, Lipschitz et al. (1999) discovered that girls have a higher rate of self-mutilation than boys. In contrast, DiClemente et al. (1991) failed to obtain gender differences in DSH rates.

Researchers are beginning to study the prevalence of self-mutilation among homeless and runaway youth. Using a sample of 428 homeless youth, ages 16–19 years, Tyler et al. (2003) found that 69 % of their sample engaged in self-mutilation one time or more. The investigators discovered that the most prevalent types of DSH were cutting or craving one's skin on purpose, burning one's skin with a cigarette or match on purpose, intentionally hitting oneself, and intentionally biting oneself on the mouth.

Tyler et al. (2003) did not find gender differences in the number of different acts of self-mutilation. However, they discovered some gender differences in the types of DSH behaviors. Homeless male youth were more likely to hit themselves intentionally and burn themselves with a cigarette or match on purpose than homeless female youth. Homeless male young people also had a greater likelihood of inserting objects under their nails or skin on purpose than homeless female young people. In contrast, homeless female young people had a greater probability of pulling their hair out intentionally than their male counterparts.

Self-harm behaviors can occur among street youth in different countries. For example, Sherman et al. (2005), using a sample of street children in Lahore, Pakistan, discovered that 40 % indicated that they had cut themselves.

In addition to engaging in DSH, runaway and homeless young people may think about self-mutilation such as cutting themselves with a blade (Broken 2014, November 29; https://confessionsofateenagerrunaway.wordpress.com/). According to one self-report, a runaway girl wrote that she frequently had feelings of hopelessness and suicidal ideation and frequently hears about individuals who engage in self-mutilate or commit suicide. She indicated that she would never cut herself or commit suicide.

Stress Theory and Affect Regulation

Many young people are able to cope with stress with developing major psychosocial difficulties (Tyler et al. 2003; Suyemoto 1998). However, runaway and homeless youth are not able to effectively cope with the trauma of street life, especially since many have suffered childhood abuse and neglect and other problems. According to stress and affect regulation theories, these vulnerable children and adolescents may engage in DSH to communicate and control emotions that are intolerable. DSH may help young people regain control over their world and their sense of self.

Risk Factors for Self-Mutilation

Risk factors for self-mutilation among homeless and runaway youth and other individuals are similar to the risk factors for suicidal behavior. For example, Jorgensen et al. (2009) note that family impairment, family loss such as the death of a parent, spouse, or close friend; feelings of betrayal and abandonment; poor mental and physical health; and personal difficulty increase the risk for suicidal ideation. These risk factors and other conditions also may increase the likelihood of self-mutilation. Below is a summary of factors that increase the risk of DSH and suicidal behavior among individuals in the general population and in clinical and forensic settings, and among runaway and homeless youth.

Family Impairment

Family dysfunction may increase the risk of self-mutilation and suicidal behaviors among runaway and homeless young people (Jorgensen et al. 2009). Families characterized by drug and alcohol abuse and addiction may crease the risk of DSH in runaway and homeless young people. In Williams et al.'s (2001) investigation of former runaway and homeless youth, Kameka, a 21-year-old African American woman, engaged in DSH to deal with the pain of having a drug-addicted mother.

Major Family-of-Origin Stressors Including Sexual, Physical, and Emotional Abuse; Neglect; and Abandonment by Family Members

Homeless and runaway youth may have a history of being physically, emotionally, and sexually abused and neglected and abandoned by family members. These young people also may be abused by the friends of family members. In response to the intense trauma, anger, low self-esteem and low self-worth, stigma, and social isolation resulting from family abuse and neglect and feelings of family betrayal and abandonment, these young people may suffer from post traumatic stress disorder (PTSD), depression, anxiety, and other mental health problems. These victims of family abuse may resort to self-mutilation to control and regulate the overwhelming emotions associated with trauma, stigma, and social isolation related to their abuse and neglect (Strong 1999).

In an analysis of the sexual abuse of boys, Valente (2005) reported that self-mutilation and other psychosocial responses such as anxiety, denial, and dissociation are some of the frequent ways that children respond to sexual abuse.

In R.'s self-report narrative, physical and sexual abuse were prominent parts of her life history (Homeless People-Rebecca's Story, n.d.). R. reported that her father "used to beat the hell out of us." She also noted that after she reached the age of 13, her mother's new partner who lived in her home would rape her on a regular basis. In addition, R. reported that he would abuse her younger sisters.

Williams et al. (2001) discuss the case study of K. who engaged in self-harm to cope with the pain of being sexually and physically abused and neglected by her mother. K., who was the oldest child, was frequently left to supervise her younger sibling.

Marschall (2014) discusses the case study of M., who ran away from home at the age of 17 because of emotional, physical, and sexual abuse; possible neglect; and abandonment. M. cut himself in response to the emotional pain resulting from these traumatic experiences.

The death of a family member may cause significant trauma for homeless and runaway children and adolescent that increase their risk for DSH (Marschall 2014).

Street-Based Victimization and Trauma

While on the street, runaway and homeless young people often suffer from extreme stressors that may worsen the traumatic effects of family abuse and neglect (Tyler et al. 2003; Tyler, Whitbeck, et al. 2001; Ross and Heath 2002). Those youth living on the streets often encounter food insecurity; an increased risk for sexual assault and rape victimization; harsh weather conditions; unsanitary living conditions; unsafe, illegal, and unstable sleeping arrangements; and little or no access to health care, all of which increase their stress on the streets. Leaving home or becoming homeless at an early age also may increase the stress for runaway and homeless youth. According to Tyler et al. (2003), young people who ran away at a younger age had an increased risk of engaging in self-mutilation. In addition, the investigators found that having ever remained on the streets was associated with an increased risk of DSH.

To control and regulate emotions associated with these highly stressful living conditions, some runaway and homeless youth may resort to self-mutilation. As these young people spend more time on the streets, their risk of responding to street life through self-mutilation may increase.

R., in her self-report narrative, indicated that she would sleep in abandoned residences and buildings (Homeless People-Rebecca's Story, n.d.). R. stated that she stayed on the streets with young persons who were similar to her. R. noted that she had to leave her suburban area and live on city streets.

Human Trafficking Victimization

While on the streets, runaway and homeless young people who become human trafficking victims may be at increased risk of engaging in self-harm behaviors (Kiss et al. 2015).

Deviant and Illegal Subsistence Methods

Runaway and homeless youth frequently rely on subsistence strategies such as survival sex, shoplifting, and assault to survive on the street (Tyler et al. 2003). R.'s self-report narrative describes her experiences with survival sex (Homeless People-Rebecca's Story, n.d.). R. reports that she would live with friends and then sleep with males. She had to "play to stay" (Homeless People-Rebecca's Story, n.d.).

By engaging in survival sex and other subsistence strategies, young people like R. increase their risk of sexual and physical violence victimization and potentially fatal outcomes. In responses to these often overwhelming stressors, runaway and homeless young people may attempt to control the psychosocial effects of these stressors by engaging in self-mutilation. In Tyler et al.'s (2003) investigation, homeless youth who participated in deviant subsistence techniques had a higher probability of participating in DSH.

Runaway and homeless young people encounter significant other stress and trauma because of their participation in these deviant and illegal subsistence strategies. These homeless and runaway youth face stigma because of their participation in these deviant and illegal behaviors.

As they participate in subsistence strategies, runaway and homeless young people face harassment by the police and face the risk of being arrested and sent to juvenile detention. In other cases, they may be transferred to an emergency shelter, a group home, or foster care setting. In other instances, they fear being returned to their families and the possibility of being further victimized. In response to these stresses, stigma, and social isolation, the runaway and homeless youth may resort to DSH.

Overwhelming Feelings Including Anger, Hopelessness, Self-Punishment, PTSD, Depression, Anxiety, Substance Abuse, and Other Mental Health Problems

Runaway and homeless youth who develop mental health problems such as PTSD, depression, anxiety, intense and persistent feelings of anger, self-punishment, guilt, and other mental health problems may be more likely to engage in self-mutilation (Tyler et al. 2003). For example, in an investigation of street children in Lahore, Pakistan, researchers discovered that 40 % indicated that they self-mutilate mostly in order to deal with their feelings of anger (Sherman et al. 2005).

While on the streets, young people who become human trafficking victims are at risk of developing PTSD and engaging in self-harm (Kiss et al. 2015).

Tyler et al. (2003), in their study, found that homeless young people who suffered from major depression were at risk for engaging in DSH. In one self-report from another analysis, the runaway girl, R., noted that she would get very depressed and upset to the point of wanting to commit suicide (Homeless People-Rebecca's Story, n.d.).

Youth who are trafficked also have an increased likelihood of suffering major depression and participating in self-harm (Kiss et al. 2015).

According to Guertin et al. (2001), adolescent suicide attempters with a history of self-mutilation had a higher probability of being diagnosed with oppositional defiant disorder, major depression, and dysthymia. Moreover, adolescent suicide attempters with a history of DSH exhibited more loneliness, anger, and hopelessness.

DSH and recurring suicidal behaviors are prevalent among patients with borderline personality disorder (BPD) (Oumaya et al. 2008; Yen et al. 2013). In a review of the literature of self-mutilation and suicide among persons with BPD, Oumaya et al. (2008) suggest that self-mutilating behaviors can both protect against suicide and increase the risk of completed suicide. On the one hand, self-mutilating behaviors in persons with BPD can help prevent suicide by allowing them to escape from their dissociative state. In this ways, individuals now are more likely to feel that they are alive again. On the other hand, repeated self-mutilation in persons with BPD may lead to greater dysphoria. Their dysphoria may only be reduced with subsequent suicidal behaviors. Oumaya et al. (2008) found that persons with BPD who repeatedly engage in self-mutilation are about two times more likely to commit suicide than individuals with BPD who do not self-mutilate repeatedly.

Risk Taking and Reckless Behaviors

Runaway and homeless young who take risks and engage in reckless behaviors may have a higher probability of engaging in DSH. Guertin et al. (2001) discovered that adolescent suicide attempters with a history of self-mutilation had a higher probability of engaging in risk taking and reckless behavior than adolescent suicide attempters without a history of self-mutilation. In addition, adolescents with BPD and impulsive and aggressive behaviors may increase the risk of suicidal behavior (Horesh et al. 2003).

Runaway and homeless young people who use and abuse drugs may be at risk for self-harming behaviors. Based on an investigation of street children in Lahore, Pakistan, Sherman et al. (2005) discovered that drug use was positively linked to DSH (ever having engaged in self-cutting).

Guertin et al. (2001) demonstrated that adolescent suicide attempters with a history of DSH had a higher probability of using alcohol than the adolescent suicide attempters without a history of self-mutilation. For example, in her self-report narrative, R. noted that she began to take drugs in order to deal with the pain of being physically abused by her father and later began extensive self-harming behaviors (Homeless People-Rebecca's Story, n.d.).

Stigma and Feelings of Low Self-Worth, Low Self-Esteem, and Low Self-Confidence

As victims of family abuse and neglect and while on the street, feeling stigmatized and having low self-worth, low self-esteem, and low self-confidence may increase the likelihood that homeless and runaway youth will self-mutilate (Tyler et al. 2003). R., in her self-report narrative, indicated that low self-confidence prevents street youth like her from trying to take corrective action (Homeless People-Rebecca's Story, n.d.).

Social Isolation and Lack of Social Support

Social isolation and little or no social support may increase the likelihood that runaway and homeless young people will self-harm (Tyler et al. 2003). Homeless and runaway young people often lack social support since they have lost contact with many of their previous friends. While on the street, they face exploitation and abuse by friends, acquaintances, and strangers. Homeless and runaway youth are often wary of others because of the exploitation and trauma that they face on the street.

In her self-report narrative, R. notes that just knowing that a person cares about her plight on the street helps her to continue living (Homeless People-Rebecca's Story, n.d.). She stated that lack of social support is a major problem for street youth.

Runaway and homeless children and adolescents may be victims of human trafficking, and they often are socially isolated by their human traffickers (Family and Youth Services Bureau, National Clearinghouse on Families & Youth, n.d.). These trafficked street youth may be abducted, isolated from their family members and friends, and threatened with death if they try to contact them (Morewitz 2008, 2016).

Minority Sexual Orientation

Homeless gay, lesbian, bisexual, and transgender youth may be at increased risk of harming themselves (Tyler et al. 2003). Homeless sexual minorities may have increased rates of self-mutilation because they encounter discrimination, harassment, stigma, and social isolation associated with their lifestyles, resulting in an increased probability of mental health problems such as depression, anxiety, anger, and hopelessness. Homeless and runaway youth who are sexual minorities may engage in self-mutilation to better control their fear and anxiety over being victimized.

Self-Mutilation and Risk of Suicide

Individuals who self-mutilate may not intend to commit suicide since their self-mutilating behaviors generally do not result in life-threatening injuries (Favazza 1998; Feldman 1988; Suyemoto 1998; Vesper 1996). For example, in one self-report narrative, R. noted that she regularly self-mutilated not to commit suicide but in order to deal with the emotional pain "of the past" (Homeless People-Rebecca's Story, n.d.). However, runaway and homeless youth and other persons who engage in DSH may be at greater risk of having suicidal thoughts and feelings (Unger et al. 1997; Brodsky et al. 2001; Burns and Patton 1999; Cooper et al. 2005; Douglas et al. 2002).

DSH among some young people may be linked to more severe suicidal ideation. In fact, youth who self-mutilate may be more likely to try to commit suicide than those who do not engage in self-mutilation. According to research, young people who harm themselves have a 30 times higher rate of trying to commit suicide than those who do not self-harm (Cooper et al. 2005; Penn et al. 2003).

Guertin et al. (2001) compared adolescent suicide attempters with a history of DSH with adolescent suicide attempters without such a history and found that the former had more symptoms of cognitive, affective, and behavioral disorders. Adolescent suicide attempts with a history of self-mutilation had a higher probability of being diagnosed with oppositional defiant disorder, major depression, and dysthymia. Moreover, adolescent suicide attempters with a history of self-mutilation exhibited more loneliness, anger, hopelessness, risk taking, and reckless behavior. They also used alcohol more than the adolescent suicide attempters without a history of DSH.

The self-reported runaway girl, R., indicated that she engaged in both self-harming behaviors and suicide attempts (Homeless People-Rebecca's Story, n.d.). R. stated that she would slash her arm and try to kill herself with a syringe.

The severity of the DSH behaviors may be linked to greater suicide risk. For example, young people who received medical care for their self-harming behaviors have a higher probability for committing suicide (Cooper et al. 2005; Douglas et al. 2002; Goldsmith et al. 2002). In the case of the self-reported runaway girl who attempted suicide, R., noted that she would cut herself 100 times if she were having a "shocker week" (Homeless People-Rebecca's Story, n.d.). R. stated that she did not resort to cutting herself 100 times that often. In addition to cutting herself in a suicide attempt, R. reported that she would sniff glue in order to lose consciousness (Homeless People-Rebecca's Story, n.d.). R. would try to kill herself because she no longer could cope with the painful "reality of life." After one suicide attempt, R. noted that a person discovered her lying in an alley and called in a medical emergency (Homeless People-Rebecca's Story, n.d.).

Interventions

School officials, mental health professionals, and other individuals are developing strategies to deal with the problems of DSH. Linden (2015) reported that schools are implementing programs to teach mental health personnel and teachers about ways to recognize and intervene with students who are participating in self-harm behaviors. A number of interventions use dialectical behavior therapy (DBT) to assist youth in controlling their emotional expression and avoid the desire to self-harm. More research is necessary to evaluate the effectiveness of therapeutic interventions such as DBT for self-harm behaviors (Ougrin et al. 2015; Saewyc and Edinburgh 2010).

Chapter 12
Sexual Risks

Runaway and homeless youth often participate in early sexual activity, survival sex, and use and abuse of alcohol and other drugs and engage in other behaviors that increase their sexual risks and related adverse consequences (Halcon and Lifson 2004; Marshall et al. 2009).

This chapter analyzes the risks for unplanned pregnancies, sexually transmitted infections (STIs), including human immune virus (HIV)/acquired immunodeficiency syndrome (AIDS), among runaway and homeless young people as they struggle to survive on the streets. Certain runaway and homeless children and adolescents are at increased risk for sexual health problems. In this chapter, the risk factors for sexual health problems such as age and gender of the street youth, subsistence strategies on the streets, unemployment, homelessness, partner coercion and violence, sexual victimization, and substance abuse are presented.

Risk Amplification Model

Whitbeck et al. (1999), in their risk amplification model, suggest that runaway and homeless children and teens who come from dysfunctional families, e.g., characterized by physical, sexual, and psychosocial abuse and neglect, are at increased risk for sexual victimization and associated sexual risks while on their own. According to the risk amplification model, runaway and homeless youth are likely to have risky lifestyles and daily routines while on the streets. They have a greater probability of developing coercive and abusive coping styles. Those homeless and runaway youth who have suffered early childhood sexual abuse are more likely to interact with deviant peers and others; engage in unprotected sex; have multiple sexual partners; participate in survival sex, e.g., exchanging sex for money, food, shelter, and other desirable goods and services and in other deviant subsistence strategies; and use and abuse of alcohol and other drugs that increase their sexual risks (Whitbeck et al. 1999).

S.J. Morewitz, *Runaway and Homeless Youth*,
DOI 10.1007/978-3-319-30863-0_12

Analysis of the results of the National Incidence Studies of Missing, Abducted, Runaway, and Thrown-away Children (NISMART) indicated that many runaway youth and those kicked out of their home (thrown-aways) have faced different sexual risks (Hammer et al. 2002). During the runaway/thrown-away incidents, some children were sexually assaulted. Children participated in survival sex, e.g., exchanging sex for resources such as money, drugs, food, or shelter. During the runaway/thrown-away incidents, children also were in the company of a sexually exploitative individual.

Survival Sex, Prostitution, and Sex Trafficking

Runaway and homeless young people often have difficulty finding employment that can provide them with a livable income. They frequently cannot give employers their real names since they may get taken into custody for being a runaway (Mishriki 2001–2013). Therefore, runaway and homeless youth resort to sex survival and prostitution as one of multiple subsistence strategies. For example, one self-reported female 15-year-old runaway noted that a runaway cannot eat without engaging in theft or prostitution because of the difficulties of finding suitable employment while on the streets (Mishriki 2001–2013).

Human traffickers may kidnap and coerce or lure runaway and homeless young people into sex trafficking (Family & Youth Services Bureau, National Clearinghouse on Families & Youth, n.d.; Morewitz 2016; Silverman et al. 2007). Because of their dire need for money, food, shelter, clothing, and other resources, runaway and homeless youth are particularly vulnerable to human traffickers. According to one report, about 17 % of human trafficking victims were girls and 10 % were boys (Ark of Hope for Children (2014, February 22). Around the world, two million children are trafficked for the sex trade (Ark of Hope for Children (2014, February 22).

According to the Family & Youth Services Bureau and National Clearinghouse on Families & Youth (n.d.), about 55 % of girls on the streets participate in prostitution and 75 % of them have a pimp. About 20 % of these street girls are part of a national crime network; these girls must travel a great distance from their families and friends and are kept isolated from them.

The prevalence of survival sex among runaway and homeless young people may vary depending on the youth's setting. Based on a representative national sample of youth from shelters and a multi-city sample of youth from the streets, Greene et al. (1999) demonstrated that street youth (27.5 %) were more likely to participate in survival sex than shelter youth (9.5 %).

Based on two investigations in Los Angeles, CA, the prevalence of survival sex among homeless young people was more than 33 % (Greenblatt and Robertson 1993; Kipke et al. 1995). According to Huba et al. (2000), the rates of survival sex among homeless youth were much lower (7.8–9.7 %).

Gender and Survival Sex

Gender may help to predict participation in survival sex among homeless and runaway young people. According to Greene et al. (1999), males in the shelter sample (11.1 %) reported that they were more likely than their female counterparts (8.3 %) to engage in survival sex. However, in the street sample, significant gender differences were not obtained.

Age and Survival Sex

The age of homeless and runaway youth may be related to their chances of participating in survival sex. In Greene et al.'s (1999) analysis, older runaway and homeless youth were more likely to have ever engaged in survival sex. In the 20–21 age group, 18.0 % of the youth from the shelter sample and 36.3 % of the youth from the street sample reported that they had ever participated in survival sex. In the 18–19 age group, 13.9 % of shelter sample and 28.7 % of the street sample reported that they had ever participated in survival sex. In contrast, in the 12–13 age group, 4.7 % of the youth from the shelter sample and 14.3 % of youth from the street sample indicated that they had ever engaged in survival sex.

Race/Ethnicity and Survival Sex

Some studies have found mixed results regarding the link between race/ethnicity and survival sex among runaway and homeless youth. In Greene et al.'s (1999) investigation of shelter youth, Whites were more likely than African Americans and other racial groups to engage in survival sex. An association between race and survival sex was not found in the street sample. In contrast, Walls and Bell (2010) found that African American homeless young people had a higher probability of engaging in survival sex than White heterosexual young people.

Days Away from Home and Survival Sex

Increased duration away from home may increase the probability that runaway and homeless young people will participate in survival sex. According to Greene et al. (1999), the number of days away from home was linked to engaging in survival sex in both the shelter sample and the street sample.

Street Experiences

Street experiences may increase the likelihood of survival sex among runaway and homeless young people. Greene et al. (1999) found that having ever stayed the night in a public setting, in a vacant building, in a vehicle, outside, in a subway, or with a stranger was associated with engaging in survival sex among the shelter sample.

Increased spending time on the streets among homeless and runaway youth may increase their exposure to survival sex, substance abuse, theft, and other problematic behaviors (Chen et al. 2004).

While on the streets, participating in certain types of social networks and interacting with deviant peers increase runaway youth's probability of participating in risky sexual activity (Ennett, Bailey, et al. 1999; Whitbeck et al. 1999; Tyler, Hoyt, et al. 2001a, b).

Desire for Love

Runaway and homeless teens may engage in sexual activity on the streets because of their desire to be in love. For example, in one self-report, a runaway teen noted that after she ran away, she had sex merely so she could feel the "love of a man" (Mishriki 2001–2013).

Previous Victimization and Survival Sex

Previous victimization may increase the homeless and runaway youth's likelihood of engaging in survival sex and other deviant subsistence strategies (Whitbeck et al. 1999). Runaway and homeless youth often have suffered different forms of abuse and neglect in their home environment. Youth who have been victims of child sexual abuse are at increased risk for different types of sexual victimization while on the streets (Tyler, Hoyt, et al. 2001a, b; Marshall et al. 2009; Noell, Rohde, Seeley, et al. 2001).

Gender Differences in Effects of Early Childhood Sexual Abuse

Female runaway youth may be more likely than male runaways to have suffered childhood sexual abuse (Tyler, Hoyt, et al. 2001a, b). As a result, female runaways may be at greater risk for sexual victimization and related sexual risks than their male counterparts. The risk amplification model helps to explain these findings (Whitbeck et al. 1999).

Delinquent/Criminal Activities

Prior participation in delinquent/criminal activities may increase the probability that homeless and runaway young people get involved in survival sex. According to Greene et al. (1999), homeless and runaway youth in the shelter sample who had engaged in theft, assault, drug trade, and weapon carrying had an increased risk of participating in survival sex. Only youth in the street sample who was involved in theft had an increased probability of participating in survival sex.

Substance Use and Abuse

While on the streets, runaway and homeless youth often use and abuse alcohol and other drugs. For example, in Halcon and Lifson's (2004) research, 51.7 % of the homeless young people indicated that they had an average of five or more alcoholic drinks per week. Other studies show that youth on the streets have high rates of using alcohol and other drugs (Kipke, Montgomery, et al. 1997; Koopman et al. 1994). Street young people also interact with peers who report that they use alcohol and other drugs weekly. The risk amplification model by Whitbeck et al. (1999) and Tyler, Hoyt, et al. (2001a, b) would suggest that youth who have come from dysfunctional families and have suffered early childhood abuse are more likely to use and abuse alcohol and other drugs to fulfill their need for attention and combat feelings of depression.

Homeless and runaway youth who use alcohol and other drugs may have an increased likelihood of engaging in survival sex, especially since survival sex may involve having sex in exchange for alcohol and other drugs.

Halcon and Lifson (2004), in an investigation of homeless young people, revealed that heavy alcohol assumption (15 or more alcohol drinks each week) was linked to an increased probability of exchanging sex for goods. The authors showed that male homeless youth did not differ from their female counterparts regarding the association between heavy alcohol use and survival sex.

Greene et al. (1999) evaluated runaway and homeless youth's substance use from 30 days prior to the young person running away until the day of the study interview and found that their use of marijuana, cocaine, and other drugs were related to survival sex among shelter and street youth. Alcohol use was associated with survival sex in the shelter sample but not in the street sample. Injection drug use may increase sexual risks among street youth (Marshall et al. 2009) and also was related to survival sex in the shelter and street samples. Illicit drug use by a family member was associated with survival sex in the shelter sample but not in the street sample.

Youth on the streets who participate in survival sex to obtain highly addicting drugs that also stimulate sexual desires face sexual risks and drug addiction (Lubotsky et al. n.d.). Lubotsky et al. (n.d.) point out that lesbian, gay, bisexual, and transsexual or transgender (LGBT) youth face sexual risks because they are befriended by elder panders who initiate them into drug addiction by providing them with methamphetamine, a highly addictive drug that also stimulates sexual desires.

Being High or Intoxicated and Not Using Protection During Sexual Intercourse

Substance use and abuse increases sexual risks among homeless and runaway young people since substance use and abuse can impair use of contraceptives. While under the influence of alcohol and other drugs, runaway and homeless youth may not be aware of the need for contraceptives. In addition, their psychomotor functioning may be so impaired that they forget to use contraceptives, are not motivated to use them, or cannot effectively use them.

In Halcon and Lifson's (2004) research, almost 33 % of the homeless young people indicated that they had been intoxicated or high on drugs during at least 50 % of the occasions that they had sex without using barrier protection in the past month. Kral et al. (1997) showed that 75 % of homeless young people in their investigation reported that they were "under the influence of alcohol or drugs" during sex (Kral et al. 1997; Tyler et al. 2004). Intoxicated youth also may use fewer strategies to avoid victimization, including sexual victimization (Felson 1997; Tyler et al. 2004).

Injection Drug Use and Lack of Barrier Protection During Sex

Runaway and homeless LGBT youth are at risk of acquiring human immune deficiency virus (HIV)/acquired immunodeficiency syndrome (AIDS) because they may be intravenous (IV) drug users (Marshall et al. 2010; Yates et al. 1988). Trafficked street youth may be especially at risk of becoming IV drug users. In their investigation of runaway and non-runaway youth at an outpatient medical clinic, Yates et al. (1988) found that 34.5 % of the runaway youth reported IV drug use. Among the runaway youth, 9.1 % identified themselves as bisexual and 7.3 % self-reported as homosexual.

Runaway and homeless youth who are IV drug users may be less likely to use contraceptives. According to Halcon and Lifson (2004), homeless youth who injected drugs had a lower probability of using barrier protection at least one time during sex in the previous month.

Depression

Street youth who are suffering from depression may have an increased risk of developing sexually transmitted infection (STIs) (Rohde et al. 2001).

Suicide Attempts

Homeless and runaway young people who attempt suicide may be more likely to get involved in survival sex. According to Greene et al.'s (1999) analysis, attempting suicide was linked to increased odds of engaging in survival sex in the shelter and street samples.

Prior Psychiatric Hospitalization

Runaway and homeless youth who have been previously hospitalized in a psychiatric facility may be more likely to engage in survival sex. In Greene et al.'s (1999) study, a previous psychiatric hospitalization was linked to an increased risk of engaging in survival sex in both the shelter and street samples.

Inconsistent Contraceptive Use/Unprotected Sex

As discussed above, a number of investigations have demonstrated that homeless and runaway young people report sexual activity without the using protection (Halcon and Lifson 2004). Kral et al. (1997) showed that 34–47 % sexually active homeless young people in three cities used a condom during each sexual encounter. In a study of sexually active runaway young people, Rotheram-Borus and Koopman (1991) discovered that less than 50 % of either females or males reported using a condom at last sexual intercourse. MacKellar et al. (2000) demonstrated that homeless and runaway young people had higher rates of unprotected sex than in the Rotheram-Borus and Koopman's (1991) investigation. Wenzel et al. (2000), using a sample of homeless females in the 15–44 age group, showed that about 67 % reported having unprotected sex in the past year. In an investigation of condom use in the most recent sexual intercourse, Bailey et al. (1998) revealed that approximately 33 % of homeless teens did not use a condom.

Some reports show that male homeless youth are more likely to use a condom than their female counterparts (Halcon and Lifson 2004; Bailey et al. 1998; Mackellar et al. 2000). For example, based on an investigation of homeless young people, Halcon and Lifson (2004) discovered that female homeless youth were less likely to use barrier protection during intercourse than their male counterparts. However, Rotheram-Borus and Koopman (1991) showed that male runaways did not have higher condom use rates than female runaways.

Sexually Transmitted Infections and HIV

STIs are prevalent among runaway and homeless teens (Halcon and Lifson 2004). Reliable information about the incidence and prevalence of STIs may be problematic since teens may not accurately report that they have STIs (Tyler, Whitbeck, et al. 2000).

In Halcon and Lifson's (2004) research, almost 33 % of the homeless youth indicated that they had acquired at least one STI. According to other investigations, 17–28 % of homeless teens report having a STI history (Clatts and Davis 1999; Huba et al. 2000). In a study in Texas, Rew et al. (2002) found that 25 % of homeless teens had a history of gonorrhea, 8.7 % chlamydia, and 8.0 % AIDS. In 2001, Wagner et al. (2001) discovered that the most prevalent STI reported among homeless youth in Seattle was chlamydia.

MacKellar et al. (2000) and Noell, Rohde, Ochs, et al. (2001) showed that female runaway and homeless youth had higher STI rates than their male counterparts. For example, Noell, Rohde, Ochs, et al. (2001) found that *C. trachomatis* was 6.30 % for female adolescents and 4.17 % for male adolescents. In their investigation, herpes simplex virus type 2 was 12.50 % for female youth and 5.73 % for male youth. However, Greene et al. (1999) and Kral et al. (1997) discovered that male runaway and homeless youth had higher survival sex rates than female runaway and homeless young people.

Survival sex among homeless and runaway youth is linked to an increased risk of acquiring HIV and other STIs (Allen et al. 1994; Stricof et al. 1991; Halcon and Lifson 2004). Street youth who are sex trafficking victims also may be at increased risk for HIV/AIDS and other STIs. HIV risks increase the probability that homeless and runaway young people will participate in survival sex (Haley et al. 2004). Greene et al. (1999) also found that having an STI was linked to a higher probability of engaging in survival sex. In addition to participating in survival sex, being sexually victimized and using and abusing alcohol and other drugs results in unsafe sex and increased risks for STIs.

Alcohol Use and Sexually Transmitted Infection History

Alcohol use is associated with a history of having an STI among runaway and homeless young people (Halcon and Lifson 2004). While on the streets, homeless and runaway children and adolescents who drink alcohol have an increased probability of engaging in unsafe sex that results in a history of STIs. Alcohol use impairs judgment and memory about using barrier methods during sex. Using alcohol can impair motor skills resulting in effective use of contraceptives. Using alcohol is also linked to increased violence that prevents the use of contraceptives during sexual intercourse.

Treatment for Sexually Transmitted Infections

Runaway and homeless young people who have obtained treatment for STIs may be at risk for additional STIs (Halcon and Lifson 2004). These individuals may already have more risk factors for acquiring STIs in the future.

Sexual Orientation

Homeless and runaway gay, lesbian, bisexual, and transsexual or transgender (GLBT) youth engage in sex in exchange for various resources such as money, food, a place to stay, and drugs (Koopman et al. 1994; Saewyc et al. 2006). In Whitbeck et al.'s (2004) report, homeless and runaway gay male young people were more likely to engage in survival sex than their heterosexual males. Marshall et al. (2010) also found that sexual minority males were more likely to engage in survival sex than heterosexual male street-involved youth. Runaway and homeless LGBT youth who engage in survival sex are at increased risk of acquiring STIs, including HIV (Cochran et al. 2002; Whitbeck et al. 2004; Yates et al. 1988).

History of Earlier Sexual Intercourse

Homeless young people have a higher probability of engaging in earlier sexual intercourse, and a history of earlier sexual intercourse increases their sexual risks (Halcon and Lifson 2004). In one self-report case, a 16-year-old girl who later ran away from her family and later from a group home noted that she had sex for the first time the day before her 14th birthday (Mishriki 2001–2013).

Sexual orientation may affect homeless and runaway youth's age at the time of their first sexual intercourse. In Cochran et al.'s (2002) study, homeless LGBT youth were more likely to be younger at the time of their first sexual intercourse than homeless heterosexual youth.

Early sexual intercourse may increase the risk of STIs and unwanted and unplanned pregnancy among female homeless and runaway youth. According to one self-report, a runaway girl who had sex at age 14 was concerned having STIs and being pregnant (Mishriki 2001–2013).

Recent History of Sexual Intercourse

A recent history of sexual intercourse may increase sexual risks, and several investigations have demonstrated that homeless young people have a recent history of sexual intercourse regardless of their gender (Kral et al. 1997; Wagner et al. 2001; Halcon and Lifson 2004). In Halcon and Lifson's (2004) research, 55 % of male homeless youth indicated that they had sex with a female in the past 30 days. A larger percentage of female homeless teens (73.8 %) reported that they had sexual intercourse with a male in the past 30 days.

Multiple Sexual Partners

While living on the streets, runaway and homeless hang out with multiple individuals, increasing their risk of having sex with multiple partners and also participating in survival sex with multiple sexual partners, which increase sexual risks. In Halcon and Lifson's (2004) report, 25.1 % of the homeless young people indicated that they had two or more sexual partners in the last 30 days.

According to one self-report story, a 12-year-old female runaway indicated that she had sex with two older male teenagers who helped her find shelter (Mishriki 2001–2013). The girl noted that she had sex with both boys because she felt obligated to them.

In another self-report, a runaway 16-year-old girl reported that after living with different male friends over time, she was concerned about having STIs and being pregnant after living with multiple male friends who always wanted "something" (Mishriki 2001–2013).

Various demographic, social, behavioral, and psychological factors may influence homeless and runaway's patterns of multiple sex partners. Male homeless and runaway young people have been found to have a higher number of sexual partners than their female counterpart (MacKellar et al. 2000; Rotheram-Borus and Koopman 1991; Wagner et al. 2001).

Heavy substance use and abuse may be linked to an increased risk of having multiple sexual partners among runaway and homeless young people (Halcon and Lifson 2004). In one report, homeless young people who consumed 15 or more alcoholic drinks each week had a greater probability of having multiple sexual partners in the last 30 days (Halcon and Lifson 2004).

Halcon and Lifson (2004) also found both gender and substance use/abuse factors were linked to differences in having multiple sex partners among homeless young people. For example, the authors demonstrated that homeless young people who drank five or more alcoholic drinks each week had a greater probability of having multiple sexual partners only among female homeless youth.

According to Cochran et al. (2002), homeless LGBT young people had a higher probability of having more lifetime sexual partners than homeless heterosexual young people. In Cochran et al.'s (2002) analysis, homeless LGBT youth were more likely to engage in unprotected sex than homeless heterosexual youth.

Sexual Victimization

While on the streets, runaway and homeless young people face sexual risks from being sexually assaulted and raped. Their participation in survival sex also may increase their risk of being raped, sexually assaulted, and physically assaulted by violent customers, friends, acquaintances, and others (Tyler et al. 2004). The use of alcohol and other drugs by runaway and homeless young people during survival sex may increase the likelihood of sexual assault, rape, and other forms of victimization (Tyler et al. 2004). Homeless and runaway youth's routine activities and lifestyle place them at risk for sexual victimization. According to an online source, some teens in Broward County, FL, reportedly engage in "hunching" in which boys will surround a girl on the streets and "have sex with her" (CYC, n.d.).

Runaway and homeless LGBT youth are at risk of acquiring HIV because they may be sexually abused and raped (Marshall et al. 2010; Yates et al. 1988). In their investigation of runaway and non-runaway youth at an outpatient medical clinic, Yates et al. (1988) found that 21.8 % of runaway young people reported sexual abuse.

Other Social and Behavioral Factors

Other social and behavior factors form a risk clustering of multiple behaviors that may increase the sexual health risks among youth while on the streets (Halcon and Lifson 2004). Runaway and homeless young people suffering from conduct disorder (CD) may have increased drug- and sex-associated HIV risk behaviors (Booth and Zhang 1997). In addition, the lack of social networks among runaway and homeless young people may increase their risky behaviors (Ennett, Bailey, et al. 1999).

Sexually Transmitted Infections May Increase the Probability of Other Health Problems

STIs may increase the Risk of various health problems. STIs may increase the risk of HIV/AIDS and early death. STIs also have been linked to an increased probability of acquiring cancer. In addition, STIs are associated with an increased likelihood of developing chronic pain. Moreover, having STIs is linked to developing infertility (World Health Organization, Task Force on the Prevention and Management of Infertility 1995).

Pregnancy

Female youth on the streets who engage in unprotected sex are at increased risk for pregnancies (Greene and Ringwalt 1998). In Halcon and Lifson's (2004) analysis of homeless young people, 53 % of the female youth reported being pregnant at least one time.

Female street teens also faced an increased probability of having multiple pregnancies (Halcon and Lifson 2004). According to Halcon and Lifson (2004), 28 % of the female street youth had two or more pregnancies.

Runaway and homeless young people who get pregnant after engaging in risky sexual behaviors can suffer various adverse outcomes such as having miscarriages. In one self-report, a runaway girl who reportedly got pregnant while selling drugs indicated that she "lost the baby" because of a miscarriage (Mishriki 2001–2013). In Halcon and Lifson's (2004) investigation, 69 % of the homeless female teens who got pregnant had one or more miscarriages.

Ethnic factors may be linked to a history of pregnancy among runaway and homeless female adolescents (Halcon and Lifson 2004). In one investigation, Whites had the highest rate (51 %) of pregnancy compared to female teens classified as "Other" ethnic identities (37 %) and African Americans (12 %) (Halcon and Lifson 2004).

Possible Effects of Runaway Behavior on STIs in Adulthood

Do runaways have an increased probability of developing STIs in adulthood? In a longitudinal study of runaway youth, Benoit-Bryan (2011) showed that former runaways had a 53 % higher probability of having a recent diagnosis of an STI as an adult compared to those who did not run away. Individuals who were younger, females, African American, homosexual, and victims of verbal or physical abuse also had an increased likelihood of having a recent STI as an adult.

Chapter 13
Pregnancy

In this chapter, the prevalence, risk factors, and consequences of adolescent pregnancy among runaway and homeless young people and adolescents in the general population are presented. Low socioeconomic status (SES), demographic factors, family dysfunction, school difficulties, survival sex, sex trafficking, low condom use, multiple sexual partners, partner coercion and violence, and substance use are some of the conditions that may increase the risk of teen pregnancy among female street youth. The extent to which teen mothers may suffer miscarriages and other adverse health outcomes is analyzed. This chapter also discusses conditions such as the pregnant teens' limited access to health care, poor nutrition and other health problems, ineffective social support, unstable living arrangements, and other difficult living situations that may increase the likelihood of poor maternal, neonatal, and child health outcomes.

Teen pregnancy in the USA is declining (Schuyler Center for Analysis and Advocacy, 2008, December). In the USA, between 1991 and 2005, teen pregnancy rates had decreased by 25 %. However, by 2006, the rate increased by 3 % (Hamilton et al. 2007). Although adolescent pregnancy rates have gone up and down, the USA has the highest rate of adolescent pregnancies and birth compared to other western developed countries. Forty-one of 1000 female teens aged 15–19 gave birth, resulting in 415,262 live births (Martin et al. 2006). These statistics indicate that adolescent pregnancy continues to be a major social problem.

Correlates of Adolescent Pregnancy

Researchers have evaluated possible correlates of pregnancy among female adolescents. Demographic, SES, risky sexual behavior, inconsistent contraceptive use, alcohol and other drug use, violence and abuse, mental health problems, poor family functioning, school difficulties, friendship patterns, and cognitive factors may be associated with adolescent pregnancy.

S.J. Morewitz, *Runaway and Homeless Youth*,
DOI 10.1007/978-3-319-30863-0_13

Using data from the National Vital Statistics System, Gavin et al. (2009) showed that pregnancy rates were much higher among female Hispanic and non-Hispanic African Americans aged 15–19 (132.8 and 128.0 per 1000 population) than their female non-Hispanic White counterparts (45.2 per 1000 population).

In terms of SES, pregnant teens may be more likely to have lower SES. In one investigation, Uzun et al. (2013) found that the families of teen mothers were more likely to be below the poverty line than adult mothers. In another report, Guijarro et al. (1999) showed that economic challenges were associated with an increased likelihood of adolescent pregnancy. A community's poor physical environment, which is associated with low SES, may be linked to teen pregnancy among males in Baltimore, Maryland, and among study participants in Johannesburg, South Africa (Brahmbhatt et al. 2014).

Low condom use and risky sexual behavior may increase the likelihood of teen pregnancy. Holden et al. (1993) discovered that pregnant adolescents had a lower probability of using condoms. Female adolescents may participate in risky sexual behavior with high rates of changing sexual partners and have low levels of contraceptive use, including condom use (Slater and Robinson 2014). In another investigation, Brahmbhatt et al. (2014) showed among female adolescents in Baltimore, Maryland, and Johannesburg, South Africa, use of condoms at first sexual intercourse reduces the probability of adolescent pregnancy.

Early initiation of sexual intercourse may be linked to adolescent pregnancy. For example, Brahmbhatt et al. (2014) found that early sexual intercourse initiation was associated with an increased probability of adolescent pregnancy among study participants in Johannesburg, South Africa, and among females in Baltimore, Maryland.

Female adolescents' use of alcohol and binge drinking may lead to an increased likelihood of teen pregnancy. Based on an investigation of adolescent pregnancy in urban disadvantaged settings in five cities, Brahmbhatt et al. (2014) discovered that alcohol consumption and binge drinking in the previous month among study participants in Baltimore, Maryland, increased the risk of teen pregnancy.

Female adolescents who are the victims of partner violence may be at increased risk of unplanned pregnancy (Sahin and Sahin 2003; Gazmararian et al. 1995; Morewitz 2004). Violent partners may oppose the use of condoms and also coerce their adolescent partners into unprotected sexual intercourse. Violent partners and others may sexually assault female adolescents, increasing their risk for unplanned pregnancies and sexually transmitted infections (STIs).

Sexual abuse may be correlated with teen pregnancy. According to Guijarro et al. (1999), pregnant teens had higher rates of sexual abuse than nonpregnant teens. Donaldson et al. (1989) discovered that among 142 adolescents at a prenatal clinic who gave birth in a recent year, 10.6% indicated that they were a past or current victim of sexual abuse. The adolescents were most likely to report that they were sexually abused by a family member.

Mental health difficulties and associated poor family functioning may increase the probability of adolescent pregnancies and adverse pregnancy-related outcomes (Williams et al. 2001). In a study of trauma and resiliency among former runaway and homeless youth, Williams et al. (2001) present the case of Y., a 19-year-old

Caucasian, who became pregnant at age 17. Y. reported that her mother suffered from schizophrenia and did not comply with her medication. The youth noted that her family had much conflict possibly caused by her mother's mental disorder. In response to the conflicts in her family, Y. ran away at the age of 13 and had two or possibly more involuntary psychiatric inpatient admissions. She also went into foster care and had dropped out of school. In another case study, S., a 21-year-old, African American woman, suffered a stillborn at the age of 16 (Williams et al. 2001).

Community violence may be linked to adolescent pregnancy. According to Brahmbhatt et al. (2014), increased community violence was associated with teen pregnancy in Baltimore, Maryland, and among study participants in Johannesburg, South Africa.

Impaired family functioning and certain structural characteristics of families may affect teen pregnancy. Guijarro et al. (1999) discovered that lower levels of communication between mother and daughters and between father and daughters were linked to a greater probability of teen pregnancy. In their study, pregnant teens had a lower probability of getting support for their difficulties from their family or others.

In terms of family structural characteristics, Brahmbhatt et al. (2014) discovered that female teens in Johannesburg, South Africa, who were brought up by someone who was not their two parents had an increased likelihood of being pregnant.

Female adolescents who have school problems may have a greater likelihood of becoming pregnant during adolescence. Guijarro et al. (1999) found that pregnant teens had lower school performance than nonpregnant teens. In their investigation, pregnant teens also had lower expectations of school achievement than nonpregnant teens.

Holden et al. (1993) also demonstrated that pregnant adolescents were more likely to have poor school performance compared to nonpregnant adolescents. Brahmbhatt et al. (2014) discovered that in two cities, Baltimore, Maryland, and Johannesburg, South Africa, female teens who were currently in school had a decreased likelihood of being pregnant.

Pregnant teens may have a higher rate of school dropout than nonpregnant teens. In Uzun et al.'s (2013) investigation, the school dropout rate was higher among adolescent mothers than adult mothers.

Adolescent pregnancy may increase the risk that girls will run away or become homeless. For example, in one case study, M., a runaway boy, reported that his older sister who ran away was pregnant (Marschall 2014). M. indicated that life with his father was chaotic. They moved often. At times the family lived with his father's sister, her husband, and four children. Marco stated his father and aunt did not get along. Other times they lived with his father's girlfriend, whom M. referred to as stepmom, along with five half siblings. An addition to the family system occurred when M.'s younger sister, age 13, had a baby boy. M. stated that he experienced "normal" discipline when he was young, such as getting hit with a belt. Verbal and physical abuse from his father intensified when M. was 13, particularly when his older sister ran away because she was pregnant

Having a relative or friend who is pregnant also may be linked to adolescent pregnancy. For example, Holden et al. (1993) found that pregnant teens were more likely to have a relative or friend was a teen mother.

Cognitive factors may be related to adolescent pregnancy. According to Holden et al. (1993), pregnant adolescents had a higher probability of expecting motherhood to be easier than their nonpregnant counterparts.

Outcomes of Adolescent Pregnancy

What are the outcomes of adolescent pregnancies? Adolescent mothers are especially vulnerable because they may come from low-SES backgrounds, lack insurance, have limited access to health care, and lack adequate social/family support. As a result, teen mothers face adverse maternal, infant, and child outcomes (Thompson et al. 2008).

Adverse Maternal, Fetal, and Neonatal Outcomes

Teen mothers may suffer miscarriages and other health problems due to partner violence (Morewitz 2004). The risk of these health problems are also increased because of the pregnant teens' limited access to health care, poor nutrition and other health problems, ineffective social support, unstable living arrangements, and other difficult living conditions.

Social Outcomes

Adolescent mothers are more likely to encounter school difficulties than their nonpregnant counterparts (Thompson et al. 2008). For example, they have a greater risk of dropping out of school. Teen mothers are more likely to have very low income (Thompson et al. 2008). In addition, adolescent mothers have a greater chance of remaining single than nonpregnant teens (Thompson et al. 2008).

Teen mothers may feel stigmatized by their pregnancy and face prejudice, discrimination, and social isolation. One investigation of 925 low-income teens that were evaluated at a postpartum unit within 48 h of delivery showed that 39.1 % of the teens indicated that they felt stigmatized by their pregnancy (Wiemann et al. 2005). Stigmatized adolescents were more likely to seriously contemplate getting an abortion, were afraid to inform their parents about their pregnancy, believe that that their parents and teachers felt that their pregnancy was a mistake, and felt abandoned by the father of their baby.

Brand et al. (2014) suggest that research is showing the multidimensional and positive aspects of adolescent pregnancy and that health professionals should regard pregnant adolescents in terms of this evolving positive model of teen pregnancy and motherhood.

Infant Care

Adolescent mothers may encounter more difficulties caring for their infants than adult mothers. In Uzun et al.'s (2013) investigation, teen mothers were more likely to indicate that they felt inadequate in caring for their infant than adult mothers.

Infant Outcomes

Infants born to adolescent mothers have a greater probability of being born prematurely at a low birth weight (Thompson et al. 2008; Martin et al. 2006). Infants born to adolescent mothers are more likely to die during their first year of life compared to infants born to mothers more than 20 years of age (Bensussen-Walls and Saewyc 2001).

Child Outcomes

The children of teen mothers face a greater likelihood of living in very low-SES, single-parent families (Thompson et al. 2008; Martin et al. 2006). These children are also more likely to participate in the child welfare system (Thompson et al. 2008; Martin et al. 2006).

Prevalence of Pregnancy Among Runaway and Homeless Youth

Studies indicate that as many as 20 % of homeless female adolescents get pregnant (Thompson et al. 2008; Halcon and Lifson 2004). Various reports have shown that female adolescent runaways have higher rates of pregnancy compared to female youth in households. Using data from the Longitudinal Study of Adolescent Health, Thrane and Chen (2012) discovered that among girls between 11 and 17 years, the probability of pregnancy in the following year was 1.67 times more likely for runaway girls. Berry et al. (2000) found that runaway and homeless female adolescents are more than four times likely to get pregnant than their peers who do not run away or become homeless.

Researchers have investigated the pregnancy history among homeless youth. Using a sample of 203 homeless young people 15–22 years of age, Halcon and Lifson (2004) discovered that 53 % of the females reported at least one pregnancy. In this sample, 28 % indicated that they had two or more pregnancies. About 43 % had an abortion. Almost 24 % had one or more live births. Almost 10 % of those who had been pregnant were currently pregnant.

Homeless and runaway pregnant teens may face an increased probability of having adverse pregnancy outcomes. In Halcon and Lifson's (2004) study of homeless youth, 69 % of the pregnant adolescents reported have one or more miscarriages.

Prior to running away or becoming homeless, girls and adolescents may have a history of rape, pregnancy, and adverse pregnancy outcomes. For example, in Lindsey et al.'s (2000) interview study of former homeless and runaway young people, the authors discuss the case of S., a young Caucasian woman, who at the age of 16 reportedly had been raped by a friend's father and later that year got pregnant and suffered a miscarriage.

Correlates of Pregnancy Among Runaway and Homeless Female Youth

An ecological system approach can help clarify pregnancy risks for runaway and homeless female adolescents (Zweig et al. 2002). Individual, family, and school/community factors may influence runaway and homeless female youth's chances of getting pregnant (Thompson et al. 2008). Many of these same factors increase the risk of pregnancy among housed female youth.

Living on the Streets and in Shelters

Living on the streets without money for food, shelter, and other necessities makes female runaways vulnerable to an increased risk of pregnancy. Female runaways may have to exchange sex for necessities such as shelter and food. In many of these instances, the female runaways do not use contraceptives and the individuals that they have sex with also do not use contraceptives.

Female street youth who are kidnapped and coerced or tricked into sex trafficking (Family & Youth Services Bureau, National Clearinghouse on Families & Youth, n.d.) are at risk of becoming pregnant and developing STIs, including HIV/AIDS.

In one self-report, a female teen runaway noted that while on the streets she would go "from house to house' to stay with male friends, but they would always want "something" in exchange for food and shelter (Mishriki 2001–2013). The female adolescent reported that she was fearful that she might be pregnant and also have STIs.

Greene and Ringwalt (1998) and Ringwalt et al. (1998) also demonstrated that female street youth had the highest lifetime rates of pregnancy compared to shelter youth and young people living in households (48 %, 33 %, and less than 10 %, respectively). Their results revealed that regardless of recent experiences of running away or becoming homeless, female shelter youth and those living on the streets had the greatest likelihood of lifetime pregnancy rates.

Longer durations away from home or institutional care may increase the likelihood that homeless and runaway female adolescents will get pregnant. In Thompson et al.'s (2008) investigation, longer duration of being away from home was linked to an increased probability of pregnancy among teen homeless and runaway girls.

Other conditions associated with pregnancy among homeless and runaway teens are similar to the factors linked to teen pregnancy in the general population. For example, ethnic factors may be associated with pregnancy among female runaway adolescents. Based on data from the Runaway/Homeless Youth Management Information System consisting of a national sample of young people who are requesting crisis shelter services, Thompson et al. (2008) showed that female runaway adolescents from ethnic minority backgrounds were more likely to be pregnant.

In one investigation, Halcon and Lifson (2004) also found that ethnicity predicted having a history of pregnancy. The authors showed that Whites had the highest rate (51 %) of a history of pregnancy than those who reported themselves as other ethnic identities (37 %), and African Americans (12 %). Age did not predict a history of pregnancy.

Romantic Involvement

Female runaway and homeless teens may have sex and get pregnant in order to feel loved. According to one self-report, a runaway girl reported that she had sex just to experience love (Mishriki 2001–2013). Female runaway and homeless adolescents who are romantically involved may have a greater chance of becoming pregnant. In their longitudinal investigation, Thrane and Chen (2012) showed that romantic involvement was related to pregnancy among female homeless and runaway youth.

Violence and Abuse

While on the streets, female runaway and homeless youth face rape and other types of violence and are at increased risk of getting pregnant. According to one self-report story, a female runaway reported being raped two times and discovered that she was pregnant (Mishriki 2001–2013).

Associating with violent male youth and developing sexual relations with these violent boys may increase the likelihood of pregnancies among runaway and homeless girls while on the streets. Violent males may resist the use of contraceptives whether they are on the streets or living at home (Morewitz 2004). Violent males are likely to coerce the girls into having sexual intercourse without the use of contraceptives, which increases the probability of unplanned pregnancies. Violent males may be impulsive and sexually assault and rape runaway and homeless females while on the streets, increasing the risks of unplanned pregnancies. In one self-report, a female runaway girl reported that she got pregnant the second time after dating another abusive male (Mishriki 2001–2013). She got pregnant this time after beginning to date an abusive 17-year-old male. Thrane and Chen (2012) also demonstrated that among females between the ages of 11 and 17, a sexual assault history was associated with an increased probability of pregnancy.

Emotional abuse may be linked with adolescent pregnancy. In Thompson et al.'s (2008) investigation, runaway and homeless adolescents who reported being emotionally abused by their mother had an increased chance of being pregnant.

Sex Trafficking

While on the streets, girls are vulnerable to being trafficked for prostitution, sex slavery, and prostitution. These girls are especially susceptible to being coerced or lured into sex trafficking by organized criminal networks. As a result, they are at increased risk of becoming pregnant due to unsafe sex and sexual, physical, and emotional violence.

Feelings of Abandonment

Feelings of being abandoned by family members may be associated with an increased likelihood of teen pregnancy among runaway and homeless teens. Feelings of abandonment by family members predicted teen pregnancy among homeless and runaway teens in Thompson et al.'s (2008) investigation.

Wanting a Sense of Belonging

In response to feeling abandoned, female runaway and homeless teens may get pregnant in order to feel part of a social unit that they have frequently lacked in their lives. One runaway girl, Yvonne, got pregnant at the age of 17 (Williams et al. 2001). She reportedly had intended to get pregnant and wanted to achieve "a sense of belonging."

Female runaway and homeless youth may get pregnant to develop feelings of belong in relation to the future father of her baby. For example, one pregnant runaway girl wanted to have a baby to increase the bond that she had with the baby's father.

Single-Parent Families

Other family factors may be related to an increased probability of pregnancy among runaway and homeless adolescents. According to Thompson et al. (2008), residing in a household that is headed by a single parent increases the odds of pregnancy among homeless and runaway female youth.

School Factors

School factors may influence the odds that runaway and homeless teens become pregnant. Thompson et al. (2008) showed that runaway and homeless teens that dropped out of school had an increased probability of being pregnant.

Sexually Transmitted Infections

Having a sexually transmitted infection (STI) may be linked to pregnancy among adolescent female runaway and homeless youth Findings from Thompson et al. (2008) revealed that having a STI was linked to pregnancy among runaway and homeless female adolescents. A female runaway in one self-report story noted that she may have STIs and be pregnant after being forced to have sex in exchange for shelter (Mishriki 2001–2013). These results are consistent with the high rates of STIs and unwanted pregnancy among adolescents in general (Gavin et al. 2009; Slater and Robinson 2014).

Runaway and Homeless Teens Experience Pregnancy

While on the streets, female runaway teens may report getting pregnant (Mishriki 2001–2013). For example, in one self-report story, a teen runaway who had broken into houses for sale noted that she was raped twice and got pregnant (Mishriki 2001–2013).

According to another self-report narrative, one female adolescent who ran away and lived on the streets stated that she decided to get married to an individual after several months (Mishriki 2001–2013). The girl indicated that she and her future husband dated for a year and became very much in love.

Like pregnant teens in general, pregnant runaways may experience encounter prejudice and discrimination because of their pregnancy. For example, a 14-year-old female runaway reported that her mother became extremely angry when the mother found out that her daughter was pregnant (Mishriki 2001–2013).

Another pregnant teen runaway, who was staying at the home of a friend's friend, noted that she got kicked out of her temporary residence when the friend discovered that she was pregnant (Mishriki 2001–2013).

While on the streets, female teen runaways may wonder if they may have an unplanned pregnancy. For example, one female 12-year-old runaway noted that she had missed her period and may be pregnant (Mishriki 2001–2013).

Interventions for Pregnant Runaways

Little is known about what percentage of runaway and homeless youth receive family planning services during patient care visits. In one study of runaway and non-runaway young people at initial visits to an outpatient medical clinic, Yates et al. (1988) discovered that 20.3 % of runaway youth received family planning services compared to 37.5 % of non-runaway young people.

Outcomes for Pregnant Runaways

Social service agencies may intervene when teen runaways become pregnant or face the possibility of pregnancy. For example, in one self-report story, a female teen runaway who reported that she had to have sex with a male in order to stay in a shelter noted that she may be pregnant (Mishriki 2001–2013). The teen indicated that a social service department sent her to a locked institution. The girl had noted that the social service agency went against her mother who wanted her daughter to come back home.

Pregnant runaway and homeless teen report pregnancy-related complications such as miscarriages because they are victims of violence. For example, according to one self-report narrative, a pregnant 13-year-old runaway reported that she had a miscarriage (Mishriki 2001–2013). The girl stated that she got pregnant again but lost her baby after her abusive, 17-year-old boyfriend repeatedly physically attacked her.

In another self-report, a pregnant adolescent had a miscarriage at the age of 16 (Williams et al. 2001). The girl indicated that as an adolescent she had been betrayed and abandoned by her parents and she had also abused drugs during different periods of time. At the age of 12, she reportedly became a chronic runaway when she learned that her drug-addicted mother was still alive.

Runaway and homeless teens that have been pregnant also may have an increased likelihood of participating in survival sex. In an investigation by Greene et al. (1999), a history of pregnancy was related to an increased probability of participating in survival sex.

Chapter 14
HIV-/AIDS-Risk Behaviors

This chapter analyzes the prevalence and risk factors of human immune virus (HIV)/acquired immunodeficiency syndrome (AIDS) among street young people are discussed. Demographic risk factors such as gender and age are analyzed. Various environmental influences, including homelessness and unstable housing, are discussed as possible risk factors for HIV and sexually transmitted infections (STIs). The effects of peer group social networks on HIV-/AIDS-risk behaviors are presented. Early family abuse, depression, and relationship status and other conditions are evaluated. In addition, survival sex, sex trafficking, multiple partners, substance use, and other factors such as sexual decision making and partner coercion and violence among runaway and homeless youth are presented.

The populations of homeless and "street-involved" young people are increasing in North America (Marshall et al. 2009). For example, according to DeMatteo et al. (1999), up to about 150,000 youth are homeless and in the streets of Canada. These young people face adverse health outcomes, including those related to sexual and reproductive health, such as STIs, including HIV/AIDS (Frankish et al. 2005; Feldmann and Middleman 2003; Roy et al. 1999, 2001, 2003).

The prevalence of HIV among youth in general is 0.2 % (Sweeney et al. 1995). In contrast, the HIV rate is higher among homeless youth. Roy et al. (1999, 2001, 2003), Pfeifer and Oliver (1997), and Noell, Rohde, Ochs, et al. (2001), Noell, Rohde, Seeley, et al. (2001) have reported high incidence and prevalence of diseases such as HIV, STIs, hepatitis B, and hepatitis C. In Montreal, Roy et al. (2000) found the prevalence of HIV to be about 2 %. Likewise, in Toronto, DeMatteo et al. (1999) estimated the prevalence of the HIV to be 2 %. Other investigators have found higher HIV prevalence rates. In New York, Stricof et al. (1991) reported a 5.3 % HIV prevalence rate. Schalwitz et al. (1990) reported a rate of 8.2 %, and Pfeifer and Oliver (1997) reported the HIV rates to be 11.5 in Hollywood.

S.J. Morewitz, *Runaway and Homeless Youth*,
DOI 10.1007/978-3-319-30863-0_14

Demographic Characteristics

Researchers have evaluated the relationship between demographic characteristics and HIV-risk behaviors among runaway and homeless youth. In Johnson et al.'s (1996) investigation, males had a higher likelihood of engaging in HIV-/AIDS-risk behaviors. With regard to age, Ennett, Bailey, et al. (1999) discovered that increasing age is linked to a greater risk of HIV among homeless young people.

Homelessness and Unstable Housing

Various environmental influences, including homelessness and unstable housing, lead to an increased amount of participation in street life, which may increase HIV and STI risk (Marshall et al. 2009; Coady et al. 2007). Researchers have found a link between homelessness and the spread of HIV in adults (Wolitski et al. 2007; Marshall et al. 2009). Johnson et al. (1996) revealed that study participants who were interviewed on the streets had a higher likelihood of participating in HIV-/AIDS-risk behaviors.

According to Corneil et al. (2006), unstable housing among injection drug users is related to their higher incidence of HIV. An investigation of high HIV-risk incarcerated women demonstrated that the larger the number of residences that they lived in, the greater their chances of participating in unprotected sex (Weir et al. 2007). Elifson et al. (2007) discovered that female drug users who stayed in unstable housing situations had a lower probability of reducing HIV-associated risk behaviors than those who obtained a stable housing environment.

Research on young men also has found that housing instability and homelessness is associated with sexual- and drug-associated risks for HIV. For example, Kipke et al. (2007) and Clatts et al. (2005) have shown that among men who have sex with other men (MSM), housing instability and homelessness increase their sexual and drug risks for HIV.

Marshall et al. (2009) suggests that among homeless and runaway youth, the association between homelessness and housing instability and HIV risks is mixed. Huba et al. (2000) found that homelessness was linked to being HIV positive.

In Coady et al.'s (2007) study of HIV-risk behaviors among young injection drug users, the researchers showed that risk for HIV differed depending on the young injection drug users' housing situation. They found that highest HIV risk occurred among homeless injection drug users.

The more days that homeless and runaway young people spend away from home and on their own, the more likely that they will engage in survival sex, which increases HIV risks (Tyler et al. 2001a, b; Greene et al. 1999). In addition, Chen et al. (2004) found that increased time on the streets among homeless and runaway youth may increase their risk of substance abuse, theft, and other problematic behaviors (Chen et al. 2004).

In Greene et al.'s (1999) investigation of shelter and street-involved youth, the number of days away from home predicted an increased probability of participating in survival sex in both the shelter sample and the street-involved sample. Among runaway and homeless youth, having ever stayed the night in a public place or vacant building may be linked to an increased probability of engaging in survival sex among runaway and homeless young people. Greene et al. (1999) found that having ever stayed the night in a public setting, in a vacant building, in a vehicle, outside, in a subway, or with a stranger predicted an increased risk of participating in survival sex among the shelter sample.

Ennett, Federman, et al. (1999) discovered that the severity of homeless is linked to HIV-risk behaviors among both male and female homeless young people. Homeless youth who ever slept in a public place over night had an increased risk for HIV. The authors also found that ever staying with a stranger and being thrown out of the residence increased homeless young people's HIV risk.

Homelessness may lead to inconsistent use of condoms (Marshall et al. 2009). For example, using data from the At-Risk Youth Study, Marshall et al. (2009) showed that the longer the period of homelessness, the greater the likelihood that street-involved young people would inconsistently use condoms. Unprotected sex and inconsistent use of condoms and other contraceptives may increase HIV/AIDS risk among homeless and runaway youth (Moon et al. 2001; de Carvalho et al. 2006; Milburn et al. 2006; Podschun 1993; Marshall et al. 2010; Johnson et al. 1996). In Ennett, Bailey, et al.'s (1999) investigation, 38.5 % had never or infrequent use of condoms. In their study of 196 homeless young people in 10 urban shelters in Chicago, Johnson et al. (1996) showed that 83.7 % indicated that they engaged in at least one risk factor for AIDS, including inconsistent use of condoms.

Unstable housing may increase the likelihood that homeless and runaway young people will have more sexual partners. For example, Marshall et al. (2009) demonstrated that unstable housing was linked to having a higher number of sexual partners among homeless youth.

Other severe aspects of homelessness may increase HIV risks. According to Ennett, Federman, et al. (1999), homeless young people who received support from illegal behaviors had an increased risk for HIV. In addition, being hungry during the current period of homelessness was linked to a greater HIV risk.

Social Network Characteristics and Peer Group Affiliation

Studies have shown that peer group social networks can exert considerable influence in promoting or discouraging HIV-/AIDS-risk behaviors (Kipke, Montgomery, et al. 1997; Rice et al. 2007; Tyler 2008).

Different peer group affiliation may influence the risk of HIV/AIDS among runaway and homeless young people (Kipke, Simon, et al. 1997). Homeless youth may form subcultural peer groups that promote certain behaviors and lifestyles. According to peer cluster theory, adolescents join clusters of peers that have a substantial impact on substance use (Oetting and Beauvais 1987). These peer cluster can exert considerable influence on the runaway and homeless youth's other behaviors as well.

In their investigation of 309 homeless young people aged 13–23, Kipke, Montgomery, et al. (1997) discovered that group affiliation influenced patterns of drug use and HIV-risk behaviors. Homeless and runaway young people may view themselves as members of certain peer groups that reflect certain social and political beliefs and values. In other instance, these members of these peer groups engage in certain risk behaviors or have specific physical characteristics. Kipke, Simon, et al. (1997) found that homeless and runaway youth considered themselves members of such groups as gay/bisexual males and females, hustlers, deadheads, punks, skinheads, skaters, and surfers. The investigators discovered that homeless youth who considered themselves part of the "punker" group had a higher probability for engaging in unprotected sex and sharing needles during injection drug use. The gay/bisexual and hustler groups had a higher likelihood of participating in survival sex.

Those runaway and homeless young people who do not have a social network may be at risk for engaging in HIV-/AIDS-risk behaviors (Ennett, Federman, et al. 1999). One investigation demonstrated that runaway and homeless young people without a social network had a higher probability than those with a social network to engage in the following HIV-/AIDS-risk behaviors: using illegal drugs, having multiple sex partners, and participating in survival sex (Ennett, Bailey, et al. 1999).

Johnson et al. (1996) also found that homeless youth who had personal needs that were not being met were associated with HIV-/AIDS-risk activities.

In Weber et al.'s (2002) study of prostitution among female street young people, the authors discovered that all girls, both prostitutes and those not involved in prostitution, had low rates of consistently using condoms for anal, vaginal, and oral sex.

Early Family Abuse

Early family abuse may increase the risk that homeless and runaway youth will engage in risky sexual behavior, which increases their likelihood of acquiring HIV/AIDS (Stoltz et al. 2007; Noell, Rohde, Seeley, et al. 2001; Whitbeck et al. 1999).

Homeless and runaway young people with a history of childhood sexual abuse may be at greater risk for using drugs, which is an HIV-risk factor. For example, Chen et al. (2004) found that female runaway and homeless young people with a history of early sexual abuse had an increased risk of using drugs, which increases their risks for HIV. Johnson et al. (1996) also reported that having a history of sexual abuse was linked to HIV/AIDS behavior.

Depression

Researchers have found that depression is associated with sexual risk behaviors among street youth (Rohde et al. 2001). In a study of older homeless youth, Rohde et al. (2001) discovered that 12.2 % had a current diagnosis of major depression and

6.5 % had the diagnosis of dysthymia. Females and older youth had higher rates. The researchers indicated that depression occurred before the youth became homeless and was linked to an increased probability of having STIs in older young people. Depression was also linked to infrequent use of condoms, a nonheterosexual orientation in older young people, and a lifetime homosexual episode.

Relationship Status

Relationship status may influence the risk of HIV and STI transmission. For example, Marshall et al. (2009) found that being single or dating casually was associated with a greater number of sex partners, which can increase the risk of HIV and STI transmission. However, Marshall et al. (2009) also discovered that being single predicted consistent condom use.

Among injection drug users, Evans et al. (2003) showed that females had a higher probability than males to indicate that they had intravenous-drug-user partners and to have sexual intercourse recently.

Sexual Decision Making

Sexual decision making among runaway and homeless youth may influence their risk of STIs and HIV/AIDS. In a study of young women who were injection drug users or partners of injection drug users, Harvey et al. (2003) discovered that female injection drug users who indicated that they were involved in making decisions about condom use and when to have sex had seven and 19 times, respectively, greater likelihood of reporting recent condom use than other individuals.

Drug and Alcohol Use

Certain types of drug use may increase HIV/AIDS risk among runaway and homeless young people (Weber et al. 2002; Gleghorn et al. 1998). Among homeless and runaway youth, intravenous drug use can co-occur with alcohol and drug use, increasing the risk of HIV/AIDS risk. Moreover, alcohol and drug use can co-occur with risky sexual behaviors such as survival sex, increasing HIV/AIDS risk among runaway and homeless young people. In Weber et al.'s (2002) investigation, female street young people who engaged in prostitution had a two times greater likelihood of binging on alcohol and five times greater chance of binging on drugs.

Runaway and homeless youth who use intravenous drugs are at risk for HIV/AIDS. In Greene et al.'s (1997) report, 17.1 % of current street youth and 3.6 % of current shelter youth used intravenous drugs. In their investigation of homeless youth in Chicago, Johnson et al. (1996) demonstrated that intravenous drug use was one of the risk factors for AIDS.

Homeless and runaway youth who participate in prostitution and trafficked street youth may be at increased risk of engaging in injection drug use. For example, Weber et al. (2002) demonstrated that female street youth who participated in prostitution were four times more likely to have a history of intravenous drug use. These female homeless youth had a 2.5 times greater likelihood of injecting cocaine as their drug choice.

Violence and Abuse

Runaway and homeless young people suffer rape and other types of violence and as a consequence are at increased risk of getting STIs such as HIV/AIDS. In one self-report story, a female runaway youth indicated that she had been raped two times and discovered that she was pregnant (Mishriki 2001–2013). This girl is at increased risk of acquiring HIV/AIDS if her rapists had been infected with the HIV virus.

While on the streets, interactions with HIV-positive violent youth and developing sexual relations with these violent individuals may increase the likelihood of acquiring HIV/AIDS and other STIs among runaway and homeless young people. HIV-positive, violent persons may resist the use of condoms whether they are on the streets or living at home (Morewitz 2004). These HIV-positive violent individuals may force their victims into having sexual intercourse without the use of condoms, which increases the probability of HIV/AIDS. HIV-positive, violent persons may be impulsive and sexually assault and rape runaway and homeless youth while on the streets, increasing the risks of HIV/AIDS. In one self-report, a female runaway girl reported that she got pregnant the second time after dating another abusive male (Mishriki 2001–2013). After starting to date an abusive 17-year-old male, this girl became pregnant this time. This youth is at increased risk for HIV/AIDs if her abusive male partner is HIV positive.

Risky Sexual Behaviors and Survival Sex, Sex Trafficking, and Prostitution

When confronted with few legitimate ways to make money, runaway and homeless young people are coerced or resort to survival sex, sex trafficking, prostitution, and pornography (Tyler et al. 2001a, b; Family & Youth Services Bureau, National Clearinghouse on Families & Youth n.d.). As a result, they are at increased risk for STIs, including HIV/AIDS and other life-threatening consequences (Ennett, Bailey, et al. 1999; Kipke et al. 1995; Weber et al. 2002; Marshall et al. 2010; Greene, Ennett, et al. 1997; Greene et al. 1999; Revaz n.d.).

In the USA, Canada, and other countries, various investigations have shown that street youth may be victims of sex trafficking, and 25 % of street young people engage in survival sex, e.g., having sex in exchange for money, a place to stay, alcohol and other drugs, or other desirable items and services (Kipke et al. 1995; Greene et al. 1999; Weber et al. 2002).

According to Family & Youth Services Bureau, National Clearinghouse on Families & Youth (n.d.), 55 % of girls on the streets participate in prostitution. Seventy-five percent of these street girls have a pimp. Approximately 20 % of these girls perform sex work as part of national criminal networks, which force the girls to travel long distances from their families and friends and keep the girls isolated and imprisoned.

Ennett, Federman, et al. (1999) found that 43.4 % of the homeless youth engaged in survival sex. In Greene et al.'s (1999) investigation, 27.5 % of the youth in the street sample and 9.5 % in the shelter sample reportedly had been involved in survival sex. Marshall et al. (2010) discovered that 11.3 % of 558 participants in the At-Risk Youth Study reported participating in survival sex. These findings highlight the risks of HIV/AIDS faced by street youth who engage in this high-risk sexual behavior.

Homeless and runaway young people who engage in survival sex are especially at risk for HIV/AIDS because they are in a high-risk environment, are embedded in social-sexual networks that have high HIV prevalence, and are exposed to violence and criminal activities (Roy et al. 2003; Shannon et al. 2009; Blankenship and Koester 2002; Ennett, Federman, et al. 1999). Runaway and homeless youth who engage in survival sex may face obstacles in negotiating consistent and effective condom use with their sexual partners. As runaway and homeless young people participate in survival sex, they may face violence from their sexual partners, which will prevent them from successfully negotiating such condom use.

Multiple Sex Partners

Homeless and runaway youth may have a number of sexual partners, and having multiple sex partners may increase the risk for HIV/AIDS among runaway and homeless young people (Ennett, Bailey, et al. 1999; Moon et al. 2000; Zimet et al. 1995; Montgomery et al. 2002). Those young people who engage in survival sex, sex trafficking, and prostitutions are likely to have multiple sexual partners. Ennett, Federman, et al. (1999) showed that 37.8 % of the homeless young people reported having more than ten sexual partners. Johnson et al. (1996), in their study of homeless youth, found that having multiple sex partners was one of the risk factors for AIDS. Several investigations have shown that in the past 6 months, the median number of sexual partners among homeless and runaway youth ranged between 1 and 6 (Moon et al. 2000; Zimet et al. 1995; Montgomery et al. 2002).

Sexual Victimization

Engaging in survival sex and prostitution and having multiple sexual partners increase the risk that homeless and runaway young people will be sexually assaulted (Tyler et al. 2001a, b). In Ennett et al.'s (1999) report, having been sexually victimized was related to an increase in HIV risk.

Runaway and homeless youth, because they face few legitimate ways to financially support themselves on the streets, may be coerced or tricked into prostitution, which increases their HIV risks (Tyler et al. 2001a, b).

High-Risk Partners

Having high-risk partners can increase the probability of HIV/AIDS among runaway and homeless youth. According to Johnson et al. (1996), having high-risk partners was one of the prevalent risk factors for AIDS in their sample of homeless youth. However, in Ennett et al.'s (1999) study, only 1.7 % of the homeless young people in the investigation reported having an HIV-positive sexual partner.

Youth who participate in survival sex, sex trafficking, and prostitution are more likely to have high-risk partners. For example, Weber et al. (2002) showed that female street youth who engaged in prostitution had a greater probability of having more high-risk sexual partners.

Male-to-Male Sex

Having sex with other men is an HIV-risk behavior, and these behaviors may vary in different populations. In Ennett et al.'s (1999) research, 17.1 % of the men reported engaging in male-to-male sex.

Anal Sex

Anal sex is one of the risky sexual behaviors that may be prevalent among homeless and runaway young people, especially among those who engage in survival sex and prostitution and increases their HIV risk. In Weber et al.'s (2002) investigation, female street youth who engaged in prostitution were two times as likely to report having anal sex. In another investigation of homeless youth, Ennett et al. (1999) found that 34 % of the study participants reported having anal sex. According to Johnson et al. (1996), anal sex is one of the risk factors for AIDS in a sample of homeless youth.

Sex with an Intravenous Drug User

An HIV-risk behavior is having sex with an intravenous drug user and the rates may vary among different populations. Ennett et al. (1999) discovered that only 4.9 % of homeless young people in their study had an intravenous drug user as a sexual partner.

HIV Testing

HIV testing of homeless and runaway youth may lead to an increase in their participation in survival sex and thus increase their HIV/AIDS risk. Walls and Bell (2010), in their multistate study of 1625 homeless individuals aged 10–28, discovered that having been tested for HIV was actually related to an increased involvement in survival sex.

History of Sexually Transmitted Infections

Homeless and runaway youth with a history of STIs are at increased risk for HIV/AIDS. With regard to being diagnosed with an STI, 32.6 % of the homeless young people in Ennett et al.'s (1999) investigation reported such a diagnosis. Johnson et al. (1996) showed that an STI history was one of the prevalent risk factors for HIV among homeless youth.

Conduct Disorder

Having a conduct disorder (CD) may increase the risks of HIV (Booth and Zhang, 1997). Based on an investigation of 219 runaway and homeless youth from a drop-in center, Booth and Zhang (1997) found that 50 % of the male adolescents and 60 % of the female adolescents received the diagnosis of CD. Their results showed that CD had the strongest predictive capacity for predicting the runaway and homeless young people's lifetime use of heroin and cocaine. CD was also the strongest predictor of participating in survival sex, e.g., exchanging sex for drugs, money, food, and shelter. The disorder also was the strongest predictor of the number of drugs that the street youth used and the number of sex partners that they had in the 3 months prior to the study.

Sexual Orientation

A number of investigations have reported an association between sexual minority orientation and increased risk for STIs and HIV. For example, Whitbeck et al. (2004) discovered that homeless and runaway gay males had a higher probability of participating in survival sex than their heterosexual counterparts. In Marshall et al.'s (2010) research, sexual minority males had a higher likelihood of participating in survival sex than heterosexual male street youth. Runaway and homeless LGBT youth who participate in survival sex have increased odds of getting STIs, including HIV (Cochran et al. 2002; Whitbeck et al. 2004; Yates et al. 1988).

Interventions to Reduce Sexually Transmitted Infections and HIV/AIDS Transmission

Interventions to reduce the risks of STIs and HIV/AIDS should meeting the basic needs of runaway and homeless youth in order to reduce their participation in high-risk subsistence strategies such as survival sex (Johnson et al. 1996). Runaways and homeless young people should receive education about available services, especially since they may not about available services (Johnson et al. 1996).

Service providers should perform additional outreach activities to target runaways and homeless young people who are especially difficult to reach (Johnson et al. 1996). More emphasis should be placed on substance use reduction efforts and needle exchange programs, and other harm reduction efforts (Johnson et al. 1996). Early identification and prevention of childhood abuse and other risk factors may help reduce the risks of STIs and HIV/AIDS (Johnson et al. 1996).

Chapter 15
Mortality

Although runaway and homeless youth may be at risk for health problems such as sexually transmitted infections (STIs), human immune deficiency virus (HIV) infection, substance abuse, viral hepatitis, mental health difficulties, and injuries, knowledge about mortality rates in this vulnerable population is scarce (Roy et al. 2004). This chapter reviews mortality rates and the causes and predictors of mortality among runaway and homeless youth and adults. This analysis also examines social, behavioral, technological, and organizational factors related to the forensic classification of death. Both statistical reports and media reports of incidents involving the death of runaway and homeless young people will be included.

Mortality Rates

Several investigations have determined mortality rates for homeless adults. These reports show that mortality ratios vary among study settings. Barrow et al. (1999) relied on a sample of New York City homeless shelter residents and discovered a mortality ratio of 2.7 for men 20–24 years of age. Hwang (2000) evaluated mortality among men at Toronto, Ontario, Canada, homeless shelters and found a mortality ratio of 8.3 among men ages 18–24 years of age.

In an investigation of homeless adults in Boston, Hwang et al. (1997) demonstrated that the mortality ratio for men aged 18–24 years was 5.9, and for women in the same age group, the mortality ratio was 11.8. Nordentoft and Wandall-Holm (2003) revealed that among users of hostels for homeless people in Copenhagen, Denmark, females aging 15–24 years had a mortality ratio of 28.5. For males in the same age group, the mortality ratio was 13.3. In research on mortality among street youth and adults in the UK, Shaw and Dorling (1998) showed that among men aging 16–29 years without a fixed address (also known as "rough sleepers"), the

S.J. Morewitz, *Runaway and Homeless Youth*,
DOI 10.1007/978-3-319-30863-0_15

mortality ratio of 37.3 was obtained. Roy et al. (2004) demonstrated that, using a sample of Montreal, Quebec, Canada, street young people aging 14–25 years obtained a mortality ratio of 11.4.

Causes of Death

Runaway and homeless young people die from homicide, suicide, drug overdose, accidental death and injury, and medical conditions.

Homicide

Homicide is a cause of death among homeless and runaway youth and young adults. While on the street, youth and young adults may be killed by friends, acquaintances, and strangers.

In an investigation of the cause of death among homeless male adults, 18–24, in Boston, MA, Hwang et al. (1997) demonstrated that homicide was a main cause of death. Homicide was also a primary cause of death among homeless females in the same age group.

According to one media account, a runaway 13-year-old girl was reportedly tortured and killed (Stout 1996, August 16). After running away from her home on Long Island, New York, the girl was reportedly found tortured and killed in Easton, Pennsylvania. One suspect is in police custody and the police are seeking two more individuals in the alleged torture and murder of the runaway girl.

Homeless and runaway teen homicide victims may be linked to crimes such as prostitution, illicit drug activities, and robbery. According to one media report, a 13-year-old runaway girl who was found dead may have been associated with people involved in prostitution and drug activities (Stout 1996, August 16). Another female teen runaway who was found dead had reportedly told her mother that she had participated in occasional prostitution (Manning 2014, September 22).

Homeless and runaway youth who are killed may be victims of shootings. For example, in one media report, a 16-year-old runaway girl was found dead with gunshot wounds (Claytor 2014, March 22). The police regarded the death as a homicide.

Runaway and homeless youth may be killed by blunt trauma. In one media report, a 14-year-old runaway girl who was found dead reportedly had sustained extensive and severe head injuries (Williams 2000, October 16). Law enforcement had regarded the death as a homicide.

Single or multiple homicide victims may be found at the crime scene. For example, Claytor (2014, March 22) reported about two homicide victims: a 16-year-old girl and a 22-year-old male. In another media report, one possible homicide victim, a 14-year-old girl, was found (Williams 2000, October 16).

Homicide victims are found in both indoor and outdoor settings, and in outdoors the homicide victims may be hidden in wooded areas and other difficult-to-find locations. According to a media report, the body of a 17-year-old runaway boy was found in a wooded area. A passerby had discovered the body before 5 a.m. (baynews9.com, 2014, February 22). The police are treating the death as a possible homicide and have initiated a homicide investigation. The body of another runaway teen homicide victim, a 14-year-old girl, was found in horse racetrack that was no longer in business (Williams 2000, October 16).

Suicide

Another cause of death among homeless and runaway young people is suicide. In Montreal, Quebec, Canada, Roy et al. (2004) ascertained the cause of death for 22 homeless males aging 14–25 years and discovered that 12 had committed suicide. Cause of death was determined for four female street youth and adults, and one of the four had taken her own life. Suicide is also a leading cause of death among male Quebec residents in the 15–19 and 20–24 age groups. Hwang (2000) showed that suicide was a cause of death among men using homeless shelters in Toronto, Canada.

Investigators have analyzed the methods that runaway and homeless youth and adults use to commit suicide. In Roy et al.'s (2004) report, 13 individuals committed suicide (12 males and one female). Nine died by hanging themselves and two by jumping from a bridge. The two remaining youth committed suicide by running or jumping in front of a vehicle that was moving.

Runaway and homeless teens may commit suicide by shooting themselves with firearms. For example, in one media account, a male teen runaway and another male teen may have killed themselves after attempting an armed robbery (news9.com, n.d.).

Drug Overdose

Drug overdose is also a cause of death among runaway and homeless young people and young adults. According to Hwang (2000), unintentional drug overdoses was the third leading cause of death among male users of shelters in Toronto, Canada.

In Roy et al.'s (2004) analysis, drug overdose was the second leading cause of death among male street youth and adults 14–25 in Montreal, Quebec, Canada. Drug overdose was the leading cause of death among female street youth and adults in the same age group.

According to one media report, a runaway girl in Columbus, Ohio, was found dead after a drug overdose (Manning 2014, September 22). The news story indicated that the runaway girl had taken a large number of pills.

Accidents and Injuries (Other Than Motor Vehicle)

Accidents and injuries are a cause of death among runaway and homeless youth and adults. In their investigation, Hwang et al. (1997), in their study of homeless adults in Boston, MA, demonstrated that a cause of death among homeless males, 18–24, was poisoning and injuries besides motor vehicle accidents. Hwang (2000) discovered that accidents (besides motor vehicle accidents and poisoning) were the leading cause of death among male users of shelters, 18–24, in Toronto, Canada.

Runaway and homeless teens who abuse alcohol and other drugs are at increased risk of dying accidentally from the adverse effects of these substances. For example, according to one media account, a 16-year-old female runaway had died accidentally from the adverse consequences of heroin and diphenhydramine (Barton 2013, November 13).

Homeless and runaway young people also may die accidentally from weapons-related shootings. The media reported that a 16-year-old runaway girl was shot accidentally by a man who was the girl's boyfriend and who was living in the same home (Pulkkinen 2011, July 21). The man was arrested and charged with first-degree manslaughter. He had reportedly shot the girl with a revolver that was manufactured without a safety bar.

Motor Vehicle Accidents

Among homeless female youth and adults 18–24, Hwang et al. (1997) determined that motor vehicle accidents were a cause of death. Runaway and homeless teens, like teens in general, may engage in risky driving behaviors such as speeding and failure to follow other safe driving practices because of their lack of driving experience, poor judgment, the distractions and negative social influence of driving with their friends, and use of alcohol and other drugs (Morewitz and Goldstein 2014). Runaway teens fleeing their residence or institutional care setting may be especially at risk for motor vehicle fatalities because of the trauma of leaving home or care can distract them from driving safely. Homeless and runaway teens also may not be using their seatbelts or may be driving without a learner's permit or valid license because of their runaway or homeless status, placing them at higher risk for dangerous driving behaviors that result in motor vehicle-related fatalities. In addition, homeless and runaway young people are not likely to drive with supervising drivers because of their homeless/runaway status.

A variety of other conditions may increase the risk that runaway and homeless teens will die in motor vehicle crashes. For example, unsafe road and weather conditions place runaway and homeless young people at increased risk for motor vehicle-related fatalities. Some teen drivers may lack the experience and skills in handling unsafe road conditions.

According to one media report, a 16-year-old female runaway was killed in a motor vehicle crash (abc.net.au 2009, October 28). The police had indicated that at the time of the crash, the girl did not have a supervising driver with her. Moreover, the highway where her crash had occurred had been the site of two previous fatal crashes that week. A political party leader stated that the condition of the highway had played a role in all of the deaths.

Diseases

Roy et al. (2004) determined that one of the deaths among street youth and adults, 14–25, was fulminant hepatitis A. Another cause of death in their investigation was a noninfectious heart condition.

The Impact of Social, Behavioral, Technological, Organizational, and Other Factors that May Affect the Forensic Classification of Death

Mortality rates are based on the forensic classification of death, and the police and forensic specialists may be faced with uncertainty in their determination of the cause of death. For example, the police and forensic specialists may have difficulty distinguishing homicide from suicide. According to one media report, a 17-year-old female runaway and a man were discovered shot to death in a motel room (abcnewsradioonline.com 2012, September 17). The police were investigating the shoot deaths as either a murder-suicide or a double suicide.

The police and forensic specialists also must distinguish homicides from accidental deaths. They use a variety of evidence such as demographic, behavioral, physical, financial, and technologically based data to help them make those determinations in cases where the evidence is unclear.

The police and forensic specialists regard clues such as blood, physical condition of the body and clothes, location of the body, and the time that the decedent had run away or gone missing in determining the cause of death. In one death involving a 15-year-old female runaway, the police were regarding the death as suspicious and were conducting a homicide investigation (Reavy 2012, March 14). One of the girl's sneakers, which had blood on it, was discovered on a pedestrian bridge, and her body was found farther down in a river.

In the case of a 15-year-old female runaway whose body was found in a river, the police suspected that her death was a homicide because her body was found wrapped in a bag (Annable 2014, August 18).

In another death investigation, the police suspected foul play involving a missing teen who was discovered dead in a park (Bowen 2013, February 2). A passerby found the naked body of this girl, who was reported missing by her legal guardian a day earlier.

The police and forensic specialists increasingly are relying on technology to help them classify the cause of death in ambiguous cases. The police and forensic experts may review the decedents' Facebook accounts and other social media sites and computer hard drives to obtain motivational insights about the decedents and whether they previously run away or gone missing, used drugs, or had been prior victims of human trafficking, stalking, death threats, bullying, date rape, partner abuse, kidnapping, and other violent and threatening behaviors, which suggest that they might be homicide, suicide, or drug overdose victims (Morewitz 2003, 2004, 2008, 2016; Morewitz and Sturdy Colls forthcoming 2016).

Global positioning systems can be used to not only locate a runaway teen but also can be employed to help the police and forensic experts determine if the teen had been a victim of possible foul play. In one case involving the possible homicide of a 15-year-old girl who had gone missing, the girl's family had used cell phone global positioning systems to find her location (Reavy 2012, March 14). The police could determine if her location was where her family expected her to be, and if not, her location might indicate possible foul play.

In a case involving a 16-year-old female runaway who was discovered dead in an upper- socioeconomic status neighborhood, the police reportedly searched the decedent's Facebook accounts (Barton 2013, November 13). The police searched for writings or photographs to help them determine what had happened to the runaway girl on the night of her death.

Social factors such as the attempts of families and friends of the decedent to persuade the police to change their classification of death may affect the ultimate forensic classification of death. For example, parents may want the police and forensic specialists to view the death of their runaway and homeless child as a homicide rather than a suicide. For example, in the case of a 13-year-old female runaway who reportedly died from smoke inhalation, the mother of the girl rejected the police's theory that her daughter had left a candle burning in a motor home where she was staying (Brown 2005, June 17). The mother reportedly "stopped short of" of saying that her daughter's death was a result of foul play. She considered her daughter to be very "smart and streetwise" and that her daughter would have escaped the burning motor home if she could have done so.

Other social, institutional, and political factors can influence the forensic classification of death. For example, in cases of the death of homeless and runaway teens in police custody, some police personnel would prefer to have the death classified as a suicide instead of a homicide committed by the police. As a consequence, the reliability of the results may be adversely affected by misclassifications.

In analyzing drug overdose cases, forensic experts may have a problem distinguishing intentional from unintentional drug overdoses (Heale et al. 2003; Darke and Ross 2001). This problem may be especially relevant for females. Runaway and homeless female young people and adults, like females of the same age group in the general population, may be more likely to commit suicide using drug overdoses and other less violent methods than their male counterparts (Brent et al. 1999). As a result, these drug overdoses may appear to be unintentional when in fact they are intentional suicidal acts.

Mortality Risk Factors

Investigators have assessed factors that increase the mortality risk among homeless youth and adults (Roy et al. 2004). Roy et al. (2004) discovered that HIV infection was the best predictor of mortality risks among homeless youth and adults, 14–25, in Montreal, Quebec, Canada. In their report, four of the deceased persons had acquired HIV infection. Other predictors of mortality risks in their study were daily alcohol use in the previous month, homelessness in the previous 6 months, injection of drugs in the previous 6 months, and male gender.

Other researchers have found substance abuse to be a predictor of mortality among homeless individuals (Nielsen et al. 2011). In an investigation of psychiatric disorders and mortality among individuals 16 and older in homeless shelters in Denmark, Nielsen et al. (2011) discovered that those with a registered substance abuse disorder were linked to the highest risk of mortality.

Chapter 16
Street Youth in Different Countries

This chapter describes the diverse life experiences of street youth in different countries. In various nations, young people may live at home, go to school, and work in the streets or live and work on the streets without going to school. In many cases, street youth's participation in family, school life, and street activities changes over time, and the meanings of street life may vary in different settings. This chapter assesses such conditions as demographic characteristics, family abuse and neglect, family conflict, low socioeconomic status (SES), behavioral problems in school, the lack of educational and occupational opportunities, and child trafficking are analyzed. In this chapter, the problems of street life are discussed. This chapter also discusses the role of governments and organizations in developing policies and interventions to assist young people on the streets.

In various nations, leaders of governments and private sector organizations have been very concerned about the problems of street youth and related problems such as child trafficking. In some countries, governments and organizations have developed policies and interventions to assist young people on the streets. For example, interventions have been designed to reunify street youth with their families and provide opportunities for them to live as emancipated youth (Scanlon et al. 1998).

Government officials and leaders of social service agencies increasingly recognize the underlying problems that cause youth to leave their homes such as child trafficking, family abuse and neglect, family conflict, low SES, behavioral problems in school, and the lack of educational and occupational opportunities (Zhao et al. 2012). Street youth in many countries are being trafficked for prostitution, sex slavery, forced labor, and military, paramilitary, and guerilla warfare. Governmental and private organizations are developing policies and programs to help youth and their families with these underlying problems.

Governmental and private sector interventions may be based on mainly negative images of street children. For example, Ennew (2003) notes that street youth are often viewed as antisocial and incorrigible. People may pity or fear these street young people.

S.J. Morewitz, *Runaway and Homeless Youth*,
DOI 10.1007/978-3-319-30863-0_16

Who Are Street Youth?

Street children and adolescents in various countries are not homogeneous (Aptekar and Heinonen 2003). They may live at home, go to school, and work in the streets or live and work on the streets without going to school. In many cases, street youth's participation in family, school life, and street activities changes over time. Young people on the streets may be victims of child trafficking. They may be trafficked for prostitution, pornography, sex slavery, and forced labor.

According to Ennew (2003), the meanings of street life vary in different settings. The notion of living on the street can differ in various parts of the same city. Living on the street may mean socializing with peers, places where social and economic activities occur in financially depressed areas, and areas where consumers and employees move around. Street life may also vary depending on the level of urbanization.

Researchers may not assess street youth's actual life experiences (Ennew 2003; Panter-Brick 2002). Young people on the streets may not be asked about their own perceptions and beliefs about their lives on the streets (Ennew 2003). According to Panter-Brick (2002), investigators emphasize studying the lifestyle of street youth and neglect to study the range and depth of the young people's experiences on the streets. Instead, researchers may rely on reports from the youth's parents, teachers, or staff of other organizations (Ennew 2003).

Living at Home and/or Living on the Streets

Experts have noted that young people on the streets are a highly diverse group of people. Some youth live at home and work on the streets; other children and adolescents live and work on the streets. Specialists characterize this latter group as being "of the street." Aptekar and Heinonen (2003) also note that some youth may be "on and off" the street.

Aptekar and Heinonen (2003) note that the differentiation between "of" and "on" the street does not reflect the complexities of street life in large urban areas. Children and adolescents have a variety of living arrangements and may change their arrangements frequently, blurring the distinction between "of" and "on" the streets.

Age Characteristics

Lalor (1999) found that a majority of street children around the globe ranged in age from 10 to14 years. In Ali et al.'s (2004) study of street children in Pakistan, the average age that children became street youth was under 10 years.

In their analysis of street youth in Nazareth, Ethiopia, Beyene and Berhane (1997) found that the age of the young people ranged from 5 to 18 with a mean of 12.9 (standard deviation).

What is the youngest age that children become street youth? Some parents may be very hesitant to allow children younger than 10 years of age to enter the streets because they perceive the streets to be very harsh (Veale 1993; Lalor 1999). At the other end of the age range, certain street children by the age of 14 or 15 may be less able to beg effectively because they no longer have childlike appearance, which previously had helped them generate sympathy among passersby (Aptekar 1989a).

Gender

In many nations around the world, males are more likely than females to become street youth (Lalor 1999). In two investigations (Felsman 1981; Aptekar 1988), males made up the entire study samples. The authors in these two studies note that people in Columbia tend to view girls on the streets as prostitutes instead of street youth. In their analysis of street children in Aracaju, Brazil, Abdelgalil et al. (2004) discovered that males were more likely to be street youth than their female counterparts. Similarly, in their analysis of street youth in Pakistan, Ali et al. (2004) discovered that 81 % of the respondents were males.

Gender and work roles, values, and norms may help to account for these differences. Male street youth may be more visible to authorities and researchers if they are living and working in outside locations compared to female street young people who may be more likely than males to work as employees inside buildings. For example, Abdelgalil et al. (2004) reported that female street children were employed as housemaids, shop assistants, and restaurant and bar employees, while male street youth worked on the streets.

Cultural traditions in rural regions may reduce the likelihood that girls will take to the streets (Lalor 1999). In rural areas, such as Nepal, families depend on girls for home and agricultural work, and this dependence on girls may keep them from becoming street youth.

Similarly, in some urban regions, families may want girls to perform childcare duties for their younger siblings and assist with home chores, which allow mothers to work in nonfamily-based employment settings (Lalor 1999). According to Connolly (1990), this cultural tradition is in place in Latin American nations. As a result, girls are discouraged from working on the streets.

People may also fear that girls face significant threats to their safety while working outside the home (Lalor 1999). For example, in Chatterjee's (1992) investigation, parents in India did not want to have males pay attention to their daughters during puberty, and the girls often had to stop working outside the household at that time.

The Worldwide Prevalence of Street Youth

According to the United Nations (UN) Department of International Economic and Social Affairs, the number of street youth under 18 years of age who were employed (part-time or full-time) or resided on the streets ranged from 30 million to 170 million (Dewees and Klees 1995). According to the UN Children's Fund (UNICEF), the number of street young in Latin America ranged from 25 million to 45 million (Lusk 1992). In 1988, Childhope, an advocacy organization serving the international community, estimated that 100 million young people were on the streets (Dewees and Klees 1995).

Many young people live and work on the streets because they were trafficked for prostitution, sex slavery, pornography, forced labor, and armed conflict. Child trafficking involves recruiting, transporting, transferring, or receiving youth for the goal of exploitation (UNICEF n.d.; Morewitz 2016). According to the International Labour Organization in 2002, 1.2 million children are trafficked annually (UNICEF n.d.). According to UNICEF, about one million children are victims of sex trafficking in Southeast Asia each year (Revaz n.d.). UNICEF estimates that another one million are sex trafficking victims around the world.

Researchers have difficulty obtaining reliable and valid estimates of this highly mobile population (Gurgel et al. 2004; Lusk 1992). Street young people may frequently move back and forth from residing on the streets to living at home with their family, making reliable and valid estimates difficult to make.

Investigators use different criteria and definitions of being a street youth (Scanlon et al. 1998). Analysts also employ varying sampling procedures that may lead to different prevalence and incidence data. In addition, investigators use different criteria in determining who is a street child or adolescent.

Risk Factors for Street Young People

Factors that increase the probability that young people will become street youth in different countries may differ depending on whether the young people work in streets (are "on" the street) or live on the streets (are "of" the street) (Rosa et al. 1992). Various social, cultural, economic, family, and educational factors may push or pull children and adolescents into these situations (Yiu and Khong 2009).

Global Factors

Global factors such as high demand for human trafficking; rapid social, technological, and economic changes, including poverty; the worldwide expansion of international corporations; modernization of agricultural methods; urbanization; migration/immigration; the collapse of governments; political violence; armed conflict; the human immune virus (HIV)/acquired immunodeficiency syndrome (AIDS) epidemic; and natural disasters lead to disruptions in traditional community and family systems, which increase the risk that young people will become street children (Abdelgalil et al. 2004; Zhao et al. 2012; Veale and Dona 2003; Stephenson 2001; Hollingsworth 2012).

Human Trafficking

According to the International Labour Organization, 20.9 million individuals, both adults and children, are victims of human trafficking around the world (National Human Trafficking Resource Center n.d.a, b). Street youth around the world face the risk of being kidnapped and coerced or tricked into sex and forced labor trafficking, organ trafficking, and armed conflicts (International Labour Organization n.d.; UNHCR n.d.; Family and Youth Services Bureau, National Clearinghouse on Families and Youth n.d.; National Human Trafficking Resource Center n.d.a, b; Revaz n.d.; Hollingsworth 2012; Morewitz 2016; Morewitz 2008).

According to the Coalition to Stop the Use of Child Soldiers, approximately 300,000 children in more than 40 nations around the globe are coerced or tricked into serving as child soldiers in armed conflicts (Revaz n.d.; Hollingsworth 2012). The Coalition to Stop the Use of Child Soldiers estimates that another 500,000 children serve in paramilitary, guerilla, and civil military units in over 85 nations. Runaway and homeless youth are especially vulnerable to being coerced or tricked into becoming child soldiers. In addition, children are susceptible into becoming child soldiers because of their lack of maturity.

Child soldiers are frequently forced to commit atrocities (Revaz n.d.). In addition, child soldiers are coerced into going into minefields, the front lines of armed conflicts, and other dangerous settings and are forced to go on suicide missions. They may also be used as sex servants. In addition, traffickers may provide alcohol and other drugs to the child soldiers in order to help the children feel courageous during armed conflicts.

Various forms of human trafficking are very profitable and the demand for children is especially high. For example, sex trafficking for the purposes of prostitution, pornography, and sex slavery is a multi-billion dollar industry (Revaz n.d.). Internet advertising has greatly facilitated sex trafficking, and sex tourists (individuals who travel to another country to have sex with prostitutes) and pedophiles take advantage of Internet advertising and the ease of global travel to expand the demand for sex trafficking.

Children who become AIDS orphans, e.g., lose their parents to AIDS, and other children who are victims of famine, drought, and other economic difficulties are also at risk of becoming street youth and are susceptible to becoming sex, forced labor, and organ trafficking victims (Hollingsworth 2012). For example, in sub-Saharan Africa, millions of AIDS orphans are being created by the HIV/AIDS pandemic. These AIDS orphans often become street youth and are at increased risk of becoming victims of sex and forced labor trafficking (Hollingsworth 2012).

Drought and famine in Somalia has been associated with an increase in human trafficking. For example, Kahare (n.d.) reports the case of one girl in Somalia, A.S., who was trafficked into Kenya and sold into employment as an attendant for her buyer.

Urbanization, which is stimulated by economic development, can lead to a reduction of employment opportunities in rural areas. For example, in China, economic development has triggered migration from rural to urban areas (Zhao et al. 2012). One trend is that parents in rural regions may migrate to cities and leave their children under the care of grandparents or other relatives. Left-behind children many run away from these rural areas to search for their parents.

Abdelgalil et al. (2004) revealed that the families of street children in Aracaju, Brazil, had a history of migration, which could mean a lack of strong ties to the local community. As a result of a history of migration, recent arrivals may be less able to adjust socially and financially in their new home areas, increasing the risk of that their children will become street youth.

Poverty and Low Socioeconomic Status

Poverty and low SES are major risk factors for children and adolescents becoming street youth in different countries (Abdelgalil et al. 2004; Rosa et al. 1992; Zhao et al. 2012). Abdelgalil et al. (2004), in a study of the family characteristics of street children in Aracaju, Brazil, found that most of the families lived in very low-income communities. These families have experienced conditions associated with low SES such as a high degree of illiteracy and unemployment.

In an investigation of street youth of Recife, Brazil, Rosa et al. (1992) showed that a family's financial need was the primary reason for the youth being "on" the street. Children "on" the street were often more likely to come from families that were headed by the mother, families that did not have running water, and those that did not have toilet facilities.

In Zhao et al.'s (2012) analysis of runaways in China, children and adolescents who desired to escape poverty was a reason for running away from home. In China, government officials recognize the need to deal with severe inequality in SES since the gap between low- and high-SES groups has increased. The problem of SES inequality is especially apparent in rural regions of China where many people are poor and have to perform strenuous manual labor. These rural areas also lack job opportunities, and youth may run away or leave home to seek employment opportunities in urban areas.

Family Disintegration

The breakup of families may increase the risk that young people will become street youth. In Abdelgalil et al.'s (2004) study of street children in Aracaju, Brazil, most of the families were headed by a single, female parent. Rosa et al. (1992), in their analysis of street youth in Recife, Brazil, discovered that children "on" the streets and "of" the streets were 3 and 3.7 times, respectively, more likely to come from families that had a female parent or her male partner.

Relations with Parents and Other Family Members

In some nations, children and adolescents run away and become street youth because of family difficulties such as conflicts with parents and problems in communicating with them (Yiu and Khong 2009; Zhao et al. 2012). Youth may feel that their parents are making unrealistic expectations about family responsibilities and rules and may run away from home to escape the stigma and trauma of not meeting their parents' expectations.

In contrast, Lalor (1999) reports that street youth often have good relations with their family members. Street youth may meet regularly or occasionally with family members. In Lusk's (1989) analysis of Columbian street youth, 90 % indicated that they occasionally or regularly contacted their family members. In another study of Columbian street youth, Aptekar (1989b) found that 16 % "had no known family to contact." Felsman (1981) discovered that only a very small percentage (2.5 %) of the Columbian children had been abandoned by their family. In a study of street youth in Lima, Peru, Boyden (1986) noted that an estimated 3 % of the 200,000 children who worked on the streets actually resided on the streets.

Drug Use

Families that are characterized by drug use may be more likely to have children who become street youth in different countries. Parents who are addicted to alcohol and other drugs may become abusive and neglectful, which increase the risks that their children will run away or become street youth (Zhao et al. 2012). In an investigation of street children in Aracaju, Brazil, Abdelgalil et al. (2004) reported that a majority of families of street youth had high rates of drug use.

In different nations, youth's use of alcohol and drugs may increase their probability of running away from home. For example, Abdelgalil et al. (2004) discovered that parents indicated that drug use was a major factor that caused their children to live on the streets.

Abuse, Violence, and Neglect

Physical, sexual, and emotional abuse increase the risk that young people will run away and/or become street youth (Zhao et al. 2012; Yiu and Khong 2009). For example, in a study of juvenile delinquents, a history of child abuse was linked to an increased likelihood of running from home (Kim et al. 2009; Zhao et al. 2012). As previously noted, parental addiction to alcohol and other drugs increase the likelihood that parents will become abusive and neglectful, increasing the chances that their children will turn to the streets (Zhao et al 2012).

In their investigation of runaway young people in Singapore, Yiu and Khong (2009) discovered that parent–child conflict, poor communication, and "violence with parents and siblings" increased the risk that the youth would run away from home. In their study of runaway young people in China, Zhao et al. (2012) describe a case of a stepmother who reportedly was angry with her stepson for wetting his bed. She made him sleep face down and place his sexual parts in a hole so that he would wet his bed. In addition, she would beat him and not feed him if he did not do his chores in an acceptable way.

Peer Influence and Desire for Independence and Fun

Many young people have an intense desire to associate with their peers, and their motivation in interacting with their friends increases the likelihood that they will run away and/or become street children (Yiu and Khong 2009). Youth may see running away and street life as a way to have fun by avoiding the discipline of family life and school work (Zhao et al. 2012). Moreover, youth often seek independence from their parents and run away or become street children to get their independence from their parents (Yiu and Khong 2009).

Parents may recognize the impact of peers in pulling their children to the streets. For example, Abdelgalil et al. (2004) showed that parents believed that peers played a major role in influencing whether their children decided to go to the streets.

School-Associated Problems

In various countries, youth who are having school-associated difficulties such as poor grades, truancy, school absences, behavioral difficulties in class, and problems interacting with teachers and school administrators have an increased risk of becoming dissatisfied with school and dropping out or being expelled from school and becoming runaways and street youth (Yiu and Khong 2009; Zhao et al. 2012).

Pressure from teachers and parents about educational expectations may trigger some youth to run away from home (Zhao et al. 2012). Teachers and school administrators may respond negatively to students who exhibit behavioral problems in schools, which may increase the students' chance of poor school achievement, school absences, truancy, suspensions, and expulsions. As a result of these problems, students may be more likely to run away from home.

Teachers and administrators may identify or learn about students who are potential runaways and try to persuade them not to run away (Zhao et al. 2012). The teachers and administrators may work with the student's parents in preventing the student from running away.

Breaking the Law

In different nations, children and adolescents who run away and/or become street youth may have engaged in criminal behavior and have been arrested, and their criminal behavior and experience with the criminal justice system may increase their chances of running away and/or becoming street youth (Zhao et al. 2012).

Street youth with a history of criminal behavior often run away from home. These students often frequently perform poorly in school and become truant, increasing their likelihood of police contact (Zhao et al. 2012).

Internet-Related Factors

In different nations, children and adolescents may run away or leave home because they are spending too much time on the Internet and playing video games and have become addicted to these activities (Zhao et al. 2012). In China, government authorities have expressed concern that young people are addicted to the Internet and are exposed to the unhealthy effects of Internet-related juvenile delinquency, pornography, and other negative Internet influences (Zhao et al. 2012). For example, young people might become juvenile delinquents because of their participation in Internet activities.

In terms of promoting running away and leaving home, Zhao et al. (2012) described how many young people in China are truant and spend time in Internet bars. Youth often stayed in Internet bars for hours without wanting to go home, which trigger arguments with their parents. The youth's participation in Internet bars may eventually lead to them to running away or leaving home.

Another reason why children and adolescents run away or leave home is that they fall in love as a result of Internet-related communication and relationships (Zhao et al. 2012). In China and other nations, young people through the Internet may fall in love with "virtual" boyfriends or girlfriends or they never actually meet. In other cases, the children and adolescents may first connect through the Internet and then later meet in person. In some instances, girls may be lured into prostitution as a result of their participation in relationships with virtual boyfriends.

Young people in China and in other nations may fear that their parents will oppose their virtual relationships and run away from home as a consequence. Zhao et al. (2012) discussed the case of 15-year-old girl who met a person on the Internet and fell in love with this person who she had never met in person. Her father was very angry that she had this Internet relationship, and he notified her teachers who also tried to convince her to break off this virtual relationship. Despite her father's and teachers' efforts, the girl ran away to locate her virtual boyfriend. She could not find her virtual boyfriend in the city where he allegedly lived and became a street youth so that she could continue to search for him.

Media Portrayal of Street Life and Lifestyle Factors

The media may portray cities as glamorous and fun, encouraging rural and suburban youth to run away or leave home to flee their boring lifestyle. In addition, young people may be influenced by the media such as movies, videos, and print media that promote running away and street life as exciting and fun (Zhao et al. 2012).

In one case, a 14-year-old boy in China reportedly saw movies and was influenced by them to such an extent that he ran away (Zhao et al. 2012). When on the street, the boy reportedly joined a gang after running out of money. The police reportedly arrested him when he attempted to rob an individual.

Zhao et al. (2012) also reported that two adolescent girls reportedly ran away from home after watching movies and television programs about gang life. The two girls reported that they had run away to become gang members in the "underground society." They resisted to go back to their parents after the police arrested them and were angry with law enforcement and their parents for keeping them from their stimulating lifestyle.

Street Life Experiences

Various conditions in different countries influence the life experiences of street youth. Youth who live at home but work on the streets may differ in their experiences than young people who are "of the streets," e.g., those who both live and work on the streets (Campos et al. 1994). In addition, street youth in countries with high levels of poverty, unemployment, family dysfunction, and low levels of education may suffer extreme deprivation and violent victimization on the streets. Nations that use highly punitive and violent approaches to deal with young people on the streets may also suffer violence at the hand of the police and security personnel.

Income-Generating Activities Among Street Youth

Street youth who are "on" the street often contribute their street-based income to their families (Rosa et al. 1992). Children "on" the street may bring some or all of their earnings from the street to their families. For example, Rosa et al. (1992) reported that 94 % of the youth "on" the street bring between 50 and 100 % of their income to their families.

Sherman et al. (2005), in their investigation of street children in Lahore, Pakistan, showed that the street youth performed odd jobs, begged, and pick pocketed people as their main sources of reported income. In a study of street children in Nazareth, Ethiopia, Beyene and Berhane (1997) discovered that a majority of the street youth worked odd jobs.

In their investigation of street children in Aracaju, Brazil, Abdelgalil et al. (2004) found gender difference in work. The investigators showed that males were more likely to be employed on the streets, while females tended to work in homes, shops, restaurants, and bars.

The type of income-generating activities that street youth engage in may vary depending on how much time youth spent on the streets (Forster et al. 1996). In their study of street youth in southern Brazil, Forster et al. (1996) showed that youth who stayed on the streets all day and slept there engaged in theft. In contrast, young people who lived with their families had a higher probability of reporting that they sold food, washed cars, or polished shoes.

Street-Based Work Exploitation

In their research on street children in Recife, Brazil, Rosa et al. (1992) demonstrated that street-based work exploitation was widespread. For those "of" the street, more than 75 % made less than the minimum wage. Fifty percent of these children made less than half of the minimum wage.

School Attendance and Educational Performance Among Street Youth

A major obstacle for street youth in different countries is that many of them do not attend school or have limited attendance, which impairs their opportunities to have gainful employment and related successes in the future. Based on a study of 5138 street children in Nazareth, Ethiopia, Beyene and Berhane (1997) reported that 18.3 % were going to school at the time of the study. In an investigation of street children in Recife, Rosa et al. (1992) discovered that more than a third of the street children were not in school.

In fact, many young people drop out of school when they become street youth. In Rosa et al.'s (1992) study, 87 % of the street youth in Recife dropped out of school after "going on the street."

For street children who are able to attend school, their school performance may suffer because their street activities interfere with their school work. In a report on street children in Aracaju, Brazil, Abdelgalil et al. (2004) found street children performed poorly in school and had high rates of school dropout. Rosa et al. (1992) showed that street youth who were going to school were behind one or two grade levels based on their age.

Drug and Alcohol Use Among Street Youth

In different countries, many young people on the streets use alcohol and other drugs. Sherman et al. (2005) found in their investigation of street children in Lahore, Pakistan, that street children may use drugs as a coping mechanism. Based on interviews of 565 male and female children in five Brazilian state capitals, Noto et al. (1997) discovered that 74.3 % had reported using drugs (excluding alcohol and tobacco) at least one time during their life.

In their study of 347 street children in Lahore, Pakistan, Sherman et al. (2005) discovered that 67.1 % of the youth reported drug use in the month prior to registering in a mobile social and health services program for street youth. Seventeen percent of the respondents indicated that they had never taken drugs and 15.9 % stated that they were ex-drug users.

Street youth may vary in the types of drugs that they use. Noto et al. (1997) found that respondents most frequently reported using solvents and marijuana. The investigators also found regional variations in drug use among street young people. Street young people in the southeast region of Brazil were more likely to use cocaine, including crack. In contrast, street youth in the northeast region of Brazil had a higher likelihood of taking psychotropic drugs.

Young people's use of alcohol and other drugs on the streets may differ depending on how much time they spent on the streets (Forster et al. 1996). Based on their analysis of street youth in southern Brazil, Forster et al. (1996) revealed that young people who stayed on day on the streets and slept on the streets were more likely to report using both alcohol and tobacco. More than 25 % of the youth who spent all day on the streets and sleeping there were more likely to report alcohol use. Fifty-eight percent of this subgroup of street youth reported tobacco use. This subgroup also reported regularly abusing inhalant (40 %). Twenty-six percent of young people in this subgroup also reported regular marijuana use.

In contrast, less than 12 % of children and adolescents who lived with their families and attended school took illegal drugs (Forster et al. 1996). Only 4 % of this subgroup reported regular marijuana use. Also, only 4 % of youth who went to school reported sniffing solvents.

Which factors increase the risk of alcohol and other drug use among street children and adolescents? In Sherman et al.'s (2005) study, various conditions were associated with current drug use compared to never using drugs. Youth who were 13 years of age or older, those who reported income on a daily basis, and having a criminal history were more likely to be current drug users. Moreover, street youth who indicated that they wanted to go home, experienced hatred from the public, and participated in survival sex for items such as drugs or food were more likely to currently use drugs.

Survival Sex

In various nations, street youth may engage in survival sex, e.g., exchange sex for drugs, food, shelter, money, and other positive resources (Sherman et al. 2005; Raffaelli et al. 1993). In Lahore, Pakistan, Sherman et al. (2005) discovered that 48 % of the street children in their investigation indicated that they had participated in survival sex. According to the authors, street children engage in survival sex as a coping mechanism.

Delinquency and History of Arrests While on the Streets

Youth on the streets may have extensive contact with the police or security personnel and have been arrested (Sherman et al. 2005). These street young people are often viewed as a threat or nuisance, and the police have derogatory slang words for them. In Ethiopia, the police refer to street young people as "vermin" (Lalor 1999). In Columbia, the police call street youth "the plague" or "dirty faces." In Cameroon, the police refer to them as "mosquitoes."

Street youth may engage in illegal activities on the streets such as theft and alcohol and drug use that increase their risk of being arrested. In other instances, street youth beg on the streets, which also may increase their risk of being arrested. In their investigation, Sherman et al. (2005) found that 52.7 % of the street youth had been arrested during their life.

During their adolescent years, youth on the streets may start out participating in petty theft such as stealing from shops and then increasingly engage in more serious crimes such as robberies (Lalor 1999; Felsman 1981; Aptekar 1988; Lusk 1989). In his analysis of street youth in Colombia, Lusk (1989) formulated a three-stage model to describe the ways in which youth go from delinquents to adult criminals. In the first stage, children who are preadolescent or pre-*gamin* tend to live with their family but are on the street part of the time in order to help financially support their family members. If the opportunity comes up, the pre-*gamin* may participate in petty theft. In the second stage, adolescents who may have less involvement with their families and may sleep on the streets are known as *gamins*. The *gamins* may live with other delinquents and use their delinquent acts to financially support themselves. Delinquents in the third stage, who are known as the *largos*, are older adolescents who have embraced the culture and ideology of street life and have an increased probability of becoming criminals in adulthood.

Researchers have discovered similar patterns of street delinquency in other countries (Lalor 1999). The lack of conventional opportunities for advancement may reinforce the street delinquents' perceptions of themselves as delinquents (Aptekar 1988). In Ethiopia, UNICEF (1993) found that street youth became more involved in delinquent acts throughout their adolescence. In their study, older boys (ages 13–15) reported two times the rate of theft than boys, ages 10–12. Older street boys (ages 16–18) had a higher rate of imprisonment than those in the 11–15 age group. These older street youth also were more like to smoke, use alcohol, and chew *khat*, a mild narcotic plant than the younger-age street youth. The investigation revealed that the older-age street young people engage in theft to support their expensive substance abuse, while younger street youth engaged in theft to obtain food. More youth were in the latter group. Researchers also discovered that in Addis Ababa, a small group of street delinquents participated in a variety of crimes such as rape, assault of younger individuals, consorting with prostitutes, and heavy alcohol consumption.

Street young people may differ in their adherence to conventional values and beliefs, which affects their delinquency patterns (Lalor 1999). For example, street youth in Addis Ababa may be less violent than street youth in Latin America. The former may be more likely to hold traditional values of discipline and respect. In contrast, Aptekar (1988), in his analysis of street youth in Colombia, described them as "nonconformist."

The operations of the police and security forces can affect the behaviors and values of street delinquents (Lalor 1999). For example, for several years, soldiers from the Ethiopian Peoples' Revolutionary Democratic Front policed the streets and reportedly shot looters, many of whom were street boys. This type of policing may have resulted in low rates of crime.

Victimization Among Street Youth in Different Countries

Street young people face the risks of being victimized. Males may be at risk of being physically assaulted (Lalor 1999). In an analysis of street young people in Addis Ababa, Lalor (1999) reported that more than 50 % of male street youth interviewed indicated that they had been physically assaulted on a regular basis. These males also noted that their injuries were often severe. They reported being the victims of stabbings, razor blade slashes, and fractures, including skull fractures. The male youth indicated that they often suffered these injuries during attacks with other street youth. They would regularly fight over who had the right to work in a given location. Moreover, fights would often occur when street youth felt insulted.

Street young people reported that they were regularly the victims of theft (Lalor 1999). In Lalor's (1999) study, youth on the streets are often "robbed of anything remotely valuable." The victims are frequently robbed by older youth on the streets. Those who can find a secure location for their valuable can avoid being robbed.

In different countries, street youth may be at increased risk of being murdered. For example, death squads, which were allegedly established by the police, allegedly were responsible for killing street children in different areas of Latin America (Lalor 1999). According to two cochairmen of the Independent Commission on International Humanitarian Issues, a radio station in one major city in South America that had an official license allegedly ask people to kill street youth (Agnelli 1986). This type of activity allegedly resulted in repeated killings of street youth (Lalor 1999).

In Lalor's (1999) report, older male youths in Addis Ababa were likely to threaten, intimidate, and rob younger female street youth. For example, the author found that 78 % of the girls reported that they had been beaten. Street girls might be reluctant to give the older boys their money so the boys would beat the girls until they did. Older male street youth would also trick naïve girls who had come from rural areas. For example, the older street males would offer to carry their luggage and then rob them of their luggage.

Female street youth face the risk of sexual assaults and rape. In Lalor's (1999) analysis, 44 % of the female street children reported that they had been raped. In the study, male street youth indicated that they would rape street girls since the male street youth did not have money to pay for the services of prostitutes. Male street youth also noted that they felt that unlike prostitutes, the female street youth did not have AIDS and other sexually transmitted infections (STIs). Lalor (1999) also showed that an additional 26 % of the female street youth indicated that they had been the victim of sexual attacks. Girls on the streets would try to avoid rape and other sexual attacks by trying to go inside buildings before darkness.

In Lalor's (1999) study of street youth in Addis Ababa, 75 % of the female youth reported that they had been solicited for sex. A majority of street girls are solicited for sex if they are sexually mature, appeared pregnant, or had a child. In this investigation, 25 % of the street girls had experienced pregnancy.

Lalor (1999) discovered that victimization was less for girls who were "on" the street than street girls "of" the streets. For example, the investigator showed that the girls on the streets suffered milder physical assaults and occurred less often than the girls of the streets. The boys also robbed the girls on the streets of smaller quantities of their goods compared to the girls of the streets. The girls on the streets also suffer less sexual victimization than the girls of the streets.

Street youth also may be more likely to have a history of victimization even before they enter the streets. Scanlon et al. (1998) noted that street children around the world may be violence victims before they arrive on the streets.

Peer Influence, Gangs, and Lifestyle

Peer influence, gangs, and lifestyle can have a significant impact on young people on the streets. Young people join gangs to help protect themselves from the police and security forces, other street youth, passersby, and customers (Lusk 1989; Connolly 1990; Lalor 1999). Gangs also provide the functions of a family such nurturance and love for youth who may have limited on no relations with their families (Agnelli 1986).

Campos et al. (1994) showed that youth who lived on the streets were more likely to engage in substance use than those who lived at home. Noto et al. (1997) found that a group lifestyle can lead to street youth initiating their use of drugs. Moreover, a group lifestyle can promote the maintenance of drug use among young people on the streets.

HIV/STI Risks Among Street Youth in Various Countries

Youth living on the streets may have an increased exposure to early onset of sexual behaviors that increase their risk for human immunodeficiency virus (HIV)/STIs (Luna and Rotheram-Borus 1992). In their study of street children and adolescents in Belo Horizonte, Brazil, Campos et al. (1994) found that young people living on the streets were more likely to have early onset of sexual behaviors.

Street youth participate in sexual activities as a coping mechanism that increases their risk of HIV and other STIs. As noted by Sherman et al. (2005), in their study of street youth in Lahore, Pakistan, the high prevalence of survival sex (48 %) increases the youth's risk for HIV and other STIs.

Likewise, Raffaelli et al. (1993) discovered that young people, aged 9–18 years in a Brazilian city, participated in sexual practices that increase their risk for HIV and other STIs. According to Raffaelli et al. (1993), sexual activity among street youth is caused by multiple factors and is a recurring behavior in this vulnerable population.

Drug use is associated with survival sex and the risk for HIV and STIs. In Sherman et al.'s (2005) investigation, ever engaging in survival sex was linked to current drug use among street children. In their analysis of homeless and runaway young people, Farrow et al. (1992) discovered that alcohol and drug use is related to deficits in child and adolescent development and emotional immaturity, which both may increase their risk for HIV and other STIs.

Young people on the streets may lack effective knowledge and beliefs to prevent the transmission of HIV and other STIs. In one investigation of 379 street youth from one major city in Brazil, Raffaelli et al. (1995) found mixed results regarding the young people's HIV-/AIDS-associated knowledge. The researchers found that 84 % of the street youth knew about the transmission of HIV. However, only 54 % were correct about the casual transmission of HIV. The study results also revealed that 64 % of the street youth had correct knowledge about HIV prevention. Only 37.5 % of those young people interviewed indicated that they had talked to a person about the disease. According to the results, 54 % of the interviewees reported that they had recently heard something AIDS.

Street youth in various countries may not take effective precautions HIV/AIDS. In Raffaelli et al.'s (1995) study, more than 50 % of the young people indicated that they used HIV-risk reduction strategies. However, only a low percentage of the street youth used effective procedures. In their investigation, among 65 % of the youth who had started sexual activity, only 18 % of the street youth reported ever using a condom in their lifetime. In addition, only 10 % of the young people indicated that they had used a condom at their most recent sexual intercourse. Overall, Raffaelli et al. (1995) demonstrated that street youth who had more HIV/AIDS knowledge had a higher probability of taking disease-prevention strategies.

Self-Harm Behaviors Among Street Youth

In response to the stress and trauma of the streets, young people on the streets in different countries may be at increased risk of engaging in self-harming behaviors such as cutting themselves (Sherman et al. 2005). Based on their investigation of street youth in Lahore, Pakistan, Sherman et al. (2005) discovered that 40 % of the children sampled indicated that they had engaged in self-harm behaviors (cutting themselves). These street youth noted that they cut themselves in order to deal with their anger issues.

Mental and Social Health Problems and Social Development Among Street Youth in Different Countries

Some analysts have focused on the good mental health of street youth who are able to adapt to the harsh nature of street life by developing intense, close relations with their friends on the streets (Aptekar 1989a). Street youth who work may obtain positive social developmental effects, and their early participation in work may help them with their future (Alaraudanjoki 2000; Stephenson 2001).

However, some street youth frequently develop a wide range of social, emotional, and mental health problems and disabilities because of the physical, emotional, and mental abuse, conflict, and low SES that they experienced in their families as well as their victimization and use of drugs and alcohol on the streets (Sherman et al. 2005; Farrow et al. 1992; de Oliveira et al. 1992; Campos et al. 1994).

The amount of time that youth spend on the streets may influence the number and severity of their mental health problems (Campos et al. 1994). Young people who live on the streets are especially at risk of suffering poor social and psychological outcomes.

Low SES increases the probability that street children will suffer mental health and social problems. de Oliveira et al. (1992) note that negative psychosocial problems are more likely to develop in low-SES children, making street children especially vulnerable to adverse social and mental health difficulties.

Other Social Conditions on the Street in Different Countries

Street youth, especially those who live on the streets, are more likely to suffer from other various social problems. For example, those young people who live on the streets have a higher probability of suffering loss of parents and reduced social support.

Nutritional Status and Physical Development of Street Youth

Living on the streets can lead to increased health risks (Campos et al. 1994). For example, street life can impair the nutritional status and physical growth of youth. Based on an evaluation of height and weight in relationship to age, Ali et al. (2004) discovered that 20 % of a sample of street children in Rawalpindi and Islamabad, Pakistan, was stunted. The investigators also found that 12 % of the youth exhibited wasting. In terms of gender differences, the investigators found that boys were more stunted than girls. However, the rates of wasting were equal between girls and boys.

Governments' Use of Punitive Measures to Remove Street Youth

Street youth in different nations are highly stigmatized; they are often viewed as worthless members of society (Scanlon et al. 1998). Some governments will use violent approaches to punish young people on the streets and remove them from the streets.

Chapter 17
Police Responses to Runaway and Homeless Youth

In this chapter, the diverse techniques that the police use in dealing with street youth are presented. In this chapter, the ways in which the police come into contact with street young people are described. This chapter assesses the police's use of discretion in responding to youth living on the streets. In this chapter, data on arrest rates of street youth and the conditions that may affect whether the police arrest these young people are presented. Different factors such as the police's danger assessment, demeanor of youth, co-occurring status offenses and crimes, school problems, and family issues are discussed. This chapter evaluates the obstacles that law enforcement personnel face in responding effectively to street youth.

Because the issue of runaway and homeless youth is a multidimensional social problem that involves a breakdown in family, school, community, law enforcement, and governmental functioning, police responses can only affect a portion of the runaway and homeless youth population (Johnson 2010).

Of all missing children who are reported to law enforcement, those who run away or are "thrown away" (e.g., kicked out of their home by their parents) make up 45 % (Hammer et al. 2002). The number of runaway/thrown-away children who are reported to the police is much larger than those children who are reported to law enforcement because they have been abducted by a family member or stranger or have been lost or injured.

Police come into contact with children and adolescents who become homeless or runaway youth while patrolling their assigned areas (Johnson 2010). Police meet runaway and homeless children and adolescents while investigating missing persons reports.

Families may notify the police that their children have run away from home. For example, in one self-report, parents notified the police that their 11-year-old daughter had run away from home (Mishriki 2001–2013). In this case, the father later found his daughter hitch hiking on a road, and he brought her home.

In another case, a mother of a teen runaway filed a missing persons report when her son ran away, and the police then searched for the child near a shopping mall where youth were known to go skateboarding (Perry 2015, June 15).

S.J. Morewitz, *Runaway and Homeless Youth*,
DOI 10.1007/978-3-319-30863-0_17

Parents may request that the police arrest their runaway child. In one self-report, a runaway girl reported that her mother had the police arrest her because her mother was afraid that she might harm her runaway daughter (Mishriki 2001–2013).

In other instances, schools may contact the police to have a runaway child arrested (Kawano 2014, January 28). School officials contacted the police when a 17-year-old runaway boy reportedly tried to register for school and became unruly. The child had a lengthy juvenile record that included resisting arrest, theft, and numerous runaway episodes.

Runaway youth may be arrested during the course of police criminal investigations when they may be victims, suspects, or witnesses of crimes. Young people who run away may commit various crimes such as prostitution, theft, assault, and robbery. In one self-report, a 15-year-old runaway girl wrote that a runaway like herself cannot have food to eat unless she or he participates in theft or prostitution because employment is unavailable to them while on the streets (Mishriki 2001–2013).

One famous runaway, Frank Abagnale, Jr., who was played by Leonardo DiCaprio in the movie, *Catch Me If You Can*, engaged in check forgery and impersonated a physician, attorney, and airline pilot, while on the run (Alter 2014, April 21).

Another male teen runaway violated airport security by stowing away in the wheel well of a plane that flew from San Jose, California, to Hawaii (Alter 2014, April 21). Another teen, a female runaway, stowed away on a British Navy submarine in Baltimore, MD, bound for Great Britain (Alter 2014, April 21).

Teens may run away from home after violating the law. In Kentucky, a 13-year-old girl and her 18-year-old boyfriend ran away from home after the police notified the boy's mother about their "underage relationship" (Warren 2015, January 15). The runaway teen couple then reportedly went on a crime spree in which they stole a truck before escaping from the police and crashing the vehicle. The teen couple then stole another truck that had a firearm inside.

A 9-year-old male runaway in Washington reportedly stole a motor vehicle to visit his grandfather in Texas (Alter 2014, April 21). The boy took the police on a high-speed chase and had more police involvement when he allegedly stole a yo-yo from a store.

Runaway youth often have conduct and behavioral problems. They have problems in dealing with authority, and these difficulties increase their chances of violating the law and getting into confrontations with the police.

For example, when three police officers in Hawaii came to arrest a 17-year-old runaway boy who was attempting to register for school and acting disorderly, the runaway boy was accused of punching two police officers and beginning to slash a third officer with a kitchen knife (Kawano 2014, January 28). One police officer reportedly shot at the teen two times and hit him in the arm.

In another case, a deputy in San Diego County reportedly used a Taser to subdue a 13-year-old who had run away from home for a day and a half and was resisting arrest (Perry 2015, June 15). The police officer allegedly made repeated commands for the runaway boy to get into the patrol car so that he could return him to his mother. The youth, who reportedly was 5 ft, 6 in. tall and weighed 145 lb, refused the police officer's repeated commands. The deputy then tried to handcuff the boy, and then the youth bit the police officer on the forearm. The deputy used the Taser after the boy bit him.

The police may arrest runaway and homeless young people, and they are later held in juvenile detention facilities. In one self-report case, a runaway was placed in juvenile detention for 2 weeks and then became an orphan in social service custody (Mishriki 2001–2013).

Law enforcement personnel have discretion in dealing with runaway and homeless youth depending on their behaviors, their relationship to caregivers, and other factors (Johnson 2010). Many children and adolescents who run away from home or substitute care are not actually living on the streets. They live for different periods of time with friends, acquaintances, and family members. Law enforcement personnel may not arrest runaway youth, especially if they believe that the youth are not at risk for harm and do not pose a danger to the public. Instead of arresting runaway children and adolescents, the police may try to reunite them with their families.

In other instances, law enforcement personnel may try to work with agencies to place the youth in emergency shelters, foster care, and group homes. In addition to the police, other agencies may be involved in locating and placing runaway youth. For example, in one self-report narrative, a female 12-year-old runaway stated that when she was on the streets, Children's Aid located her and placed her in a foster home in her home town (Mishriki 2001–2013).

In another self-report, F, a 16-year-old runaway girl was placed in a group home, which was a locked facility (Mishriki 2001–2013). The teen had run away from multiple times after having many conflicts with her mother, skipping school, and having failing school grades.

The police may not be able to arrest runaway youth if the youth decides to return home, even if just on a temporary basis. For example, according to one self-report narrative, a female teen decided to run away by trying to hitchhike 1 day (Mishriki 2001–2013). Her father called the police; however, by the time the police arrived, the father had found his daughter and brought her to her current parent's home. The police told her parents that they could not take any action at this time since she was already at home.

In other instances, the police may arrest the parents of the runaway child or other family members. For example, in one case, the police in Louisville, Kentucky, arrested a 35-year-old mother of a runaway girl for refusing to allow her to come back home even though her juvenile daughter had no other place to reside and weather conditions in February were extremely cold and windy (wdrb.com 2015, February 19). The police reported that the mother cursed them, was belligerent, and attempted to strike one of the officers when they came to her house to return her runaway juvenile daughter. The mother also allegedly started to kick the officers. The police arrested the mother, and she faces several charges including abandonment of a minor, criminal abuse, resisting arrest, and assaulting a police officer or probation officer.

Runaway and Homeless Youth Arrest Data

According to Snyder (2001a, b), 150,700 youth were arrested for running away in 1999. This statistic represents less than 10 % of all runaways in that same year (Snyder 2001a, b; U.S. Department of Justice 2003, March). According to a National

Council on Crime and Delinquency (NCCD) survey of juvenile detention and correctional settings, 100,000 children were held in county jails and police lockups (Howell 1995).

Researchers have also studied the arrest data for selected samples of runaway and homeless youth. Stricof et al. (1991), in their survey of 168 runaway and homeless adolescents at the Covenant House in New York, found that 62 % had reported being arrested.

In McCarthy and Hagan's (1992) investigation of homeless young people in Toronto, Canada, 45.5 % had been incarcerated at least one time since becoming homeless. Most of them had been jailed for nonstatus offenses. In Ontario, youth can leave home legally at the age of 16; therefore, running away is not a status offense for those 16 years old or older.

Chen et al. (2006), using a sample of 428 homeless and runaway young people, showed that more than 50 % had been arrested at least one time since their first runaway incident, and they had been arrested an average of 4.4 times.

Young juveniles face being arrested for running away from home or substitute care. In one self-report narrative, a 12-year-old female runaway reported that she had a warrant for her arrest. She had been on the streets for several months.

In 1997, 8 % of juvenile arrests involving youth younger than age 13 were for running away. In 1997, 15,700 juveniles younger than age 13 were arrested for running away, 2100 younger than age 10, and 13,500 between the ages of 10 and 12.

Youth who participate in illegal activities on the streets are at risk for getting arrested or placed in juvenile detention for different crimes and delinquent activities. For example, Mitchell et al. (2010) estimated that 1450 arrests or detentions occurred for cases of juvenile prostitution on a national basis. The problems that the police face in regularly monitoring and detecting juvenile offenses limit the reliability and validity of arrest statistics.

Adults who are former runaways may have an increased risk of getting arrested. In Benoit-Bryan's (2011) investigation of adults who were former runaway youth, 25.4 % of the former runaways had been arrested after they were 18 years of age, compared to 11.7 % of adults who had not run away from home. Former runaways were 2.72 times more likely to have been arrested after the age of 18 than non-runaways. The researchers discovered that being African American and having a history of verbal and physical abuse increased the probability of getting arrested after age 18. In contrast, being female and Asian decreased the likelihood of getting arrested.

Researchers also have studied instances in which the police are contacted. Using the results of the National Incidence Studies of Missing, Abducted, Runaway, and Thrown-away Children (NISMART), Hammer et al. (2002) discovered that of the total number of estimated runaway/thrown-away episodes (1,682,900), police were contacted in 32 % of the episodes (539,100). Thrown-away youth have been kicked out of their home by their parents. Police were contacted for a various reasons. In 29 % of the estimated runaway/thrown-away incidents, police were contacted in order to locate a missing child. Police were contacted in 5 % of the episodes to recover a youth from a known location. Other reasons accounted for 9 % of the police contacts in the estimated runaway/thrown-away episodes. In 57 % of the estimated episodes of runaway/thrown-away incidents, reasons for contacting the police were not available.

The investigators also analyzed why police were not contacted during the runaway/thrown-away episodes. In 21 % of the estimated runaway/thrown-away incidents, caretakers knew the youth's location. Police were not contacted in 18 % of the estimated episodes because the parents or guardians did not believe that law enforcement was necessary. Another reason the police were not contacted is that the youth was not away from home long enough (8 %). In 7 % of the estimated runaway/thrown-away incidents, the child was expected to return home. Caretakers did not want the child to get arrested or in trouble 4 % of the estimated episodes. Other reasons for not contacting law enforcement were given in 10 % of the estimated runaway/thrown-away incidents. In 29 % of the episodes, no information was provided about why the police were not contacted.

Hammer et al. (2002) suggest that the NISMART results do not indicate that caretakers should increase their reporting of runaway/thrown-away episodes to the police. The data are inconclusive as to whether the families and involved youth would benefit from more or less police participation. According to Hammer et al. (2002), caretakers may be accurately judging when they should contact law enforcement during runaway/thrown-away incidents.

Runaway and Homeless Youth Try to Evade Police

Runaway children and adolescents frequently will try to evade police detection by lying to the police about their status as runaways, decreasing their visibility in public places, and using other evasive strategies (Mishriki 2001–2013). L., a self-reported 14-year-old male runaway, in one self-report narrative reported that 1 day a police car drove up to him (Mishriki 2001–2013). The police officer got out of his vehicle and asked him where he was going. He told the police officer that he was returning from a sleep over and that he was walking home. The police officer ordered the youth to get in his police car, and the police officer drove him to his home. L. told him to drive to the next exit and when they got to a nearby neighborhood, the youth pointed to what appeared to be an empty house and indicated that it was his home. L. knocked on the door of the house, and no one answered. The police officer glared at L. and warned him to keep away from the highway.

Runaway youth will live in abandoned houses and other hidden locations to avoid detection. If detected, they might be returned to their home, sent to substitute care, or face other undesirable outcomes (Mishriki 2001–2013). For example, a 15-year-old female runaway reported that while on the streets she frequently slept over night behind a grocery store (Mishriki 2001–2013). The runaway youth stated the she would wake up early in the morning to avoid being detected by the delivery truck drivers who would deliver goods to the store.

In a self-report case, a 13-year-old runaway girl wrote that she was "constantly running from the cops" (Mishriki 2001–2013). The youth indicated that she would break into "for sale" houses to stay in them overnight. She reported that she sold drugs to make money and a drug dealer attempted to shoot her. The girl also wrote that she had been raped two times. The youth reported that the police finally arrested her and contacted her mother to have her retrieved.

As runaway children and adolescents are faced with the dilemma of surviving on the street without employment or other financial resources, they often turn to theft as one of several subsistence strategies (Mishriki 2001–2013). In one self-report narrative, a 15-year-old female runaway stated that she was arrested for shoplifting at a grocery store, where she had been regularly sleeping over night behind the store (Mishriki 2001–2013). The police officer asked her if she wanted to stay the night in jail and said that it would be better than living on the street. The youth reported that she had spent a few days in juvenile detention.

Runaway and Homeless Youth May Resist Arrest

While on the streets, runaway and homeless youth may resist arrest. For example, In Noblesville, Indiana, two runaway adolescent girls allegedly led police on a chase while driving a stolen vehicle. At the end of the police chase, the girls crashed their vehicle and then fled from the scene. After being treated for minor injuries, the two runaway girls were arrested and charged with running away from home, possessing a stolen vehicle and resisting police. They were taken to a juvenile detention facility.

Risk Factors Associated with Getting Arrested

In the juvenile justice system, gender may affect outcomes for juvenile offenders. Although the arrest rates for both female and male juveniles have decreased, Bright et al. (2014) report that females have lower rates of decrease than males.

Gender may play a role in whether runaway youth are arrested (McCarthy and Hagan 1992). The police may be more likely to arrest runaway girls than their male counterparts because the police follow traditional gender and sex role beliefs. For example, the police may treat runaway girls more harshly than runaway boys because the police are concerned about the possible sexual exploitation of runaway girls and that they are more vulnerable to other dangers than runaway boys. In other instances, the police may treat female juveniles involved in prostitution as victims of commercial sexual exploitation or delinquents (Mitchell et al. 2010).

Gender may play a factor in whether runaway juveniles are formally processed by having a petition filed in juvenile court (Hockenberry and Puzzanchera 2015; Development Services Group, Inc. 2015). Based on an analysis of petitioned status offense cases, Hockenberry and Puzzanchera (2015) showed that girls had a higher percentage of petitioned status offenses for running away than boys. In contrast, boys made up a majority of petitioned status offenses for alcohol-related offenses, ungovernability, skipping school, and violations of curfew.

Racial and ethnic factors may affect whether runaway youth are arrested and have a petition filed. Hockenberry and Puzzanchera (2015) discovered that White youth had a higher rate of petitioned runaway offenses than their Black counterparts (Hockenberry and Puzzanchera 2015; Development Services Group, Inc. 2015).

Older youth may be more likely than younger juveniles to have a petition filed for running away and other status offenses (Hockenberry and Puzzanchera 2015; Development Services Group, Inc. 2015). However, between 1995 and 2013, the rates of petitioned status offenses for running away and three other status violations (curfew, alcohol, and ungovernable) went down. In addition, the socioeconomic status (SES) of the runaway young people may influence whether the police will arrest them.

Drug and Alcohol Offenses

Children and adolescents who run away engage in risky behaviors that increase their risk of getting arrested. For example, runaway and homeless young people who use and abuse alcohol and other drugs may be at increased risk of getting arrested. Minors in possession of alcohol face arrests. Youth who are found in possession of tobacco products also are at risk for police contact. In Chen et al.'s (2006) investigation, runaway and homeless youth who abused substances were more likely to be arrested. Based on a convenience sample of 349 adolescents using runaway shelter services in Texas and New York, Thompson and Pillai (2006) showed that 17.4 % of the teens had a drug possession/drug distribution charge.

Runaway and homeless youth may get arrested for alcohol-related status offenses, e.g., possession of alcohol by a minor. The potential for runaway and homeless young people getting arrested is significant because many use alcohol and other drugs. For example, Thompson and Pillai (2006) discovered that 60.2 % of youth using runaway emergency shelter services had ever consumed alcohol. In one self-report, a teen runaway who had been living with a friend and his parents went drinking alcohol with his friends and got arrested for being a minor in possession of alcohol (Mishriki 2001–2013). The child had to go to court and was sentenced to 30 days in juvenile detention.

Street youth with a history of substance use and abuse may have a higher probability of getting arrested than those without a substance use and abuse history. In one self-report, a teen runaway with a history of abusing drugs while on the streets was arrested by the police and placed in juvenile detention for 2 weeks (Mishriki 2001–2013).

Runaway and homeless young people who have peers with an arrest history may be more likely to get involved in hard drugs themselves. For example, CA, using data from a sample of newly homeless and runaway youth in Los Angeles, CA, Rice et al. (2007) discovered that having peers who have been arrested may have an increased probability that newly homeless and runaway juveniles will take hard drugs.

Vagrancy Arrests

While on the streets, runaway and homeless adolescents face arrests for vagrancy (Snyder 2001a, b). Those who are visible on the streets are especially at risk for vagrancy arrests.

Vandalism and Property Damage

The police may arrest runaway and homeless youth who vandalize or damage property. Homeless and runaway young people may get arrested for causing property damage in the course of leading police on high-speed chases.

Other Juvenile Status Offenses

Runaway and homeless youth may be arrested for committing other juvenile status offenses, which are violations that if perpetrated by an adult would not be considered criminal violations. According to one self-report story, a female runaway reported that she had been charged twice for truancy (Mishriki 2001–2013). The juvenile noted that she received 1-year probation for the second time.

Arrests of Runaways' Friends

Youth who run away from home or substitute care also report that their friends are arrested, indicating the importance of peers in police arrests. For example, in one self-report narrative, a female 11-year-old runaway noted that her best friend, a 20-year-old male, was arrested by the police (Mishriki 2001–2013).

Runaway and homeless young people who participate in social networks that consist of peers who have been arrested, had been in a gang, stole from individuals, or suffered a drug overdose may have a greater probability of using hard drugs (Rice et al. 2007). Hard drug use by these runaway and homeless young people may increase the risks that they will be arrested.

Community, Law Enforcement, and State/National Factors

Various community, law enforcement, and legislative factors may affect whether runaway and homeless young people are harassed and arrested by the police. Analysts discuss the ways in which some communities enact laws to criminalize the street behaviors committed by many runaway and homeless youth (Esmonde 2002; O'Grady et al. 1998). Laws may be enacted to criminalize loitering and vagrancy. In Ontario, the Safe Streets Act was passed to curb squeegeeing by homeless and runaway youth.

Demeanor and Behavioral Characteristics

The demeanor and behavioral characteristics of runaway and homeless youth may affect police's use of discretion in handling runaway and homeless youth. Runaway and homeless youth who have CD and/or use drugs may be at increased risk of committing delinquent acts and getting arrested (Chen et al. 2006). The police may use discretion in deciding whether to arrest runaway young people. Extra-legal aspects of their behavior may affect whether they are arrested and other criminal justice outcomes. The police may take into consideration the runaway child's demeanor, in deciding the juvenile's outcome. For example, the police may be more likely to arrest runaway young people who appear defiant (Mann 1980). Runaway young people who display defiant verbal and nonverbal cues may be more likely sent to be arrested and sent to juvenile court (Mann 1980).

Mental Health Problems of Runaway Youth

Mental health problems among runaway and homeless youth may increase their likelihood of getting arrested. In Chen et al.'s (2006) study, runaway and homeless youth who had various mental health disorders, both internalizing and externalizing disorders, had a greater likelihood of getting arrested. For example, having externalizing disorders such as conduct disorder increased the probability of being arrested.

Current Living Situation

The current living situation of runaway and homeless youth may affect the probability that they will be arrested and incarcerated. Young people who are surviving on the streets may be more likely to participate in deviant and criminal activities to obtain food and other services and therefore may be more likely to get arrested and incarcerated than youth who are living in more stable residential settings (e.g., shelter or hostel) with access to food and other resources. For example, in a study of homeless young people in Toronto, Canada, McCarthy and Hagan (1992) demonstrated that homeless youth's current living situation predicted whether the young people would be incarcerated.

Length of Time on the Street

Young persons who spend more time on the streets may have an increased risk of getting arrested and incarcerated. McCarthy and Hagan (1992) showed that the homeless youth's length of time was positively linked to the likelihood of incarceration. The investigators also found that the duration of time on the streets increased the probability that homeless young people would participate in prostitution.

Survival Strategies on the Streets

Street-based runaway children and adolescents may be more likely to be arrested for property crimes than other juveniles because they participate in these property crimes as a survival strategy on the streets. Runaway children and adolescents who live on the streets are more likely to be arrested for these disorderly conduct offenses than other juveniles because of their visibility in the streets.

Runaway young people who live on the streets and engage in survival sex as an adaptation strategy are more likely to be arrested for prostitution and commercialized vice offenses because of their visibility on the streets and their vulnerability to victimization and sexually transmitted infections, including human immune virus (HIV)/acquired immunodeficiency syndrome (AIDS). In McCarthy and Hagan's (1992) research on homeless youth in Toronto, Canada, 29.7 % indicated that they participated in prostitution since becoming homeless. Runaway young people frequently will exchange sex for food, housing, alcohol and other drugs, clothes, and other commodities. Runaway children and adolescents face the possibility of being recruited, coerced, or tricked into prostitution. In addition, runaway youth may be more likely to be arrested for violent crime offenses because they commit aggravated assault, other assaults, and robbery as a survival strategy on the streets.

Obstacles that Law Enforcement Face in Responding to Runaway Children and Adolescents

The extent to which law enforcement personnel can respond effectively to runaway youth may be affected by the extensive amount of time and effort involved in dealing with runaway young people (Posner 1992; Finkelhor et al. 1990; Hammer et al.

2002). A considerable amount of time and effort may be needed to handle juveniles who run away from substitute care.

Another obstacle is that the police may spend a considerable amount of time involved in transporting runaway youth (Posner 1992). The police frequently are limited in dealing with runaway juveniles because the police must respond to more serious crimes (Maxson et al. 1988; Posner 1992). Another difficulty is that police may want to return the runaway child to her or his parents, but parents frequently do not want their child to come back home (Posner 1992). In addition, the runaway does not want to return home (Posner 1992). The characteristics of the family may be an obstacle for the police in returning the runaway youth to their family (Widom 1995, March).

The police also may be limited in their responses since runaway children and adolescents often run away again after law enforcement personnel return the youth to their families (Newiss 1999; Posner 1992). The lack of placement facilities is another obstacle that the police confront in handling runaway youth (Smart 1991; Posner 1992; Collins et al. 1993; Joe 1995; Newiss 1999; National Law Center on Homelessness and Poverty 2003).

The police perceptions of the parents' beliefs may affect law enforcement practices regarding runaway children. For example, the police may believe that parents and substitute care providers want the police to discipline or guard their runaway child (Posner 1992).

Do Runaways Have an Increased Risk of Criminal Justice Involvement as Adults?

Youth who run away may be also at increased risk of being arrested as adults (Benoit-Bryan 2011). In the Runaway Youth Longitudinal Study, Benoit-Bryan (2011) discovered that former runaway young people were more than two and a half times as likely to be arrested after age 18 compared to non-runaways.

Chapter 18
Court Responses to Runaway Offenses and Other Juvenile Status Violations

In this chapter, the ways in which the courts respond to youth who run away from home and commit other offenses is discussed. Runaway youth may be classified as status offenders. Status offenses are non-criminal behaviors that are treated as violations only because the offender is a minor. Classifying juvenile behavior as status offenses is designed to restrict the youth's behavior in order to promote their safety and health. States may classify runaways and other status violators as delinquents, while in other states status offenders are considered neglected or abused dependents. Some states classify status violators as a separate category. Status offenders may be referred to juvenile court or the runaway's first contact is with a state child welfare agency. In other states, the status offender may be sent to a residential facility or the juvenile is required to participate in community-based interventions. If these informal strategies are not successful, juvenile courts will formally process them. In addition, A Child in Need Supervision petition can be filed with the court to assist juveniles who repeatedly commit status violations such as running away from home. This chapter also analyzes factors that increase the likelihood that juveniles will commit status offenses and the disparities in the juvenile justice system.

Status offenses are non-criminal behaviors that are treated as violations only because the offender is a minor (Development Services Group, Inc. 2015). Classifying juvenile behavior as status offenses is designed to restrict youth's behavior in order to promote their safety and health (getlegal.com, n.d.). These laws protect youth from the dangers of staying away from home, skipping school, becoming addicted to alcohol and tobacco, and suffering from other dangerous conditions. The court may decide to divert status offenders away from formal processing in the justice system. In other instances, the court may decide to formally process the status violator by filing a petition.

Running away from home is one type of status violation. According to the Office of Juvenile Justice and Delinquency Prevention (OJJDP), a runaway is a "child (who) leaves home without permission and stays away overnight" (Development Services Group, Inc. 2015; Snyder and Sickmund 1999). According to the *OJJDP Statistical Briefing Book Online* (n.d.), 39 states in 2013 had specified juvenile

S.J. Morewitz, *Runaway and Homeless Youth*,
DOI 10.1007/978-3-319-30863-0_18

runaway behaviors or chronic behaviors away from home in their statues (*OJJDP Statistical Briefing Book Online*. n.d.). State laws can have their own classification of running away.

How many runaways have contact with the juvenile justice system? According to a US General Accounting Office (1989) investigation, 17 % of runaway young people using runaway shelters had "been in trouble with the juvenile justice system" (US General Accounting Office 1989; Walsh and Donaldson 2010).

In addition to being charged as a runaway, teen runaways may be caught violating other status offenses such as truancy, curfew, and alcohol laws. Because of their multiple status offenses, these youth may face an increased likelihood of being treated more severely.

A majority of juveniles run away from home for a short period of time; they generally come back home within a few days (Beharry 2012; Development Services Group, Inc. 2015). These youth are referred to as "situational runaways." Other youth run away from home for long periods of time and may never return home. These latter runaways often are escaping family sexual, physical, and emotional abuse and neglect (Beharry 2012; Development Services Group, Inc. 2015). Youth also may have been kicked out of their homes and are known as "throwaways" (Beharry 2012). These thrown-aways may be classified by the police as runaways. Other young people reside in substitute care and cannot return home or refuse to do so.

A juvenile may be charged with truancy, which is defined as "habitual, unexcused absences from school, which exceed the number allowed under state law" (Development Services Group, Inc. 2015). States differ in their determination of the number of unexcused school absences that are allowed before a child is considered truant. Schools also vary in their school attendance laws that specify the age at which a child begins school and is permitted to drop out of school.

Violations of juvenile curfews are also a status offense (Development Services Group, Inc. 2015). Curfew laws vary in terms specific conditions, such as the hours that the laws are in effect, the day of week, and the age groups that are affected by the law. States have exceptions to curfew laws. For example, a child is permitted to stay out later to attend school-related functions or go to work.

Another status offense is underage drinking (Development Services Group, Inc. 2015). Underage drinking is a widespread problem among adolescents. According to the 2012 National Survey on Drug Use and Health, 25 % of young people aged 12–24 consume alcohol (Substance Abuse and Mental Health Services Administration 2013). In the survey, 15 % of the young people engaged in binge drinking and 1.7 million were determined to be heavy drinkers.

A teen runaway, according to a self-report narrative, had been residing with a friend and his parents. On one occasion, this youth went drinking alcohol with his friends and was arrested for being a minor in possession of alcohol (MIP) (Mishriki 2001–2013). The adolescent received a 30-day sentence in juvenile detention.

A small percentage of individuals aged 18–20 can be charged with underage drinking and would be classified as criminal offenders because they are classified as adults in their respective states. In 2010, youth charged with MIP cases were no longer treated as status offenders and were now classified as criminal offenders (Development Services Group, Inc. 2015). Nevertheless, the OJJDP still recommends against securely detaining both minors and adults charged with MIP violations.

Juveniles may use tobacco, and possession and use of tobacco by a minor is another status offense. Tobacco use among juveniles is widespread and can cause serious health problems including cancer, heart disease, and lung disease.

In a majority of states, a minor may be charged with being an incorrigible/ungovernable youth (Development Services Group, Inc. 2015). Youth may disobey their parents so frequently and severely that the parents feel that they cannot control them. These parents may obtain legal assistance by having their child charged as "incorrigible" or "ungovernable" (Hockenberry and Puzzanchera 2015).

Another status violation is loitering in locations that are forbidden by law enforcement personnel (getlegal.com). Violations of a valid court order (VCO) that regulate a juvenile's behavior are also a type of status offense.

Status offenses such as teen runaway, truancy, underage drinking, and curfew violations may reflect individual, social, family, school, and community problems (Development Services Group, Inc. 2015; Chuang and Wells 2010). These juveniles may have a higher probability of suffering from substance use and abuse, becoming victimized, and suffering other health problems. Youth who commit status violations may turn to more serious forms of delinquency (Development Services Group, Inc. 2015; Michon n.d.; Huizinga et al. 1995).

However, this "precursor to delinquency" perspective is too simplistic since it does not consider that many young people normally experiment with deviant behavior and do not become career criminals (Development Services Group, Inc. 2015). Youth often temporarily experiment with deviance and learn from their behaviors to become law-abiding citizens. According to Kelley et al. (1997), a majority of young people who commit status violations do not participate in major criminal activities later. According to Snyder and Sickmund (1999), about 54 % of male and 73 % of female youth who have been arrested will not have any additional experience with the juvenile justice system. The precursor to delinquency approach also does not consider many factors that may contribute to future criminal behaviors in adulthood.

How Are Status Offenses Handled?

Traditionally, status offenders were handled in the juvenile justice system (Michon n.d.). Criminal justice experts and policy makers felt that status offenders might become future criminals and therefore required more "supervision and support." Officials designed strategies that had three basic goals: further the safety of the public, maintain family cohesion, and prevent delinquency and criminal behaviors.

States vary in how they handle children who commit status offenses (Michon n.d.). States may classify status violators as delinquents (Development Services

Group, Inc. 2015). In other states, status offenders are considered neglected or abused dependents. Other states classify status violators as a separate category.

The classification type will determine how the state responds to status violators (Development Services Group, Inc. 2015). The classification category will affect whether a juvenile receives treatment and the types of services available to status offenders (Kendall 2007).

A status offender may be referred to juvenile court or the status offender's first contact is with a state child welfare agency (Michon n.d.). In other states, the status violator may be sent to a residential facility or the juvenile is required to participate in community-based interventions. If these informal strategies are not successful, juvenile courts will formally process them. In addition, A Child in Need Supervision petition can be filed with the court to assist juveniles who repeated commit status violations such as running away from home.

Few states treat status offenders as delinquents on a de jure basis. However, states use probation violations to treat status offenders as de facto delinquents (Development Services Group, Inc. 2015). Status violators are treated as de facto delinquents when they receive probation for their status offense and then are later incarcerated for a technical violation of their probation. These juveniles would not have been incarcerated for their original status violation. Thirty states have probation as a disposition for a status offense (Szymanski 2006; Development Services Group, Inc. 2015).

States vary in the penalties that they impose on juvenile status offenders (Michon n.d.; Development Services Group, Inc. 2015). Courts may suspend the status violator's driver's license or require the child to pay a fine or restitution (Michon n.d.; Development Services Group, Inc. 2015). The court may decide to place the child with an individual other than a parent or guardian or in a foster home or group home. The status offender may be ordered to participate in counseling or educational programs. In most courts, courts can order a juvenile detained in a locked facility for violating a court order. The parents of the juveniles also may be required to participate in counseling and parenting interventions.

A juvenile may get a formal juvenile record if the court determines during the adjudication stage that the child committed a status offense (getlegal.com, n.d.). This formal record can be expunged when the child reaches the age of majority. The juvenile may receive a risk factor score for being a repeat offender. If the child is adjudicated again for another status offense, her or his risk factor may help justify a more severe punishment for the child.

If the court decides that the child has committed a status offense, he or she may get deferred adjudication in which the child does not have a formal probation or formal ruling that the child committed the status offense. Deferred adjudication occurs as long as the juvenile does not commit a status offense for a specified time period (getlegal.com n.d.).

The court may determine that the child should be placed on probation and allowed to continue to live at home (getlegal.com, n.d.). Previous contacts with the court and the seriousness of the current offense may determine the duration of the probation period.

The court also may make a disposition, which is determined based on the type of status violation and the parents' desire to take back the child, that the child should be boarded at a state school for a specified time period (getlegal.com, n.d.). States that receive federal funding from the OJJDP must follow the JJDP Act of 1974 (Development Services Group, Inc. 2015) regarding separation of incarcerated juveniles and adults and the deinstitutionalization of status offenders.

The JJDP emphasizes diverting status offenders away from formal processing in the juvenile justice system to avoid the stigmatizing juvenile delinquent label and instead placing them in "less restrictive, service-intensive" community interventions (Development Services Group, Inc. 2015; Chesney-Lind 1989). States have not fully accepted the federal government's goal of deinstitutionalization. Moreover, states have not complied with the federal government's goal of diverting status offenders.

In 1980, an amendment to the JJDP Act provided for a VCO exception to the deinstitutionalization of status offenders main requirement of the Act, which enables the court to detain status violators if they have violated a direct court order (Yeide and Cohen 2009; Development Services Group, Inc. 2015).

Risk Factors for Committing Status Offenses

Which juveniles are at risk for committing status offenses? Various legislative, criminal justice, demographic, social, behavioral, mental health, socioeconomic status, family, school, and environmental factors may increase the risk that minors will become a status offender or a more serious delinquent (Bright et al. 2014). For example, juveniles, especially female adolescents who suffer sexual and physical abuse and neglect, may be more likely to run away from these traumatic family environments (Chesney-Lind 1989). Female adolescents may be more susceptible to depression and other internalizing behaviors associated with abuse than their male counterparts. As a result, female adolescents may have different rates of delinquent behaviors than boys (Bright et al. 2014).

Disadvantaged minority youth, when faced with such problems as family abuse and violence, poverty, inadequate community social control, and ineffective schools, may have a higher probability of engaging in status offenses and more serious delinquent behaviors.

According to Loeber et al. (1993, 1997), youth may go through different developmental pathways that lead some to exhibit disruptive behaviors. In a so-called overt pathway, children participate in shoplifting and lying and later may become aggressive and bully others. These youth then participate in physical fighting and violent offenses (Gorman-Smith and Loeber 2005; Loeber et al. 1993, 1997).

Disparities in the Juvenile Justice System

Various characteristics of juveniles may affect the extent to which juvenile courts process youth formally by filing a petition, which can result in placement in detention and confinement facilities. Racial and ethnic disparities, including racism in the juvenile justice system, may influence the extent to which minors' status offenses are treated more harshly, e.g., whether they are formally processed by filing a petition (Hoytt et al. 2003; Development Services Group, Inc. 2015). Minority youth may be more likely to be placed in juvenile detention than White youth. Hockenberry and Puzzanchera (2015), in an investigation of case records from 2400 courts, showed that race played a role in the rates of status offenses. For example, in 2013, Whites had a higher rate of runaway offenses than Blacks (Hockenberry and Puzzanchera 2015; Development Services Group, Inc. 2015). Whites also had a higher rate of alcohol offenses than Blacks. However, Blacks had a higher rate of ungovernable violations than Whites.

Gender disparities, including sexism, can lead female youth to be at greater risk for being treated more severely than their male counterparts (Federle 2000; Gavazzi et al. 2006; Chesney-Lind and Shelden 2003; Chesney-Lind 1989; Development Services Group, Inc. 2015). According to Chesney-Lind (1989), the police are likely to treat female delinquents more harshly. Juvenile courts may be more likely to file a petition when female youth commit status offenses. Chesney-Lind (1989) showed that juvenile courts have a double standard in their treatment of female juveniles. For example, female juveniles have a higher probability of receiving a more severe court disposition especially for running away from home or engaging in "sexual promiscuity" than their male counterparts. In Hockenberry and Puzzanchera (2015)'s study of petitioned status-offense cases, female juveniles had a higher rate of runaway offenses than their male counterparts. However, the authors showed that male juveniles were involved in most of the total petitioned status-offense cases.

Age disparities may influence whether juvenile courts formally process a youth for a status offense (Development Services Group, Inc. 2015). Older juveniles may be treated more severely than their younger counterparts. For example, Hockenberry and Puzzanchera (2015) revealed that 16-year-old juveniles had a rate of petitioned status-offense cases that was twice that of 14-year-old youth. However, between 1995 and 2013, the rate of petitioned runaway offenses and three other status offenses (alcohol violations, ungovernable, and curfew violations) went down for almost all age groups (Hockenberry and Puzzanchera 2015; Development Services Group, Inc. 2015).

Socioeconomic status (SES) and other factors may affect the degree to which the courts formally process minors. Low-SES children and adolescents may face a greater risk of being formally processed by juvenile courts than upper-SES youth. Other conditions such as the demeanor of youth who commit status offenses may impact whether the courts will file a petition against a youth for a status offense.

Hockenberry and Puzzanchera (2015) evaluated various outcomes for status offenders. If a court determines that the juvenile should be formally processed, the court may file a petition. In 2013, Hockenberry and Puzzanchera (2015) found that 109,000 status offenses were petitioned in juvenile courts in the USA in 2013. The researchers found that 8 % of petitioned status offenses involved runaways. A majority of the cases consisted of truancy violations.

In 2013, Hockenberry and Puzzanchera (2015) showed that juveniles were placed in juvenile detention in 7300 petitioned status violations. Children charged with running away from home had the highest probability of being detained, while those charged with truancy had the lowest probability of being detained.

In regard to adjudication, 44 % of petitioned status violations were adjudicated in 2013 (Hockenberry and Puzzanchera 2015). Juveniles were mostly adjudicated for alcohol-related status offenses. In 2013, among all adjudicated status violations, 54 % involved probation (Hockenberry and Puzzanchera 2015). Eight percent involved the court ordering an out-of-home placement of the juvenile. The juvenile received court-ordered treatment or counseling, restitution or fine, or community service in 38 % of the adjudicated status offenses.

Chapter 19
Juvenile Detention

When runaway children and adolescents are faced with the dilemma of surviving on the street without money, food, stable housing, employment, or other resources, they often turn to crimes such as theft as one of several subsistence strategies and face getting arrested and placed in juvenile detention (Mishriki 2001–2013). Runaway and homeless youth also engage in substance use and abuse and other deviant behaviors, which increases their risks of getting arrested and placed in juvenile detention. In this chapter, various historical perspectives, investigations, and self-report narratives provide insights into the juvenile detention system. This chapter discusses societal trends and the philosophy and history of the juvenile justice system, changes in the way that juvenile courts respond to runaway youth and other status offenders, the goals of juvenile detention, the decision to place juveniles in secure detention and commitment, the demographic and behavioral characteristics of confined juveniles, and the conditions facing juveniles in detention and other correctional facilities. This chapter also evaluates the effectiveness of secure detention and confinement and the impact of different types of juvenile settings, such as residential programs, including camps, community-based programs, and residential treatment, including training schools on juvenile re-offending rates. Improvements in custody classification and other aspects of the juvenile justice system are also discussed.

When runaway children and adolescents are faced with the dilemma of surviving on the street without money, food, stable housing, employment, or other resources, they often turn to crimes such as theft as one of several subsistence strategies and face getting arrested and placed in juvenile detention (Mishriki 2001–2013). Runaway and homeless youth also engage in substance use and abuse and other deviant behaviors, which increases their risks of getting arrested and placed in juvenile detention. In this chapter, various historical perspectives, investigations and self-report narratives provide insights into the juvenile detention system.

Juveniles may get arrested for offenses such as shoplifting. One self-reported 15-year-old female runaway stated that she was arrested for shoplifting at a grocery store, where she had been regularly sleeping over night behind the store (Mishriki

S.J. Morewitz, *Runaway and Homeless Youth*,
DOI 10.1007/978-3-319-30863-0_19

2001–2013). The police officer asked her if she wanted to stay the night in jail and said that it would be better than living on the street. The youth reported that she had spent a few days in juvenile detention.

Children and adolescents may get arrested for status offenses such as alcohol violations, e.g., status as a runaway youth, possession of alcohol by a minor, curfew violations, and truancy. Runaways who get arrested may be placed in different facilities. For example, in one self-report case, a runaway youth was arrested, placed in juvenile detention for 2 weeks, and then made an orphan in the custody of social services (Mishriki 2001–2013).

The potential for runaway and homeless young people getting arrested is significant because many use alcohol and other drugs. For example, Thompson and Pillai (2006) discovered that 60.2 % of youth using runaway emergency shelter services had ever consumed alcohol.

According to one self-report, a teen runaway who had been living with a friend and his parents went drinking alcohol with his friends and got arrested for being a minor in possession of alcohol (Mishriki 2001–2013). The child had to go to court and was sentenced to 30 days in juvenile detention.

Societal Trends and the Juvenile Court System's History and Philosophy

Beginning in the nineteenth century, the US government started to promote rehabilitating or punishing youthful offenders (Steinhart 1996). In this context, states started to change its laws, no longer requiring delinquents to receive the same punishment as adult offenders. Legislation at this time sought to remove delinquents from their dysfunctional families and other unhealthy environments that were thought to cause their misconduct.

The "child-saving" movement of the Progressive Movement in the nineteenth century led to the establishment of organizations such as houses of refuge in order to care of juvenile delinquents (Steinhart 1996). At the same time, several states started to adjudicate youth in juvenile courts instead of courts for adults (Desai et al. 2006). The first such court was established in Illinois in 1899 (Steinhart 1996). Child advocates viewed juvenile courts as a central part of a system to reform the adjudication of delinquents.

The founders of juvenile court believed that juveniles had a greater likelihood of being the victim of abuse and to be vulnerable to developing a career as a criminal because of their association with older inmates (Mears et al. 2014). Those who started the juvenile court believed that setting up the juvenile court was a moral necessity (Mears et al. 2014). For example, Judge Mack (1909) believed that juveniles should be regarded by the court as neglected and court reform should be a major goal (Mears et al. 2014; Mack 1909).

During this period, juvenile courts were established because many people began to regard children and adolescents as different from adults in terms of their socio-emotional development and therefore these at-risk youth needed to be tried in juvenile courts that met their socio-developmental needs (Desai et al. 2006). Instead of getting punished for their crimes, juvenile offenders now could be steered toward more healthy and productive pathways out of childhood and adolescence.

This viewpoint reflected the child-saving approach (Platt 1977; Mears et al. 2014). Proponents of this approach viewed juveniles as youth who are growing "physically, mentally and morally" (Tanenhaus 2004; Mears et al. 2014) and was embodied in the principle of *parens patriae* or "the state as parent" (Feld and Bishop 2012; Mears et al. 2014).

Following *parens patriae*, juvenile court was established as a separate civil court for juvenile offenders instead of a criminal court (Feld 1999; Mears et al. 2014). This juvenile court has different goals and standards of evidence than criminal court. The goal of the juvenile court is to achieve outcomes that are in the "best interest" of the juveniles (Feld 1999; Mears et al. 2014). In this context, the court, like a caring parent, decides whether goals such as rehabilitating or punishing the young offender will achieve the most desired behavioral changes.

One interpretation of *parens patriae* is that the courts should intervene even in minor acts of deviance (Emerson 1969; Mears et al. 2014). These juvenile court interventions employ some mix of services, treatment, and punishment to help the youth avoid becoming a criminal (Guarino-Ghezzi and Loughran 2004; Krisberg 1997; Mears 2012; Mears et al. 2014).

States in this time period gave juvenile courts wide authority to assist youth who were accused of criminal behaviors as well as those who were thought to be neglected and ungovernable or whose life was in danger (Steinhart 1996). Juvenile courts were less interested in distinguishing between criminal and non-criminal activities. Instead, they sought to rehabilitate youth so they could become functioning members of society.

When juveniles needed to be detained for their own safety and protect the public, the juvenile court system was designed to detain these juveniles in settings that were similar to a safe home environment (Desai et al. 2006). These early detention facilities were often not locked.

The growth of the juvenile delinquent population after World War II, especially in metropolitan areas, led to the building of many correctional facilities for juvenile delinquents (Desai et al. 2006). These establishments, which were frequently known as reform schools, sought to educate and discipline the juveniles and also meet their health needs. At the same time, smaller juvenile detention facilities were built. These facilities held juveniles until they received a disposition decision and adjudication (Desai et al. 2006).

Juvenile detention facilities in the 1960s lacked funding and many settings could not provide comprehensive educational and employment programs (Desai et al. 2006). During this period, experts in child welfare and policy criticized the juvenile detention facilities for being too much like jails that were punishment-oriented. In fact, youth during this period increasingly were held in larger facilities that were more secure than in period times. Child specialists also complained that the juveniles were not receiving appropriate services.

The juvenile detention facilities from the 1960s to the 1990s varied extensively in their approaches to juveniles (Desai et al. 2006). Many juveniles might receive a therapeutic-based intervention, while other juveniles might get harsh punishment. The juvenile courts had to adjust to a rapid increase in serious juvenile crime. Juveniles were increasingly arrested for violent offenses and drug-related violations (Parent et al. 1994). In response to these trends, policy makers passed harsher punishment for violent and habitual juvenile offenses. During this period, states also enabled juvenile offenders who were accused of violent offenses to be waived to adult criminal courts.

The US Department of Justice and the Office of Juvenile Justice and Delinquency Prevention (OJJDP) in the 1990s attempted to use a balanced approach to juvenile offenders (Desai et al. 2006). The OJJDP's balanced approach consisted of providing full adherence to due process for juveniles and also emphasized diverting juveniles away from formal processing in the juvenile justice system. In addition, the OJJDP focused on having youthful offenders be held accountable for their offenses and on promoting the safety of the public.

A recurring problem has been the institutionalization of status offenders, those youth who engage in illegal behaviors such as running away and violating curfew that if they were adults would not be committing crimes. In response to this problem, the Juvenile Justice and Delinquency Prevention (JJDP) Act was enacted (Development Services Group, Inc. 2015). When the law was passed, the Act had two main requirements: separating juveniles and adults during incarceration and not holding status offenders and abused or neglected youth in juvenile detention facilities. Keeping status offenders out of detention facilities is known as the deinstitutionalization of status offenders (DSO).

The JJDP Act was amended in 1980 so that juvenile courts could have a valid court order (VCO) exception to the DSO requirement (Development Services Group, Inc. 2015). This VCO exception allowed the juvenile courts to have discretion in detaining status offenders if they have violated a direct court order such as "attending school regularly." As a result, status offenders could be placed in detention facilities who would not normally be incarcerated.

Austin et al. (2005) argued against holding status offenders in detention facilities for mere violations of court orders. The authors also suggested that status offenders do not constitute a threat to the safety of the community. The investigators found that one-third of all young people in detention facilities had been held for status offenses and probation violations of a technical nature.

Goals of Juvenile Detention

Based on *parens patriae*, the courts seek to maintain the well-being of juveniles held in custody by ensuring that they are safe and secure and the community is also protected. In juvenile courts, although the types of services that they provide vary, they are required to offer adequate education, recreation, health-care evaluation, mental health services, and other services for the juveniles.

Secure Detention and Confinement

Juveniles can be held or placed in different settings and programs (Desai et al. 2006). Before adjudication, juveniles may be held in juvenile detention facilities, also known as secure detention and "juvenile hall." Juveniles may also be held in juvenile detention facilities during the post-adjudication phase as they wait for placement in a residential program or other setting. Juveniles whose cases have already been adjudicated may be placed in corrections centers (Desai et al. 2006).

In contrast to secure detention, juveniles may be placed in secure confinement (Austin et al. 2005). Youth who have been placed in secure confinement have been adjudicated delinquent and are placed or committed to a correctional facility. The duration of their secure confinement in these facilities varies from months to several years. Secure confinement facilities have more diverse programs than detention facilities.

Why are juveniles placed in juvenile detention facilities? They may be placed in these facilities because they are considered at risk of carrying more criminal activity and therefore a threat to the community (Desai et al. 2006). Juveniles may be kept in juvenile detention facilities because they have been charged with serious crimes, which necessitate automatic detention. Youth may be detained in juvenile facilities because their case has not yet been adjudicated, and they may not be likely to appear in juvenile court as required. Juveniles may be held in juvenile detention because adequate adult supervision or placement in another setting is not available. Desai et al. (2006) also note that parents can ask juvenile court to have their child sent to juvenile detention because they are ungovernable. As noted above, as a result of the VCO exception under the JJDP Act, status offenders are also held in detention facilities.

The Detention Decision

Some experts claim that the courts often rely on stereotypes and nonlegal characteristics such as the youth's demeanor, style of dress, gender, race, and socioeconomic status when they adjudicate juveniles (Cohen and Kluegel 1979; Cicourel 1968; Schur 1973). Youth who display a threatening demeanor before the judge may have an increased probability of receiving a harsh punishment. Juveniles dressed like gang members may have greater likelihood of receiving punishment.

Judges may take into consideration the testimony of the juvenile's family members. According to one self-report narrative, a runaway boy wrote that when he went before the judge on the charge of being a minor in possession of alcohol (MIP), his father took the stand and testified against him (Mishriki 2001–2013). The runaway boy stated that his father told the judge "more lies" about him. The youth believed that as a result of his father's false testimony, the judge sentenced him to 30 days in a juvenile detention facility. In this self-report narrative, the runaway boy noted that after spending 30 days in juvenile detention for being MIP, his stepfather would not take custody of him, so he ended up in a foster home as a ward of the state (Mishriki 2001–2013).

Wrongful conviction of juveniles can be a serious problem (Drizin and Luloff 2007), and the use of broad discretionary authority among juvenile court judges and other factors may increase the rate of wrongful convictions of juveniles. Traditionally, juveniles have not been accorded the same constitutional rights as adults, and this approach can lead to wrongful detention and convictions (Antieau 1961). For example, juveniles have been "detained overnight or longer without even" appearing in juvenile court (Antieau 1961).

Drizin and Luloff (2007) note that even when the so-called due process revolution of the 1960s occurred and juveniles were accorded the same rights to due process as adults, the juvenile court system was still inadequate. These new rights meant little when juveniles were still not capable of ensuring their rights to due process.

Another major problem is that juveniles, like adults, frequently have been coerced into making false confessions and being wrongfully incarcerated (Drizin and Luloff 2007; Davis and Leo 2014). For example, five juveniles falsely confessed to attempted murder and rape in the case involving the "Central Park Jogger," *People v. Salaam*, 666 N.Y.S.2d 881 (1997). Davis and Leo (2014) describe the many ways in which the police deliberately employ physical and psychosocial distress on criminal suspects in order to coerce them into confessing to crimes that they did not commit. The police also use lie trickery, lie detection, and other techniques to extract false confessions from criminal suspects.

Because of their socio-developmental stage and level of maturity, youth are especially vulnerable to interrogation-induced false confessions (Drizin and Luloff 2007). Youth often have difficulty judging risks, are susceptible to peer influence, and are unable to appreciate the long-term effects of their behaviors. During police interrogations, juvenile suspects may be more "compliant and suggestible" than adult offenders. As a result of these and other psychosocial and behavioral limitations, children and adolescents have an increased probability of making false confessions.

Cohen and Kluegel (1979) evaluated the impact of social characteristics and legal factors in two juvenile courts in metropolitan areas. The authors found that the juveniles' present activity (conventional activity or idle), the juveniles' prior juvenile record, and the court's orientation to juvenile court decision making were factors that predicted whether the juvenile was placed in juvenile detention or released.

Crowding

Juveniles have been exposed to crowded detention and confinement facilities. Crowding has become more prevalent in these settings (Parent et al. 1994; Austin et al. 2005). Thirty-six percent of youth were confined in facilities that went over their design capacity by 1987 (Parent et al. 1994). Crowding has occurred because of increased rates of incarceration. For example, between 1985 and 1995, the number of youth placed in juvenile detention increased 72 % (Hoytt et al. 2003).

Demographic and Behavioral Characteristics of Confined Juveniles

In the late 1980s, the demographic profile of confined youth changed significantly (Parent et al. 1994). The percentage of minority youth in detention facilities increased from 53 to 63 % between 1987 and 1991 (Parent et al. 1994). Blacks had the largest increase in the proportion who were held in detention during this period (from 37 to 44 %). The rate of confined Hispanic juveniles rose from 13 to 17 %. Minority youth continue to be disproportionately held in detention facilities (Desai et al. 2006). Hoytt et al. (2003) offers strategies for reducing racial disparities in juvenile detention settings. The authors recommend eliminating individual-based and institutional-based racism.

Researchers have found that female delinquents may be treated more harshly than male delinquents (Lederman et al. 2004). These extralegal aspects play a more important rule in adjudicating youth than the juveniles' alleged delinquent behaviors.

Youth who were held in detention settings for offenses against persons rose 22–28 % between 1987 and 1991 (Parent et al. 1994). Juveniles detained for crimes against property declined from 40 to 34 %. Youth who were confined for drug-associated crimes increased from 6 to 10 %.

Conditions of Confinement in Juvenile Detention and Correction Facilities

The US Congress in 1988 directed the OJJDP to evaluate aspects of juvenile offenders' confinement in correctional facilities, including private juvenile detention centers, training schools, camps, and ranches (Parent et al. 1994). The OJJDP study revealed many deficits in meeting basic needs; ensuring order and security; providing adequate education, recreation, and treatment programming; and ensuring juvenile rights (Parent et al. 1994).

With regard to fulfilling basic needs, the OJJDP report demonstrated that only 43 % of the facilities met the criteria for providing adequate living space. Forty-nine percent of juvenile correctional settings provided adequate accommodations based on the criteria assessed. According to the OJJDP report, only 35 % of juvenile facilities met the criteria for providing food, clothing, and hygiene (Parent et al. 1994).

The OJJDP report revealed that only 35 % of the settings fulfilled the criteria for offering health-care services to meet the juveniles' basic needs. Adequate health-care services are critical because juveniles in these facilities may have serious health problems. Detainees may be sexually active and at risk for sexually transmitted infections (STIs) and are not using contraception (Kelly et al. 2000; Bell et al. 1985). In one investigation of adolescent detainees in two juvenile detention settings, Kelly et al. (2000) found that almost of the juveniles in the sample reported being sexually active. In their study, 22.2 % of the female detainees and 8.7 % of the male detainees were infected with chlamydia. The researchers discovered that injection drug use increased the risk of having the chlamydia infection.

Bell et al. (1985) discovered that 18 % of females detainees at a juvenile detention center in King County, Washington, had *Neisseria gonorrhoeae* and 20 % had *Chlamydia trachomatis*. The investigators found that 68 % of the detainees did not use contraception.

Public health interventions in juvenile facilities may help to reduce the rates of STIs and other health problems in this vulnerable population. For example, Kelly et al. (2000) recommend the use of educational programs and community services to reduce the rate of the Chlamydia infection in adolescent detainees.

Desai et al. (2006) also discussed problems related to providing mental health care in juvenile detention facilities. The authors note that overcrowding and the large percentage of juveniles in detention centers who have mental disorders have resulted in an increase prevalence of injuries and suicides in these facilities. One investigation by Teplin et al. (2002) discovered that the 6-month prevalence of any psychiatric or substance abuse disorder in the juvenile detention facility in Cook County, Illinois, was 73.8 % in female juvenile offenders and 66.3 % in male juvenile inmates. The authors found that the disorders that were most prevalent were substance-use disorder, conduct disorder, anxiety disorders including post-traumatic stress disorder (PTSD), and affective disorders.

In another study of juveniles at a large, temporary detention setting in Cook County, Illinois, Abram et al. (2004) showed that 92.5 % of the detainees in the sample had suffered one or more traumas. The investigators demonstrated that more male detainees reportedly suffered at least one trauma than female detainees (93.2 % vs. 84.0 %). The researchers showed that 11.2 % fulfilled PTSD criteria for the prior year. For those suffering from PTSD, more than 50 % reportedly was a witness to violence.

Only 27 % of the correctional settings met the criteria for providing security for its juvenile inmates (Parent et al. 1994). According to the OJJDP investigation, an estimated 24,200 juvenile-on-juvenile injury incidents occurred per year. In addition, an estimated 6900 juvenile-on-staff and 106 staff-on-juvenile injury incidents took place per year.

The OJJDP report found that only 51 % of the juvenile correctional settings met the criteria for controlling suicidal behavior, which included suicide attempts, suicidal gestures, and self-mutilation. This problem is particularly serious since youth in detention settings have a high risk of making suicide attempts and committing suicide (Rohde et al. 1997). According to the OJJDP report, an estimated 17,600 incidents involving suicidal behaviors occurred in juvenile correctional facilities per year. The OJJDP report found that only 50 % of juveniles are in settings that monitor suicidal youth at least every 4 min.

Personnel at juvenile facilities may benefit from knowing about the risk factors for suicidal behaviors, PTSD, and other mental health problems among juveniles. For example, Rohde et al. (1997) discovered that boys at a county juvenile detention center who exhibited suicidal behaviors were more likely to be depressed and have low social support, while girls at the facility who had suicidal behaviors had a higher probability of being impulsive and unstable.

Another problem is that many juvenile facilities do not have effective inspections and emergency preparedness (Parent et al. 1994). In the OJJDP report, only 55 % of the settings met the criteria for effective policies and procedures in these areas.

According to the OJJDP investigation, many juvenile settings were deficient in offering adequate programming for juvenile inmates. Only 57 % of the facilities fulfilled the criteria for providing effective education services, and only 60 % met the criteria for offering treatment services. The report found that 85 % of the juvenile settings fulfilled the criteria for recreation programming.

The OJJDP also showed that many juvenile settings were deficient in ensuring the rights of juvenile inmates (Parent et al. 1994). Only 25 % of the facilities met the criteria for providing juveniles with access to the community. The report revealed that 76 % of the settings fulfilled the criteria for limiting the use of discretion by correctional staff.

One concern is that juveniles are being placed in solitary confinement. For example, a lawsuit was filed against the state of Ohio over this issue (New York Times, The Editorial Board, 2014, June 8).

Questions About the Effectiveness of Secure Detention and Confinement

Many juveniles are confined in traditional settings such as large training schools, which can house 100–500 juveniles (Austin et al. 2005). Research has shown that youth committed to these secure facilities have high recidivism rates (Wiebush et al. 2005; Krisberg 2005; Winner et al. 1997). Within 1 or 2 years of being releases, up to 50–70 % of confined juveniles are arrested again.

Youth in these traditional settings face significant separation from their communities, making reintegration into these communities after release problematic (Austin et al. 2005). Youth who receive long-term sentences, although they can receive various services, still confront obstacles to community reintegration.

Different Juvenile Settings

Agencies often manage a variety of juvenile settings including detention facilities and out-of-home programs. For example, in the District of Columbia, the Department of Youth Rehabilitation Services (DYRS) has authority for placing juveniles in a range of settings: "detention, commitment, and after-care programs" (Wikipedia n.d., Youth detention center). The DYRS manages the New Beginnings Youth Development Center, a 60-bed secure facility for the most serious male juvenile offenders in D.C.

Juvenile courts may send juveniles to other types of out-of-home placement such as residential programs, including camps, community-based programs, and residential treatment, including training schools (Wikipedia n.d., Youth detention center; Austin et al. 2005).

The Connecticut Juvenile Training School (CJTS) is a residential treatment for male juveniles, ages 12–17 (Wikipedia n.d., Youth detention center). Between 1998 and 2005, CJTS was plagued by scandals and controversial issues. The Connecticut Department of Children and Families improved the facility in 2008, and the new program focuses on therapeutic interventions.

Policy makers should emphasize alternatives to secure detention and confinement, especially since many juveniles after they are arrested will have no additional contact with the juvenile justice system (Austin et al. 2005) For example, Snyder and Sickmund (1999) showed that about 54 % of male and 73 % of female youth who have been arrested will not have additional involvement with the juvenile justice system.

Alternatives to secure detention include outright release of the youth to their families before adjudication, supervised release, home detention, electronic monitoring, and intensive supervision (Austin et al. 2005). Investigators have studied the impact of using these alternatives. One investigation of juveniles in Kentucky by Kihm and Block (1982) showed that the number of rearrests before final disposition did not increase after the number of juveniles released to their families or non-secure settings increased significantly.

Supervised release may be appropriate if the child is considered likely to re-offend or not show up for adjudication (Austin et al. 2005). Supervised release programs have been implemented to meet the requirement of reducing the number of juveniles in secure detention settings.

Home detention differs from outright release in that it requires the child to stay at home during specific periods of time (Austin et al. 2005). Home detention may involve other requirements such as drug testing. Outreach staff may be employed to supervise and mentor the juveniles. Ball et al. (1988) discovered that home detention was less costly than secure and non-secure facilities. Smykla and Selke (1982) showed that juveniles in home detention did not have a greater chance of re-offending than those in pre-adjudication detention. Other studies revealed that a large percentage of juveniles in home detention had positive outcomes (Ball et al. 1988; Austin et al. 2005).

Home detention frequently uses electronic monitoring and can reduce the expenses associated with supervision and the rate of placement in secure detention facilities (Austin et al. 2005). One investigation by Roy and Brown (1995) revealed that juvenile detained at home with electronic monitoring had a lower re-offending rate than those who did not get electronic monitoring.

For juveniles who have been adjudicated, intensive supervision programs (ISPs) are alternatives to secure confinement (Austin et al. 2005). The Detention Diversion Advocacy Program (DDAP) in San Francisco is a model intervention that emphasizes rehabilitation approaches that are customized to the juveniles' needs. One investigation indicated that juveniles in the DDAP intervention had lower re-offending rates than a group of children who were detained for a minimum of 3 days (Sheldon 1999).

Another alternative to secure confinement is day and evening reporting centers, which are nonresidential settings that require juveniles to report to case managers on a daily basis (Austin et al. 2005). Day and evening reporting centers are different from ISPs; the former settings provide more varied services such as drug treatment and job training. Cook County, Illinois, has a model day and evening reporting center program for juveniles who have been charged with violating probation or have been arrested on warrant. This program achieves a 92 % success rate (e.g., did not re-offend while in the program) for the period December 1995 to August 2001.

Skills training program are also an alternative to secure detention. Fresh Start, which is in Baltimore, Maryland, is an example of a 40-week nonresidential skills training program for delinquents, ages 16–19 (Austin et al. 2005). Young people in this program get education in practical skills such as carpentry. Between 1997 and 2000, graduates had lower rearrest rates (19 %) than children in other juvenile justice programs in Maryland.

Residential programs are another alternative to secure detention (Austin et al. 2005). They are designed for youth who are unable to go home or would not be suitable for secure detention facilities. Residential programs include foster homes and residential programs for runaway young people.

With regard to group homes, Mishriki (2001–2013) reported the case of a 16-year-old female runaway who had been placed in a group home, which was a locked facility. The youth had run away a number of times after having substantial problems such as fights with her mother, truancy, and school failure.

Investigations have shown that well-organized community-based treatment programs such as group homes, intensive supervision, probation, and day and evening reporting centers are better able to reduce repeat offenses among juvenile delinquents than conventional juvenile justice settings such as training schools (Howell 1995; Austin et al. 2005). These community-based programs also have been shown to enhance youth's adjustment within the community. According to Howell (1995), even when participation in community-based treatment facilities leads to less positive outcomes, these programs have been found to be more cost-effective than training schools.

In Massachusetts, juvenile justice personnel emphasizes the use of small secure settings for serious juvenile offenders instead of using secure detention facilities (Austin et al. 2005). In addition, juvenile justice officials rely on a full range of community-based treatment programs for most of the committed juveniles. Studies have shown that these settings can help the juvenile connect with their families, schools, and support systems in the community and can reduce future contact with the juvenile justice system (Coates et al. 1978; Krisberg et al. 1989).

Another investigation evaluated detention homes, foster homes, and runaway youth programs and showed that juveniles had negligible rates of new violations during pre-adjudication (Young and Pappenfort 1979). The study also revealed rates of 10 % or less of running away from programs.

In many areas, juvenile justice officials implement interventions that combine residential settings and different at-home programs (Austin et al. 2005). In one investigation, Lubow (1999) assessed three Juvenile Detention Alternatives Initiative (JDAI) programs that included a combination of day or evening reporting centers, home confinement, and temporary non-secure settings in different communities.

Some participants received electronic monitoring. The authors discovered that participation in these settings reduced failure to appear in court by half. One of the sites of the intervention was Cook County, Illinois. Ninety-three percent of the juvenile assigned to home confinement there completed the program, and 92 % of the juveniles placed in evening reporting centers completed the program. In addition, 94 % of juveniles assigned to electronic monitoring and 96 % placed in non-secure settings completed the program in Cook County, Illinois.

The Gulf Coast Trades Center (GCTC) is a residential skills program that does not include at-home component (Austin et al. 2005). The results from September 1999 through August 2000 revealed that 84 % of the juveniles in the intervention completed the program. Children who graduated the program in 1999–2000 had a lower rearrest rate (16 %) than the rate for all juveniles released from the Texas Youth Commission.

Juvenile justice officials provide a number of alternatives to secure confinement such as diversion, ISPs, community-based treatment and therapy, and residential treatment (Austin et al. 2005). Police and the courts can use their discretion in diverting juveniles away from formal processing in the juvenile justice system and into alternative treatments and supervision. Diversion of juveniles became popular with officials in the 1970s due to overcrowding in juvenile facilities and associated decline in the conditions within these settings.

Analysts have found that diversion results in mixed outcomes (Austin et al. 2005). Some investigations show that diversion lowers re-offending rates, while other studies reveal no positive consequences. Other research indicates that diversion have mixed findings (Stanford 1984; Ezell 1992; Austin et al. 2005). In Massachusetts, Coates et al. (1978) discovered that participation in community-based programs resulted in a lower re-offending rate when different types of programs were available to the juveniles.

ISPs may not be very intensive and may be similar to traditional supervision (Austin et al. 2005). Greenwood and Turner (1993) and Murray and Cox (1979) discovered that ISPs and traditional supervision had similar re-offending rates. However, in Pennsylvania, Sontheimer and Goodstein (1993) demonstrated that juveniles who received intensive supervision and aftercare had lower recidivism than those who only participated in traditional probation. In a study in North Carolina among juveniles who were mainly status offenders, Land et al. (1990) revealed that these juveniles who were in intensive supervision and aftercare had lower recidivism than those in traditional supervision.

One intensive probation program in Texas, the Tarrant County Advocate Program-North (TCAP) relies on mentors or advocates in order to help juveniles and their families in accessing community-based programs (Austin et al. 2005). The TCAP is customized to the needs of the juveniles and includes services such as anger management, youth employment, and tutoring. Ninety-six percent of the juveniles remained in the community or were diverted from being committed to the Texas Youth Commission or out-of-home facilities.

Community-based treatment and therapy such as multisystemic therapy (MST) may be effective in helping violent and chronic juvenile offenders (Austin et al. 2005). Juveniles in MST stay at home and get therapy that focus on difficulties such as their problems with peers, family members, and school performance. Studies indicate that

MST may be a very effective intervention (Lipsey and Wilson 1998; Krisberg and Howell 1998; Cullen and Gendreau 2000). In a review of the literature, Henggeler (1997) found that MST programs in various southern states had lower rates of re-offending among juveniles who were violent and chronic offenders.

Mihalic et al. (2001) showed that participation in MST resulted in lower re-offending rates among violent and chronic juvenile offenders. In addition, those juveniles who were in MST had a reduction in mental health difficulties and improvements in their family's functional status. Other investigations have demonstrated that participation in MST improved the juvenile offenders' problems, such as anxiety, aggressive tendencies, and level of maturity (Henggeler et al. 1998; Kazdin and Weisz 1998; Thorton et al. 2000). Moreover, these investigations reveal that youth who receive MST have better relationships with their families and reduced rates of self-reported violations.

The Family and Neighborhood Services (FANS) intervention is an MST project that provides for small caseloads for therapists who are working with juveniles and their families for 4 months on average. Participants in FANS have extensive delinquency histories including arrest and confinement records. In one investigation, Henggler et al. (1992) discovered that participation in FANS resulted in reductions in rates of rearrest and confinement compared to juveniles in a control group. FANS participants also had better family functioning and lower aggressive interactions with their peers. The study also found that FANS was more cost-effective than placement in correctional facilities.

Community residential centers such as group homes supervise primarily nonviolent juveniles on a 24-h basis. Austin et al. (2005) note that research on group homes in the 1970s revealed that group homes had better outcomes or at least did not produce worse results that state facilities. One investigation by Lipsey and Wilson (1998) evaluated the effectiveness of teaching family homes which have a small group of juveniles who live with supervising adults who work on changing the juveniles' problematic behaviors. The authors discovered that this setting reduced re-offenses.

Another program type, treatment foster care (TFC) is designed to separate juveniles from their negative peers by relying on adult mentors and conventional peers (Austin et al. 2005). TFC provides intensive treatment in different settings such as the juvenile's home, school, and community settings and are designed for chronic and serious offenders. Chamberlain and Mihalic (1998) demonstrated that juveniles who were in TFC had reduced stays in confinement and had fewer runaway episodes than those in a control group.

Camps also provide juveniles with a range of interventions in order to reduce juvenile recidivism and foster rehabilitation (OJJJDP n.d.; Austin et al. 2005). For example, juvenile boot camps, which developed from the model for adult offender boot camps, have been established in a number of states (OJJJDP n.d.). Juvenile boot camps are designed to expose juveniles to a military-type routine, provide discipline for the youth, offer physical condition, and provide a range of educational, counseling, and substance abuse programs. One study of three juvenile boot camp programs revealed that the programs had high rates of attrition associated with youth not complying, being absent from the programs, and getting arrested again (OJJJDP n.d.).

At VisionQuest, a nationwide intervention, offenders with serious delinquent histories participate in wilderness camps and other outdoor interventions for several months (Austin et al. 2005). After participating in the outdoor program, juveniles are placed in a community-based residential home for 5 months in order to prepare them to make the transition to their families and local communities. Based on an evaluation of VisionQuest in San Diego, California, Greenwood and Turner (1987) demonstrated that VisionQuest participants had lower rearrest rates than a control group that consisted of juveniles who had been incarcerated in a country correctional facility. Before the intervention, youth in the VisionQuest group also had a history of more serious violations than those in the country correctional setting.

Ranches can provide a wide range of interventions for juvenile offenders. For example, the James Ranch, a 96-bed facility for boys ages 15 and half to 18, is managed by the Superior Court of California, County of Santa Clara, Juvenile Probation Department. The James Ranch provides GED tutoring, work programs, drug and alcohol counseling and treatment, sex offender intervention, victim awareness, and sports activities.

Another program, the Log Cabin Ranch School (LCR), is managed by the San Francisco Juvenile Probation Department. The LCR is a post-adjudication, 24-h residential treatment and rehabilitation program for male delinquents. LCR offers educational, mental health, health-care, and cognitive-behavioral-oriented interventions.

One approach to reducing detention and confinement is to expand special program initiatives (Austin et al. 2005). These programs, which are funded by governments or private sources, are designed to encourage juvenile justice officials to design alternative interventions.

Legislative reform can be used to expand the use of alternatives to secure detention and confinement (Austin et al. 2005). In contrast to special program initiatives, legislative reforms do not require the implementation of treatment programs. State legislators can enact legislation that reduces the population of juvenile correctional facilities. For example, legislators can enact laws that allow juveniles in pretrial detention to be released on bail. Laws can also be enacted to provide juveniles with credit for time spent in pretrial detention. These laws apply to adults and also can be applied to juveniles.

Administrative reforms also can be effective in reducing the population of juvenile correctional settings (Austin et al. 2005; Annie E. Casey Foundation 2000). The use of objective screening criteria and risk assessment protocols may reduce unnecessary use of secure detention and confinement settings. Improvements in risk assessment can improve the process after a juvenile is arrested to determine if the juvenile should be placed in secure detention. Risk assessment can assist courts in determining dispositional alternatives. Improvements in custody classification can ensure that youth are placed in a facility with an appropriate custody level. Innovations in the processing of juvenile cases such as innovative police referral practices and fast-track hearings can reduce the population of juveniles in secure detention and confinement settings. These types of innovations can reduce overcrowding and the costs of operating the juvenile facilities.

In addition, reform of the system of secure detention and confinement can be achieved through litigation (Austin et al. 2005). However, litigation can be lengthy and costly and produce adversarial relations.

Chapter 20
Runaway and Homeless Youth Interventions

This chapter describes the effectiveness of primary and secondary intervention approaches in responding to runaway and homeless young people. Primary prevention approaches seek to prevent homelessness and runaway behaviors and other adverse behavioral consequences among youth in the general community. Primary prevention can use a youth development model that has been effective in helping youth with a variety of problems. Secondary prevention targets young people who have run away or become homeless. Investigators and practitioners believe that these secondary intervention approaches should be comprehensive and customized to meet the needs of the runaway and homeless young people. These interventions should also address the street youth's criminal/delinquent activities, school truancy, substance abuse, risks for sexually transmitted infections (STIs) including human immune virus (HIV)/acquired immunodeficiency syndrome (AIDS), and other mental health, social, and behavioral problems. Program outcomes such as reducing rates of runaway/homeless behavior, improving psychosocial functioning, reducing HIV risk behaviors, and strengthening family relationships are discussed.

In various countries, practitioners and researchers are analyzing the most effective methods to respond to runaway and homeless young people (Slesnick et al. 2009). Interventions for runaway and homeless young people may benefit from taking into account the risk amplification model proposed by Whitbeck et al. (1999). According to this model, runaway and homeless youth often come from dysfunctional families. These children and adolescents frequently have suffered from sexual, physical, and emotional abuse and neglect in their family environments, which places them at increased risk for sexual violence, human trafficking victimization, and other adverse outcomes while on the streets.

Investigators should use both qualitative and qualitative research methods to develop the most effective responses to runaway and homeless youth (Slesnick et al. 2009). Interventions should include both qualitative and quantitative data in the same studies. According to Slesnick et al. (2009), qualitative investigations are more prevalent in international research, while in the USA, quantitative-oriented research dominates the intervention field.

S.J. Morewitz, *Runaway and Homeless Youth*,
DOI 10.1007/978-3-319-30863-0_20

Meade and Slesnick (2002) also recommend that interventions with runaway and homeless young people should follow ethical practices. For example, service providers and researchers must obtain informed consent in order for runaway and homeless youth to participate in research and treatment. Informed consent is a requirement of the US Department of Health and Human Services and other organizations (Office for Protection from Research Risks 1979; Meade and Slesnick 2002).

Primary and Secondary Intervention Approaches

Practitioners and researchers have two approaches to deal with the diverse problems of runaway and homeless youth (Robertson and Toro n.d.). Primary prevention approaches seek to prevent homelessness and runaway behaviors and other adverse behavioral consequences among youth in the general community. Primary prevention can use a youth development model that has been effective in helping youth with a variety of problems (Family and Youth Services, Bureau 1996; Durlak and Wells 1997).

According to Robertson and Toro (n.d.), primary intervention might identify those young people who have a high probability of suffering from unstable housing situations and becoming homeless. Researchers and practitioners could target risk factors such as low socioeconomic status (SES), family violence, alcohol and other drug problems, conduct disorder, and juvenile delinquency (Morewitz 2004; Goldstein and Morewitz 2011; Robertson and Toro n.d.).

Researchers and practitioners can use families to implement primary prevention (Robertson and Toro n.d.). They are especially useful in intervening with dysfunctional family dynamics such as ineffective parenting, poor communication, divorce, family violence, and substance abuse (Morewitz 2003, 2004, 2008).

Primary prevention can rely on school settings to help at-risk youth avoid homelessness and runaway behaviors (Robertson and Toro n.d.). Teachers and school administrators can identify and work with young people who truant and absent from school for periods of time. Primary prevention can focus on reducing young people's delinquent activities, school truancy, substance use and abuse, and other high-risk behaviors that increase their probability of running away and becoming homeless.

Primary intervention can help children and adolescents who are suffering from mental health problems that place them at high risk for running away and becoming homeless. For example, school officials are developing programs to train mental health personnel and teachers to recognize and intervene with school children who are engaging in deliberate self-harm, which occurs among runaway and homeless youth (Linden, 2015). Researchers are evaluating the most effective therapeutic interventions for youth who self-harm (Ougrin et al., 2015).

Practitioners and investigators can use primary prevention approaches that rely on peer groups (Robertson and Toro n.d.). For example, Pedro-Carroll et al. (1986) used peer groups in a preventive intervention with children of divorce.

Primary prevention can target residential institutions such as psychiatric settings, foster care, and juvenile detention facilities to help young people avoid homelessness and runaway behaviors (Robertson and Toro n.d.). Emphasizing comprehensive discharge planning may reduce the risks of homelessness and runaway behavior in these vulnerable populations. The development of independent living skills services can help youth in different settings transition to conventional life. Robertson and Toro (n.d.) recommend extending support to former foster care youth for 1–2 years after they leave foster care may help reduce homelessness. In addition, training for foster care parents with youth at risk for becoming runaways and homeless may be a viable approach.

Secondary prevention targets young people who have run away or become homeless. Investigators and practitioners believe that these intervention approaches should be comprehensive and customized to the needs of the runaway and homeless young people (Robertson and Toro n.d.). They should take into account the fact that these individuals may be used to taking care of themselves while on the streets and are often distrustful of service providers and others in authority. These services should also address the street youth's criminal/delinquent activities, school truancy, substance abuse, and other mental health and social problems.

Kidd (2003) suggests that researchers previously have neglected views and experiences of runaway and homeless young people. Understanding the views of street youth is essential for developing effective intervention programs, especially since their participation in programs is voluntary (Karabanow and Rains 1997). Studies in different countries and different service settings show that runaway and homeless young people frequently are not satisfied with service providers and their organizations (Slesnick et al. 2009). Researchers recommend implementing interventions that emphasize the strengths of the runaway and homeless young people rather their deficits and are comprehensive and individualized based on the life experiences of the youth (Kidd 2003; Nebbitt et al. 2007).

Various researchers have found that successful interventions should promote trust, caring, and nonjudgmental views toward runaway/homeless youth (Kidd 2003; Thompson et al., 2006; Karabanow and Rains 1997). In addition, studies indicate that young people in these interventions prefer service providers who follow inclusionary practices rather than exclusionary ones (Darbyshire et al. 2006). For example, runaway and homeless youth oppose being punished for missing appointments, and interventions that are inclusionary have the best chances of being successful.

Rice et al. (2007) suggest that interventions should target conventional or prosocial peers in the social networks of homeless young people. For example, the presence of peers who go to school, are employed, or have good relationships with their families can reduce the likelihood of HIV risk behaviors.

Edinburgh and Saewyc (2009) evaluated an intensive home visiting and case management program for runaway, sexually assaulted girls, ages 10–14. The home visits were centered on the participants and used a "strengths-based or positive development" focus.

Secondary prevention approaches can focus on preserving families in crisis. For example, Slesnick and Prestopnik (2009) assessed the effects of a home-based intervention that follows a family preservation approach to assisting families in crisis. The program known as Ecologically Based Family Therapy (EBFT), which follows the Homebuilders family preservation perspective, targets families who have runaway youth at shelters or children who have been removed from the family. EBFT seeks to help substance-using children in runaway shelters and also assist their families improve their ability to function. The researchers discovered that youth in the EBFT group had fewer days using alcohol or other drugs at two follow-up periods (9- and 15-month follow-ups) compared to juveniles in a control group. However, the investigators did not find improvements in other variables related to using alcohol and other drugs.

Other secondary intervention emphasizes other behavioral and cognitive issues. For example, the Aggression Replacement Training (ART) program is designed to help aggressive youth with anger management, social skills, and "moral-reasoning education" (Nugent et al. 1998; Development Services Group, Inc 2015). The ART program is designed to assist youth at runaway shelters and other short-term residential settings deal with their aggressive and violent tendencies. Youth at runaway shelters often have suffered abuse in their home environments, which may increase the likelihood that they will engage in violence (Wilson et al. 2009). Based on a sample of 522 shelter-living teens, Nugent et al. (1998) discovered that participating in the ART program was associated with a 20 % reduction in the episodes of antisocial behavior per participant and a 17.2 % drop in the mean number of antisocial behavior episodes per day.

Secondary prevention programs that are community based may be more likely to reduce the runaway and homeless youth's rate of delinquent behaviors. Various researchers have found that community-based treatments that reinforce positive family interactions and social control processes are better than juvenile detention in reducing crime rates in the future (Hughes 2011; Holman and Ziedenberg 2006; Development Services Group, Inc 2015).

Evaluation of Service Settings

Researchers and practitioners have evaluated program outcomes in different service settings such as runaway drop-in centers and shelters (Slesnick et al. 2009). Drop-in centers, which are unstructured and meet the immediate needs of runaway and homeless youth such as food and bathing facilities, may help these individuals return to conventional society. According to a 1999 National Survey of Homeless Assistance Providers and Clients, the US had only 14 drop-in centers for young people and 22 outreach settings, which are much fewer than the programs available to homeless adults (17,900 adult drop-in centers and 3310 adult outreach programs) (Burt et al. 1999; Slesnick et al. 2009).

The Runaway and Homeless Youth Act's Basic Centers Program provides funding to runaway shelters in order to facilitate family reunification (Teare et al. 1994; Thompson et al. 2000; Nebbitt et al. 2007; Slesnick et al. 2009). Some analysts have found that some young people who went back home after a stay at a runaway shelter exhibited improved psychosocial functioning (Teare et al. 1992; Thompson et al. 2000; Slesnick et al. 2009). These individuals had lower levels of depression, less suicidal thought, and reduced feelings of hopelessness than those young people who were discharged from other settings. In contrast, various investigations have shown that discharged youth, regardless of which service setting discharges them, often have a high rate of returning to runaway shelters (Baker et al. 2003). In one investigation, Baker et al. (2003) discovered that 34 % of individuals who were "repeat runaways" and 18 % of first-time runaways came back to the shelter within 12 months of being discharged.

Reducing Rates of Runaway/Homeless Behavior

To what extent do runaway shelters and specific interventions reduce runaway behaviors? Based on a sample of 371 runaway/homeless young people, Pollio et al. (2006) evaluated the degree to which youth who were using crisis shelter services had lower rates of running away. At the time of their enrollment in the investigation, 62 % had run away at least one time. Most of the youth had more than two running away incidents for more than 7 days. Before the incident that triggered their use of emergency shelters, 81 % of these children and adolescents had been residing with their families

Pollio et al. (2006) discovered that runaway and homeless youth who used the crisis shelter services showed a decrease in the number of days on the run at the 6-week, 3-month, and 6-month study periods compared to the number of days that they were on the run at the time that they were enrolled in the study. These youth also had decreases in the number of days on the run from the 6-week to the 3-month study periods. However, the young people in the investigation had an increase in the number of days on the run at the 6-month study period compared to the 6-week and 3-month study periods.

Behavioral and Mental Health Problems

Runaway and homeless young people often suffer from serious mental health problems such as conduct disorder (CD) and suicidal behaviors. To what degree do shelters and other settings reduce behavioral and emotional difficulties of runaway and homeless young people? In one investigation, Barber et al. (2005) showed that homeless young people's use of shelter services was associated with fewer behavioral problems and emotional difficulties at a 6-month follow-up.

Using a Community Reinforcement Approach (CRA) that emphasizes operant principles and behavioral and cognitive treatment that is ecologically based, Slesnick et al. (2007) showed that participation in the CRA group increased the homeless youth's social stability compared to those who participated in the treatment-as-usual intervention (58 % compared to 13 %). Participation in the

CRA group was associated with a greater reduction in depression symptoms compared to youth in the treatment-as-usual group (40 % vs. 23 % reduction).

Booth and Zhang (1997) recommend that interventions target runaway and homeless young people who have CD since this having this disorder may increase the risks of sexually transmitted infections (STIs) and human immunodeficiency virus (HIV)/acquired immune deficiency syndrome (AIDS) transmission.

Relationship with Family Members

Based on their analysis, Pollio et al. (2006) showed that runaway and homeless children and adolescents who used emergency shelter services had a higher rate of contacting their families at each study period compared to the start of the investigation.

In terms of runaway and homeless youth's perceptions of family support, Pollio et al. (2006) found that perceived family support increased at each follow-up period compared to the start of the investigation. However, between other study periods, no significant findings were obtained.

Substance Use and Abuse

To what degree can interventions reduce substance use and abuse among runaway and homeless young people? Pollio et al. (2006) discovered that runaway and homeless youth who had used shelter services exhibited significant reductions in current substance use at all three study periods compared to the start of the investigation. However, this trend reversed itself in later periods. In one investigation, Steele and O'Keefe (2001) found that homeless teens that used emergency shelter services had a lower rate of substance use at the time of discharge. Using the CRA approach, Slesnick et al. (2007) showed that participants in the CRA had reduced substance use compared to young people in the treatment-as-usual group (a reduction of 37 % compared to 17 %).

To what extent can substance-abuse interventions that involve both substance-abusing runaway adolescents and their families reduce the homeless and runaway youth's substance-abuse patterns? Based on a sample of 179 individuals from a shelter, Slesnick et al. (2013) found that different interventions have the potential to reduce substance abuse in homeless youth. However, some homeless adolescents in their sample fluctuated in their rates of substance use.

Delinquency and Criminal Behavior Reduction

Research specialists and service providers can design interventions to reduce street youth's delinquency/criminal activities. While on the streets, young people may have high rates of delinquent and criminal activity in order to survive on the streets with employment, food, or shelter and face getting arrested and processed in the juvenile justice system. According to one study of runaway and homeless youth by Chen et al. (2006), more than 50 % of the children had been arrested at least once since their first runaway incident. In their investigation, street youth had been arrested an average 4.4 occasions. In another investigation, Booth (2006) found 65 % of homeless young people in Adelaide, Australia, committed theft as part of their food acquisition strategies. Street youth also may resort to other deviant strategies such as scavenging in dumpsters, known as dumpster surfing, which also increases their chances of getting arrested. Interventions should evaluate the extent to which offering employment, job training, employment readiness, and educational services can reduce rates of delinquency and criminal activity, lower arrest rates, and reduce placement in correctional facilities.

HIV/AIDS Prevention and Sexual Health Risk Reduction Strategies

Pollio et al. (2006) discovered that the rate of sexual behavior among runaway and homeless youth using shelter services increased at the 6-month study period compared to the onset of the investigation.

Two investigations have found that interventions can reduce risk behaviors for HIV among runaway adolescents (Rotheram-Borus et al., 2003; Rotheram-Borus and Koopman 1991). Based on an evaluation of a ten-session group-based HIV intervention, researchers showed that condom use increased and high-risk activities were reduced at a 6-month follow-up (Rotheram-Borus and Koopman 1991). At a 2-year follow-up, female youth had a lower level of unprotected sex (Rotheram-Borus et al., 2003).

Several other investigations of drop-in centers and outreach programs did not reveal reductions in HIV risk outcomes such as improvements in sexual risk behaviors and thinking related to HIV (Rew et al. 2007; Booth et al. 1999; Auerswald et al. 2006). One study by Gleghorn et al. (1997) showed that outreach on the streets was associated with homeless young people using a new needle at their last injection at a 6-month follow-up.

Other interventions can emphasize reducing runaway and homeless youth's participation in survival sex and prostitution (Halcon and Lifson 2004; Tyler et al. 2000a, b). These interventions are crucial since street youth frequently participate in prostitution. In McCarthy and Hagan's (1992) research, about 30 % of the homeless young people reported that they engaged in prostitution.

Pregnancy Prevention

Interventions can focus on reducing the pregnancy rates among runaway and homeless females. While on the streets, female adolescents are at high risk due to their participation in high-risk sexual activity including survival sex, prostitution, and sex with multiple partners. These female teens also face the risks of sexual assault and rape. According to research, up to 20 % of homeless female adolescents get pregnant (Thompson et al. 2008; Halcon and Lifson 2004).

Improving School Outcomes

How effective are runaway/homeless interventions in improving youth's educational outcomes such as reduced rates of school detention and suspension? In their investigation, Pollio et al. (2006) only discovered a significant decrease in the percentage of youth receiving a detention, suspension, or expulsion between the 6-week and 3-month study periods. The researchers did not find a pattern for individual forms of adverse school incidents.

Enhancing Employment and Vocational Training Outcomes

In their investigation of runaway and homeless youth using crisis shelter services, Pollio et al. (2006) showed that the percentage of runaway and homeless youth currently employed did not increase by the 6-month study period compared to the start of the investigation. The percentage of runaway and homeless young people who were terminated from their job actually increased by the 6-month follow-up period compared to the onset of the investigation.

Improving Vocational Training

Based on a sample of homeless young people from a sample of drop-in centers, Ferguson and Xie (2008) discovered that participants in a vocational training program had higher levels of satisfaction with life and more contact with their families than those not participating in the intervention. However, participants in the vocational training had more sexual risk activities than nonparticipants. The authors did not investigate vocational outcomes in this study.

Effects of Service Utilization

Pollio et al. (2006) found only few favorable outcomes when studying the impact of service utilization on different outcomes. In terms of the few positive findings, only use of alcohol/drug treatment and employment services was associated with a decrease in number of days on the run for certain time periods. Use of employment services was associated with an increase in self-esteem for certain time periods. Health services utilization was linked to greater perceived parent support.

Case Management

Community-based mental health facilities rely on case management to assist homeless and runaway children and adolescents (Sosin and Durkin 2007; Slesnick et al. 2009; Edinburgh and Saewyc 2009). Based on a study of youth from a drop-in center, Cauce et al. (1994) discovered that Project Passage, an intensive case management program for homeless young people, did not produce better outcomes than regular case management. The authors suggest that short-term case management may be as effective as longer case management strategies.

Mental Health Treatment for Runaway and Homeless Youth

Researchers have evaluated the effectiveness of interventions to reduce mental health problems among homeless and runaway youth. For example, one investigation by Guo et al. (2014) found that ecologically based family therapy (EBFT) shows promise in reducing symptoms of depression among runaway youth who are substance abusers.

International Research

According to Toro et al. (2007), international studies on the problem of homelessness started in the latter part of the 1990s. A majority of these investigations analyzed homeless adults who were single. Slesnick et al. (2009) identified several countries such as Israel, China, and Uganda that have implemented research on runaway and homeless young people.

In one intervention, government officials in Uganda relocated street young people from the capital to families or organizations (Jacob et al. 2004). At the end of 12 months, 700 juveniles had been resettled by law enforcement personnel. However, a follow-up investigation revealed that 50 % of the youth visited were no longer in their new locations. Children who were interviewed reported that they were assaulted or had observed other children who were assaulted.

In Israel, Dekel et al. (2003) evaluated young people who had been discharged from runaway shelters and found that a majority had gone to their family's residence. However, at follow-up, only 54 % had remained there. Twenty-eight percent of the youth were on the streets or with their friends. Eighteen percent of the young people in the study had been placed in out-of-home settings. The investigators suggest that due to the limited options following discharge from shelters, and as a result, youth are inappropriately discharged to home or other settings.

Hyun et al. (2005), in Seoul, Korea, assessed shelter youth who participated in group-based cognitive behavioral therapy (CBT). The investigators discovered that young people in the CBT group indicated that their self-efficacy improved and reduced their depression symptoms compared to those in the control group.

In China, the central government of China set up Protection and Education Centers for Street Children in order to meet their basic needs and reunify the youth with their families. However, Lam and Cheng (2008) discovered that most of the youth do not use these settings because they restrict their behaviors. In addition, the children avoid these organizations because they do not want to go back to their families. The investigators showed that most of the respondents went back to the streets after using these settings.

Taylor et al. (2007), in the United Kingdom, also found a high dropout rate in a study of homeless youth who received mental health treatment from 18 homeless shelters in various regional areas. The researchers showed that 50 % of the young people who went for mental health services stopped participating after the first visit.

Methodological Concerns

Methodological problems limit the success of evaluating the impact of programs on runaway and homeless adolescents (Slesnick et al. 2009). For example, investigators have not used control groups, which reduce the effectiveness of their research. In addition, evaluators have not conducted long-term follow-up of young people who have participated in interventions. This deficit is particularly important because the positive effects of interventions are often temporary. Some researchers also have not offered empirical justification for their intervention approaches.

Chapter 21
Runaway and Homeless Youth Needs: Legislation and Policy Options

In this chapter, the diverse needs and problems facing street youth and the legislation and policies that have been enacted to help meet their needs are presented (National Conference of State Legislatures 2013, October 1; Robertson and Toro n.d.; Slesnick et al. 2009). Effective legislation and policy options are essential because of the large number of runaway/thrown-away and homeless young people in the USA and other countries. For example, in the USA, the National Incidence Studies of Missing, Abducted, Runaway, and Thrown-away Children estimated that 1,682,900 runaway/thrown-away incidents occurred in 1999 (Hammer et al. 2002). In this chapter, issues such as identifying children and adolescents who are at early risk for running away and becoming homeless, promoting family reunification and community-based emergency shelter and social services, and meeting the need for permanent supportive housing are assessed.

In addition, this chapter evaluates the need for notifying parents, guardians, or custodians and parental responsibility for damages caused by their runaway children. In the USA, state and federal policies related to runaway and homeless youth are presented.

Identifying Homeless and Runaway Youth

Homeless and runaway young people are highly transient and mobile, and many are engaged in problematic behaviors, including prostitution, survival sex, substance abuse, school failure, truancy, and delinquent/criminal behaviors. In addition, runaway and homeless youth may have conduct disorder, depression, anxiety, and physical health problems, including malnutrition and food insecurity, and are at risk for sexually transmitted infections and HIV/AIDS, pregnancy, suicidal behaviors, and early death (Anderson 2013; Yates et al. 1988). Homeless and runaway youth may come from dysfunctional families and are escaping sexual, physical, and emotional/mental abuse and neglect. Many youth are considered thrown-aways since they have been thrown out by their parents.

S.J. Morewitz, *Runaway and Homeless Youth*,
DOI 10.1007/978-3-319-30863-0_21

One major difficulty in providing services to meet the extensive needs of homeless and runaway youth population is that service providers, policy makers, and researchers do not have reliable data on the prevalence of homeless and runaway youth (Anderson 2013). Services providers, researchers, and policy makers use different definitions and categories of homeless and runaway youth. Homeless young people can be classified as unaccompanied youth or youth who live in families. According to the McKinney–Vento Homeless Assistance Act (42 USC 11431-11435, 2001), an unaccompanied youth is "a youth not in the physical custody of a parent or guardian" (42 USC 1143a(6), 2001). Anderson (2013) notes that analysts have difficulty measuring the number of unaccompanied youth in the community since the unaccompanied youth rarely take advantage of shelters or other services. Unaccompanied young people frequently become homeless because of severe family dysfunction, including conflict, sexual, physical, and emotional abuse and neglect. They also become homeless after they leave foster care or jail. Most unaccompanied homeless young people ran away from home or were thrown out by their parents or guardians.

The Homeless Management Information Systems (HMIS) only measures homeless persons who are sheltered. The HMIS also excludes "doubled up persons," low socioeconomic status (SES) persons, or family members who are staying with friends, relatives, or others due to financial difficulties) and families in its definition of homeless. In addition, the HMIS does not count persons who use domestic violence shelters and homeless individuals who use certain homeless programs.

Another method for measuring the prevalence of homeless individuals is the point-in-time (PIT) count, which measures on a single night the prevalence of sheltered and unsheltered homeless persons in a specific community (Anderson 2013). The PIT does not differentiate youth who are homeless; it reports only the number of individuals living in families with children.

Service providers also differ in their definition of runaway youth based on the age of the runaway. Some service providers classify runaway youth as those who are under 18 years of age, while others consider the age of 21 as the age limit for runaways (National Conference of State Legislatures 2013, October 1, Minnesota).

Prevalence of Homeless People

What is known about the prevalence of homeless people and the subgroup, homeless, and runaway youth? The US Congress mandated that the Annual Homeless Assessment Report (AHAR) be prepared to collect and analyze data on the homeless population. The 2009 AHAR reported between October 1, 2008, and September 30, 2009, 1,558,917 people were in an emergency shelter or transitional housing. According to the Second National Incidence Studies of Missing, Abducted, Runaway, and Thrown-away Children (NISMART-2), an estimated 1,682,900 young person experienced a runaway or thrown-away incident in 1999 (Hammer et al. 2002). The National Survey on Drug Use in 2002 reported that 1.6 million young persons aged 12–17 were runaways and had slept on the streets in the prior year (Benoit-Bryan 2010).

Identifying Youth Who Are at Early Risk for Running Away and Becoming Homeless

Experts can identify young people who are at early risk for running away and becoming homeless and can design policies to reduce these outcomes. For example, Hammer et al. (2002) discovered that age is linked to running away. Youth ages 15–17 have a higher probability of running away than those younger than 15 years of age. Investigators have also discovered that girls have a greater likelihood of running away than boys (Courtney and Zinn 2009; Sanchez et al. 2006). According to the National Runaway Switchboard (NRS) (2008), 75 % of those who called the NRS were female.

Family Reunification and Community-Based Emergency Shelter and Social Services

Youth can benefit from using community-based emergency shelter and social services because they are designed to offer short-term resolution of crises and custodial services and achieve family reunification (Nebbitt et al. 2007). Runaway and homeless young people should be reunited with their families if this reunification provides a suitable environment for youth (Nebbitt et al. 2007). Unfortunately, family reunification is frequently not in the best interest of the runaway/homeless child. Policy makers can fund research and interventions that rebuild dysfunctional families and prevent children and adolescents from running away or becoming homeless (Slesnick et al. 2009; National Conference of State Legislatures 2013, October 1, Indiana).

Runaway and homeless youth, because of their potentially life-threatening conditions, can receive significant help from community and street outreach and social and health services (Slesnick et al. 2009). However, the provision of these services is hampered by the fact that runaway and homeless youth often distrust individuals in authority. In fact, runaway youth frequently have conduct problems such as conduct disorder and oppositional defiant disorder, which make them resentful and antagonistic toward those in authority. Street youth may be suffering from food insecurity, substance abuse, and other severe health problems that limit their use of vital social and health services. Service providers should assess the outreach and social services needs and perceptions of the young people and adjust the delivery of outreach and social services accordingly (Thompson et al. 2006a).

Runaway and homeless young persons may need drop-in services because these services help to meet immediate needs such as food, clothing, showers, and laundry (Slesnick et al. 2009). Drop-in centers also may offer case management based on the organization's level of funding. Runaway and homeless youth have an opportunity to develop trust with service providers, which may encourage the young person to request more drop-in services. These shelters also offer social skills training (Slesnick et al. 2009). Policies can be enacted to ensure that effective skills training are provided.

Notification of Parent, Guardian, or Custodian

Parents, guardians, or custodians frequently do not know the whereabouts of their runaway or homeless child even though the child may be receiving homeless/runaway services at an emergency shelter or other organization. Policies can be designed to require individuals who harbor runaway and homeless youth and shelters and other facilities that provide services to homeless and runaway young people notify the child's parents, guardian, or custodian (National Conference of State Legislatures 2013, October 1, Nevada; Utah). Researchers and policy makers should investigate the extent to which parental notification would lead to successful reunification of youth with their families.

Parental Responsibility for Damages Caused by Their Runaway Children

Runaway and homeless young people can cost local communities and government agencies substantial money, and their parents are not often held liable for these costs. Policies can be implemented to make parents liable for the damages caused by their runaway children (National Conference of State Legislatures 2013, October 1, Connecticut).

Foster Care

Youth in foster care often suffer from social-emotional problems, and as result, they frequently run away, necessitating increased resources to find the runaway youth within a certain time period. Running away from care is complicated by the fact that the foster care system itself has been criticized for being a "national disgrace" (Crosland and Dunlap 2014). According to MacLean et al. (1999), 18 % of young people at a Seattle shelter indicated that they had run away from care. In a study of four states in the Midwest by Whitbeck et al. (1997a, b), 13 % of the young people from street and shelter settings had run away from care. In an investigation of 2000 young people in 18 states, Kurtz et al. (1991a) showed that 18 % of young people in shelters ran away. Bass (1992a 1992a, b) surveyed 170 runaway shelters and discovered that 25 % of the runaway young people had been directly from a foster home or group home. An investigation of homeless young people in Canada showed that 68 % of the youth had been directly from foster care, group homes, or a youth facility and 43 % had involvement with child protection services (Raising the Roof 2009).

Policies can be implemented to improve the provision of foster care and reduce the prevalence of running away from foster care and associated interruptions in school and employment training (Crosland and Dunlap 2014; National Conference of State Legislatures 2013, October 1). Policies that promote interventions that take into account the youth's motivation for running away may help decrease foster care placements and provide stability for these placements (Clark et al. 2008).

Transitional Living Needs and Permanent Supportive Housing with Social Services

Policies can be designed to assist runaway and homeless youth in long-term residential facilities develop strategies for obtaining permanent supportive housing (National Conference of State Legislatures 2013, October 1, New Mexico). In addition, experts recognize that runaway and homeless youth can benefit from permanent supportive housing that is combined with social services (Anderson 2013). Having permanent supportive housing can help runaway and homeless young people apply for jobs or receive vocational training and other educational programs that allow them to make the transition to conventional society. The provision of permanent supportive residences helps street youth reduce health problems associated with the lack of stable and safe housing.

Lack of Transportation

Runaway and homeless young people often lack access to transportation that increases their risk of obtaining adequate food, employment, education, shelter, health care, social services, and other essential services (National Center for Homeless Education 2013, Spring). Without transportation, runaway and homeless youth have difficulty finding food at shelters and other locations that provide food for homeless and runaway youth.

Lack of access to transportation also limits homeless and runaway youth's access to shelter and other housing services. Moreover, their difficulties in accessing transportation limit their ability to go to school, get a job, or receive job training. Moreover, without transportation runaway and homeless young people have difficulty obtaining health-care and social services at designated locations.

Educational Barriers

In addition to difficulties in accessing transportation to and from school and jobs, homeless and runaway young people face other barriers in enrolling in school, having stable attendance, and completing school (National Center for Homeless Education 2013, Spring; De Rosa et al. 1999; Slesnick et al. 2009; National Conference of State Legislatures 2013, October 1, New York). For example, in De Rosa et al.'s (1999) investigation of service utilization among homeless and runaways in Los Angeles, CA, only two individuals reportedly used GED services.

Lack of housing, inadequate support from adults, lack of adequate nutrition and basic health services, and lack of school supplies are some of the many barriers that homeless and runaway youth face in participating effectively in school.

Runaway and homeless young people are often fearful of persons in authority and may be afraid of being arrested or sent to substitute care. They may be suffering from substance-abuse problems and other mental health problems that limit their ability to go to school.

Another educational obstacle that runaway and homeless youth face is the lack of immunization records, which is required to enroll in school (National Conference of State Legislatures 2013, October 1, Tennessee; National Center for Homeless Education 2013).

Employment Training, Employment Opportunities, and Job Referrals

To help runaway and homeless young people leave the streets and reintegrate into society, policy makers and social services professionals are developing ways to expand and improve access to employment services, including job training, employment readiness, and educational programs (Thompson et al. 2006a; Slesnick et al. 2009). Runaways and homeless juveniles may be reluctant to use employment services or lack the knowledge about available services. These young people may not have a valid identification, a permanent mailing address, suitable clothes, bathing facilities, access to the Internet, and other resources to help them apply for jobs. De Rosa et al. (1999) discovered that only 14 % of homeless young people in their investigation used employment services.

Living Independently as an Emancipated Adult

Common law and specific statutes enable youth to become an emancipated adult under specific circumstances, and these laws can be passed or modified to facilitate the emancipation of these young people (Price 2009, April 30). Policies can be developed to provide more support and resources to homeless and runaway youth who are seeking emancipation (National Conference of State Legislatures 2013, October 1, Illinois).

Mental Health and Medical Services

Policies can be designed to expand and improve the treatment of the physical, mental, and emotional health problems of runaway and homeless youth (Anderson 2013; National Conference of State Legislatures 2013, October 1, Kansas, dental hygiene; Slesnick et al. 2009; Thompson et al. 2006a). While on the streets, runaways and homeless young people suffer a variety of physical, sexual, and emotional victimization and other health problems related to food insecurity, a lack of shelter and clothes, and other difficulties associated with street survival.

Although homeless and runaway youth may get food from different sources, they often suffer from food insecurity and nutritional vulnerability (Tarasuk et al. 2005). For example, Tarasuk et al. (2005), in an investigation of homeless young people in Toronto, Canada, discovered that homeless male young people had lower intake of energy and nutrients when compared to a sample of housed youth based on the Ontario Food Survey.

The lack of stable and safe housing also increases the risks that youth on the streets will suffer medical and mental health problems. Despite the prevalence of physical and mental health problems of runaways and homeless young people, street youth have low utilization rates of medical and mental health services. De Rosa et al. (1999) showed that only 28 % of homeless young people in their sample used medical care services and a much lower percent (9 %) used psychological services. The assessment, treatment, and prevention of these medical and mental health problems should be a major priority.

Delinquency and Deviant Behavior Prevention Interventions

To get food, shelter, clothing, and other resources, homeless and runaway young people may engage in illegal activities such as theft and assault and get arrested. One investigation showed that more than a half of a sample of runaways and homeless children had been arrested at least once since their initial runaway episode. In addition, young people on the streets had been arrested an average 4.4 occasions (Chen et al. 2006). Street youth also may resort to various deviant strategies such as scavenging in dumpsters, known as dumpster surfing, which also increases their chances of getting arrested. Policy makers and social services professionals are focusing on expanding employment services, job training, employment readiness, and educational programs to prevent delinquent and deviant behavior among runaway and homeless youth, reduce their contacts with the justice system, and help them reintegrate into conventional society.

Survival Sex, Prostitution, Sex Trafficking, and Sexually Transmitted Infections, Including HIV/AIDS

While on the streets, runaways and homeless young people suffer sexual abuse and assaults; engage in survival sex, e.g., exchanging sex for food, money, and shelter; participate in other forms of prostitution; face the possibility of becoming sex trafficking victims; have multiple sexual partners; practice unsafe sex; and are at risk for acquiring sexually transmitted infections (STIs) and human immune virus (HIV)/acquired immune deficiency syndrome (AIDS). In one investigation of nationwide cases of arrests or detentions for juvenile prostitution, Mitchell et al. (2010) estimated that 1450 arrests or detentions occurred in cases involving juvenile prostitution.

Rew et al. (2002), in a study of homeless youth in Texas, discovered that the young people had a history of STIs and AIDS: 25 % gonorrhea, 8.7 % chlamydia, and 8.0 % AIDS. In other studies, HIV rates among homeless young people have been reported to be more than 8 % (Rew et al. 2002; Pfeifer and Oliver 1997). The prevention of prostitution, sexual assault, STIs, and HIV/AIDS are substantial policy issues (Slesnick et al. 2009). A related policy concern is the rate of pregnancy among runaway and homeless female youth.

Mental Health Policy Initiatives

Mental health policies should be designed to help reduce the prevalence and adverse of anxiety, depression, and self-harm and suicidal behaviors among runaway and homeless youth. For example, many runaway and homeless youth engage in self-mutilation and are at risk for engaging in suicidal behavior.

Homeless and runaway youth are also especially at risk for developing other health problems because of their limited or no access to health-care services while on the streets. Some policies address the dental hygiene of runaway and homeless young people (National Conference of State Legislatures 2013, October 1, Kansas, dental hygiene).

Drug and Alcohol Treatment

Policy makers can develop programs to improve substance-abuse treatment for street youth. While on the streets, young people may have low rates of using drug and alcohol treatment services. De Rosa et al. (1999) revealed that only 10 % of the homeless young people in their investigation used substance-abuse treatment services and 10 % accessed 12-step program services. Effective treatment for substance-abuse programs can help runaways and homeless young people leave the streets.

Runaway and Homeless Lesbian, Gay, Bisexual, and Transgendered (LGBT) Youth

LGBT youth may be especially at risk for harassment, discrimination, and sexual/physical victimization in the home environment and while on the streets. According to an investigation by Whitbeck et al. (2004), homeless and runaway LGBT youth were more likely to be sexually abused by their adult caretakers (44.3 %) compared to heterosexual young people (22.3 %). In addition, young people who are lesbians had a higher probability of reporting physical abuse and neglect by an adult caretaker than heterosexual females. Legislators can develop laws to take into account the needs of homeless and runaway LGBT young people.

Evaluation of Outcomes

To measure the success of interventions, researchers need to evaluate the outcomes of their program activities. In recognition of this need, policy makers are passing legislation that requires evaluation of outcomes (National Conference of State Legislatures 2013, October 1, Nebraska; Connecticut).

Agency-Based Tracking of Runaway and Homeless Youth

While on the streets, young people are especially difficult to track, thus reducing the ability of agencies to measure the effectiveness of their program interventions. In one study, Pollio et al. (2000) discovered that 69 % of homeless young people in St. Louis, MO, were located. The investigators were able to interview 59 % of the sample. Policies can be implemented to improve the tracking of this hard-to-reach population.

Federal Policies

The Runaway and Homeless Youth Act (RHYA) in the USA authorizes support for street youth programs (RHYA (Juvenile Justice and Delinquency Prevention Act Pub. L. 93-415, Sept. 7, 1974, 88 Stat. 1109 (Title 42, Sec. 5601 et seq.), as amended by the Runaway, Homeless, and Missing Children Protection Act of 2003 (Public Law 108-96). The RHYA funds three programs which are designed to prevent the victimization of homeless young people and provide them with access to various services, including job training, education, and substance-abuse treatment. The RHYA's Basic Centers Program offers funds to runaway shelters in order to provide emergency shelter for young people under the age of 18.

The John H. Chafee Foster Care Independence Program under the Foster Care Independence Act (HR 3443 and 1802HR 3443 and 1999), previously called the Independent Living Program, is the second program. This program assists foster youth, ages 16–21, in achieving the transition to independent living after they graduate from foster care.

The third program, the Sexual Abuse Prevention Program or the Runaway Prevention program (also called the Street Outreach Program), funds outreach and educational activities to runaway, homeless, and other street youth. Many of these individuals have been victims of sexual abuse or they have an increased probability of suffering from such abuse.

The Runaway and Homeless Youth Inclusion Act of 2013 – H.R. 2955 requires grant applicants to offer services to sexual minorities, maintain demographic data on the sexual orientation or gender identity, and offer culturally competent services such as transitional living programs to young people. The Act also requires that sexual abuse prevention programs provide certification to the US Department of Health and Human Services that these programs are ensuring culturally competent services to all participants.

In the USA, the federal McKinney–Vento Homeless Assistance Act is a conditional funding act that provides federal funds for homeless shelter programs to ensure homeless youth's access to education (The McKinney–Vento Homeless Assistance Act (MVHAA) of 1987; Pub. L. 100-77, July 22, 1987, 101 Stat. 482, 42 U.S.C. § 11301 et seq.). The MVHAA provides for children's transportation to and from school free of charge, permitting youth to go to their school "of origin" (the last school that they enrolled in or the school that they went to when they were initially homeless). They can attend this school even though their family lives in another district. In addition, the MVHAA requires that schools register homeless youth even if they do not possess immunization records and other mandatory records.

In order to implement the MVHAA, states are required to have a statewide homeless coordinator who evaluates policies and established procedures such as procedures for resolving disputes about school attendance. The MVHAA also requires that school districts have local education liaisons who make sure that school personnel know about the rights of homeless children and provide public notice to homeless families at shelters and schools and promote homeless children's access to schools and transportation.

Some states have complied with the MVHAA, while other states have not. Many lawsuits have been filed over the noncompliance of states. For example, in *Lampkin v. District of Columbia*, 27 F. 3d 605 (D.C. Cir. 1993), remanded to trial at 879 F. Supp 116(D.D.C. 1995), the District of Columbia avoided following the MVHAA by not accepting additional federal funds. However, eventually the District of Columbia changed its stance and started obtaining federal funds and improving its implementation process. Two legal cases, *Nat'l Law Ctr. on Homelessness and Poverty v. New York*, 224 F.R.D. 314 (E.D.N.Y. 2004); and *Bullock v. Maryland*, 210 F.R.D. 556 (D. Md 2002), were successful in implementing the MVHAA. Another case, which has been under litigation, is *Kaleuati v. Tonda*, CV07-504 (D. Haw).

The Family and Youth Services Bureau (FYSB) (n.d.) also supports organizations and communities that seek to eliminate youth homelessness and other social problems. FYSB's Transitional Living Program funds activities that offer long-term residential services to homeless youth ages 16–22 on a long-term basis.

State Policies

In the USA, some states have passed homeless and runaway youth legislation (National Conference of State Legislatures 2013, October 1). Below is a discussion of some of the areas of concern that these state laws have addressed.

Definition of Being Runaway/Homeless

Some states are developing policies that define who constitute runaway or homeless young people. The state of Nevada enacted legislation that classified runaway or homeless young people as under 18 years of age (National Conference of State Legislatures 2013, October 1). In contrast, the state of Minnesota passed the Runaway and Homeless Youth Act in 2006 that classified a homeless young person as an individual who is 21 years of age or younger who does not have a "fixed, regular, or adequate nighttime residence" (National Conference of State Legislatures 2013, October 1).

Comprehensive and Transitional Living Programs

States have enacted laws that facilitate the development of comprehensive interventions and transitional living programs for runaway and homeless children and adolescents. In Maine, the state created a comprehensive intervention for homeless and runaway young people to facilitate street- and community-based outreach, emergency shelters, transitional living, and drop-in services (National Conference of State Legislatures 2013, October 1).

The state of Minnesota introduced a bill to appropriate funding from the general fund to the Commissioner of Human Services for the Runaway and Homeless Youth Act in fiscal years 2010 and 2011 National Conference of State Legislatures 2013, October 1). The state also introduced a measure to appropriate funds to implement programs to meet the needs of youth who are homeless on a long-term basis.

In New Mexico, the state introduced a bill to fund a transitional living program for runaway and homeless young people in Bernalillo County (National Conference of State Legislatures 2013, October 1). This transitional program provides runaway and homeless young people, ages 16–21, with short-term shelter, board, training in living skills, behavioral health, and social services.

Legislators in Illinois introduced a law to provide shelter and transitional housing and assistance in employment for young people who are homeless (National Conference of State Legislatures 2013, October 1).

In Hawaii, lawmakers introduced the idea of a task force to facilitate resources for children who are homeless (National Conference of State Legislatures 2013, October 1).

Mental Health Services

Legislators in California introduced a law that mandated counties to offer counseling services to young people who are homeless as well as at-risk youth (National Conference of State Legislatures 2013, October 1).

Research on Runaway and Homeless Youth

A few states are enacting laws to facilitate research on the prevalence of runaway and homeless youth and their use of programs and services. The state of Minnesota enacted the Runaway and Homeless Youth Act, which mandated that the state Commissioner of Human Services prepare a report on homeless young people and those youth who are at risk for running away or becoming homeless (National Conference of State Legislatures 2013, October 1).

In Nebraska, the state introduced a bill to research the homeless youth problem. In addition, the law will fund research on the capabilities of existing government programs for homeless young people. The bill also will develop alternative strategies to address the increased prevalence of homeless youth.

Performance-Based ProgramsLegislation and policies:

As a part of its comprehensive program for homeless and runaway youth, the state of Maine mandated that the Maine Department of Health and Human Services rely on performance-based contracts with organizations that are licensed by the department to offer comprehensive runaway and homeless youth services (National Conference of State Legislatures 2013, October 1).

Shelters

Some states enacted legislation that involved the delivery of runaway and homeless youth services. States such as Indiana and Kansas have passed legislation that affect shelter services (National Conference of State Legislatures 2013, October 1). The state of Indiana enacted legislation that facilities that offer services to homeless or low-income persons may provide shelter and other services without obtaining consent from the youth's parent or guardian. The state of Kansas passed a law that allows runaway and homeless programs and shelters to offer dental hygiene services to youth who are under their care.

Foster Care

The state of Illinois created a program that provides adolescent foster youth with transitional discharge from foster care (National Conference of State Legislatures 2013, October 1). This program enables former foster adolescents under the age of 21 to obtain necessary supports and services for those who have encountered substantial difficulties after emancipation. These young people must reconnect with the Department of Children and Family Services and the Juvenile Court to obtain these resources, which will enable them to learn to live independently as adults.

Notification

State legislators have been concerned about different aspects of notification regarding runaway and homeless children and adolescents. Since 2006, the state of Nevada enacted a law that required approved shelters to make a bona fide, reasonable effort to notify a parent, guardian, or custodian about the location of a homeless or runaway youth except in instances of suspected neglect or abuse (National Conference of State Legislatures 2013, October 1).

The state of Utah passed a law that mandates any person who harbors a runaway young person to notify the minor's parent or legal guardian and Division of Child and Family Services within a time period of 8 h from the time that the individual began to harbor the runaway youth. According to the statue, the individual who harbors the runaway youth under certain conditions must notify a peace officer or a detention facility within the same time period.

Placement Issues

States may be interested in assessing trends in the placement of runaway and homeless youth to facilitate program effectiveness and the enactment of laws or modification of existing ones. The state of Connecticut enacted legislation that requires the Department of Children and Families "review and monitor" the placement of runaway and homeless youth who are out of state (National Conference of State Legislatures 2013, October 1). The law also requires that the Department of Children and Families prepare a report for the state General Assembly regarding their placement activities.

School Issues

A few states are enacting laws that are designed to improve school access for homeless and runaway youth or improve the accountability of school expenditures for homeless and runway youth.

In Alaska, state legislators introduced a law that mandates the governing body of a school district be required to adhere to the requirements for continuing the public education of homeless students in their school of origin (National Conference of

State Legislatures 2013, October 1). The law would also offer "comparable" schooling and transportation for youth while they were homeless.

The state of Tennessee enacted a law that prevents a school from blocking school admission for a child who has not been immunized or cannot provide immunization records because of her or his homeless status (National Conference of State Legislatures 2013, October 1).

The state of Washington passed a law that mandates the Superintendent of Public Instruction to follow extra expenditures associated with providing transportation of students who are homeless (National Conference of State Legislatures 2013, October 1).

In New York, legislators introduced a bill to amend their education law so that it is consistent with the federal McKinney–Vento Assistance Act (National Conference of State Legislatures 2013, October 1). The bill would enable the homeless youth to designate a public school as the youth's "school of origin." This bill also would mandate that the school district would offer the homeless child transportation to school.

Parental Responsibility for Damages Caused by Their Runaway Children

The state of Connecticut introduced a law to conduct research on whether parents should be held responsible for damages that are generated by their runaway children (National Conference of State Legislatures 2013, October 1).

Appendix A: Runaway Youth Project (RYP) Research Methods

Researchers are investigating how social, behavioral, and demographic factors may influence why and how children and adolescents run away from home and substitute care. The method used is data from self-report narratives and the Runaway Youth Project (RYP), which are based on a random sample of 200 missing-person reports (MPRs) involving runaway children and adolescents, are used to describe possible demographic, social, psychological, and behavioral characteristics of runaway and homeless youth.

The RYP is part of the Missing Persons Project, which is based on a random sample of 966 MPRs that were filed between 1991 and 2016 and published on the North American Missing Persons Network and the National Center for Missing and Exploited Children websites. Each MPR was coded using a protocol that contains 291 variables. The coded data were entered into a data file and statistical analysis was then performed using Systat 9 for Windows program (1999). In addition, selected MPRs were analyzed qualitatively to illustrate possible social and behavioral issues related to running away from home (Tables A.1, A.2, A.3, A.4, and A.5).

S.J. Morewitz, *Runaway and Homeless Youth*,

DOI 10.1007/978-3-319-30863-0

Table A.1 Demographic and socioeconomic status characteristics of endangered runaways (N=200)

Variable	Percentage (%)	Frequency		
Gender				
Male	34.0	68		
Female	66.0	132		
Chi-square=22.6, df=1, $p<.000$				
Racial/ethnic background				
White	33.5	67		
African American	30.5	61		
Hispanic	31.0	62		
Asian/Pacific Island	2.0	4		
Others	3.0	6		
Chi-square=53.5, df=1, $p<.000$				
Age (mean/S.D.)				
Endangered runaways	15.7 ± 1.6			
Non-endangered	23.3 ± 19.3			
Runaways				
$p<.000$				
Region of country				
North	7.5	15		
South	45.0	90		
East	4.5	9		
West	19.5	39		
Midwest	11.0	22		
Southwest	12.5	25		
Hawaii	0.0	0		
Alaska	0.0	0		
Chi-square=41.3, df=7, $p<.000$				
Runaway during				
Fall	40.5	81		
Winter	12.0	24		
Spring	24.5	49		
Summer	23.0	46		
Chi-square=23.6, df=3, $p<.000$				

Table A.2 Behavioral characteristics of endangered runaways ($N = 200$)

Variable	Percentage (%)	Frequency
# of years reported missing (mean ± S.D.)		
Endangered runaways	2.6 ± 4.[illegible]	
Non-endangered	8.8 ± 6.4	
Runaways $p < .000$		
May be in the local area		
Yes	27.0	54
No	73.0	146
Chi-square = 72.3, df = 1, $p < .000$		
Traveled with adult(s)		
Yes	11.0	22
No	89.0	178
Chi-square = 37.1, df = 1, $p < .000$		
Traveled out of state		
Yes	14.2	27
No	85.8	163
Chi-square = 72.3, df = 1, $p < .000$		
Uses an alias or nickname		
Yes	22.5	45
No	77.5	155
Chi-square = 7.3, df = 1, $p < .007$		

Table A.3 Additional forensic and behavioral characteristics of endangered runaways ($N = 200$)

Variable	Percentage (%)	Frequency
Has a history of violence		
Yes	11.0	22
No	89.0	178
Chi-square = 24.6, df = 1, $p < .000$		
Auto used		
Yes	4.0	8
No	96.0	192
Chi-square = 15.8, df = 1, $p < .000$		
May travel to another country		
Yes	3.5	7
No	96.5	193
Chi-square = 40.8, df = 1, $p < .000$		
Has a criminal history		
Yes	2.0	4
No	98.0	196
Not statistically significant		
Uses alcohol or illicit drugs		
Yes	0.0	0
No	100.0	200
Chi-square = 7.5, df = 1, $p < .006$		

Table A.4 Forensic and health characteristics of endangered runaways ($N=200$)

Variable	Percentage (%)	Frequency
Foul play is suspected		
Yes	1.5	3
No	98.5	197
Chi-square = 163.6, df = 1, $p<.000$		
Is depressed		
Yes	0.0	0
No	100.0	200
Chi-square = 4.1, df = 1, $p<.044$		
Has a medical condition		
Yes	2.5	5
No	97.5	195
Chi-square = 37.1, df = 1, $p<.000$		
Has a physical disability		
Yes	0.0	0
No	100.0	200
Chi-square = 8.7, df = 1, $p<.003$		
Has a mental disability		
Yes	1.0	2
No	99.0	198
Chi-square = 10.2 df = 1, $p<.001$		

Table A.5 Selected possible travel locations of the runways ($N=24$)

Variable	Percentage (%)	Frequency
Mexico	12.5	3
Newberry, SC	12.5	3
Texas	12.5	3
Miami, FL	8.3	2
Out of state	8.3	2
Salt Lake City, UT	8.3	2
Baltimore, MD	8.3	2

References

Aarons, G. A., James, S., Monn, A. R., et al. (2010). Behavior problems and placement change in a national child welfare sample: A prospective study. *Journal of the American Academy of Child and Adolescent Psychiatry, 49*, 70–80.

abc.net.au. (2009, October 28). Runaway teen killed in car crash. http://www.abc.net.au/news/2009-10-28/runaway-teen-killed-in-car-crash/1120242.

abcnewsradioonline.com. (2012, September 17). Runaway California teen found dead in motel room. http://abcnewsradioonline.com/national-news/runaway-california-teen-found-dead-in-motel-roon.html.

Abdelgalil, S., Gurgel, R. G., Theobald, S., et al. (2004). Household and family characteristics of street children in Aracaju, Brazil. *Archives of Disease in Childhood, 89*, 817–820.

Abram, K. M., Teplin, L. A., Charles, D. R., et al. (2004). Posttraumatic stress disorder and trauma in youth in juvenile detention. *Archives of General Psychiatry, 61*(4), 403–410.

Abram, K. M., Teplin, L. A., McClelland, G. M., et al. (2003). Comorbid psychiatric disorders in youth in juvenile detention. *Archives of General Psychiatry, 60*(11), 1097–1108.

Administration for Children's Services (1992). Children absent without leave from foster care. Procedure No. 90.

Agnelli, S. (1986). *Street children: A growing urban tragedy*. London, UK: Weidenfeld and Nicolson.

Alaraudanjoki, E. (2000). Child labour. A multi-disciplinary review. pp. 157–202. In: Leppanen, S. & Kuortti, J. (Eds.), Inescapable horizons: Culture and context, papers of the 5th Summer School of Cultural Studies, University of Jyvaskyla, Research Centre for Contemporary Culture.

Ali, M., Shahab, S., Ushijima, H., et al. (2004). Street children in Pakistan: A situational analysis of social conditions and nutritional status. *Social Science & Medicine, 59*(8), 1707–1717.

Allen, D. M., Lehman, J. S., Green, T. A., et al. (1994). HIV infection among homeless adults and runaway youth, United States, 1989–1992. *AIDS, 8*, 1593–1598.

Almeida, J., Johnson, R. M., Corliss, H. L., et al. (2009). Emotional distress among LGBT youth: The influence of perceived discrimination based on sexual orientation. *Journal of Youth and Adolescence, 38*, 9397.

Alter, J. (2014, June 29). Catch me if you can. Retrieved from www.youtube.com/watch?v=ur0ff96jxqA.

American Psychological Association, n.d.; Effects of Poverty, Hunger, and Homelessness on Children and Youth. Retrieved from http://www.apa.org/pi/families/poverty.aspx#).

Anderson, S. A. (1990). Core indicators of nutritional state for difficult-to-sample populations. *The Journal of Nutrition, 120*, 1559–1600.

S.J. Morewitz, *Runaway and Homeless Youth*,
DOI 10.1007/978-3-319-30863-0

Anderson, C.L. (2013). Opening doors: Preventing youth homelessness through housing and education collaboration. Seattle J for Social Justice, 11(2), Article 3. http://digitalcommons.lawu.edu/sjsj/vol11/iss2/3.

Angenent, H. L. W., Beck, B. M., & Shane, P. G. (1991). Structural problems in institutional care for youth. *Journal of Health and Social Policy, 2*, 83–98.

Annable, K. (2014, August 18). Teen runaway's body found in Red River. Police treating the case as a homicide. Winnipeg Sun.

Annie E. Casey Foundation. (2000). Pathways to juvenile detention reform. Baltimore, MD: Annie E. Casey Foundation.

Antieau, C. J. (1961). Constitutional rights in juvenile courts. *Cornell Law Review, 46*(3), 387.

Antoniades, M., & Tarasuk, V. (1998). A survey of problems experienced by Toronto street youth. *Canadian Journal of Public Health, 89*(6), 371–375.

Aptekar, L. (1989a). Columbian street children: Gamines and chupagruesos. *Adolescence, 24*(96), 783–794.

Aptekar, L. (1989b). Characteristics of the street children of Columbia. *Child Abuse & Neglect, 13*, 427–437.

Aptekar, L. (1988). *Street children of Cali*. Durham, NC & London, UK: Duke University Press.

Aptekar, L., & Heinonen, P. (2003). Methodological implications of contextual diversity in research on street children. *Children, Youth & Environments, 13*(1), 202–219.

Aseltine, R. H., Jr., & DeMartino, R. R. (2004). An outcome evaluation of the SOS suicide prevention program. *American Journal of Public Health, 94*, 446–451.

Auerswald, C. L., Sugano, E., Ellen, J. M., et al. (2006). Street-based STD testing and treatment of homeless youth are feasible, acceptable and effective. *Journal of Adolescent Health, 38*, 208–212.

Austin, J., Johnson, K.D., & Weitzer, R. (2005). Alternatives to the secure detention and confinement of juvenile offenders. Washington, D.C.: U.S. Department of Justice, Office of Justice Programs, Office of Juvenile Justice and Delinquency Prevention.

Aviles, A., & Helfrich, C. (2004). Life skill service needs. Perspectives of homeless youth. *Journal of Youth and Adolescence, 33*(4), 331–338.

Bailey, S. L., Camlin, C. S., & Ennett, S. T. (1998). Substance use and risky sexual behavior among homeless and runaway youth. *Journal of Adolescent Health, 23*(6), 378–388.

Baker, A. J. L., McKay, M. M., Lynn, C. J., et al. (2003). Recidivism at a shelter for adolescents: First-time versus repeat runaways. *Social Work Research, 27*, 84–93.

Ball, R., Huff, C., & Lilly, J. (1988). *House arrest and correctional policy: Doing time at home*. Beverly Hills, CA: Sage Publication.

Barber, C. C., Fonagy, P., Fultz, J., et al. (2005). Homeless near a thousand homes: Outcomes of homeless youth in a crisis shelter. *The American Journal of Orthopsychiatry, 75*, 347–355.

Barnett, J. K., Papini, D. R., & Gbur, E. (1991). Familial correlates of sexually active pregnant and nonpregnant adolescents. *Adolescence, 26*(102), 457–472.

Baron, S. W. (1997). Risky lifestyles and the link between offending and victimization. *Studies on Crime and Crime Prevent, 6*, 53–71.

Baron, S. W. (2003). Self-control, social consequences and criminal behavior: Street youth and the general theory of crime. *Journal of Research in Crime and Delinquency, 40*, 403–425.

Baron, S. W., & Hartnagel, T. F. (1998). Street youth and criminal violence. *Journal of Research in Crime and Delinquency, 35*, 166–192.

Baron, S. W., Kennedy, L. W., & Forde, D. R. (2001). Male street youths' conflict: the role of background, subcultural, and situational factors. *Justice Quarterly, 18*, 759–789.

Barrow, S. M., Herman, D. B., Cordova, P., et al. (1999). Mortality among homeless shelter residents in New York City. *American Journal of Public Health, 89*, 529–534.

Barton, M.A. (2013, November 13). Teenage girl found dead in Vienna in August death ruled 'accidental'. http://patch.com /virginia/vienna/ teenage-girl-found-dead-in-vienna-in-august-death-ruled-accidental.

Bass, D. (1992a). *Helping vulnerable youths: Runaway and homeless adolescents in the United States*. Washington, DC: NASW Press.

Bass, M. J. (1992b). Assessing functional status in family practice. *Family Medicine, 24*, 134.

baynews9.com. (2014, February 22). Lakeland teen found dead after being reported as runaway. http://www.baynews9.com/content/news/baynews9/news/article.html/content/news/articles/bn9/2014/2/22/Lakeland_teen_found_.html.

Bearman, P. S., & Moody, J. (2004). Suicide and friendship among American adolescents. *American Journal of Public Health, 94*, 89–95.

Beharry, M. S. (2012). Health issues in the homeless youth population. *Pediatric Annals, 41*(4), 154–156.

Bell, T. A., Farrow, J. A., Stamm, W. E., et al. (1985). Sexually transmitted diseases in females in a juvenile detention center. *Sexually Transmitted Diseases, 12*(3), 140–144.

Bennum, I., & Phil, M. (1983). Depression and hostility in self-mutilation. *Journal of Suicide and Life Threatening Behaviour, 13*, 71–84.

Benoit-Bryan, J. (2010). National Runaway Switchboard 2010 reporter's source book on runaway and homeless youth. 14–16. http://www.1800runaway.org/assets/1/7/2010reporterssourcebookv07152010.pdf.

Benoit-Bryan, J. (2011, September). The runaway youth longitudinal study. National Runaway Switchboard. Retrieved from www.1800RUNAWAY.org

Bensussen-Walls, W., & Saewyc, E. M. (2001). Teen-focused care versus adult-focused care for the high-risk pregnant adolescent: An outcomes evaluation. *Public Health Nursing, 18*, 424–435.

Berry, E. H., Shillington, A. M., Peak, T., et al. (2000). Multi-ethnic comparison of risk and protective factors for adolescent pregnancy. *Child and Adolescent Social Work Journal, 17*, 79–96.

Beyene, Y., & Berhane, Y. (1997). Characteristics of street children in Nazareth, Ethiopia. *East African medical journal, 74*(2), 85–88.

Biehal, N., & Wade, J. (2000). Going missing from residential and foster care: Linking biographies and contexts. *British Journal of Social Work, 30*(2), 211–225.

Blankenship, K. M., & Koester, S. (2002). Criminal law, policing policy, and HIV risk in female street workers and injection drug users. *The Journal of Law, Medicine & Ethics, 30*, 548–559.

Bolger, N., Downey, G., Walker, E., et al. (1989). The onset of suicidal ideation in childhood and adolescence. *Journal of Youth and Adolescence, 18*, 175–189.

Bolognini, M., Plancherel, B., Laget, J., et al. (2003). Adolescent's suicide attempts: Populations at risk, vulnerability, and substance use. *Substance Abuse & Misuse, 38*, 1651–1669.

Bontempo, D. E., & D'Augelli, A. R. (2002). Effects of at-school victimization and sexual orientation on lesbian, gay, or bisexual youths' health risk behavior. *Journal of Adolescent Health, 30*(5), 364–374.

Booth, R. E., Kwiatkowski, C., Iguchi, M. Y., et al. (1998). Facilitating treatment entry among out-of-treatment injection drug users. *Public Health Reports, 113*, 116–128.

Booth, R. E., & Zhang, Y. (1997). Conduct disorder and HIV risk behaviors among runaway and homeless adolescents. *Drug and Alcohol Dependence, 48*(2), 69–76.

Booth, R. E., Zhang, Y., & Kwiatkowski, C. F. (1999). The challenge of changing drug and sex risk behaviors of runaway and homeless adolescents. *Child Abuse & Neglect, 23*(12), 1295–1306.

Booth, S. (2006). Eating rough: Food sources and acquisition practices of homeless young people in Adelaide, South Australia. *Public Health Nutrition, 9*(2), 212–218.

Bowen, A. C. L., & John, A. M. H. (2001). Gender differences in presentation and conceptualization of adolescent self-injurious behavior: implications for therapeutic practice. *Counselling Psychology Quarterly, 14*(4), 357–379.

Bowen, C. (2013, February 2). Missing Fairfield teen found dead in park; Police suspect foul play. http://www.timesheraldonline.com/ci_22505522/missing-fairfield-teen-found-dead-in-park-police-suspect.

Boyden, J. (1986). *Children in development: Policy and programming for especially disadvantaged children in Lima*. Oxford, UK: UNICEF.

Brahmbhatt, K., Emerson, D., et al. (2014). Prevalence and determinants of adolescent pregnancy in urban disadvantaged settings across five cities. *Journal of Adolescent Health, 55*(6 Suppl), S48–S57.

Brand, G., Morrison, P., & Down, B. (2014). How do health professionals support pregnant and young mothers in the community? A selective review of the research literature. *Women Birth, 27*(3), 174–178.

Brent, D. A., Baugher, M., Bridge, J., et al. (1999). Age- and sex-related risk factors for adolescent suicide. *Journal of the American Academy of Child and Adolescent Psychiatry, 38*, 1497–1505.

Brent, D. A., Kalas, R., Edelbrock, C., et al. (1986). Psychopathology and its relationship to suicidal ideation in childhood and adolescence. *Journal of the American Academy of Child Psychiatry, 25*, 666–673.

Bridge, J. A., Goldstein, T. R., & Brent, D. A. (2006). Adolescent suicide and suicidal behavior. *Journal of Child Psychology and Psychiatry, 47*, 372–394.

Briere, J., & Gil, E. (1998). Self-mutilation in clinical and general population samples: Prevalence, correlates, and functions. *The American Journal of Orthopsychiatry, 68*, 609–620.

Bright, C. L., Kohl, P. L., & Jonson-Reid, M. (2014). Females in the juvenile justice system: Who are they and how do they fare? *Crime & Delinq, 60*(1), 106–125.

Brockington, I. (2001). Suicide in women. *International Clinical Psychopharmacology, 16*, 7–19.

Brodsky, B. S., Oquendo, M., Ellis, S. P., et al. (2001). The relationship of childhood abuse to impulsivity and suicidal behavior in adults with major depression. *The American Journal of Psychiatry, 158*, 1871–1877.

Broken. (2014). Comments. November 29. Retrieved from https://confessionsofateenagerrunaway.wordpress.com/)

Brooks, R. A., Milburn, N. G., Rotheram-Borus, M. J., et al. (2004). The system-of-care for homeless youth: Perceptions of service providers. *Evaluation and Program Planning, 27*, 443–451.

Brown, J.M. (2005, June 17). Teen runaway from Vallejo found dead; police: no foul play. Times-Herald. http://www/timesheraldonlline.com.

Brown, L. L., et al. (1997). Adolescents with psychiatric disorders and the risk of HIV. *J of the Amer Acad of Child & Adolesce Psychiat, 36*(11), 1609–1617.

Buckner, J., & Bassuk, E. (1997). Mental disorders and service utilization among youths from homeless and low-income housed families. *J of Amer Acad of Child & Adolesc Psychiatry, 36*, 890–990.

Bucy, J., & Obolensky, N. (1990). Runaway and homeless youths. In M. Rotheram-Borus, J. Bradley, & N. Obolensky (Eds.), *Planning to live: Evaluation and treating suicidal teens in community settings* (pp. 333–353). Tulsa, OK: University of Oklahoma Press.

Bullock v. Maryland, 210 F.R.D. 556 (D. Md 2002).

Burns, J. M., & Patton, G. C. (1999). Preventive interventions for youth suicide: A risk factor-based approach. *The Australian and New Zealand Journal of Psychiatry, 34*, 388–407.

Burt, M. R., Laudan, Y. A., Douglas, T., et al. (1999). *Homelessness: Programs and the people they serve; Findings of the national survey of homeless assistance providers and clients: Summary.* Washington, D.C.: Urban Institute Press.

Campos, R., Raffaelli, M., Ude, W., et al. (1994). Social networks and daily activities of street youth in Belo Horizonte, Brazil. *Child Development, 65*(2), 319–330.

Carlson, G. A., & Cantwell, D. P. (1982). Suicidal behavior and depression in children and adolescents. *Journal of the American Academy of Child and Adolescent Psychiatry, 21*, 361–368.

Carpenter, S. C., Clyman, R. B., Davidson, A. J., et al. (2001). The association of foster care or kinship care with adolescent sexual behavior. *Pediatrics, 108*(3), E46.

Cauce, A. M., Morgan, C. J., Lohr, Y., et al. (1994). Effectiveness of intensive case management for homeless adolescents: Results of a 3-month follow-up. *Journal of Emotional and Behavioral Disorders, 2*, 219–227.

Cauce, A.M., Paradise, M., Embry, L., et al. (1997). Homeless youth in Seattle: Youth characteristics, mental health needs, and intensive case management. Unpublished manuscript. Department of Psychology, University of Washington.

Cauce, A. M., Paradise, M., & Ginzler, J. A. (2000). The characteristics and mental health of homeless adolescents: Age and gender differences. *Journal of Emotional and Behavioral Disorders, 8*, 230–239.

Chamberlain, P., & Mihalic, S. (1998). *Blueprints for violence prevention. Book eight: Multidimensional treatment foster care*. Boulder, CO: Center for the study and prevention of violence.

Champion, H. L., & Durant, R. H. (2001). Exposure to violence and victimization and the use of violence by adolescents in the United States. *Minerva Pediatrica, 53*(3), 189–197.

Chatterjee, A. (1992). *India: The forgotten children of the cities*. Florence, Italy: UNICEF.

Chen, X., Thrane, L., Whitbeck, L. B., & Johnson, K. (2006). Mental disorders, comorbidity, and postrunaway arrests among homeless and runaway adolescents. *Journal Research on Adolescence, 16*(3), 379–402.

Chen, X., Thrane, L., Whitbeck, L. B., Johnson, K. D., & Hoyt, D. R. (2007). Onset of conduct disorder, use of delinquent subsistence strategies, and street victimization among homeless and runaway adolescents in the Midwest. *Journal of Interpersonal Violence, 22*(9), 1156–1183.

Chen, X., Tyler, K., Whitbeck, L. B., et al. (2004). Early sexual abuse, street adversity, and drug use among female homeless and runaway adolescents in the Midwest. *Journal of Drug Issues, 34*(1), 1–21.

Chesney-Lind, M. (1989). Girls' crime and woman's place: Toward a feminist model of female delinquency. *Crime & Delinquency, 35*, 5–29.

Chesney-Lind, M., & Shelden, R. G. (2003). *Girls, delinquency, and juvenile justice*. Belmont, CA: West/Wadsworth.

Chiu, S. H., & DiMarco, M. A. (2010). A pilot study comparing two developmental screening tools for use with homeless children. *Journal of Pediatric Health Care, 24*(2), 73–80. Epub 2009 Jul 18.

Chuang, E., & Wells, R. (2010). The role of inter-agency collaboration in facilitating receipt of behavioral health services for youth involved with child welfare and juvenile justice. *Children and Youth Services Review, 32*(12), 1814–1822.

Chun, J., & Springer, D. W. (2005). Correlates of depression among runaway adolescents in Korea. *Child Abuse & Neglect, 29*(12), 1433–1438.

Cicourel, A. V. (1968). *The social organization of juvenile justice*. New York: Wiley.

Clark, H. B., Crosland, K. A., Geller, D., et al. (2008). A functional approach to reducing runaway behavior and stabilizing placements for adolescents in foster care. *Research on Social Work Practice, 18*, 429–441.

Clark, R., & Robertson, M. J. (1996). *Surviving for the moment: A report on homeless youth in San Francisco*. Berkeley, CA: Alcohol Research Group.

Clatts, M. C., & Davis, W. R. (1999). A demographic and behavioral profile of homeless youth in New York City: Implications for AIDS outreach and prevention. *Medical Anthropology Quarterly, 13*(3), 365–374.

Clatts, M. C., Goldsamt, L., Yi, H., et al. (2005). Homelessness and drug abuse among young men who have sex. *Journal of Adolescence, 28*(2), 201–214.

Claytor, S.M. (2014). Runaway teen found dead in a home. March 22. https://www.youtube.com/watch?v=tJ6G5Yr68d8).

Coady, M. H., Latka, M. H., et al. (2007). Housing status and associated differences in HIV risk behaviors among young injection drug users (IDUs). *AIDS and Behavior, 11*(6), 854–863.

Coates, R., Miller, A., & Ohlin, L. (1978). *Diversity in a youth correctional system*. Cambridge, MA: Ballinger.

Cochran, B. N., Stewart, A. J., Ginzler, J. A., et al. (2002). Challenges faced by homeless sexual minorities: Comparison of gay, lesbian, bisexual, and transgender homeless adolescents with their heterosexual counterparts. *American Journal of Public Health, 92*(5), 773–777.

Cohen, L. E., & Felson, M. (1979). Social change and crime rate trends: A routine activity approach. *American Sociological Review, 44*, 588–608.

Cohen, L. E., & Kluegel, J. R. (1979). The detention decision: A study of the impact of social characteristics and legal factors in two metropolitan juvenile courts. *Social Forces, 58*(1), 146–161.

Cole, D. A. (1989). Psychopathology of adolescent suicide: Hopelessness, coping beliefs, and depression. *Journal of Abnormal Psychology, 98*, 248–255.

Coleman, J. S. (1988). Social capital in the creation of human capital. *American Journal of Sociology, 94*(Suppl), S95–S120.

Collins, J., Powers, M., McCalla, C., et al. (1993). *Law enforcement policies and practices regarding missing children and homeless youth: Research summary*. Washington, D.C.: U.S. Department of Justice, Office of Juvenile Justice and Delinquency Prevention.

Connolly, M. (1990). Adrift in the city: A comparative study of street children in Bogota, Columbia, and Guatemala City. *Child and Youth Services, 14*(1), 129–149.

Cooper, J., Appleby, L., & Amos, T. (2002). Life events preceding suicide by young people. *Social Psychiatry and Psychiatric Epidemiology, 37*, 271–275.

Cooper, J., Kapur, N., Webb, R., et al. (2005). Suicide after deliberate self-harm: A 4-year cohort study. *The American Journal of Psychiatry, 162*, 297–303.

Corneil, T. A., Kuyper, L. M., Shoveller, J., et al. (2006). Unstable housing, associated risk behaviour, and increased risk for HIV infection among injection drug users. *Health and Place, 12*(1), 79–85.

Courtney, M. E., Pajarita, C., Okpych, N. J., et al. (2014). *Findings from the California Youth Transitions to Adulthood Study (CalYOUTH): Conditions of foster youth at age 17*. Chicago: Chapin Hall at the University of Chicago.

Courtney, M. E., Skyles, A., Miranda, G., et al. (2005). *Youth who run away from substitute care*. Chicago: Chapin Hall at the University of Chicago.

Courtney, M. E., & Zinn, A. (2009). Predictors of running away from out-of-home care. *Children and Youth Services Review, 31*, 1298–1306.

Craig, T. K., & Hodson, S. (1998). Homeless youth in London: I. Childhood antecedents and psychiatric disorder. *Psychological Medicine, 28*(6), 1379–1388.

Crawford, D. M., Whitbeck, L. B., & Hoyt, D. R. (2011). Propensity for violence among homeless and runaway adolescents: An event history analysis. *Crime & Delinquency, 57*(6), 950–968.

Crespi, T. D., & Sabatelli, R. M. (1993). Adolescent runaways and family strife: A conflict-induced differentiation framework. *Adolescence, 28*, 867–878.

Crosland, K., & Dunlap, G. (2014). Running away from foster care: What do we know and what do we do? J Child Family Studies, Online First, May; 1–23.

Cullen, F., & Gendreau, P. (2000). Assessing correctional rehabilitation: Policy, practice, and prospects. In: J. Horney (Ed.). Criminal Justice 2000, Vol. 3. Washington, D.C.: U.S. Department of Justice, Office of Justice Programs, National Institute of Justice, pp. 109–160.

CYC. (no date). Runaways face tough life on streets. Retrieved from http://www.cyc-net.org/features/ft-runaways.html).

Dachner, N., & Tarasuk, V. (2002). "Homeless "Squeegee Kids:" Food insecurity and daily survival. A study of food habits among homeless youth in Toronto. Centre for Urban and Community Studies Research". Bulletin, #7, May; 1–5.

Darbyshire, P., Muir-Cochrane, E., Fereday, J., et al. (2006). Engagement with health and social care services: Perceptions of homeless young people with mental health problems. *Health, 14*(6), 553–562.

Darke, S., & Ross, J. (2001). The relationship between suicide and heroin overdose among methadone maintenance in Sydney, Australia. *Addiction, 96*, 1443–1453.

D'Augelli, A. R., & Hershberger, S. L. (1993). Lesbian, gay, and bisexual youth in community settings: Personal challenges and mental health problems. *American Journal of Community Psychology, 21*, 421–448.

D'Augelli, A. R., Hershberger, S. L., & Pilkington, N. W. (2001). Suicidality patterns and sexual orientation-related factors among lesbian, gay, and bisexual youths. *Suicide & Life-Threatening Behavior, 31*, 250–264.

Davis, D., & Leo, R. A. (2014). The problem of interrogation-induced false confession: Sources of failure in prevention and detection. In S. J. Morewitz & M. L. Goldstein (Eds.), *Handbook of forensic sociology and psychology*. New York: Springer.

de Carvalho, F. T., Neiva-Silva, L., Ramos, M. C., et al. (2006). Sexual and drug use risk behaviors among children and youth in street circumstances in Porto Alegre, Brazil. *AIDS and Behavior, 10*(Suppl 1), S57–S66.

Dekel, R., Peled, E., & Spiro, S. E. (2003). Shelters for homeless youth: A follow-up evaluation. *Journal of Adolescence, 26*(2), 201–212.

DeMan, A. F., & LeDuc, C. P. (1995). Suicidal ideation in high school students: Depression and other correlates. *Journal of Clinical Psychology, 51*, 173–181.

DeMatteo, D., Major, C., Block, B., et al. (1999). Toronto street youth and HIV/AIDS: Prevalence, demographics, and risks. *Journal of Adolescent Health, 25*(5), 358–366.

de Oliveira, W., Baizerman, M., & Pellet, L. (1992). Street children in Brazil and their helpers: Comparative views on aspirations and the future. *International Social Work, 35*(2), 163–176.

De Rosa, C. J., Montgomergy, S. B., Kipke, M. D., et al. (1999). Service utilization among homeless and runaway youth in Los Angeles, California: Rates and reasons. *Journal of Adolescent Health, 24*, 449–458.

Desai, R. A., Goulet, J. L., Robbins, J., et al. (2006). Mental health care in juvenile detention facilities: A review. *Journal of the American Academy of Psychiatry and the Law, 34*(2), 204–214.

Development Services Group Inc. (2015). *Status offenders. Literature review*. Washington, D.C.: Office of Juvenile Justice and Delinquency Prevention.

Dewees, A., & Klees, S. J. (1995). Social movements and the transformation of national policy: Street and working children in Brazil. *Comparative Education Review, 39*(1), 76–100.

DiClemente, R. J., Hansen, W. B., & Ponton, L. E. (1996). Adolescents at risk: A generation in jeopardy. In R. J. DiClemente, W. B. Hansen, & L. E. Ponton (Eds.), *Handbook of Adolescent Health Risk Behavior* (pp. 1–4). New York: Plenum.

DiClemente, R. J., Ponton, L. E., & Hartley, D. (1991). Prevalence and correlates of cutting behavior: Risk for HIV transmission. *Journal of the American Academy of Child and Adolescent Psychiatry, 30*, 735–739.

District of Columbia Public Schools. (2007). *Youth risk behavior survey sexual minority baseline fact sheet: Senior high school YRBS 2007 baseline findings for GLBQ items*. Washington, D.C.: District of Columbia Public Schools, HIV/AIDS Program.

Donaldson, P. E., Whalen, M. H., & Anastas, J. W. (1989). Teen pregnancy and sexual abuse: Exploring the connection. *Smith College Studies in Social Work, 59*(3), 289–300.

Douglas, J., Cooper, J., Amos, T., et al. (2002). Near-fatal deliberate self-harm: Characteristics, prevention & implications for the prevention of suicide. *Journal of Affective Disorders, 79*, 263–268.

Drizin, S. A., & Luloff, G. (2007). Are juvenile courts a breeding ground for wrongful convictions? *Northern Kentucky Law Review, 34*(2), 257.

DuRant, R. H., Treiber, F., Goodman, E., & Woods, E. R (1996). Intentions to use violence among young adolescents. *Pediatrics, 98*(6 Pt 1), 1104–1108.

Durlak, J. A., & Wells, A. M. (1997). Primary prevention mental health programs for children and adolescents: A Meta-Analytic Review. *American Journal of Community Psychology, 25*, 115–152.

Dusenbury, L., Epstein, J. A., Botvin, G. J., & Diaz, T. (1994). Social influence predictors of alcohol use among New York Latino youth. *Addictive Behaviors, 19*(4), 363–372.

Eberle, J. A., & Maiuro, R. D. (2001). Review Introduction and commentary: Developmental perspectives on violence and victimization. *Violence and Victims, 16*(4), 351–354.

Edinburgh, L. D., & Saewyc, E. M. (2009). A novel, intensive home-visiting intervention for runaway, sexually exploited girls. *Journal for Specialists in Pediatric Nursing, 14*(1), 41–48.

Elifson, K. W., Sterk, C. E., & Theall, K. P. (2007). Safe living: The impact of unstable housing conditions on HIV risk reduction among female drug users. *AIDS and Behavior, 11*(Suppl 2), S45–S55.

Emerson, R. M. (1969). *Judging delinquents: Context and process in juvenile court*. Chicago, IL: Aldine.

Ennett, S. T., Bailey, S. L., & Federman, E. B. (1999). Social network characteristics associated with risky behaviors among runaway and homeless youth. *Journal of Health and Social Behavior, 40*(1), 63–78.

Ennett, S. T., Federman, E. B., Bailey, S. L., et al. (1999). HIV-risk behaviors associated with homelessness characteristics in youth. *Journal of Adolescent Health, 25*(5), 344–353.

Ennew, J. (2003). Difficult circumstances: Some reflections on 'street children' in Africa. Children, Youth and Environ, 13(1). Retrieved from http://cye.colorado.edu.

Esmonde, J. (2002). Criminalizing poverty: The criminal law power and the Safe Streets Act. *Journal of Law and Social Policy, 17*, 63–86.

Evans, J. L., Hahn, J. A., Page-Shafer, K., et al. (2003). Gender differences in sexual and injection risk behavior among active young injection drug users in San Francisco (the UFO Study). *Journal of Urban Health, 80*(1), 137–146.

Ezell, M. (1992). Juvenile diversion: The ongoing search for alternatives. In I. Schwartz (Ed.), *Juvenile justice and public policy*. New York: Lexington.

Family and Youth Services Bureau. (1996). Reconnecting youth and community. A youth development approach. Washington, D.C.: U.S. Department of Health and Human Services, Administration for Children and Families.

Family and Youth Services Bureau. (no date). TLP fact sheet. Retrieved from http://www.acf.hhs.gov/programs/fysb/resource/tlp-fact-sheet).

Family and Youth Services Bureau. (no date). Transitional Living Program. Retrieved from (http://www.acf.hhs.gov/programs/fysb/resource/tlp-fact-sheet).

Fanshel, D., Finch, S. J., & Grundy, J. F. (1990). *Foster children in a life course perspective*. New York: Columbia University Press.

Farmer, E., & Pollock, S. (1998). *Sexually abused and abusing children in substitute care*. Chichester: Wiley.

Farrow, J. A., Deisher, R. W., Brown, R., et al. (1992). Health and health needs of homeless and runaway youth: A position paper of the Society for Adolescent Medicine. *Journal of Adolescent Health, 13*(8), 717–726.

Favazza, A. R. (1998). The coming of age of self-mutilation. *The Journal of Nervous and Mental Disease, 186*, 259–268.

Federle, K. (2000). The institutionalization of female delinquency. *Buffalo Law Review, 48*, 881–895.

Feitel, B., Margetson, N., Chamas, J., et al. (1992). Psychosocial background and behavioral and emotional disorders of homeless and runaway youth. *Hospital & Community Psychiatry, 43*, 155–159.

Feld, B. C. (1999). *Bad kids: Race and the transformation of the juvenile court*. New York: Oxford University Press.

Feld, B. C., & Bishop, D. M. (2012). Transfer of juveniles to adult court. In B. C. Feld & D. M. Bishop (Eds.), *The Oxford handbook of juvenile crime and juvenile justice*. New York: Oxford University Press.

Feldman, M. D. (1988). The challenge of self-mutilation: A review. *Comprehensive Psychiatry, 29*, 252–269.

Feldmann, J., & Middleman, A. B. (2003). Homeless adolescents: Common clinical concerns. *Seminars in Pediatric Infectious Diseases, 14*(1), 6–11.

Felsman, J.K. (1981). Street urchins of Cali: On risk, resiliency and adaptation in childhood. Harvard University, MA: Unpublished Ph.D. thesis.

Felson, R. B. (1997). Routine activities and involvement in violence as actor, witness, or target. *Violence and Victims, 12*, 209–221.

Ferguson, K. M., & Xie, B. (2008). Feasibility study of the social enterprise intervention with homeless youth. *Research on Social Work Practice, 18*(1), 5–19.

Finkelhor, D., Hotaling, G., & Sedlak, A. (1990). *Missing, abducted, runaway, and thrownaway children in America – First report: Numbers and characteristics national incidence studies*. Washington, D.C.: U.S. Department of Justice, Office of Juvenile Justice and Delinquency Prevention.

Flick, U., & Röhnsch, G. (2007). Idealization and neglect: health concepts of homeless adolescents. *Journal of Health Psychology, 12*(5), 737–749.

Forster, L. M. K., Tannhauser, M., & Barros, H. M. T. (1996). Drug use among street children in southern Brazil. *Drug & Alcohol Dependence, 43*(1–2), 57–62.

Fortenberry, J. D. (1995). Adolescent substance use and sexually transmitted disease risk: A review. *Journal of Adolescent Health, 16*, 304–308.

Foster Care Independence Act (HR 3443 and 1802HR 3443 and 1999).

Frankish, C. J., Hwang, S. W., & Quantz, D. (2005). Homelessness and health in Canada: Research lessons and priorities. *Canad Journal of Public Health 96*(Suppl 2), S23–S29.

Friedman, R. C., Corn, R., Hurt, S. W., et al. (1984). Family history of illness in the seriously suicidal adolescent. *American Journal of Orthopsychiatry, 54*, 390–397.

Gaetz, S., & O'Grady, B. (2002). Making money. Exploring the economy of young homeless workers. *Work, Employment & Society, 16*(3), 433–456.

Garofalo, R., Wolf, R. C., Wissow, L. S., et al. (1999). Sexual orientation and risk of suicide attempts among a representative sample of youth. *Archives of Pediatrics and Adolescent Medicine, 153*(5), 487–493.

Garrison, C. Z., Addy, C. L., McKeown, R. E., et al. (1993). Nonsuicidal physically self-damaging acts in adolescents. *Journal of Child and Family Studies, 2*, 339–352.

Gavazzi, S. M., Yarcheck, C. M., & Chesney-Lind, M. (2006). Global risk indicators and the role of gender in a juvenile detention sample. *Criminal Justice and Behavior, 33*(5), 597–612.

Gavin, L., MacKay, A. P., Brown, K., et al. (2009). Sexual and reproductive health of persons aged 10–24 years – United States, 2002–2007. *MMWR Surveillance Summaries, 58*(6), 1–58.

Gazmararian, J. A., Adams, M. M., Saltzman, L. E., et al. (1995). The relationship between pregnancy intendedness and physical violence in mothers of newborns. *Obstetrics & Gynecology, 85*, 1031.

getlegal.com (no date). Retrieved from http://public.getlegal.com/legal-info-center/status-offenses/).

Ginzler, J. A., Cochran, B. N., Domenech-Rodriguez, M., et al. (2003). Sequential progression of substance use among homeless youth: An empirical investigation of the gateway theory. *Substance Use & Misuse, 38*(3–6), 725–758.

Gleghorn, A. A., Clements, K. D., Marx, R., et al. (1997). The impact of intensive outreach on HIV prevention activities of homeless, runaway, and street youth in San Francisco: The AIDS evaluation of street outreach project (AESOP). *AIDS and Behavior, 4*, 261–271.

Gleghorn, A. A., Marx, R., Vittinghoff, E., et al. (1998). Association between drug use patterns and HIV risks among homeless, runaway, and street youth in northern Calfornia. *Drug and Alcohol Dependence, 51*(3), 219–227.

Goldsmith, S. K., Pellmar, T. C., Kleinman, A. M., et al. (2002). *Reducing suicide: A national imperative*. Washington, DC: The National Academies Press.

Goldstein, M. L., & Morewitz, S. J. (2011). *Chronic disorders in children and adolescents*. New York: Springer.

Goncalves de Moura, Y., van der Meer Sanchez, Z., & Noto, A. R. (2010). Diversity of contexts in drug use among street adolescents. *Qualitative Health Research, 20*(9), 1241–1253. Epub 2010 May 17.

Gorman-Smith, D., & Loeber, R. (2005). Are developmental pathways in disruptive behaviors the same for girls and boys? *Journal of Child and Family Studies, 14*(1), 15–27.

Greenblatt, M., & Robertson, M. J. (1993). Life-styles, adaptive strategies, and sexual behaviors of homeless adolescents. *Hospital & Community Psychiatry, 44*(12), 1177–1180.

Greene, J. M., Ennett, S. T., & Ringwalt, C. L. (1999). Prevalence and correlates of survival sex among runaway and homeless youth. *American Journal Public Health, 89*(9), 1406–1409.

Greene, J. M., Ennett, S. T., & Ringwalt, C. L. (1997). Substance use in runaway and homeless youth in three national samples. *American Journal Public Health, 87*(2), 229–235.

Greene, J. M., & Ringwalt, C. (1998). Pregnancy among three national samples of runaway and homeless youth. *Journal of Adolescent Health, 23*(6), 370–377.

Greene, J. M., & Ringwalt, C. (1996). Youth and familial substance uses association with suicide attempts among runaway and homeless youth. *Substance Use & Misuse, 31*(8), 1041–1058.

Greene, J. M., Ringwalt, C. L., & Iachan, R. (1997). Shelters for runaway and homeless youths: Capacity and occupancy. *Child Welfare, 76*, 549–561.

Greene, J., Ringwalt, C., Kelley, J., Iachan, R., & Cohen, Z. (1995). Youth with runaway, thrownaway, and homeless experiences. Prevalence, drug use, and other at-risk behaviors. Administration for Children and Families. Youth Services Bureau.

Greenwood, P., & Turner, S. (1993). Evaluation of the Paint Creek Youth Center: A residential program for serious delinquents. *Criminology, 31*(2), 263–279.

Grunbaum, J. A., Kann, L., Kinchen, S. A., et al. (2004). Youth Risk Behavior Surveillance United States, 2003. *Morbidity and Mortality Weekly Report, CDC Surveillance Summaries, 53*, 1–96.

Guarino-Ghezzi, S., & Loughran, E. J. (2004). *Balancing juvenile justice*. New Brunswick, NJ: Transaction.

Guertin, T., Lloyd-Richardson, E., Spirito, A., et al. (2001). Self-mutilative behavior in adolescents who attempt suicide by overdose. *Journal of the American Academy of Child and Adolescent Psychiatry, 40*, 1062–1069.

Guijarro, S., Naranjo, J., Padilla, M., et al. (1999). Family risk factors associated with adolescent pregnancy: Study of a group of adolescent girls and their families in Ecuador. *Journal of Adolescent Health, 25*(2), 166–172.

Guo, X., Slesnick, N., & Feng, X. (2014). Reductions in depressive symptoms among substance-abusing runaway adolescents and their primary caretakers: a randomized clinical trial. *Journal of Family Psychology, 28*(1), 98–105.

Gurgel, R. Q., da Fonseca, J. D. C., Neyra-Castaneda, D., et al. (2004). Capture-recapture to estimate the number of street children in a city of Brazil. *Archives of Disease in Childhood, 89*, 222–224.

Gutierrez, P. M., Rodriguez, P., & Garcia, P. (2001). Suicide risk factors for young adults: Testing a model across ethnicities. *Death Studies, 25*, 319–340.

Guttmann-Steinmetz, S., Gadow, K. D., & Devincent, C. J. (2009). Oppositional defiant and conduct disorder behaviors in boys with autism spectrum disorder with and without attention-deficit hyperactivity disorder versus several comparison samples. *Journal of Autism and Developmental Disorders, 39*(7), 976–985.

Hagan, J., & McCarthy, B. (1997). *Mean streets: Youth crime and homelessness*. New York: Cambridge University Press.

Halcon, L. L., & Lifson, A. R. (2004). Prevalence and predictors of sexual risks among homeless youth. *Journal of Youth and Adolescence, 33*(1), 71–80.

Haley, N., Roy, E., Leclerc, P., et al. (2004). HIV risk profile of male street youth involved in survival sex. *Sexually Transmitted Infections, 80*, 526–530.

Hallfors, D. D., Waller, M. W., Ford, C. A., et al. (2004). Adolescent depression and suicide risk: Association with sex and drug behavior. *American Journal of Preventive Medicine, 27*, 224–231.

Hamilton, B. E., Martin, J. A., & Ventura, S. J. (2007). *Preliminary data for 2006: National vital statistics report*. Hyattsville, MD: National Center of Health Statistics.

Hammer, H., Finkelhor, D., & Sedlak, A.J. (2002). Runaway/thrownaway children: National estimates and characteristics. Washington, D.C: U.S. Department of Justice, Office of Justice Programs, Office of Juvenile Justice and Delinquency Prevention.

Harpin, S., Gilroy, C., & Rosenberg, E. (2013). Emergency department use among a sample of shelter-based runaway and homeless youth. J of Adolesce. *Journal of Adolescence, 52*(2), S76–S77. Suppl 1.

Hartnagel, T. F. (1989). High school dropouts, labour market success and criminal behavior. *Youth and Society, 20*, 416–444.

Harvey, S. M., Bird, S. T., De Rosa, C. J., et al. (2003). Sexual decision making and safer sex behavior among young female injection drug users and female partners of IDUs. *Journal of Sex Research, 40*(1), 50–60.

Heale, P., Dietze, P., & Fry, C. (2003). Intentional overdose among heroin overdose survivors. *Journal of Urban Health, 80*, 230–237.

Heck, N. C., Flentje, A., & Cochran, B. N. (2011). Offsetting risks: High school gay-straight alliances and lesbian, gay, bisexual, and transgender (LGBT) youth. *School Psychology Quarterly, 26*(2), 161–174.

Henggeler, S. (1997). Treating serious anti-social behavior in youth: The MST approach. Bulletin. Washington, D.C.: U.S. Department of Justice, Office of Justice Programs, Office of Juvenile Justice and Delinquency Prevention.

Henggeler, S., Melton, G., & Smith, L. (1992). Family preservation using multisystemic therapy: An effective alternative to incarcerating serious juvenile offenders. *Journal of Consulting and Clinical Psychology, 60*(6), 953–961.

Henngeler, S., Mihalic, S.F., Rone, L., et al. (1998). Multisystemic therapy. In D. Elliot (Ed.). Blueprints for violence prevention. Boulder, CO: Center for the Study and Prevention of Violence, Institute of Behavioral sciences, University of Colorado at Boulder.

Hershberger, S. L., & D'Augelli, A. R. (1995). The impact of victimization on the mental health and suicidality of lesbian, gay, and bisexual youths. *Developmental Psychology, 31*, 65–74.

Hershberger, S. L., Pilkington, N. W., & D'Augelli, A. R. (1997). Predictors of suicide attempts among gay, lesbian, and bisexual youth. *Journal of Adolescent Research, 12*(4), 477–497.

Hindelang, M. J., Gottfredson, M. R., & Garofalo, J. (1978). *Victims of personal crime: An empirical foundation for a theory of personal victimization*. Cambridge, MA: Ballinger.

Hockenberry, S., & Puzzanchera, C. (2015). *Juvenile court statistics: 2013*. Pittsburgh, PA: National Center for Juvenile Justice.

Holden, G. W., Nelson, P. B., Velasquez, J., et al. (1993). Cognitive, psychosocial, and reported sexual behavior differences between pregnant and nonpregnant adolescents. *Adolescence, 28*(111), 557–572.

Holman, B., & Ziedenberg, J. (2006). *The dangers of detention*. Washington, D.C.: Justice Policy Institute.

Homeless People-Elle's Story. http://homeless.org.au/people/elle.htm.

Homeless People-Rebecca's Story. http://homeless.org.au/people/Rebecca.htm.

Horesh, N., Orbach, I., Gothelf, D., et al. (2003). Comparison of the suicidal behavior of adolescent inpatients with borderline personality disorder and major depression. *Journal of Nervous and Mental Disease, 191*(9), 582–588.

Howell, J.C. (1995). Guide for implementing the comprehensive strategy for serious, violent, and chronic juvenile offenders. Report. Washington, D.C.: U.S. Department of Justice, Office of Justice Programs, Office of Juvenile Justice and Delinquency Prevention.

Hoyt, D. R., Ryan, K. D., & Cauce, A. M. (1999). Personal victimization in a high-risk environment: Evaluating the relative effects of exposure, attractiveness and guardianship. *Journal of Research in Crime and Delinquency, 36*, 371–392.

Hoytt, E. H., Schiraldi, V., Smith, B. V., et al. (2003). *Reducing racial disparities in juvenile detention*. Baltimore, MD: Annie E. Casey Foundation.

Huba, G. J., Melchior, L. A., Panter, A. T., et al. (2000). Risk factors and characteristics of youth living with, or at high risk for, HIV. *AIDS Education and Prevention, 12*(6), 557–575.

Hughes, D. (2011). An overview of the Juvenile Justice and Delinquency Prevention Act and the valid court order exception. *Arkansas Law Notes, 102*, 29–30.

Huizinga, D., Loeber, R., & Thornberry, T. P. (1993). Longitudinal study of delinquency, drug use, sexual activity, and pregnancy among children and youth in three cities. *Public Health Report, 108*(Suppl 1), 90–96.

Huizinga, D., Loeber, R., & Thornberry, T. P. (1995). *Urban delinquency and substance abuse: Initial findings*. Washington, D.C.: U.S. Department of Justice, Office of Justice Programs, Office of Juvenile Justice and delinquency Preventions.

Hwang, S. W. (2000). Mortality among men using homeless shelters in Toronto, Canada. *JAMA, 283*(16), 2152–2157.

Hwang, S. W., Orav, E. J., O'Connell, J. J., et al. (1997). Causes of death in homeless adults in Boston. *Annals of Internal Medicine, 126*(8), 625–628.

Hyde, J. (2005). From home to street: Understanding young people's transitions to homelessness. *Journal of Adolescence, 28*(2), 171–183.

Hyun, M., Chung, H., & Lee, Y. (2005). The effect of cognitive-behavioral group therapy on the self-esteem, depression, and self-efficacy of runaway adolescents in a shelter in South Korea. *Applied Nursing Research, 18*(3), 160–166.

Igra, V., & Irwin, C. E. (1996). Theories of adolescent risk-taking behavior. In R. J. DiClemente, W. B. Hansen, & L. E. Ponton (Eds.), *Handbook of adolescent health risk behavior* (pp. 35–51). New York: Plenum.

Jacob, J., Smith, T., Hite, S., et al. (2004). Helping Uganda's street children. *Journal of Children & Poverty, 10*(1), 3–22.

Janus, M. D., Burgess, A. W., & McCormack, A. (1987a). Histories of sexual abuse in adolescent male runaways. *Journal of Adolescence, 22*(86), 405–417.

Janus, M., McCormack, A., Burgess, A. W., & Hartman, C. (1987b). *Adolescent runaways: Causes and consequences*. Lexington, MA: Lexington Books.

Jiang, Y., Perry, D. K., & Hasser, J. E. (2010). Adolescent suicide and health risk behaviors: Rhode Island's 2007 Youth Risk Behavior Survey. *American Journal of Preventive Medicine, 38*, 551–555.

Joe, K. (1995). The dynamics of running away, deinstitutionalization policies and the police. *Juvenile and Domestic Relations District Court, 46*(3), 43–55.

Johnson, K. D., Whitbeck, L. B., & Hoyt, D. R. (2005). Predictors of social network composition among homeless and runaway adolescents. *Journal of Adolescence, 28*(2), 231–248.

Johnson, K.D. (2010). Juvenile runaways. Problem-oriented guides for police problem-specific guides series guide No. 37. Washington, D.C.: Center for Problems-Oriented Policing, Inc., U.S. Department of Justice.

Johnson, T. P., Aschkenasy, J. R., Herbers, M. R., et al. (1996). Self-reported risk factors for AIDS among homeless youth. *AIDS Education and Prevention, 8*(4), 308–322.

Jorgensen, E. L., Jorgensen, S. L., Heard, M. P., et al. (2009). Suicidal ideation among homeless youth: The impact of family dysfunction, morbidity and deliberate self-harm. *Journal of Adolescence*(June 17) [Epub ahead of print].

Kahn, A. U. (1987). Heterogeneity of suicidal adolescents. *Journal of the American Academy of Child and Adolescent Psychiatry, 26*, 92–96.

Kaleuati v. Tonda, CV07–504 (D. Haw).

Kandel, D. B., Raveis, V. H., & Davies, M. (1991). Suicide ideation in adolescents: Depression, substance use, and other risk factors. *Journal of youth and Adolescence, 20*, 289–309.

Kaplan, C. (2004). *Children missing from care: An issue brief.* Washington, D.C.: Child Welfare League of America.

Karabanow, J., & Clement, P. (2004). Interventions with street youth: A commentary on the practice-based research literature. *Brief Treatment and Crisis Intervention, 4*(1), 93–108.

Karabanow, J. M., & Rains, P. (1997). Structure versus caring: Discrepant perspectives in a shelter for street kids. *Children and Youth Services Review, 19*(4), 301–321.

Kawano. L. (2014, January 28). hawaiinewsnow.com. Retrieved from http://www.hawaiinews-now.com/story/24564506/breaking-roosevelt-high-school-campus-on-lockdown-hpd-responding-to-incident-latest-on-hawaiinewsnowcom).

Kazdin, A., & Weisz, J. (1998). Identifying and developing empirically supported child and adolescent treatments. *Journal of Consulting and Clinical Psychology, 66*(1), 19–36.

Keil, V., & Price, J. M. (2006). Externalizing behavior disorders in child welfare settings: Definition, prevalence, and implications for assessment and treatment. *Children & Youth Services Review, 28*, 761–779.

Kelley, B.T., Lorber, R., Keenan, K., et al. (1997). Developmental pathways in boys' disruptive and delinquent behavior. Bulletin. Washington, D.C.: U.S. Department of Justice, Office of Justice Programs, Office of Juvenile Justice and Delinquency Prevention.

Kelly, P. J., Bair, R. M., Baillargeon, J., et al. (2000). Risk behaviors and the prevalence of Chlamydia in a juvenile detention facility. *Clinical Pediatrics, 39*(9), 521–527.

Kendall, J.R. (2007). Families in need of critical assistance: Legislation and policy aiding youth who engage in noncriminal misbehavior. Chicago, IL: American Bar Association (ABA) Center on Children and the Law.

Kerr, T., Marshall, B.D., Miller, C., Shannon, K., Zhang, R., Montaner, J.S., & Wood, E. (2009). *Injection drug use among street-involved youth in a Canadian setting.* BMC Public Health, Jun 3; 9,171. Epub 2009 Jun 3.

Kidd, S. A. (2006). Factors precipitating suicidality among homeless youth: A quantitative follow-up. *Youth and Society, 37*(4), 393–422.

Kidd, S. A. (2003). Street youth: Coping and interventions. *Child and Adolescent Social Work Journal, 20*(4), 235–261.

Kidd, S. A. (2004). The walls were closing in, and we were trapped: A qualitative analysis of street youth suicide. *Youth & Society, 36*, 30–55.

Kienhorst, C. W. M., DeWilde, E. J., Van Den Bout, J., et al. (1990). Characteristics of suicide attempters in a population-based sample of Dutch adolescents. *British Journal of Psychiatry, 156*, 243–248.

Kihm, R., & Block, J. (1982). Response to crisis: Reducing the juvenile detention rate in Louisville, Kentucky. *Juvenile and Domestic Relations District Court, 33*(1), 37–44.

Kim, M. J., Tajima, E. A., Herrenkohl, T. I., & Huang, B. (2009). Early child maltreatment, runaway youths, and risk of delinquency and victimization. *Social Work Research, 33*(1), 19–28.

King, C. A., Hill, E., Evans, T., et al. (1993). Alcohol consumption in relation to other predictors of suicidality among adolescent girls. *Journal of the American Academy of Child & Adolescent Psychiatry, 32*, 82–88.

Kipke, M. D., Montgomery, S. B., Simon, T. R., et al. (1997a). Homeless youth: Drug use patterns and HIV risk profiles according to peer group affiliation. *AIDS & Behavior, 1*, 247–259.

Kipke, M. D., O'Connor, S., Palmer, R., et al. (1995). Street youth in Los Angeles: Profile of a group at high risk for human immunodeficiency virus infection. *Archives of Pediatrics and Adolescent Medicine, 149*, 513–519.

Kipke, M., Simon, T., Montgomery, D., et al. (1997b). Homeless youth and their exposure to violence while living on the streets. *Journal of Adolescence Health, 20*, 360–367.

Kipke, M. D., Weiss, G., & Wong, C. F. (2007). Residential status as a risk factor for drug use and HIV risk among young men who have sex with men. *AIDS and Behavior, 11*(Suppl 2), S56–S69.

Klein, J. D., Woods, A. H., Wilson, K. M., et al. (2000). Homeless and runaway youths' access to health care. *Journal of Adolescent Health, 27*(5), 331–339.

Klonsky, E. D. (2007). Non-suicidal self-injury: An introduction. *Journal of Clinical Psychology, 63*(11), 1039–1043.

Koopman, C., Rosario, M., & Rotheram-Borus, M. J. (1994). Alcohol and drug use and sexual behaviors placing runaways at risk for HIV infection. *Addictive Behavior, 19*, 95–103.

Kosciw, J. G., Greytak, E. A., & Diaz, E. M. (2009). Who, what, where, when and why: Demographic and ecological factors contributing to hostile school climate for lesbian, gay, bisexual and transgender youth. *Journal of Youth and Adolescence, 38*(7), 976–988.

Kowaleski-Jones, L., & Mott, F. L. (1998). Sex, contraception and childbearing among high-risk youth: do different factors influence males and females? *Family Planning Perspectives, 30*(4), 163–169.

Kral, A. H., Molnar, B. E., Booth, R. E., et al. (1997). Prevalence of sexual risk behavior and substance use among runaway and homeless adolescents in San Francisco, Denver and New York City. *International Journal of STD & AIDS, 8*, 109–117.

Krisberg, B. (2005). *Juvenile justice: Redeeming our children*. Thousand Oaks, CA: Sage.

Krisberg, B. (1997). *The impact of the juvenile justice system on serious, violent and chronic juvenile offenders*. San Francisco, CA: National Council on Crime and Delinquency.

Krisberg, B., Austin, J., & Steele, P. (1989). *Unlocking juvenile corrections*. San Francisco, CA: National Council on Crime and Delinquency.

Kruks, G. (1991). Gay and lesbian homeless/street youth: Special issues and concerns. *Journal of Adolescence Health, 12*(7), 515–518.

Kufeldt, K., & Nimmo, M. (1987). Youth on the street: Abuse and neglect in the eighties. *Child Abuse & Neglect, 11*, 531–543.

Kurtz, P., Jarvis, S. V., & Kurtz, G. L. (1991a). Problems of homeless youths: Empirical findings and human service issues. *Social Work, 36*, 309–314.

Kurtz, P., Jarvis, S., & Kurtz, G. (1991b). Problems of maltreated runaway youth. *Adolescence, 26*, 544–555.

Kurtz, P. D., Kurtz, G. L., & Jarvis, S. V. (1991c). Problems of maltreated runaway youth. *Adolescence, 26*, 543–555.

Kurtz, P. D., Lindsey, E. W., Jarvis, S., et al. (2000). How runaway and homeless youth navigate troubled waters: The role of formal and informal helpers. *Child and Adolescent Social Work Journal, 17*(5), 381–403.

Lalor, K. (1999). Street children: A comparative perspective. *Child Abuse & Neglect, 23*(8), 759–770.

Lam, D., & Cheng, F. (2008). Chinese policy reaction to the problem of street children: An analysis from the perspective of street children. *Children and Youth Services Review, 30*(5), 575–584.

Lampkin v. District of Columbia, 27 F. 3d 605 (D.C. Cir. 1993), remanded to trial at 879 F. Supp 116(D.D.C. 1995).

Land, K., McCall, P., & Williams, J. (1990). Something that works in juvenile justice: An evaluation of the North Carolina Court Counselors' Intensive Supervision project, 1987–1989. *Evaluation Review, 14*(6), 574–606.

Lange, A., DeBeurs, E., Dolan, C., et al. (1999). Long-term effects of childhood sexual abuse: Objective and subjective characteristics of the abuse and psychopathology in later life. *The Journal of Nervous and Mental Disease, 187*, 150–158.

Lankenau, S. E., Clatts, M. C., Welle, D., et al. (2005). Street careers: Homelessness, drug use, and sex work among young men who have sex with men (YMSM). *International Journal of Drug Policy, 16*, 10–18.

Lansford, J. E., Dodge, K. A., Pettit, G. S., et al. (2002). A 12-year prospective study of the long-term effects of early child physical maltreatment on psychological, behavioral, and academic problems in adolescence. *Archives of Pediatrics and Adolescent Medicine, 156*(8), 824–830.

Lauritsen, J. L., Laub, J. H., & Sampson, R. J. (1992). Conventional and delinquent activities: Implications for the prevention of violent victimization among adolescents. *Violence & Victims, 7*, 91–108.

Laye-Gindhu, A., & Schonert-Reichl, K. A. (2005). Nonsuicidal self-harm among community adolescents: Understanding the "Whats" and "Whys" of self-harm. *Journal of Youth and Adolescence, 34*(5), 447–457.

Lederman, C. S., Dakof, G. A., et al. (2004). Characteristics of adolescent females in juvenile detention. *International Journal of Law and Psychiatry, 27*, 321–337.

Lee, B. A., & Schreck, C. J. (2005). Danger on the streets: Marginality and victimization among homeless people. *American Behavioral Scientist, 48*, 1055–1081.

Lester, D. (2003). Adolescent suicide from an international perspective. *American Behavioral Scientist, 46*, 1157–1170.

Li, A., Dachner, N., & Tarasuk, V. (2009). Food intake patterns of homeless youth in Toronto. *Canadian Journal of Public Health, 100*(1), 36–40.

Linden, D.W. (2015). Schools face the teen cutting problem. The Wall Street Journal, July 27. Retrieved from http://www.wsj.com/articles/schools-face-the-teen-cutting-problem-1438018567.

Lindsey, E. W., Kurtz, D., Jarvis, S., et al. (2000). How runaway and homeless youth navigate troubled waters: Personal strengths and resources. *Child and Adolescent Social Work Journal, 17*(2), 115–140.

Lipschitz, D. S., Wingegar, R. K., Nicolaou, A. L., et al. (1999). Perceived abuse and neglect as risk factors for suicidal behavior in adolescent inpatients. *The Journal of Nervous and Mental Disease, 187*, 32–39.

Lipsey, M., & Wilson, D. (1998). Effective intervention for serious juvenile offenders. In: R. Loeber & D. Farrington (Eds.). Thousand Oaks, CA: Sage.

Liu, R. T., & Mustanski, B. (2012). Suicidal ideation and self-harm in lesbian, gay, bisexual, and transgender youth. *American Journal of Preventive Medicine, 42*(3), 221–228.

Liu, K., Slap, G. B., Kinsman, S. B., et al. (1994). Pregnancy among American Indian adolescents: Reactions and prenatal care. *Journal of Adolescent Health, 15*, 336–341.

Loeber, R., Keenan, K., & Zhang, Q. (1997). Boys' experimentation and persistence in developmental pathways toward serious delinquency. *Journal of Child and Family Studies, 6*, 321–357.

Loeber, R., Wung, P., Keenan, K., et al. (1993). Developmental pathways in disruptive child behavior. *Development and Psychopathology, 5*, 101–132.

Lubotsky, E., Tapu, I, & Zopp, F. (no date). Gay homeless youth and their lives on the streets of New York City. humanityinaction.org. Retrieved from http://www.humanityinaction.org/knowledgebase/83-gay-homeless-youth-and-their-lives-on-the-streets-of-new-york-city.

Lubow, B. (1999). Successful strategies for reforming juvenile detention. *Federal Probation Journal, 63*(2), 16–24.

Luna, G.C., & Rotheram-Borus, M.J. (1992). Street youth and the AIDS pandemic. AIDS Educ & Prev, Suppl, 1–13.

Lusk, M. W. (1989). Street children programs in Latin America. *Journal of Sociology & Social Welfare, 16*(1), 55–73.

Lusk, M. W. (1992). Street children of Rio de Janeiro. *International Social Work, 35*(3), 293–305.

Luthar, S. S. (1999). *Poverty and children's adjustment*. Thousand Oaks, CA: Sage.

Mack, J. W. (1909). The juvenile court. *Harvard Law Review, 23*, 104–122.

MacKellar, D. A., Valleroy, L. A., Hofmann, J. P., et al. (2000). Gender differences in sexual behaviors and factors associated with nonuse of condoms among homeless and runaway youths. *AIDS Education and Prevention, 12*(6), 477–491.

MacLean, M. G., Embry, L. E., & Cauce, A. M. (1999). Homeless adolescents' paths to separation from family: Comparison of family characteristics, psychological adjustment, and victimization. *Journal of Community Psychology, 27*, 179–187.

Mallett, S., Rosenthal, D., & Keys, D. (2005). Young people, drug use and family conflict: Pathways into homelessness. *Journal of Adolescence, 28*(2), 185–199.

Mallett, S., Rosenthal, D., Myers, P., et al. (2004). Practising homelessness: A typology approach to young people's daily routines. *Journal of Adolescence, 27*(3), 337–349.

Mann, C. R. (1980). Courtroom observations of extra-legal factors in the juvenile court dispositions of runaway boys. A field study. *Juvenile and Family Court Journal, 31*, 43–52.

Manning, A. (2014). Abuse haunted runaway teen found dead in Columbus. The Columbus Dispatch, November 15. http://www.dispatch.com/content/stories/local/2014/09/22/lost-runaway.html.

Margolis, P. A., Stevens, R., Bordley, W. C., Stuart, J., Harlan, C., Keyes-Elstein, L., et al. (2001). From concept to application: the impact of a community-wide intervention to improve the delivery of preventive services to children. *Pediatrics, 108*(3), E42.

Marschall, LeAnn K. (2014). Art therapy and runaway homeless youth: An exploration of trauma and the survival response of" (2014). LMU/LLS Theses and Dissertations. Paper 59).

Marshall, B. D. L., Kerr, T., Shoveller, J. A., et al. (2009). Homelessness and unstable housing associated with an increased risk of HIV and STI transmission among street-involved youth. *Health & Place, 15*, 783–790.

Marshall, B. D., Shannon, K., Kerr, T., et al. (2010). Survival sex work and increased HIV risk among sexual minority street-involved youth. *Journal of Acquired Immune Deficiency Syndromes, 53*(5), 661–664.

Martijn, C., & Sharpe, L. (2006). Pathways to youth homelessness. *Social Science & Medicine, 62*(1), 1–12.

Martin, G., Bergen, H. A., Richardson, A. S., et al. (2004). Sexual abuse and suicidality: Gender differences in a large community sample of adolescent. *Child Abuse and Neglect, 28*, 491–503.

Martin, J. A., Hamilton, B. E., Sutton, P. D., et al. (2006). *Births—Final data for 2003: National vital statistics reports*. Hyattsville, MD: National Center for Health Statistics.

Martinez, T. E., Gleghorn, A., Marx, R., et al. (1998) Psychosocial histories, social environment, and HIV risk behaviors of injection and noninjection drug using homeless youth. *Journal of Psychoactive Drugs, 30*(1), 1–10.

Maxson, C., Little, M., & Klein, M. (1988). Police response to runaway and missing children: A conceptual framework for research and policy. *Crime & Delinquency, 34*(1), 84–102.

Mays, V. M., & Cochran, S. D. (2001). Mental health correlates of perceived discrimination among lesbian, gay, and bisexual adults in the United States. *American Journal of Public Health, 91*(11), 1869–1876.

McCarthy, B., & Hagan, J. (1992). Surviving on the street. The experiences of homeless youth. *Journal of Adolescent Research, 7*(4), 412–430.

McCaskill, P. A., Toro, P. A., & Wolfe, S. M. (1998). Homeless and matched housed adolescents: A comparative study of psychopathology. *Journal of Clinical Child & Adolescent Psychology, 27*, 306–319.

McCormack, A., Janus, M. D., & Burgess, A. W. (1986). Runaway youths and sexual victimization: gender differences in an adolescent runaway population. *Child Abuse and Neglect, 10*(3), 387–395.

McKinney-Vento Homeless Assistance Act, Re-Authorized (2002). 42 USC 11431 et seq 725.

McMorris, B. J., Tyler, K. A., Whitbeck, L. B., et al. (2002). Familial and "On-the-Street" risk factors associated with alcohol use among homeless and runaway adolescents. *Journal of Studies on Alcohol and Drugs, 63*(1), 34–43.

Meade, M. A., & Slesnick, N. (2002). Ethical considerations for research and treatment with runaway and homeless adolescents. *Journal of Psychology, 136*(4), 449–463.

Mears, D. P. (2012). The front end of the juvenile court: Intake and informal vs. formal processing. In B. C. Feld & D. M. Bishop (Eds.), *The Oxford handbook of juvenile crime and juvenile justice*. New York: Oxford University Press.

Mears, D. P., Cochran, J. C., Stults, B. J., et al. (2014). The 'true' juvenile offender: Age effects and juvenile court sanctioning. *Criminology, 52*(2), 169–194.

Melhem, N. M., Day, N., Shear, M. K., et al. (2003). Predictors of complicated grief among adolescents exposed to a peer's suicide. *Journal of Loss and Trauma, 9*, 21–34.

Michon, K. (no date). Retrieved from http://www.nolo.com/legal-encyclopedia/juvenile-law-status-offenses-32227.html).

Mihalic, S., Irwin, K., Elliott, D., et al. (2001). Blueprints for violence prevention. Bulletin. Washington, D.C.: U.S. Department of Justice, Office of Justice Programs, Office of Juvenile Justice and Delinquency Prevention.

Milburn, N. G., Rothereram-Borus, M. J., Batterham, P., et al. (2005). Predictors of close family relationships over one year among homeless young people. *Journal of Adolescence, 28*(2), 263–275.

Milburn, N. G., Rotheram-Borus, M. J., Rice, E., et al. (2006). Cross-national variations in behavioral profiles among homeless youth. *American Journal of Community Psychology, 37*(12), 63–76.

Mishriki, J. (2001–2013). Runaway lives. Personal stories and reflections by runaways and their families. http://www2.lv.psu.edu/jkl1/runawaylives/index.html.

Mitchell, K. J., Finkelhor, D., & Wolak, J. (2010). Conceptualizing juvenile prostitution as child mistreatment: Findings from the National Juvenile Prostitution Study. *Child Mistreatment, 15*(1), 18–36.

Moffitt, T. E. (1993). Adolescence-limited and life-course-persistent antisocial behavior. A developmental taxonomy. *Psychological Review, 100*, 674–701.

Molnar, B. E., Shade, S. B., Kral, A. H., et al. (1998). Suicidal behavior and sexual/physical abuse among street youth. *Child Abuse & Neglect, 22*(3), 213–222.

Moon, M. W., Binson, D., Page-Shafer, K., et al. (2001). Correlates of HIV risk in a random sample of street youths in San Francisco. *Journal of the Association of Nurses in AIDS Care , 12*(6), 18–27.

Moon, M. W., McFarland, W., Kellogg, T., et al. (2000). HIV risk behavior of runaway youth in San Francisco: Age of onset and relation to sexual orientation. *Youth & Society, 32*(2), 184–201.

Montgomery, S. B., Hyde, J., De Rose, C. J., et al. (2002). Gender differences in HIV risk behaviors among young injectors and their social network members. *American Journal of Drug and Alcohol Abuse, 28*(3), 453–475.

Morewitz, S. J. (2008). *Death threats and violence. New research and clinical perspectives*. New York: Springer.

Morewitz, S. J. (2004). *Domestic violence and maternal and child health*. New York: Kluwer Academic/Plenum Publishers.

Morewitz, S.J. (2016, forthcoming). Kidnapping and violence. New research and clinical perspectives. New York: Springer.

Morewitz, S. J. (2003). *Stalking and violence. New patterns of trauma and obsession*. New York: Springer.

Morewitz, S.J., & Goldstein, M. (2014). (Eds.). Handbock of forensic sociology and psychology. New York: Springer.

Morewitz, S.J., & Sturdy Colls, C. (forthcoming, 2016). (Eds.). Handbook of missing persons. New trends in forensic sciences research. New York: Springer.

Morey, M. A., & Friedman, L. S. (1993). Health care needs of homeless adolescents. *Current Opinion in Pediatrics, 5*(4), 395–399.

Morris, A. (2014). The forsaken: A rising number of homeless gay teens are being cast out by religious families. Rolling Stone Magazine, September 3. Retrieved from http://www. rollingstone.com/culture/features/the-forsaken-a-rising-number-of-homeless-gay-teens-are-being-cast-out-by-religious-families-20140903?page=4.

Mundy, P., Robertson, M. J., Robertson, J. M., et al. (1990). The prevalence of psychotic symptoms in homeless adolescents. *Journal of the American Academy of Child & Adolescent Psychiatry, 29*, 724–731.

Murray, C., & Cox, L. (1979). *Beyond probation*. Beverly Hills, CA: Sage.

National Center for Health Statistics. (2005). NCHS: National Death Index. Retrieved from www. cdc.gov/nchs/ndi.htm.

National Center for Homeless Education. (2013, Spring). Who are unaccompanied homeless youth? (Brief). http://www.serve.org/nche.

National Child Traumatic Stress Network. (2007). Trauma among homeless youth. *Culture and Trauma Brief, 2*(1), 1–7. www.NCTSN.org.

National Conference of State Legislatures. (2013, October 1). Homeless and runaway youth. http://www.ncsl.org/research/human-services/homeless-and-runaway-youth.aspx#3.

National Institute for Clinical Excellence. (2004). National clinical practice guideline number 16: Self-harm (pdf). The British Psychological Society.

National Law Center on Homelessness and Poverty. (2003). *Alone without a home: A state-by-state guide to laws affecting unaccompanied youth*. Washington, D.C.: National Law Center on Homelessness and Poverty.

Nat'l Law Ctr. on Homelessness and Poverty v. New York, 224 F.R.D. 314 (E.D.N.Y. 2004).

National Network for Youth (no date). Education barriers for homeless youth. NN4Y Issue Brief. Washington, D.C. www.nn4youth.org.

National Network of Runaway and Youth Services, Inc; (1985). *To whom do they belong? A profile of America's runaways and homeless youth and the programs that help them*. Washington, D.C.: National Network of Runaway and Youth Services, Inc.

National Runaway Switchboard. (2008). Crisis call log and program services report, 2007. http:// www.1800runaway.org/news_events/call_stats.html.

Nebbitt, V. E., House, L. E., Thompson, S. J., et al. (2007). Successful transitions of runaway/ homeless youth from shelter care. *Journal of Child and Family Studies, 16*(4), 545–555.

New York Times, The Editorial Board. (2014, June 8). Juveniles placed in solitary confinement; State of Ohio lawsuit.

Newiss, G. (1999). Missing presumed…? The police response to missing persons. Police Research Series Paper 114. London: Home Office.

News9.com. (no date). Oklahoma teen runaway found dead after attempted robbery in Texas. http://www.news9.com/story/21752139/pot-co-under-sheriff-ids-body-found-in-texas).

Nielsen, S. F., Hjorthoj, C. R., Erlangsen, A., et al (2011). Psychiatric disorders and mortality among people in homeless shelters in Denmark: A nationwide register-based cohort study. *Lancet, 77*(9784), 2205–2214.

Noell, J. W., & Ochs, L. M. (2001). Relationship of sexual orientation to substance use, suicidal ideation, suicide attempts, and other factors in a population of homeless adolescents. *Journal of Adolescent Health, 29*(1), 31–36.

Noell, J., Rohde, P., Ochs, L., et al. (2001a). Incidence and prevalence of chlamydia, herpes, and viral hepatitis in a homeless adolescent population. *Sexually Transmitted Diseases, 28*(1), 4–10.

Noell, J., Rohde, P., Seeley, J., et al. (2001b). Childhood sexual abuse, adolescent sexual coercion and sexually transmitted infection acquisition among homeless female adolescents. *Child Abuse & Neglect, 25*(1), 137–148.

Nofziger, S. (2009). Deviant lifestyles and violent victimization at school. *Journal of Interpersonal Violence, 24*(9), 1494–1517. Epub 2008 Sep 19.

Nordentoft, M., & Wandall-Holm, N. (2003). 10 year follow-up study of mortality among users of hostels for homeless people in Copenhagen. *BMJ, 327*, 81.

Noto, A. R., Nappo, S. A., Galduroz, J. C. F., et al. (1997). Use of drugs among street children in Brazil. *Journal of Psychoactive Drugs, 29*(2), 185–192.

Nugent, W. R., Bruley, C., & Allen, P. (1998). The effects of aggression replacement training on antisocial behavior in a runaway shelter. *Research on Social Work Practice, 8*(6), 636–656.

Oates, K. R. (2004). Sexual abuse and suicidal behavior. *Child Abuse & Neglect, 28*, 487–489.

Oetting, E. R., & Beauvais, F. (1987). Peer cluster theory, socialization characteristics, and adolescent drug use: A path analysis. *Journal of Counseling Psychology, 34*, 205–213.

O'Grady, B., Bright, R., & Cohen, E. (1998). Sub-employment and street youths: An analysis of the impact of squeegee cleaning on homeless youths. *Security Journal, 11*, 315–323.

OJJJDP. (no date). Juvenile justice reform initiatives in states, 1994–1996. Washington, D.C.: Office of Juvenile Justice and Delinquency Prevention, U.S. Department of Justice. Retrieved from: ojjdp.gov.

OJJDP Statistical Briefing Book. Online. (no date). Retrieved from: http://www.ojjdp.gov/ojstatbb/structure_process/qa04121.asp?qaDate=2013. Released on August 1, 2014).

Olson, L., Huyler, F., Lynch, A. W., et al. (1999). Guns, alcohol and intimate partner violence: The epidemiology of female suicide in New Mexico. *Crisis, 20*, 121–126.

Olson, L., Liebow, E., Mannino, F. V., & Shore, M. F. (1980). Runaway children. Twelve years later. *Journal of Family Issues, 1*, 165–188.

Ougrin, D., Tranah, T., Stahl, D., et al. (2015). Therapeutic interventions for suicide attempts and self-harm in adolescents: Systematic review and meta-analysis. *Journal of the American Academy of Child and Adolescent Psychiatry, 54*(2), 97–107.

Oumaya, M., Friedman, S., Pham, A., et al. (2008). Borderline personality disorder, self-mutilation and suicide: Literature review. *Encephale, 34*(5), 452–458.

Overholser, J., Evans, S., & Spirito, A. (1990). Sex differences and their relevance to primary prevention of adolescent suicide. *Death Studies, 14*, 391–402.

Panter-Brick, C. (2002). Street children, human rights, and public health: A critique and future directions. *Annual Review of Anthropology, 31*, 147–171.

Paradise, M., & Cauce, A. M. (2002). Home street home: The interpersonal dimensions of adolescent homelessness. *Analyses of Social Issues and Public Policy, 2*(1), 223–238.

Parent, D. G., Leiter, V., Kennedy, S., et al. (1994). *Conditions of confinement: Juvenile detention and corrections facilities*. Washington, D.C.: U.S. Department of Justice, Office of Justice Programs, Office of Juvenile Justice and Delinquency Prevention.

Pasztor, E. M., Clarren, J., Timberlake, E. M., et al. (1986). Stepping out of foster care into independent living. *Children Today, 15*(2), 32–35.

Patterson, G.R., & Yoerger, K. (1997). A developmental model for late-onset delinquency. In: Dienstbier, R., & Osgood, D.W. (Eds.). Nebraska Symposium on Motivation: Vol. 44, Motivation and delinquency. Series Ed. Vol. Ed. Lincoln, Nebraska: University of Nebraska Press, 119–177.

Pedro-Carroll, J. L., Cowen, E. L., Hightower, A. D., et al. (1986). Preventive intervention with latency-age children of divorce: A replication study. *American Journal of Community Psychology, 14*, 277–290.

Peled, E., & Cohavi, A. (2009). The meaning of running away for girls. *Child Abuse & Neglect, 33*, 739–749.

People v. Salaam, 666 N.Y.S.2d 881 (1997).

Penn, J. V., Esposito, C. L., Schaeffer, L. E., et al. (2003). Suicide attempts and self-mutilative behavior in a juvenile correctional facility. *Journal of the American Academy of Child and Adolescent Psychiatry, 42*(7), 762–769.

Pergamit, M., & Ernst, M. (2010). *Runaway youth's knowledge and access of services*. Washington, D.C.: The Urban Institute.

Perry, T. (2015, June 15). latimes.com. Retrieved from http://www.latimes.com/local/lanow/la-me-ln-sheriff-stun-gun-20150615-story.html).

Petering, R., Rice, E., Rhoades, H., et al. (2014). The social networks of homeless youth experiencing intimate partner violence. *Journal of Interpersonal Violence, 29*, 2172–2191.

Pfeifer, R. W., & Oliver, J. (1997). A study of HIV seroprevalence in a group of homeless youth in Hollywood, California. *Journal of Adolescent Health, 20*(5), 339–342.

Platt, A. (1977). *The child savers: The invention of delinquency* (2nd ed.). Chicago, IL: University of Chicago Press.

Plunkett, A. M., O'Toole, B., Swanson, H. I., et al. (2001). Suicide risk following child sexual abuse. *Ambulatory Pediatrics, 1*, 262–266.

Podschun, G. D. (1993). Teen peer outreach-street work project: HIV prevention education for runaway and homeless youth. *Public Health Reports, 108*(2), 150–155.

Pollio, D. E., Thompson, S. J., & North, C. S. (2000). Agency-based tracking of difficult-to-follow populations: Runaway and homeless youth programs in St. Louis, Missouri. *Community Mental Health Journal, 36*(3), 247–258.

Pollio, D. E., Thompson, S. J., Tobias, L., et al. (2006). Longitudinal outcomes for youth receiving runaway/homeless shelter services. *Journal of Youth and Adolescence, 35*, 859–866.

Posner, M. (1992). *The runaway risk reduction project assessment report*. Newton, MA: Education Development Center.

Price, S. (2009, April 30). Parental option for out-of-control 16-year-olds. 2009-R-0187. http://www.cga.ct.gov/2009/rpt/2009-R-0187.htm.

Pulkkinen, L. (2011, July 21). Boyfriend charged in teen runaway's death. http://www.seattlepi.com/local/article/Boyfriend-charged-in-teen-runaway-s-death-1527864.php.

Quilgars, D., Johnsen, S., & Pleace, N. (2008). Youth homelessness in U.K.: A decade of progress? New York, UK: Joseph Roundtree Foundation.

Raffaelli, M., Campos, R., & Merritt, A. P. (1993). Sexual practices and attitudes of street youth in Belo Horizonte, Brazil. *Social Science & Medicine, 37*(5), 661–670.

Raffaelli, M., Sigueira, E., Payne-Merritt, A., et al. (1995). HIV-related knowledge and risk behaviors of street youth in Belo Horizonte, Brazil. The Street Youth Study Group. *AIDS Education and Prevention, 7*(4), 287–297.

Raine, W. J. B. (1982). Self-mutilation. *Journal of Adolescence, 5*, 1–13.

Raising the Roof (2009). Youth homelessness in Canada: The road to solutions. http://www.raisingtheroof.org/RaisingTheRoof/media/RaisingTheRoofMedia/Documents/Roadt.

Reavy, P. (2012, March 14). Parents of missing teen tried finding her through cellphone GPS. http://www.ksl.com/?sid=19587097.

Rebeccas Community. (no date). http://www.homeless.org.au/people/rebecca.htm.

Resch, F., Parzer, P., Brunner, R., et al. (2008). Self mutilation and suicidal behavior in children and adolescents: Prevalence and psychosocial correlates: Results of the BELLA study. *European Child & Adolescent Psychiatry, 17*(Suppl 1), 92–98.

Rew, L., Fouladi, R. T., & Yockey, R. D. (2002). Sexual health practices of homeless youth. *Journal of Nursing Scholarship, 34*(2), 139–145.

Rew, L., Fouladi, R. T., Land, L., et al. (2007). Outcomes of a brief sexual health intervention for homeless youth. *Journal of Health Psychology, 12*, 818–832.

Rew, L., Taylor-Seehafer, M., & Fitzgerald, M. L. (2001). Sexual abuse, alcohol and other drug use, and suicidal behaviors in homeless adolescents. *Issues in Comprehensive Pediatric Nursing, 24*, 225–240.

Rice, E., Milburn, N. G., & Rotheram-Borus, M. J. (2007). Pro-social and problematic social network influences on HIV/AIDS risk behaviours among newly homeless youth in Los Angeles. *AIDS Care, 19*(5), 697–704.

Rice, E., Stein, J. A., & Milburn, N. (2008). Countervailing social network influences on problem behaviors among homeless youth. *Journal of Adolescence, 31*(5), 625–639.

Ringwalt, C. L., Greene, J. M., & Robertson, M. J. (1998). Familial backgrounds and risk behaviors of youth with thrownaway experiences. *Journal of Adolescence, 21*, 241–252.

Robertson, M.J. (1989). Homeless youth in Hollywood: Patterns of alcohol use. A Report to the National Institute on Alcohol Abuse and Alcoholism (Report No. C51). Berkeley, CA: Alcohol Research Group.

Robertson, M.J., & Toro, P.A. (no date). Homeless youth: Research, intervention, and policy. National Symposium on Homelessness Research. Washington, D.C.: U.S. Department of Housing and Urban Development; U.S. Department of Health and Human Services.

Rogers, T. R., Segal, E. A., & Graham, M. (1994). The relationship between academic factors and running away among adolescents. *Children & Schools, 16*(1), 46–54.

Rohde, P., Noell, J., Ochs, L., et al. (2001). Depression, suicidal ideation and STD-related risk in homeless older adolescents. *Journal of Adolescence, 24*(4), 447–460.

Rohde, P., Seeley, J. R., & Mace, D. E. (1997). Correlates of suicidal behavior in a juvenile detention population. *Suicide & Life Threatening Behavior, 27*(2), 164–175.

Rome, E. S., Rybicki, L. A., & Durant, R. H. (1998). Pregnancy and other risk behaviors among adolescent girls in Ohio. *Journal of Adolescent Health, 22*(1), 50–55.

Rosa, C. S. A., Borba, R. E., de Sousa, E., & Ebrahim, G. J. (1992). The street children of Recife: A study of their background. *Journal of Tropical Pediatrics, 38*(1), 34–40.

Rosario, M., Schrimshaw, E. W., Hunter, J., et al. (2002). Gay-related stress and emotional distress among gay, lesbian and bisexual youths: A longitudinal examination. *Journal of Consulting and Clinical Psychology, 70*(4), 967–975.

Ross, S., & Heath, N. (2002). A study of the frequency of self-mutilation in a community sample of adolescents. *Journal of Youth and Adolescence, 31*, 67–77.

Ross, T. (2001). *A system in transition: An analysis of New York City's foster care system at the year 2000*. New York: Vera Institute of Justice. Retrieved from http://www.vera.org/publication_pdf/153_223.pdf.

Rossow, I., Groholt, B., & Wichstrom, L. (2004). Intoxicants and suicidal behavior among adolescents: Changes in levels and associations from 1992–2002. *Addiction, 100*, 79–88.

Rotheram-Borus, M. J. (1993). Suicidal behavior and risk factors among runaway youths. *American Journal of Psychiatry, 150*, 103–107.

Rotheram-Borus, M. J., & Koopman, C. (1991). Sexual risk behaviors, AIDS knowledge, and beliefs about AIDS among runaways. *American Journal of Public Health, 81*(2), 208–210.

Roy, E., Haley, N., Leclerc, P., et al. (2003). HIV incidence among street youth in Montreal, Canada. *AIDS, 17*, 1071–1075.

Roy, E., Haley, N., Leclerc, P., et al. (2004). Mortality in a cohort of street youth in Montreal. *JAMA, 292*(5), 569–574.

Roy, E., Haley, N., Leclerc, P., et al. (2000). Prevalence of HIV infection and risk behaviours among Montreal street youth. *International Journal of STD & AIDS, 11*(4), 241–247.

Roy, S., & Brown, M. (1995). Juvenile electronic monitoring program in Lake County, Indiana: An evaluation. In J. Smykla & W. Selke (Eds.), *Intermediate sanctions: Sentencing in the 1990s*. Cincinnati, OH: Anderson Publishing.

Rubin, D. H., Erickson, C. J., San Agustin, M., et al. (1997). Cognitive and academic functioning of homeless children compared with housed children. *Pediatrics, 97*(3), 289–294.

Rudatsikira, E., Singh, P., Job, J., & Knutsen, S. (2007). Variables associated with weapon-carrying among young adolescents in southern California. *The Journal of Adolescent Health, 40*(5), 470–473. Epub 2007 Mar 9.

Runaway and Homeless Youth Act of 1974 (Juvenile Justice and Delinquency Prevention Act Pub. L. 93–415, Sept. 7, 1974, 88 Stat. 1109 (Title 42, Sec. 5601 et seq.), as amended by the Runaway, Homeless and Missing Children Protection Act of 2003 (Public Law 108–96).

Runaway and Homeless Youth Act of 1974 (Title III of the Juvenile Justice and Delinquency Prevention Act of 1974), Administration for Children and Families. As Amended by the Reconnecting Homeless Youth Act of 2008 (P.L.110-378); Prepared by the Administration for Children and Families, October 8, 2008.

Runaway and Homeless Youth Inclusion Act of 2013 - H.R. 2955) (113th Congress, 2013–2014).

Runaway, Homeless and Missing Children Protection Act of 2003 (Public Law 108–96).

Russell, S. T., & Joyner, K. (2001). Adolescent sexual orientation and suicide risk: Evidence from a national study. *American Journal of Public Health, 91*, 1276–1281.

Rutter, M., & Garmezy, N. (1983). Developmental psychopathology. In: E.M. Heatherington (Ed.). (vol. ed.). Handbook of child psychology (Vol. 4, 4th ed.).

Ryan, C., Huebner, D., Diaz, R., et al. (2009). Family rejection as a predictor of negative health outcomes in White and Latino lesbian, gay, and bisexual young adults. *Pediatrics, 123*, 346–352.

Ryan, K. D., Kilmer, R., Cauce, A. M., et al. (2000). Psychological consequences of child maltreatment in homeless adolescents: Untangling the unique effects of maltreatment and family environment. *Child Abuse & Neglect, 24*(3), 333–352.

Saewyc, E. M., & Edinburgh, L. D. (2010). Restoring healthy developmental trajectories for sexually exploited young runaway girls: fostering protective factors and reducing risk behaviors. *The Journal of Adolescent Health, 46*(2), 180–188. Epub 2009 Aug 3.

Saewyc, E. M., Skay, C. L., Pettingell, S. L., et al. (2006). Hazards of stigma: The sexual and physical abuse of gay, lesbian, and bisexual adolescents in the United States and Canada. *Child Welfare, 85*(2), 195–213.

Safe Horizon (no date). Mike's LGBT homeless youth story: HIV positive and looking for safety. Retrieved from http://www.safehorizon.org/page/mikes-lgbt-homeless-youth-story-hiv-positive-and-looking-for-safety-307.html.

Sahin, H. A., & Sahin, H. G. (2003). An unaddressed issue: Domestic violence and unplanned pregnancies among pregnant women in Turkey. *The European Journal of Contraception & Reproductive Health Care, 8*(2), 93–98.

Sampson, R. J., & Lauritsen, J. L. (1990). Deviant lifestyles, proximity to crime, and the offender-victim link in personal violence. *Journal of Research in Crime and Delinquency, 27*, 110–139.

Sanchez, R. P., Waller, M. W., & Greene, J. M. (2006). Who runs? A demographic profile of runaway youth in the United States. *Journal of Adolescent Health, 39*, 778–781.

Savin-Williams, R. C. (1994). Verbal or physical abuse as stressors in the lives of lesbian, gay male, and bisexual youths. *Journal of Consulting and Clinical Psychology, 62*, 261–269.

Savin-Williams, R.C., & Cohen, K.M. (1996). Psychosocial outcomes of verbal and physical abuse among lesbian, gay, and bisexual youths. In: R.C. Savin-Williams, & K.M. Cohen (Eds.). The lives of lesbians, gays, and bisexuals: Children to adults. pp. 181–200. Ft. Worth, TX: Harcourt Brace College Publishers.

Scanlon, T., Tomkins, A., Lynch, M., et al. (1998). Street children in Latin America. *British Medical Journal, 316*, 1596–1600.

Schalwitz, J., Goulart, M., Dunnigan, K., et al. (1990). Prevalence of sexually transmitted diseases (STDs) and HIV in a homeless youth medical clinic in San Francisco. Presented at the VI International Conference on AIDS; San Francisco, CA, June, Abstract.

Schmidtke, A., Bille-Brahe, U., DeLeo, D., et al. (1996). Attempted suicide in Europe: Rates, trends and sociodemographic characteristics of suicide attempters during the period 1989–1992. Results of the WHO/EURO Multicentre Study on Parasuicide. *Acta Psychiatrica Scandinavica, 93*(5), 327–338.

Schur, E. M. (1973). *Radical non-intervention: Rethinking the delinquency problem*. Englewood Cliffs, N.J.: Prentice-Hall.

Schuyler Center for Analysis and Advocacy. (2008). *Teenage births: Outcomes for young parents and their children*. Albany, NY: Schuyler Center for Analysis and Advocacy.

Sedlak, A. J., Finkelhor, D., Hammer, H., et al. (2002). *National estimates of missing children: An overview*. Washington, D.C.: U.S. Department of Justice Programs, Office of Juvenile Justice and Delinquency Prevention.

Shannon, K., Strathdee, S. A., Shoveller, J., et al. (2009). Structural and environmental barriers to condom use negotiation with clients among female sex workers: Implications for HIV-prevention strategies and policy. *American Journal of Public Health, 99*, 659–665.

Sharma, M. K., & Marimuthu, P. (2014). Prevalence and psychosocial factors of aggression among youth. *Indian Journal of Psychological Medicine, 36*(1), 48–53.

Shaw, M., & Dorling, D. (1998). Mortality among street youth in the UK. *Lancet, 352*, 743.

Sheldon, R. (1999). *Detention diversion advocacy: An evaluation*. Washington, D.C.: Bulletin.

U.S. Department of Justice, Office of Justice Programs, Office of Juvenile Justice and Delinquency Prevention.

Sherman, S. S., Plitt, S., ul-Hassan, S., et al. (2005). Drug use, street survival, and risk behaviors among street children in Lahore, Pakistan. *Journal of Urban Health, 82*(3 Suppl 4), iv113–iv124.

Sigrid, J. (2004). Why do foster care placements disrupt? An investigation of reasons for placement change in foster care. *Social Service Review, 78*, 601–627.

Silenzio, V. M., Penn, J. B., Duberstein, P. R., et al. (2007). Sexual orientation and risk factors for suicide ideation and suicide attempts among adolescents and young adults. *American Journal of Public Health, 97*, 2017–2019.

Simkin, D. R. (2002). Review adolescent substance use disorders and comorbidity. *Pediatric Clinics of North America, 49*(2), 463–477.

Simons, R. L., & Whitbeck, L. B. (1991). Sexual abuse as a precursor to prostitution and victimization among adolescent and adult homeless women. *Journal of Family Issues, 12*(3), 361–379.

Slater, C., & Robinson, A. J. (2014). Sexual health in adolescents. *Clinics in Dermatology, 32*(2), 189–195.

Slesnick, N., Dashora, P., Letcher, A., et al. (2009). A review of services and interventions for runaway and homeless youth: Moving forward. *Children and Youth Services Review, 31*(7), 732–742.

Slesnick, N., Erdem, G., Bartle-Haring, S., et al. (2013). Intervention with substance-abusing runaway adolescents and their families: Results of a randomized clinical trial. *Journal of Consulting and Clinical Psychology, 81*(4), 600–614.

Slesnick, N., & Prestopnik, J. J. (2009). Comparison of family therapy outcome with alcohol-abusing, runaway adolescents. *Journal of Marital and Family Therapy, 35*(3), 255–277.

Slesnick, N., & Prestopnik, J. (2004). Perceptions of the family environment and youth behaviors: Alcohol-abusing runaway adolescents and their primary caretakers. *The Family Journal, 12*, 243–253.

Slesnick, N., Prestopnik, J., Meyers, R. J., et al. (2007). Treatment outcomes for street-living, homeless youth. *Addictive Behaviors, 32*(6), 1237–1251.

Smart, D. (1991). Homeless youth in Seattle. *Journal of Adolescent Health, 12*, 519–527.

Smart, R. G., & Walsh, G. W. (1993). Predictors of depression in street youth. *Adolescence, 28*(109), 41–53.

Smith, G., Cox, D., & Saradjian, J. (1998). *Women and self-harm: Understanding, coping, and healing from self-mutilation*. London: Women's Press.

Smykla, J., & Selke, W. (1982). Impact of home detention: A less restrictive alternative to detention of juveniles. *Juvenile and Family Court Journal, 33*(2), 3–9.

Smyth, C. L., & Maclachlan, M. (2004). The context of suicide: An examination of life circumstances thought to be understandable precursors to youth suicide. *Journal of Mental Health, 13*, 83–92.

Snyder, H. (2001a). Law enforcement and juvenile crime. Juvenile Offenders and Victims: National Report Series Bulletin. Washington, D.C.: U.S. Department of Justice, Office of Juvenile Justice and Delinquency Prevention.

Snyder, H. N. (2001b). Epidemiology of official offending. In R. Loeber & D. P. Farrington (Eds.), *Child delinquents: Development, intervention, and service needs*. Thousand Oaks, CA: Sage Publications, Inc.

Snyder, H., & Sickmund, M. (1999a). *Juvenile offenders and victims: 1999 national report*. Washington, D.C.: U.S. Department of Justice, Office of Justice Programs, Office of Juvenile Justice and Delinquency Prevention.

Sontheimer, H., & Goodstein, L. (1993). Evaluation of juvenile intensive aftercare probation. *Justice Quarterly, 10*(2), 197–227.

Sosin, M., & Durkin, E. (2007). Perceptions about services and dropout from a substance abuse case management program. *Journal of Community Psychology, 35*(5), 583–602.

Stanford, R. (1984). Implementing the multigoal evaluation technique in diversion programs. In S. Decker (Ed.), *Juvenile justice policy: Analyzing trends and outcomes*. Beverly Hills, CA: Sage.

Steele, R. W., & O'Keefe, M. A. (2001). A program description of health care intervention for homeless teenagers. *Clinical Pediatrics, 40*, 259–263.

Steinhart, D. J. (1996). Status offenses. *The Future of Children, 6*(3), 86–99.

Steinhausen, H. C., & Winkler-Metzke, C. (2004). The impact of suicidal ideation in preadolescence, adolescence, and young adulthood on psychosocial functioning and psychopathology in young adulthood. *Acta Psychiatrica Scandinavica, 110*, 438–445.

Stephenson, S. (2001). Street children in Moscow: Using and creating social capital. *The Sociological Review, 49*(4), 530–547.

Stewart, A. G., Steiman, M., Cauce, A. M., et al. (2004). Victimization and posttraumatic stress disorder among homeless adolescents. *Child & Adolescent Psychiatry, 43*(3), 325–331.

Stewart, S. M., Felice, E., Claassen, C., et al. (2006). Adolescent suicide attempters in Hong Kong and the United States. *Social Science & Medicine, 63*, 296–306.

Stoltz, J. A., Kerr, K., Zhang, T., et al. (2007). Associations between childhood mistreatment and sex work in a cohort of drug-using youth. *Social Science & Medicine, 65*(6), 1214–1221.

Stout, D. (1996). Runaway girl is found dead after torture, police say. The New York Times. August 16. http://www.nytimes.com/1996/08/16/nyregion/runaway-girl-is-found-dead-after-torture-police-say.html.

Stricof, R. L., Kennedy, J. T., Natell, T., et al. (1991). HIV seroprevalence in a facility for runaway and homeless adolescents. *American Journal of Public Health, 81*(Suppl), 50–53.

Strong, M. (1999). *A bright red scream: Self-mutilation and the language of pain*. New York: Penguin Books.

Substance Abuse and Mental Health Services Administration. (2013). Results from the 2012 National Survey on Drug Use and Health: Summary of National Findings. NSDUH Series H-46, HHS Publication No. (SMA) 13–4795. Rockville, MD.

Sullivan, P. M., & Knutson, J. F. (2000). The prevalence of disabilities and maltreatment among runaway children. *Child Abuse & Neglect, 24*(10), 1275–1288.

Suyemoto, K. L. (1998). The functions of self-mutilation. *Clinical Psychology Review, 18*, 531–554.

Sweeney, P., Lindegren, M. L., Buehler, J. W., et al. (1995). Teenagers at risk of human immunodeficiency virus type 1 infection. Results from seroprevalence surveys in the United States. *Archives of Pediatrics & Adolescent Medicine, 149*, 521–528.

Snyder, H., & Sickmund, M. (1999). Juvenile offenders and victims: 1990 national report. Report. Washington, D.C.: U.S. Department of Justice, Office of Justice Programs, Office of Juvenile Justice and Delinquency Prevention.

Szymanski, L.A. (2006). Probation as a disposition for status offenders. NCJJ Snapshot, 11(4), Pittsburgh, PA: National Center for Juvenile Justice.

Tanenhaus, D. S. (2004). *Juvenile justice in the making*. New York: Oxford University Press.

Tanner, J., & Krahn, H. (1991). Part-time work and deviance among high-school seniors. *Canadian Journal of Sociology, 16*, 281–302.

Tarasuk, V., Dachnar, N., & Li, J. (2005). Homeless youth in Toronto are nutritionally vulnerable. *The Journal of Nutrition, 135*(8), 1926–1933.

Taylor, H., Stuttaford, M., & Vostanis, P. (2007). Short-term outcome of young homeless people in contact with a designated mental health service. *The Europian Journal of Psychiatry, 12*(4), 268–278.

Taylor-Seehafer, M. A. (2004). Positive youth development: reducing the health risks of homeless youth. *MCN: American Journal of Maternal Child Nursing, 29*(1), 36–40.

Teare, J. F., Furst, D., Peterson, R. W., et al. (1992). Family reunification following shelter placement: child, family, and program correlates. *American Journal of Orthopsychiatry, 62*(1), 142–146.

Teare, J. F., Peterson, R. W., Furst, D., et al. (1994). Treatment implementation in a short-term emergency shelter program. *Child Welfare, 73*(3), 271–281.

Tenner, A. D., Trevithick, L. A., Wagner, V., et al. (1998). Seattle youthcare's prevention, intervention and education program: a model of care for hiv-positive, homeless, and at-risk youth. *Journal of Adolescent Health, 12*, 515–518.

Teplin, L. A., Bram, K. M., McClelland, G. M., et al. (2002). Psychiatric disorders in youth in juvenile detention. *Archives of General Psychiatry, 59*(12), 1133–1143.

Thompson, S. J. (2005). Factors associated with trauma symptoms among runaway/homeless adolescents. *Stress Trauma and Crisis an International Journal, 8*(2–3), 143–156.

Thompson, S. J., Bender, K. A., Lewis, C. M., & Watkins, R. (2008). Runaway and pregnant: risk factors associated with pregnancy in a national sample of runaway/homeless female adolescents. *The Journal of Adolescent Health, 43*(2), 125–132. EPUB 2008 APR 11.

Thompson, S. J., Maccio, E. M., Desselle, S. K., et al. (2007). Predictors of posttraumatic stress symptoms among runaway youth utilizing two service sectors. *Journal of Traumatic Stress, 20*(4), 553–563.

Thompson, S. J., McManus, H., Lantry, J., et al. (2006a). Insights from the street: Perceptions of services and providers by homeless young adults. *Evaluation and Program Planning, 29*, 34–43.

Thompson, S. J., McManus, H., & Voss, T. (2006b). Posttraumatic stress disorder and substance abuse among youth who are homeless: Treatment issues and implications. *Brief Treatment and Crisis Intervention, 6*(3), 206–217.

Thompson, S. J., & Pillai, V. K. (2006). Determinants of runaway episodes among adolescents using crisis shelter services. *International Journal of Social Welfare, 15*, 142–149.

Thompson, S.J., & Pollio, D.E. (2006). Adolescent runaway episodes: Application of an estrangement model of recidivism. Soc Work Research, 30(4).

Thompson, S. J., Pollio, D. E., & Bitner, L. (2000). Outcomes for adolescents using runaway and homeless youth services. *Journal of Human Behavior in the Social Environment, 3*(1), 79–97.

Thornton, T. N., Craft, C. A., Dahlberg, L. L., et al. (2000). *Best practices of youth violence prevention: A sourcebook for community action*. Atlanta, GA: Centers for Disease Control and Prevention, National Center for Injury Prevention and Control.

Thrane, L. E., & Chen, X. (2012). Impact of running away on girls' pregnancy. *Journal of Adolescence, 35*(2), 443–449.

Thrane, L. E., Hoyt, D. R., Whitbeck, L. B., & Yoder, K. A. (2006). Impact of family abuse on running away, deviance, and street victimization among homeless rural and urban youth. *Child Abuse & Neglect, 30*(10), 1117–1128. Epub 2006 Oct 2.

Thrane, L. E., Yoder, K. A., & Chen, X. (2011). The influence of running away on the risk of female sexual assault in the subsequent year. *Violence and Victims, 26*(6), 816–829.

Toro, P. A., Tompsett, C. J., Lombardo, S., et al. (2007). Homelessness in Europe and the United States: A comparison of prevalence and public opinion. *Journal of Social Issues, 63*, 505–524.

Turgay, A. (2005). Treatment of comorbidity in conduct disorder with attention-deficit hyperactivity disorder (ADHD). *Essential psychopharmacology, 6*(5), 277–290.

Tyler, K. A. (2008). Social network characteristics and risky sexual and drug related behaviors among homeless young adults. *Social Science Research, 37*(2), 673–685.

Tyler, K. A., & Cauce, A. M. (2002). Perpetrators of early physical and sexual abuse among homeless and runaway adolescents. *Child Abuse & Neglect, 26*(12), 1261–1274.

Tyler, K. A., Hoyt, D. R., Whitbeck, L. B., & Cauce, A. M. (2001a). The effects of a high-risk environment on the sexual victimization of homeless and runaway youth. *Violence and Victims, 16*(4), 441–455.

Tyler, K. A., Hoyt, D. R., & Whitbeck, L. B. (2000). The effects of early sexual abuse on later sexual victimization among female homeless and runaway adolescents. *Journal of Interpersonal Violence, 15*(3), 235–250.

Tyler, K. A., Hoyt, D. R., Whitbeck, L. B., & Cauce, A. M. (2001b). The impact of childhood sexual abuse on later sexual victimization among runaway youth. *Journal of Research on Adolescence, 11*(2), 151–176.

Tyler, K. A., & Johnson, K. A. (2006). A longitudinal study of the effects of early abuse on later victimization among high-risk adolescents. *Violence and Victims, 21*(3), 287–306.

Tyler, K. A., Whitbeck, L. B., Hoyt, D. R., et al. (2000). Predictors of self-reported sexually transmitted diseases among homeless and runaway adolescents. *Journal of Sex Research, 37*(4), 369–377.

Tyler, K. A., Whitbeck, L. B., Hoyt, D. R., et al. (2004). Risk factors for sexual victimization among male and female homeless and runaway youth. *Journal of Interpersonal Violence, 19*(5), 503–520.

Tyler, K. A., Whitbeck, L. B., Hoyt, D. R., et al. (2003). Self-mutilation and homeless youth: The role of family abuse, street experiences, and mental disorders. *Journal of Research on Adolescence, 13*(4), 457–474.

Unger, J. B., Kipke, M. D., Simon, T. R., et al. (1998). Stress, coping, and social support among homeless youth. *Journal of Adolescent Research, 13*(2), 134–157.

UNICEF. (1993). *Study on street children in four selected towns of Ethiopia*. Ethiopia: Addis Ababa.

U.S. Department of Commerce. (1993). *Social and economic characteristics: United States*. Washington, D.C.: U.S. Government Printing Office.

U.S. General Accounting Office. (1989). *Homelessness: Homeless and runaway youth receiving services at federally-funded shelters*. Rockville, MD: National Institute of Justice.

U.S. Department of Justice. (2003, March). Prevalence and development of child delinquency. Washington, D.C.: U.S. Department of Justice, Office of Justice Programs, Office of Juvenile Justice and Delinquency Prevention.

Unger, J. B., Kipke, M. D., Simon, T. R., et al. (1997). Homeless youths and young adults in Los Angeles: Prevalence of mental health problems and the relationship between mental health and substance abuse. *American Journal of Community Psychology, 97*, 371–395.

Uzun, A. K., Orhon, F. S., Baskan, S., et al. (2013). A comparison between adolescent mothers and adult mothers in terms of maternal and infant outcomes at follow-ups. *The Journal of Maternal-Fetal & Neonatal Medicine, 26*(5), 454–458.

Valente, S. M. (2005). Sexual abuse of boys. *Journal of Child and Adolescent Psychiatric Nursing, 18*(1), 10–16.

Van Leeuwen, J. M., Hopfer, C., Hooks, S., et al. (2004). A snapshot of substance abuse among homeless and runaway youth in Denver, Colorado. *Journal of Community Health, 29*(3), 217–229.

Veale, A. (1993). Community study. In: Study on street children in four selected towns of Ethiopia. (pp. 89–93). Addis Ababa, Ethiopia: UNICEF.

Veale, A., & Dona, G. (2003). Street children and political violence: A socio-demographic analysis of street children in Rwanda. *Child Abuse & Neglect, 27*(3), 253–269.

Vesper, J. H. (1996). Ethical and legal considerations with self-mutilating and lethal clients. *American Journal of Forensic Psychology, 14*, 25–38.

Violent Acres. (2007). Diary of a teenage runaway. April 11. Retried from http://www.violentacres.com//archives/158/diary-of-a-teenage-runaway/.

Vladislav, R. V., Schwab-Stone, M., Koposov, R. A., et al. (2003). Suicidal ideations and attempts in juvenile delinquents. *Journal of Child Psychology and Psychiatry, 44*, 1058–1066.

Votta, E., & Manion, I. G. (2004). Suicidality, risk-taking behaviours and coping styles in homeless adolescent males. *Journal of Adolescent Health, 34*, 237–243.

Wade, J., & Biehal, N. (1998). *Going missing: Young people absent from care*. Chichester, U.K.: Wiley.

Wagner, B. M., Alice, M., Silverman, C., et al. (2003) Family factors in youth suicidal behaviors. *American Behavioral Scientist, 46*, 1171–1191.

Wagner, L. S., Carlin, L., Cauce, A. M., et al. (2001). A snapshot of homeless youth in Seattle: their characteristics, behaviors and beliefs about HIV protective strategies. *Journal of Community Health, 26*(3), 219–232.

Waldvogel, J. L., Rueter, M., Charles, N., et al. (2008). Adolescent suicide: Risk factors and prevention strategies. *Current Problems in Pediatric and Adolescent Health Care, 38*, 110–125.

Walinder, J., & Rutz, R. (2001). Male depression and suicide. *International Clinical Psychopharmacology, 16*, 21–25.

Walls, N. E., & Bell, S. (2010). Correlates of engaging in survival sex among homeless youth and young adults. *Journal of Sex Research, 25*, 1–14 [Epub ahead of print].

Walsh, S.M., & Donaldson, R.E. (2010). Invited commentary: National Safe Place: Meeting the immediate needs of runaway and homeless youth. J of Youth & Adoles, March 16 (online). Retrieved from http://link.springer.com/article/10.1007/s10964-010-9522-9/fulltext.html.

Walters, A. S. (1999). HIV prevention in street youth. *Journal of Adolescent Health, 25*(3), 187–198.

Warf, C. W., Clark, L. F., Desai, M., et al. (2013). Coming of age on the streets: Survival sex among homeless young women in Hollywood. *Journal of Adolescence, 36*(6), 1205–1213.

Warren, L. (2015, January 15). dailymail.co.uk. Runaway girl, 13, boyfriend, 18, wanted by police for crime spree. Kentucky mom confronted underage relationship. Retrieved from http://www.dailymail.co.uk/news/article-2911954/Runaway-girl-13-boyfriend-18-wanted-police-crime-spree-Kentucky-mom-confronted-underage-relationship.htm).

Warren, J. K., Gary, F. A., & Moorhead, J. (1997). Runaway youths in a southern community: Four critical areas of inquiry. *Journal of Child and Adolescent Psychiatric Nursing, 10*(2), 26–35.

wdrb.com. (2015, February 19). Police-Louisville woman refused to let runaway child return home. Retrieved from http://www.wdrb.com/story/28148855/police-louisville-woman-refused-to-let-runaway-child-return-home.

Weber, A. E., Boivin, J. F., Blais, I., et al. (2002). HIV risk profile and prostitution among female street youths. *Journal of Urban Health, 79*(4), 525–535.

Weir, B. W., Bard, R. S., O'Brien, K., et al. (2007). Uncovering patterns of HIV risk through multiple housing measures. *AIDS and Behavior, 11*(Suppl 2), S31–S44.

Whitbeck, L. B., Chen, X., Hoyt, D. R., et al. (2004). Mental disorder, subsistence strategies, and victimization among gay, lesbian, and bisexual homeless and runaway adolescents. *Journal of Sex Research, 41*(4), 329–342.

Whitbeck, L. B., Chen, X., & Johnson, K. D. (2006). Food insecurity among homeless and runaway adolescents. *Public Health Nutrition, 9*(1), 47–52.

Whitbeck, L., & Hoyt, D. (1999). *Nowhere to grow: Homeless and runaway adolescents and their families*. New York: Aldine.

Whitbeck, L. B., Hoyt, D. R., & Ackley, K. A. (1997a). Abusive family backgrounds and later victimization among runaway and homeless adolescents. *Journal of Research on Adolescence, 7*, 375–392.

Whitbeck, L., Hoyt, D., & Ackley, K. (1997b). Families of homeless and runaway adolescents: A comparison of parent/caretaker and adolescent perspectives on parenting, family violence, and adolescent conduct. *Child Abuse & Neglect, 21*, 517–528.

Whitbeck, L. B., Hoyt, D. R., & Bao, W.-N. (2000). Depressive symptoms and co-occurring depressive symptoms, substance abuse, and conduct problems among runaway and homeless adolescents. *Child Development, 71*, 721–732.

Whitbeck, L. B., Hoyt, D. R., & Yoder, K. A. (1999). A risk-amplification model of victimization and depressive symptoms among runaway and homeless adolescents. *American Journal of Community Psychology, 27*(2), 273–296.

White, J., Carrington, J., & Freeman, P. (1990). *A study of the educational status of foster children in Oregon: Research and statistics*. Portland, OR: Department of Human Resources, Children's Services Division.

Widom, C.S. (1995, March). Victims of childhood sexual abuse-Later criminal consequences. National Institute of Justice Research in Brief. Washington, D.C.: U.S. Department of Justice, Office of Justice Programs, National Institute of Justice.

Wiebush, R., Wagner, D., McNulty, B. et al. (2005). Implementation and outcome evaluation of the intensive aftercare program. Report. Washington, D.C.: U.S. Department of Justice, Office of Justice Programs, Office of Juvenile Justice and Delinquency Prevention.

Wiemann, C.M., Rickert, V.I., Berenson, A.B., et al. (2005). Are pregnant adolescents stigmatized by pregnancy? J Adolesc Health, 36(4), Apr; 352.e1-352.e7.

Wikipedia. (no date). Youth detention center. Retrieved from https://en.wikipedia.org/wiki/Youth_detention_center.

Williams, B. (2000). Teen runaway found dead. Lubbock Avalanche-Journal. October 16. http://lubbockonline.com/stories/101600/loc101600016.shtml.

Williams, C. C., & Nadin, S. (2012). Work beyond employment: Representations of informal economic activities. *Work, Employment & Society, 26*(2), 1–10.

Williams, N. R., Lindsey, E. W., Kurtz, P. D., et al. (2001). From trauma to resiliency: Lessons from former runaway and homeless youth. *Journal of Youth Studies, 4*(2), 233–253.

Willner, A. G., Braukmann, C. J., Kirigin, K. A., et al. (1977). The training and validation of youth-preferred social behaviors of child-care personnel. *Journal of Applied Behavior Analysis, 10*, 219–230.

Wilson, H. W., Stover, C. S., & Berkowitz, S. K. (2009). Research review: The relationship between childhood violence exposure and juvenile antisocial behavior: A meta-analytic review. *Journal of Child Psychology and Psychiatry, 50*(7), 769–779.

Winner, L., Lanza-Kaduce, L., Bishop, D. M., et al. (1997). The transfer of juveniles to criminal courts: Reexamining recidivism rates over the long term. *Crime & Delinquency, 43*(4), 548–563.

Witherup, L., Van Camp, C., Vollmer, T., et al. (2006) A comparison of preference assessment methodologies for use with verbal children. Paper presented at the annual meeting of the Florida Association for Behavior Analysis, Dayton Beach, FL.

Wittebrood, K., & Nieuwbeerta, P. (2000). Criminal victimization during one's life course: the effects of previous victimization and patterns of routine activities. *Journal of Research in Crime and Delinquency, 37*, 91–122.

Wolitski, R. J., Kidder, D. P., & Fenton, K. A. (2007). HIV, homelessness, and public health: Critical issues and a call for increased action. *AIDS and Behavior, 11*(Suppl 2), S167–S171.

World Health Organization, Task Force on the Prevention and Management of Infertility. (1995). Tubal infertility: Serologic relationship to past chlamydial and gonococcal infections. *Sexually Transmitted Diseases, 22*(2), 71–77.

Yates, G. L., MacKenzie, R. G., Pennbridge, J., et al. (1991). A risk profile comparison of homeless youth involved in prostitution and homeless youth not involved. *The Journal of Adolescent Health, 12*(7), 545–548.

Yates, G. L., MacKenzie, R., Pennbridge, J., et al. (1988). A risk profile comparison of runaway and non-runaway youth. *American Journal of Public Health, 78*(37), 820–821.

Yates, G. L., Pennbridge, J. N., MacKenzie, R. G., et al. (1990). A multiagency system of care for runaway/homeless youth. In M. L. Forst (Ed.), *Missing children: The law enforcement response*. Springfield, IL: Charles C. Thomas.

Yeide, M., & Cohen, M. (2009). Deinstitutionalization of status offenders: Legal definitions and legislative strategies. Technical Report. Washington, D.C.: U.S. Department of Justice, Office of Justice Programs, Office of Juvenile Justice and Delinquency Prevention.

Yen, S., Gagnon, K., & Spirito, A. (2013). Borderline personality disorder in suicidal adolescents. *Personality and Mental Health, 7*(2), 89–101.

Yiu, L., & Khong, L. (2009). Runaway youths in Singapore: Exploring demographics, motivations, and environments. *Children and Youth Services Review, 31*(1), 125–139.

Yoder, K. A., Hoyt, D. R., & Whitbeck, L. B. (1998). Suicidal behavior among homeless and runaway adolescents. *Journal of Youth and Adolescence, 27*(6), 753–771.

Young, T.M., & Pappenfort, D.M. (1979). Use of secure detention for juveniles and alternatives to its use. Report. Washington, D.C.: U.S. Department of Justice, Office of Justice Programs, National Institute of Justice.

Zhao, M., Yung, K., Bullock, L. M., et al. (2012). Newspaper coverage of runaway in China. *Children and Youth Services Review, 34*(9), 1598–1803.

Zimet, G. D., Sobo, E. J., Zimmerman, T., et al. (1995). Sexual behavior, drug use, and AIDS knowledge among Midwestern runaways. *Youth & Society, 26*(4), 450–462.

Zweig, J. M., Phillips, S. D., & Duberstein Lindberg, L. (2002). Predicting adolescent profiles of risk: Looking beyond demographics. *Journal of Adolescent Health, 31*, 343–353.

Index

S.J. Morewitz, *Runaway and Homeless Youth*,
DOI 10.1007/978-3-319-30863-0